NEW DIRECTIONS IN BOETHIAN STUDIES

NEW DIRECTIONS IN BOETHIAN STUDIES

Edited by

Noel Harold Kaylor, Jr.
and
Philip Edward Phillips

2007
Studies in Medieval Culture XLV
Medieval Institute Publications

WESTERN MICHIGAN UNIVERSITY

Kalamazoo, Michigan, USA 49008-5432

Library of Congress Cataloging-in-Publication Data

New directions in Boethian studies / edited by Noel Harold Kaylor, Jr.
and Philip Edward Phillips.
    p. cm. -- (Studies in medieval culture ; 45)
    "The boke of coumfort of Bois": P.
    Includes bibliographical references and index.
    ISBN-13: 978-1-58044-100-1 (hardcover : alk. paper)
    ISBN-13: 978-1-58044-101-8 (pbk. : alk. paper)
    1. Boethius, d. 524. De consolatione philosophiae. 2. Philosophy and
religion--Early works to 1800. 3. Happiness--Early works to 1800. 4.
Philosophy, Medieval. 5. Boethius, d. 524. I. Kaylor, Noel Harold,
1946- II. Phillips, Philip Edward. III. Boethius, d. 524. De consolatione
philosophiae. Book 1. Middle English. IV. Series.
    CB351.S83vol. 45
    [B659.D473]
    940.1 s--dc22
    [189]
                                                        2006016732

ISBN 978-1-58044-100-1 (casebound)
ISBN 978-1-58044-101-8 (paperbound)

Cover design by Linda K. Judy

Printed in the United States of America

For Paul Szarmach,
in appreciation of
his many contributions to
Boethian Studies

CONTENTS

ACKNOWLEDGMENTS

It is a great honor for the International Boethius Society that Medieval Institute Publications chose to publish a retrospective on the first decade of the organization's existence. The Society is grateful for this honor and, furthermore, acknowledges that it was conceived at meetings during the International Congress on Medieval Studies at Kalamazoo. Otto Gründler, director of the Medieval Institute, helped bring the Society into existence; Paul Szarmach, his successor, has shepherded it along and generously served as its president. It is to Paul Szarmach that the Society dedicates this volume.

The editors are especially grateful to Patricia Hollahan, Managing Editor of Medieval Institute Publications, and Juleen Eichinger of Eichinger Communications LLC, without whose diligent work this book would not have been possible.

The editors thank the members of the Society for presenting papers at Kalamazoo annually. It is because those papers delivered at those sessions have been of high quality that the Society's interdisciplinary journal, *Carmina Philosophiae,* has flourished. It then is because of the success of the journal that this volume was proposed by the editors and accepted by Medieval Institute Publications. All of the essays included in this book appeared previously in *Carmina Philosophiae.* They appear here with the permission of the authors and the Society. It is a statement of gratitude to each individual contributor that we provide the following list:

Asbell, William J., Jr. "The Philosophical Background of *Sufficientia* in Boethius's *Consolation,* Book III." *Carmina Philosophiae* 7 (1998): 1–17.

Astell, Ann W. "Visualizing Boethius's *Consolation* as Romance." *Carmina Philosophiae* 3 (1994): 23–36.

Atkinson, J. Keith. "A *Dit Contre Fortune,* the Medieval French Boethian *Consolatio* Contained in MS Paris, Bibliothèque Nationale, fr. 25418." *Carmina Philosophiae* 10 (2001): 1–22.

Cessario, Romanus, O.P. "Boethius, Christ, and the New Order." *Carmina Philosophiae* 1 (1992): 53–64.

Cropp, Glynnis M. "An Italian Translation of *Le Livre de Boece de Consolacion.*" *Carmina Philosophiae* 10 (2001): 23–30; reprinted with corrections in *Carmina Philosophiae* 11 (2002): 1–8.

Drake, Graham N. "The Muses in the *Consolation:* Responses from Late-Medieval Mythographers, 1150–1500." *Carmina Philosophiae* 4 (1995): 1–75.

Houswitschka, Christoph. "The Eternal Triangle of Writer, Patron, and Fortune in Late Medieval Literature." *Carmina Philosophiae* 1 (1992): 79–95.

Herold, Christine. "Boethius's *Consolatio Philosophiae* as a Bridge Between Classical and Christian Conceptions of Tragedy." *Carmina Philosophiae* 3 (1994): 37–52.

Kaylor, Noel Harold, Jr., Jason Edward Streed, and William H. Watts, Editors. "The Boke of Coumfort of Bois." *Carmina Philosophiae* 2 (1993): 55–104.

Masi, Michael. "Boethius, the Wife of Bath, and the Dialectic of Paradox." *Carmina Philosophiae* 1 (1992): 65–78.

Twu, Krista Sue-Lo. "This is Comforting? Boethius's *Consolation of Philosophy,* Rhetoric, Dialectic & 'Unicum Illud Homines Deumque Commercium.'" *Carmina Philosophiae* 7 (1998): 19–36.

Ziino, Francesca. "Some Vernacular Versions of Boethius's *De Consolatione Philosophiae* in Medieval Spain: Notes on their Relationship with the Commentary Tradition." *Carmina Philosophiae* (1998): 37–65.

INTRODUCTION

Noel Harold Kaylor, Jr., and Philip Edward Phillips

Anicius Manlius Severinus Boethius (ca. 475–524 C.E.) lived and wrote after the fall of the western Roman Empire during the Ostrogothic occupation of Italy in the sixth century C.E., a period often considered part of the early Middle Ages but also regarded by most scholars today as belonging to late antiquity. We know little about the life of Boethius except that his father, who died when Boethius was a child, had served as consul in Rome in 487. Upon his father's death, Boethius was adopted by Symmachus, whose patrician lineage exceeded even his own, and he later married Symmachus's daughter, Rusticiana, in 495. Boethius's father-in-law encouraged his intellectual pursuits and shared his interest in Greek philosophy. As a scholar, senator, and consul, whose life was centered in Rome and later in Ravenna, Boethius belonged to two worlds—the world of pagan antiquity and the world of the Christian Middle Ages—and his life and work embody and embrace the spirit of both. Unlike most of his contemporaries in Italy, Boethius possessed a native fluency in the Greek language. Even had he not composed his most famous literary work, *The Consolation of Philosophy,* Boethius's contributions to the *quadrivium* as well as his works on logic would have secured him lasting fame in western Europe through the influence of the monastic schools and universities. Indeed, Boethius is credited with having coined the term *quadrivium,* meaning "four-fold path," to refer to the four mathematical disciplines, including arithmetic, music, geometry, and astronomy. To many educated people in the Middle Ages, Boethius's name would have been widely known and associated with his treatises *De Institutione Arithmetica* and *De Institutione Musica*—which were used as textbooks at Oxford University and throughout Europe, even into the eighteenth century—even more so than with his *Consolation.*

Boethius embraced the Platonic belief that the philosopher has a duty to serve the state. To fulfill this belief as well as to live up to the patrician expectations of his day, Boethius served as consul in Rome in 510, and his two sons had the nearly unprecedented honor of serving as joint consuls in 522. For his exemplary public service and his notable private intellectual abilities, the orthodox Christian Boethius was chosen by the Arian King Theodoric to serve as *magister officiorum,* or "chief of staff," in spite of their religious differences. Although known for his remarkable religious tolerance and his commitment to the preservation of many traditional Roman institutions, King Theodoric nevertheless believed the charges of treason leveled against Boethius and removed him from office, stripped him of his possessions, and imprisoned him five hundred miles away near Pavia. Boethius wrote *The Consolation of Philosophy* in Pavia, before being brutally bludgeoned to death in 524 or 525.

Boethius is best known to readers and scholars today as the author of *The Consolation of Philosophy,* famously regarded by the historian Edward Gibbon as "a golden volume not unworthy the leisure of Plato or Tully" and considered by educated readers from the Middle Ages through the Renaissance as a book essential to a proper liberal education. Although neo-Platonic in its worldview, most of the arguments contained in *The Consolation of Philosophy* are not incommensurate with the author's orthodox Christianity. Boethius was, therefore, appropriately called "the last of the Romans whom Cato or Tully could have acknowledged for their countryman" by Gibbon and "the first of the scholastic theologians" by the twentieth-century translators of his *Theological Tractates,* H. F. Stewart and E. K. Rand. The latter epithet recognizes rightfully that Boethius was well known in his own day by contemporaries such as Ennodius and Cassiodorus as a preeminent and unique scholar, fluent as he was in both Latin and Greek, as well as a senator devoted to the traditions of Rome. Boethius's lifelong aim as a philosopher, however, was to reconcile the seemingly disparate philosophies of Plato and Aristotle. To that end, Boethius devoted much of his energy to the translation of Greek philosophical texts, and thus he contributed significantly to the preservation and dissemination of works that otherwise would have been unavailable to scholars in the Middle Ages. More impressive, perhaps, than the enormous influence of his mathematical and musical treatises, however, are the venerable vernacular translation and commentary traditions of *The Consolation of Philosophy*. In England alone, for example, Boethius's *Consolation* was translated into Old English by King Alfred the Great as part of his educational reform program; into Middle English by the father of English poetry, Geoffrey Chaucer; and into sixteenth-century English by Queen Elizabeth I. Notwithstanding the profound influence of *The Consolation of Philosophy* throughout the Middle Ages and into the Renaissance, a suitable appreciation for Boethius's significance and contributions as a classical, late antique, or early medieval thinker requires multidisciplinary approaches to his entire *corpus*.

The pioneering scholarship of H. F. Stewart, *Boethius, An Essay* (1891), E. K. Rand, *Founders of the Middle Ages* (1929), H. R. Patch, *The Tradition of Boethius* (1935), and H. Barrett, *Boethius, Some Aspects of His Times and Works* (1965) forms the basis for modern criticism on Boethius and has led to further significant contributions by P. Courcelle, *La Consolation de Philosophie dans la tradition littéraire* (1967), H. Chadwick, *Boethius: Consolations of Music, Logic, Theology and Philosophy* (1981), and, most recently, J. Marenbon, *Boethius* (2003). Our understanding of all aspects of Boethius's life, thought, and influence in a wide range of disciplines owes a debt of gratitude to these pioneers in Boethian scholarship.

In addition to these studies, some significant collections of essays have appeared. First is *Boethius: His Life, Thought and Influence* (1981), edited by Margaret Gibson and published by Basil Blackwell to commemorate the fifteen-hundredth anniversary of the birth of Boethius (480–1980). An aspect of the classic quality of her volume is the successful attempt she made to arrange the material of her subject as systematically and comprehensibly as possible. She presents chapters on the life of Boethius, his scholastic writings, *The Consolation of Philosophy,* and an epilogue on Boethius in the Renaissance. These chapters cover the life, the writings, and the tradition of Boethian translations up to about 1600. *Boethius and the Liberal Arts: A Collection of Essays* (1981), edited by Michael Masi, effectively examines the role and significance of the liberal arts through several interdisciplinary approaches to the multifaceted interests of Boethius as expressed principally in his *De Institutione Musica* and *De Institutione Arithmetica,* the extant works of Boethius's *quadrivium*. Alastair J. Minnis's book, *The*

Medieval Boethius: Studies in the Vernacular Translations of "De Conso-latione Philosophiae" (1987), is a collection of essays that amplify aspects of certain essays that had appeared in Gibson's collection. It does not, how-ever, attempt to be either systematic or comprehensive in adding new ma-terial to the earlier volume. *Boethius in the Middle Ages* (1997), edited by Maarten J. F. M. Hoenen and Lodi Nauta, continues the work of Minnis in contributing further materials to the systematically conceived study of Gibson. The focus in this volume does not relate specifically to commen-taries on and vernacularizations of Boethius's Latin works.

The present volume, *New Directions in Boethian Studies,* continues the work begun by Masi, Minnis, and Hoenen and Nauta by bringing together recent studies from the diverse perspectives of recent scholarship published during the first decade of *Carmina Philosophiae: Journal of the Interna-tional Boethius Society.* Moreover, the present volume seeks also to respond to the injunction of Margaret Gibson, who served as the first president of the International Boethius Society until her death, to make sound editions of texts and commentaries, both Latin and vernacular, more readily avail-able to scholars. As Gibson wrote in her first letter to the members of the society, "The sounder the textual basis, the more convincing and useful will be the articles in *Carmina Philosophiae.*" Since the founding of the society and the inaugural issue of *Carmina Philosophiae,* published in 1992, the International Boethius Society has attempted to advance Boethian studies by sponsoring annual sessions at the International Congress on Medieval Studies in Kalamazoo and at the Modern Language Association, publishing high-quality essays on Boethius, publishing book reviews and review essays on current studies of Boethius and his age, and making available through new editions previously inaccessible editions of vernacular translations of *The Consolation of Philosophy.* Several of the essays in this volume, in fact, began as papers delivered in one of the society's annual sessions on Boethi-us at the Congress in Kalamazoo. It is, therefore, fitting that this collection should now appear as part of the Medieval Institute Publication's Studies in Medieval Culture series.

The essays and the critical edition selected from the first decade of *Carmina Philosophiae* for inclusion in this volume reflect the exciting new directions that are being taken in Boethian studies. The book is divided into five sections according to the following areas of study: 1) aspects of Boethius's Latin *De Consolatione Philosophiae;* 2) vernacular translations of the *Consolatio;* 3) multidisciplinary perspectives on Boethius in art and literary history; 4) multidisciplinary perspectives on Boethius in religion and mythography; and 5) ongoing efforts to find and edit unpublished translations and major studies of Boethius's works.

The first section, consisting of three essays on Boethius's *Consolation* within the Classical tradition, begins with "The Philosophical Background of *Sufficientia* in Boethius's *Consolation,* Book 3." In this essay, William J. Asbell, Jr., offers a thorough investigation of the linguistic and philosophical background of the Latin term *sufficientia* [sufficiency], a close examination of the contexts and possible meanings of *sufficientia* in the *Consolation,* and an examination of the extent to which Boethius's unique use of the term corresponds to meanings in Greek and Latin philosophical works, the Bible, and patristic literature. In the second essay, "Boethius's *Consolatio Philosophiae* as a Bridge between Classical and Christian Conceptions of Tragedy," Christine Herold builds upon previous studies concerned with Boethius's role in the transmission of tragedy. But she takes a philosophical approach to the way in which the *Consolation* mediates Platonic and Senecan views of tragedy, demonstrated, as she argues, by the interaction between the metrical and prose passages, which dramatize the debate between poetry and philosophy. In the section's third essay, "This Is Comforting? Boethius's *Consolation of Philosophy,* Rhetoric, Dialectic and 'Unicum Illud Homines Deumque Commercium,'" Krista Sue-Lo Twu provides a thoroughly and closely argued exploration of the prisoner's journey in the *Consolation* from despair to hope under the tutelage of Philosophy, who educates her pupil in his proper identity and the nature of the *summum bonum* by means of dialectic and prayer.

The three essays in the second section focus respectively upon specimens from the French, Italian, and Spanish vernacular translations of the *Consolation.* The first, "A *Dit contre Fortune,* the Medieval French Boethian *Consolatio* Contained in MS Paris, Bibliothèque Nationale, fr. 25418," by J. Keith Atkinson, closely examines textual issues concerning a French parchment manuscript from the late fourteenth to early fifteenth century. The second, "An Italian Translation of *Le Livre de Boece de Consolacion,*" by Glynnis M. Cropp, examines an Italian version of the most widely known medieval French translation of the *Consolation* and argues that Books 1–4 are a translation of the unglossed version of *Le Livre de Boece,* with abridgements and omissions and with little amplification. The final essay, "Some Vernacular Versions of Boethius's *De Consolatione Philosophiae* in Medieval Spain: Notes on Their Relationship with the Commentary Tradition," by Francesca Ziino, examines aspects of two of the four Spanish translations of the *Consolation* produced for a growing audience of laypeople eager to read Boethius during the fourteenth and fifteenth centuries. It discusses their relationship to one another and to the tradition of Latin commentary on the *Consolation.* Collectively, these essays employ scholarship expertly in their close analysis of their respective texts and, in so doing, reveal the extent to which vernacular interest in Boethius flourished during the fourteenth and fifteenth centuries in Europe.

The essays in the third section of this collection take multidisciplinary approaches to the study of Boethius. Ann W. Astell's essay, "Visualizing Boethius's *Consolation* as Romance," examines mental images and related manuscript illuminations, comparing Boethius's *Consolation* to its amatory literary parodies, Jean de Meung's *Roman de la Rose* as well as Chaucer's *Troilus and Criseyde.* The illuminations discussed in the essay allow readers to imagine different ways of visualizing the relationship of philosopher to philosophy, and Astell's astute essay points the way toward further investigation in this promising area of inquiry. In "The Eternal Triangle of Writer, Patron, and Fortune in Late Medieval Literature," Christoph Houswitschka grapples with the problem of Fortune in the works of many medieval writers, including Christine de Pizan. That there are many attitudes toward the fickle goddess goes without saying, but Houswitschka argues that a writer's position regarding Fortune can best be understood within the context of his or her political situation and the relationship that the writer wishes to establish and maintain with his or her patron. This third section concludes with "Boethius, the Wife of Bath, and the Dialectic of Paradox," in which Michael Masi discusses the Wife of Bath's logical method that advances in the form of contrasting opposites, which is reminiscent of Boethius's philosophical method in the *Consolation.*

The two essays that comprise the fourth section address theological and mythopoetic concerns in Boethius. In "Boethius, Christ, and the New Order," Romanus Cessario, O.P., maintains the centrality of Boethius's Christianity to his life and works through closely argued discussion of the *Consolation* and the theological tractates. In "The Muses in the *Consolation: The Late Medieval Mythographic Tradition*," Graham N. Drake discusses in great detail how different commentators have reacted to Boethius's references to the Muses through the centuries.

The collection concludes with a complete edition of *The Boke of Coumfort of Bois,* a fourteenth-century Middle English translation of Book 1 of the *Consolation,* reedited by Noel Harold Kaylor, Jr., and Philip Edward Phillips from an earlier transcription and edition that appeared in *Carmina Philosophiae.* The translation is clearly indebted to Geoffrey Chaucer's *Boece* (ca. 1380), but the anonymous Oxford translator frequently makes use of available commentaries to fill out the narrative with glosses, and he includes a *vita* of Boethius at the beginning of the text. Few scholars have had access to of this manuscript, and its publication here with an introduction and textual notes will make it available for a broader scholarly audience.

The study of Boethius, his works, and his influence continues to expand as scholars turn their attention to interdisciplinary and heretofore neglected areas of research. The essays and the critical edition presented in this collection represent the thought that continues to be provoked in the minds of established and emerging scholars who are drawn to Boethius, undeniably one of the most central and most seminal thinkers in the Western tradition.

PART I

BOETHIUS'S LATIN
DE CONSOLATIONE PHILOSOPHIAE

THE PHILOSOPHICAL BACKGROUND OF *SUFFICIENTIA* IN BOETHIUS'S *CONSOLATION*, BOOK 3

William J. Asbell, Jr.

In the third book of Boethius's *Consolation of Philosophy,* Lady Philosophy sets forth the form of false happiness and leads the imprisoned Boethius to a vision of true happiness. The first half of the book focuses on the incomplete goods of *sufficientia, reuerentia, potentia, celebritas,* and *laetitia,* and the means commonly employed to gain them.[1] Most of these goods are familiar from ethical discussions in both Greek and Latin philosophical works. The Latin term *sufficientia,* however, and its cognate adjective *sufficiens,* are relative latecomers to the Latin language and have received only scant attention from scholars. Among those few who have investigated the linguistic and philosophical background of *sufficientia,* Karl Büchner thought that it was a Roman ideal that represented the individual's freedom in society.[2] Joachim Gruber, in contrast, suggests that Boethian *sufficientia* translates the Greek noun *hikanotes,* whose meanings include "competence" or "ability."[3] It is more likely, however, that *sufficientia* represents *autarkeia,* the common Greek philosophical term usually translated into English as self-sufficiency.[4] I shall first identify the Greek term that *sufficientia* represents and then consider its uses in the *Consolation.* In this way I hope to show how Boethius contributes to a centuries-old problem of ancient ethical thought.

Lexical and Semantic Evidence

Three passages from the Latin version of the Pauline epistles suggest *autarkeia* as a likely Greek forerunner for Boethius's *sufficientia.* Paul uses the noun *autarkeia* twice and the related adjective *autarkes* once. Paul tells the Corinthian Christians in 2 Corinthians 9:8 that "God is able to provide you in abundance with every gift, so that you may have all possible *autarkeia* in every situation at all times."[5] Likewise, in the sixth chapter of 1 Timothy, Paul warns against false teachers who, motivated by greed, believe that piety is an easy path to financial gain. But Paul hastens to add in 1 Timothy 6:6 and 7 that "piety with *autarkeia* is a great resource, for we brought nothing into this world and we can take nothing out of it; if we have nourishment and shelter, let us be content with these."[6] Finally, in the fourth chapter of Philippians, Paul thanks the Christians of Philippi for their offer of financial support. In 4:11, however, he politely rejects their offer, claiming to have learned how to be *autarkes,* or self-sufficient, in whatever circumstances he may find himself, whether he enjoys abundance or suffers poverty.[7] In the Vulgate version of 2 Corinthians 9:8 and 1 Timothy 6:6, *sufficientia* appears in place of *autarkeia,* Paul's term for self-sufficiency, while in Philippians 4:11, *sufficiens* corresponds to Paul's adjective *autarkes.*

Roman philosophers writing in Latin never developed a single abstract noun to render the Greek *autarkeia.*[8] Influenced by these biblical passages, however, Christian Latin writers normally employed *sufficientia* to represent the Greek *autarkeia.*[9] Boethius probably belongs to this tradition. Further evidence supports this conclusion: *autarkeia* and *sufficientia* (as Boethius defines it) share the same meaning. Throughout antiquity, freedom from need was the essential meaning of *autarkeia;* freedom from need and self-sufficiency often served as synonyms.[10] To name just two examples, Aristotle observed that self-sufficiency "makes life desirable and free from need."[11] At the other end of antiquity, Plotinus wrote in *Ennead* 5.3: "That which is absolutely simple and self-sufficient truly needs nothing."[12] Similarly, Boethius regards *sufficientia* as freedom from need. In her attack against wealth as a means to *sufficientia* in Book 3, prose 3, Lady Philosophy declares that "one who needs anything is not entirely self-sufficient."[13] Since Boethius himself had felt need even when he was wealthy, Philosophy concludes that "riches are unable to render one free from need and self-sufficient."[14] In light of these close parallels, there is little doubt that Boethian *sufficientia* is equivalent to the Greek *autarkeia.*

Autarkeia in the Philosophical and Patristic Traditions

Before we can evaluate further the philosophical background of *sufficientia* in the *Consolation,* we must consider some of the ways in which the philosophical and patristic traditions employed the concept of *autarkeia*.[15] As a theological term, self-sufficiency frequently appeared as a quality of God or the divine. Euripides in the fifth century B.C.E. was among the first to attest the growing belief that God or the gods must be free from need.[16] During the following centuries, thinkers from many different philosophical schools, including the more learned Jewish and Christian writers of the Roman empire, accepted this doctrine of divine self-sufficiency.[17] Aristotle[18] and the Middle Platonists[19] generally allotted self-sufficiency to the divine first principle. Neoplatonists such as Plotinus and Porphyry sometimes followed this older tradition and assigned self-sufficiency to their first principles[20] but sometimes placed self-sufficiency on the lower but still divine level of Intellect.[21] Moreover, God's absolute self-sufficiency appears in Hellenistic Judaism and early Christianity as well.[22]

But self-sufficiency was also an aspect of the individual and played an important part in discussions of human happiness. Members of all the ancient philosophical schools, except the Skeptics, agreed that there could be no happiness without self-sufficiency. Proclus summed up this axiom well in his commentary on Plato's *Alcibiades* when he wrote: "The common and undistorted opinion characterizes happiness with *autarkeia*."[23] Nevertheless, human self-sufficiency was the source of heated controversy in antiquity. Given the weakness of human nature, it was reasonable to ask how an individual could attain absolute freedom from need. Several solutions to this difficulty existed, each based on a different conception of *autarkeia* and proposing a different strategy to attain it. These conceptions were often in direct conflict, and sometimes stood side-by-side in the works of the same author.[24]

One such solution relied on what I call the broad conception of self-sufficiency. The proponents of this conception frankly admitted that human happiness requires a great many things. Therefore, the self-sufficient individual must possess a wide range of goods that contribute to happiness. Aristotle, the foremost supporter of the broad conception, formulates this conception in the first book of the *Rhetoric*:[25]

[The parts of happiness] must include good birth, many good friends, wealth, many good children, and a pleasant old age; moreover, they must include physical good qualities, such as good looks, strength, power, large size, athletic prowess, and a good reputation, honor, good luck, and virtue. One would be most self-sufficient if both internal and external goods were available to him, for there are no goods apart from these.

According to this conception, then, the only viable strategy to attain self-sufficiency consists of the gathering of many different goods. Ethical thinkers of the Hellenistic and Roman periods objected to this Aristotelian view, because many of these goods were vulnerable to chance and therefore could not provide a reliable foundation for happiness or self-sufficiency—as Boethius himself discovered. In response to this difficulty, the narrow conception of *autarkeia* arose. One widespread variety of the narrow conception emphasized the satisfaction of basic physical needs alone. Asceticism was the way to this type of *autarkeia;* through the rejection of wealth and the limitation of desire for anything more than the body demands, the individual could attain self-sufficiency. There is no better example of this strategy in action than Diogenes the Cynic, who eschewed all property as unnecessary, apart from his one threadbare tunic.[26] Many early Christian writers—including figures as diverse as Clement of Alexandria, Basil of Caesarea, and John Chrysostom[27]—accepted a less extreme variation of the Cynic conception; they considered self-sufficiency the virtue that regulates the individual's use of necessities such as food, clothing, and shelter. This conception of self-sufficiency was designed to protect happiness from chance: those who could suffice on minimal physical requirements alone would be less likely to suffer from the loss of family, friends, or property.

Other philosophers, above all the Stoics and Neoplatonists, proposed a second variety of the narrow conception that played an important part in discussions of human happiness. These thinkers too rejected the value of bodily and external goods on account of their instability, arguing instead that the individual attains self-sufficiency by possessing the one highest good that resides in the soul, far from the influence of fortune. Stoics such as Zeno and Chrysippus defined this good as *areté,* or virtue, the possession of which imparted happiness and self-sufficiency.[28] Neoplatonists such as Plotinus and Proclus, whom we shall presently have occasion to discuss in more detail, stipulated that self-sufficiency was something that resides in the soul of the happy individual. Their conception, however, involved a theological element lacking in Stoicism: the divine first principle must be the ultimate source of human self-sufficiency.

Broad and Narrow Conceptions of *Sufficientia* in *Consolation* 3

Like the Greek *autarkeia,* Boethian *sufficientia* is a quality of God, of the individual, and of human happiness. If my identification of *sufficientia* and *autarkeia* is correct, the third book of the *Consolation* represents Boethius's contribution to the ancient debate about self-sufficiency. Standing at the end of antiquity, Boethius, with his command of Greek and Latin philosophical texts, was in an excellent position to survey the entire debate. In fact, Boethius treats at least briefly all these different uses of self-sufficiency. We find in 3 prose 12 that *sufficientia* is a quality of human happiness and of God himself. While laying the groundwork for her defense of divine justice, Lady Philosophy notes that *sufficientia* has been included in happiness and that God is happiness itself; therefore, God must not need external assistance to govern the world, for otherwise He would not have full *sufficientia.*[29] In addition, *sufficientia* is a quality of the happy individual. In 3 prose 9, Boethius defines true and perfect happiness as "that which makes one self-sufficient, powerful, respected, famous, and delighted."[30]

But which conception of self-sufficiency does Boethius accept? Which strategy does he propose to attain it? What original contribution, if any, does he make to the *autarkeia* debate? In order to answer these questions, let us consider the argument of the third book in more detail. *Sufficientia* and related negative expressions appear first in the second prose chapter of Book 3. Lady Philosophy notes that the Good must satisfy all desire. The highest Good must subsume all goods, and if it lacked anything, it could not be the highest Good; in other words, the highest good must be self-sufficient. Happiness, Philosophy concludes, is a "state made perfect by the gathering of all goods."[31] Philosophy then surveys different conceptions of the highest Good, the first of which is freedom from need, or self-sufficiency. Although wealth fails as a strategy to satisfy need, the pursuit of freedom from need [*nihilo indigere*] is nonetheless worthwhile.[32] Philosophy asks the Boethian persona, "Certainly there is nothing else which can perfect happiness as well as a condition abounding in all goods and which needs nothing else, but is self-sufficient."[33] Near the end of prose 2, Philosophy summarizes by matching goods and the means by which people seek them: "These are the things which people wish to gain; they seek wealth, high office, kingship, glory, and pleasures, because they believe that through them they will gain *sufficientia,* respect, power, celebrity, and joy."[34]

Although Boethian scholarship has focused largely on Platonism and Neoplatonism in the *Consolation,* this description of happiness has relatively little in common with those traditions. Rather, much of the chapter's content is ultimately Aristotelian in origin. Like Boethius, Aristotle identified happiness as the highest Good and the end of human endeavor,[35] for the sake of which all other goods such as honor and pleasure are sought.[36] In addition, Aristotle insisted upon the completeness and self-sufficiency of happiness. A famous passage from his *Nicomachean Ethics* illustrates these aspects of his theory:[37]

> The perfect good seems to be a self-sufficient good; we speak of self-sufficiency not in reference to a single person who lives a life of isolation, but in reference to parents and children and a wife and in general friends and fellow citizens. . . . Moreover, we define self-sufficiency as that which alone makes life desirable and in need of nothing, and happiness appears to be such a thing. . . . Happiness, then, seems to be something complete and self-sufficient, for it is the end of action.

As we have seen, Aristotle in his *Rhetoric* accepted a broad conception of self-sufficiency in his discussions of happiness. The same conception is implied here: if happiness is to be complete and self-sufficient, it must include all other goods worth pursuing, among them friends, wealth, political power, good birth, good children, and good looks.[38] This view of the self-sufficiency of happiness remained an article of faith among subsequent Peripatetics,[39] and occasionally influenced thinkers of other philosophical schools.[40] Here in 3 prose 2, Boethius also adopts a broad conception of self-sufficiency; freedom from need requires a "condition abounding in all goods."[41]

How, then, does one attain self-sufficiency according to Boethius? The third prose chapter offers a negative answer to this question: the accumulation of wealth fails to deliver on its promise to render the individual self-sufficient by eliminating need. Three different arguments are presented in this chapter. First, appealing to Boethius's own experience with wealth,

Philosophy asks if he ever felt any desire prior to the loss of his possessions. When Boethius admits that he had, Philosophy concludes that wealth cannot provide freedom from need or self-sufficiency.[42] Second, wealth, far from eliminating need in its possessors, creates a need of its own. Since property is vulnerable to theft, the wealthy must have assistance to protect it.[43] Third, wealth cannot offer the permanent elimination of even basic physical needs such as food, water, and shelter, although riches may help to satisfy such needs.[44]

Some of these arguments were commonplace in ancient ethical discourse. The opposition between material prosperity and self-sufficiency was very widespread. The poet Horace pointed out the inability of wealth to satisfy desire;[45] likewise, Plutarch observed in his treatise entitled *Against Wealth* that money failed to purchase self-sufficiency.[46] Many others delighted in the paradox that self-sufficiency, although it required the rejection of wealth, constituted true riches.[47] While his opposition of wealth and *sufficientia* is traditional, Boethius barely alludes to the strategy of attaining self-sufficiency through the ascetic reduction of physical needs, despite its great popularity in the writings of Greek philosophers and the Church Fathers. Philosophy remarks in the penultimate sentence of prose 3: "I pass over in silence the fact that very little is enough for nature, but nothing is enough for greed."[48] Apart from this brief statement, Boethius avoids promoting the ascetic restriction of needs as the proper way to gain self-sufficiency, for he has a different strategy in mind.

After a discussion of the inadequacy of the remaining four goods in prose 4 through 8, *sufficientia* reappears in prose 9 and 10, where Boethius refines and clarifies his conception of self-sufficiency, its relation to the other partial goods, and his strategy for attaining it. In these chapters the argument takes a Platonic turn, for God is now identified as the highest Good and the source of happiness. But Boethius does not dismiss the five partial goods as irrelevant for happiness, as several of his Neoplatonic predecessors had done. Instead, he preserves them as aspects of divine goodness. Early in prose 9 we learn that the goods of self-sufficiency, power, respect, renown, and pleasure are one and the same.[49] *Sufficientia* plays a crucial part in this process of unification. Deftly exploiting the negative connotation of *sufficientia,* Lady Philosophy argues that the five partial goods must by nature be one. If the highest good lacks nothing, by definition it must also possess power; it follows that *sufficientia* and power share the same nature. The same holds true for respect, fame, and pleasure; if the highest good is truly self-sufficient, it cannot lack any of these goods. We now discover why *sufficientia* has been the first item in the list of partial goods, for the negative character of *sufficientia* as freedom from need allows Boethius to deduce all the other goods from it.

In 3 prose 3, Boethius had denied that wealth could make the individual self-sufficient, thus implying that *something* could do so. In 3 prose 10, he finally suggests a strategy that does provide *sufficientia*. Having conflated the five partial goods, Lady Philosophy now argues that God and happiness are one and the same.[50] As a corollary to this proposition, Philosophy reasons that we gain happiness through the possession of divinity. Therefore, every happy individual is a god. Although there is only one God, many can attain divinity through participation.[51]

This passage contains no explicit mention of *sufficientia*. Nevertheless, Boethius's reasoning here contains his method for gaining individual self-sufficiency. *Sufficientia* and the other partial goods are aspects of happiness. Happiness and God are in turn identical. Hence, *sufficientia* must be an aspect of God, as 3 prose 12 makes clear. Moreover, if the individual in a sense becomes a god through participation, he must possess self-sufficiency as well. Boethius thus adopts a narrow conception of self-sufficiency: the individual must acquire only the one supreme Good, which he identifies as God, in order to become self-sufficient.

Regardless of the specific sources, if any, that Boethius might have been following, it is clear that developments in Platonism over the previous centuries had prepared the way for much of the argument in prose 9 and 10. Like the Stoics, Middle and Neoplatonists had sought one self-sufficient supreme good, and they found it in the divine first principle, which they often called God. For example, the Middle Platonist Alcinous, who wrote a compendium of Platonic doctrine in the second century C.E., identified the Good with his primary deity, who is free from need.[52] The author of the ineptly written but thoroughly Platonic sixth treatise of the *Corpus Hermeticum* likewise had argued that the highest Good must be free from need. However, he took a further step in claiming that the Good is in God, or rather *is* God, since He too is free from need.[53]

Although the Neoplatonists rarely spoke of human autarky, and on occasion stated that the first principle is "beyond self-sufficiency,"[54] they too contributed several of the elements of Boethius's teaching in 3 prose 9 and 10. Plotinus and Proclus both rejected the broad conception of self-sufficiency and identified the divine as the ultimate source of human self-sufficiency. In *Ennead* 1.4, Plotinus sets forth a strategy for the individual soul to gain happiness and self-sufficiency. The soul must gain both from the One.[55] Proclus proposed participation in the divine as the best means to attain self-sufficiency. In his commentary on the pseudo-Platonic dialogue *Alcibiades I,* he sketched the emanation of self-sufficiency from the gods through the lower levels of divinity and eventually to us:[56]

> We must say that self-sufficiency exists among the gods in a primary degree, for the gods are good and are superessential goodnesses which fulfill all things that exist. They provide all other things with self-sufficiency, both intellects and divine souls and demons and us. Other things are self-sufficient through participation, the gods by substance.

The last sentence of this passage strongly suggests that Proclus, like Boethius, proposed participation in the divine as the means to attain self-sufficiency. Like these Platonists, Boethius rejects the notion that there are individual goods; instead, he identifies God as the self-sufficient highest Good.

Conclusion

Boethius, then, chose the noun *sufficientia* to translate the Greek term *autarkeia,* most likely following the lead of the translators of the Latin Bible and the Latin Church Fathers. Like his philosophical predecessors, he regarded self-sufficiency as an aspect of God, of human happiness, and of the happy individual. Early in the third book of the *Consolation,* Boethius appears to accept a number of external and bodily goods as necessary for happiness, yet in the end he settles on a transcendent, self-sufficient cause, the possession of which imparts self-sufficiency to its possessor. *Sufficientia* thus evolves from a broad, Aristotelian conception as the gathering of all goods in 3 prose 2 to a narrow Platonic conception in 3 prose 10, where self-sufficiency is the possession of God alone. But if Boethius wanted to identify God as the source of self-sufficiency, why did he not take that position from the start of Book 3? Boethius was an excellent Hellenist, well versed in both Platonic and Aristotelian thought, which in his youth he intended to reconcile. That ambitious project never came to fruition, but in my view, his reflections on *sufficientia* represent a first and, to my knowledge, unique attempt to reconcile the broad Aristotelian and narrow Platonic conceptions of self-sufficiency. This reconciliation constitutes Boethius's unique contribution to the old debate about *autarkeia*.

Notes

1. E.g., Boethius, *Consolation* 3 pr. 2.19. All citations of the *Consolation* are from the edition of Ludwig Bieler, *Corpus Christianorum* 94 (Turnholt: Brepols, 1957). Unless otherwise indicated, all translations are my own.

2. K. Büchner, "Bemerkungen zum dritten Buche des Boethius Trost der Philosophie," *Historisches Jahrbuch* 62 (1949), 39.

3. J. Gruber, *Kommentar zu Boethius De Consolatione Philosophiae* (Berlin and New York, 1978), 242.

4. G. Capone-Braga, "La soluzione cristiana del problema del 'summum bonum' in 'Philosophiae consolationis libri quinque' di Boezio," *Archivio di storia della filosofia italiana* 3 (1934), 111, compared the self-sufficiency of Boethius's conception of the Good with the *autarkeia* of Plato's Good in *Philebus* 20D and 67A, but did not identify *sufficientia* as a translation of *autarkeia*.

5. "Potens est autem Deus omnem gratiam abundare facere in uobis, ut in omnibus semper omnem sufficientiam habentes abundetis in omne opus bonum."

6. "Est autem quaestus magnus pietas cum sufficientia. Nihil enim intulimus in hunc mundum: haud dubium quod nec auferre quid possumus. Habentes autem alimenta et quibus tegamus his contenti simus."

7. "Non quasi propter penuriam dico: ego enim didici, in quibus sum, sufficiens esse. Scio et humiliari, scio et abundare (ubique et in omnibus institutus sum): et satiari, et esurire, et penuriam pati."

8. Cicero and Seneca employed cumbersome verbal expressions such as *se contentus esse* or, rarely, *sibi sufficere*. In addition, Roman writers frequently expressed the idea of self-sufficiency through negative expressions, among them *nulla re egere* and *nihil deesse*.

9. The first to do so appears to have been Tertullian, *Ad uxorem* 1.78, who declares that God provides *sufficientia* in our physical needs. Pseudo-Pelagius, *De divitiis* 5.1, employs the noun *sufficientia* in reference to wealth and the adjectival phrase *sibi sufficiens* as a quality of the individual.

10. Modern scholars often err in equating *autarkeia* and concepts such as freedom and autonomy. See, however, A. O. Lovejoy and G. Boas, *Primitivism and Related Ideas in Antiquity* (New York: Octagon, 1965), 119, who after a brief survey of self-sufficiency in Plato, Xenophon, and the Cynics, remark: "In all these applications of [*autarkeia*], even the theological and metaphysical ones, the emphasis was upon its negative sense of not-wanting. . . ." R. Nickel, "Das Verhältnis von Bedürfnis und Brauchbarkeit in seiner Bedeutung für das kynostoische Ideal der Bedürfnislosigkeit," *Hermes* 100 (1972), 45, states the meaning simply: "Der Bedürfnislose braucht—im doppelten Sinne des Wortes—keinen Besitz, er ist autark."

11. Aristotle, *Nicomachean Ethics* 1.1097b15.

12. Plotinus, *Enneads* 5.3.13.

13. Boethius, *Consolation* 3 pr. 3.9: "Qui uero eget aliquo non est usquequaque sibi ipse sufficiens."

14. Boethius, *Consolation* 3 pr. 3.11: "Opes igitur nihilo indigentem sufficientemque sibi facere nequeunt."

15. Comprehensive modern treatments of *autarkeia* are few and far between. The brief articles of P. Wilpert, "Autarkie," *Reallexicon für Antike und Christentum,* vol. 1 (Stuttgart: Hiersemann, 1950), 1039–50; W. Warnach, "Autarkie, autark," *Historisches Wörterbuch der Philosophie,* vol. 1 (Basel and Stuttgart: Schwabe, 1971), 685–90; O. Gigon, "Autarkibegreppet I den klassiska grekiska filosofin," *Ajatus* 28 (1966), 39–52; and K. Gaiser, "Das griechische Ideal der Autarkie," *Acta Philologica Aenipontana* 3 (1976), 35–37, list the best known sources and sketch the primary issues. The most extensive work is the dissertation of T. Davis, "*Autarkeia:* Historical Development of a Concept from Homer to Aristotle" (Ph.D. diss., Harvard University, 1947), but his discussion omits much material from later antiquity that is germane to Boethius.

16. Euripides, *Heracles* 1345–46.

17. For useful but incomplete surveys of major passages involving self-sufficiency, see U. von Willamowitz-Moellendorf, *Euripides Herakles,* 2nd ed., vol. 3 (Leipzig and Berlin: Teubner, 1895), 271; J. Geffcken, *Zwei griechische Apologeten* (Leipzig and Berlin: Teubner, 1913), 13–14; B. Gärtner, *The Areopagus Speech and Natural Revelation,* Acta Seminarii Neotestamentici Upsaliensis, vol. 21 (Uppsala: Gleerup, 1955), 343–44; and E. P. Meijering, *Athanasius: Contra Gentes,* Philosophia Patrum, vol. 7 (Leiden: Brill, 1984), 93–95.

18. Aristotle, *Metaphysics* 14.1091b16–21.

19. Alcinous, *Didaskalikos* 10.3; Apuleius, *De Platone* 1.190; Plutarch, *De Iside et Osiride* 374C–D; and Maximus of Tyre, *Dissertationes* 38.6.8–12 Hobein.

20. E.g., Plotinus, *Enneads* 2.9.1, 5.4.1, and 6.9.6; and Porphyry, *De abstinentia* 1.57.

21. Plotinus, *Ennead* 5.3.17; Iamblichus, *De mysteriis* 8.2.261; and Proclus, *Elements of Theology* 10.

22. Among the many instances of divine self-sufficiency in Philo of Alexandria, one of the most striking is *De virtutibus* 9, where Philo states that "God is without lack since He needs nothing, but is most self-sufficient [*autarkestatos*]." The earliest example from Christian literature may be found at Acts 17.24–25, where Paul argues that divine freedom from need precludes the value of temples and cult images in worship. See also Athanasius, *Contra gentes* 28 and *Oratio secunda contra Arianos* 41.

23. Proclus, *In Alcibiadem* 104.8–10.

24. The two most striking examples are found in Plato's *Republic* and Aristotle's *Nicomachean Ethics*. At *Republic* 2.369B5–C4, Socrates argues that human nature is so needy that individuals must look to the state to provide their self-sufficiency, but he suggests at 3.387D11–E4 that the good man [*epieikes aner*] could be so self-sufficient that he would lament neither the loss of his property nor death of a son or a brother. Similarly, Aristotle, as we shall shortly see, says at *Nicomachean Ethics* 1.1099a31–b8 that human self-sufficiency demands a variety of goods, only to reverse himself at 10.1177a27–35: the wise man, at least, needs only contemplation to be happy and self-sufficient.

25. Aristotle, *Rhetoric* 1.5.4.

26. For a concise treatment of the Cynics' view of self-sufficiency, see A. N. M. Rich, "The Cynic Conception of AUTARKEIA," *Mnemosyne* 9 (1956), 23–29.

27. See Clement of Alexandria, *Paedagogus* 1.12.4; Basil, *Regulae fusius tractatae* 364C and 365B–C; and John Chrysostom, *Homilia in Epistulam II. ad Corinthios* 19, *PG* 61, cols. 532–34.

28. For ancient sources of virtue's self-sufficiency in Stoicism, see *Stoicorum veterum fragmenta* 3.49–67, the fifth book of Cicero's *Tusculanae disputations,* and Seneca, *Epistle* 85.

29. Boethius, *Consolation* 3 pr. 12.10–11: "Nonne in beatitudine sufficientiam numerauimus deumque beatitudinem ipsam esse consensimus? . . . Et ad mundum igitur, inquit, regendum nullis extrinsecus amminiculis indigebit; alioquin si quo egeat, plenam sufficientiam non habebit."

30. Boethius, *Consolation* 3 pr. 9.26: "Nam nisi fallor, ea uera et perfecta felicitas est quae sufficientem, potentem, reuerendum, celebrem laetumque perficiat."

31. Boethius, *Consolation* 3 pr. 2.3.

32. Boethius, *Consolation* 3 pr. 2.14: "Num enim uidentur errare hi qui nihilo indigere nituntur?"

33. Boethius, *Consolation* 3 pr. 2.14: "Atqui non est aliud quod aeque perficere beatitudinem possit quam copiosus bonorum omnium status nec alieni egens sed sibi ipse sufficiens."

34. Boethius, *Consolation* 3 pr. 2.19.

35. Aristotle, *Nicomachean Ethics* 1.1094a1–22.

36. Aristotle, *Nicomachean Ethics* 1.1097b1–5.

37. Aristotle, *Nicomachean Ethics* 1.1097b7–21. This passage is responsible for an abundant growth of scholarship. I have found the following items most useful on the relationship between self-sufficiency and happiness: J. L. Ackrill, "Aristotle on Eudaimonia," *Essays on Aristotle's Ethics,* ed. A. O. Rorty (Berkeley and Los Angeles: University of California Press, 1980), 15–33; T. H. Irwin, "Permanent Happiness: Aristotle and Solon," *Oxford Studies in Ancient Philosophy* 3 (1985), 89–124; R. Heinaman, "Eudaimonia and Self-sufficiency in the *Nicomachean Ethics,*" *Phronesis* 33 (1988), 31–53; S. A. White, "Is Aristotelian Happiness a Good Life or the Best Life?" *Oxford Studies in Ancient Philosophy* 8 (1990), 103–43; and A. Kenny, *Aristotle on the Perfect Life* (Oxford: Clarendon, 1992), 23–42.

38. Aristotle, *Nicomachean Ethics* 1.1099a31–38.

39. See Aspasius, *In Ethica Nicomachea* 16.5–22, and Alexander of Aphrodisias, *De anima liber alter* 163.1–8.

40. E.g., according to Clement of Alexandria (*Stromateis* 2.133.7), Polemo, head of Plato's Academy in the late fourth and early third centuries B.C.E., argued that happiness was "*autarkeia* in all goods, or the most and greatest," while at the same time claiming that virtue alone was self-sufficient for happiness. In addition, the author of the pseudo-Platonic *Horoi* (412B6–7) defined *autarkeia* as a "complete possession of goods."

41. It is quite possible that Aristotle was Boethius's primary source for this conception of *sufficientia.* Capone-Braga, "La soluzione," 106–08, suggested that Boethius found much of the content of 3 pr. 2 in Cicero's lost *Hortensius.* It is indeed possible that Cicero presented there a broad conception of self-sufficiency, although the extant fragments contain no discussion of the topic. Cicero was indebted to the Academics for much of his ethical doctrine, and they had incorporated elements of Aristotle's eudaimonism into their system. Moreover, in view of Boethius's acquaintance with the works of Aristotle, upon which he commented extensively, it is just as possible that Aristotle himself was Boethius's source. Gruber, *Kommentar,* 242, avoids the issue by saying that the catalogue of five goods "geht von der platonischen und aristotelischen Beschreibung der Eudaimonia aus."

42. Boethius, *Consolation* 3 pr. 3.5–11.

43. Boethius, *Consolation* 3 pr. 3.12–16.

44. Boethius, *Consolation* 3 pr. 3.17–18.

45. Horace, *Odes* 3.16.17–18: "crescentem sequitur cura pecuniam / maiorumque fames."

46. Plutarch, *Moralia* 523D.

47. E.g., Epicurus, *Gnomologium vaticanum* 476 and *Principal Doctrines* 45; Porphyry, *Ad Marcellam* 27.23–28.12; *Pythagorean Sentences* 30; and Plutarch, *Numa* 6.2.

48. Boethius, *Consolation* 3 pr. 3.19: "Taceo quod naturae minimum, quod auaritiae nihil satis est." See also the similar remarks in 2 pr. 5.15–16: "Terrarum quidem fructus animantium procul dubio debentur alimentis, sed si, quod naturae satis est, replere indigentiam uelis, nihil est quod fortunae affluentiam petas. paucis enim minimisque natura contenta est. . . ." Gruber, *Kommentar,* 198, wrongly sees here an instance of the Greek notion of *autarkeia.* Contentment with little is an idea often associated but not synonymous with self-sufficiency.

49. F. Klingner, *De Boethii consolatione philosophiae,* 2nd ed. (repr. Zürich and Dublin: Weidmann, 1966), 70, compares Plato, *Protagoras* 329C–D, where Socrates discusses the connection of the parts of virtue. That passage, however, contains no mention of anything like self-sufficiency and does not depend on the logical process that Boethius here employs.

50. Boethius, *Consolation* 3 pr. 10.17–20.

51. Boethius, *Consolation* 3 pr. 10.22–26. Gruber, *Kommentar,* 295 wrongly compares this passage to the doctrine of *homoiosis theo* [the imitation of God], according to which the individual must strive to imitate the divine in order to gain happiness. The idea here is not imitation of the divine, however, but is rather the old Platonic notion of participation. For a comprehensive survey of the tradition of the imitation of God, see H. Merki, *HOMOIOSIS THEO: von der platonischen Angleichung an Gott zur Gottähnlichkeit bei Gregor von Nyssa* (Freiburg in der Schweiz: Paulusverlag, 1952).

52. Alcinous, *Didaskalikos* 10.3.

53. *Corpus Hermeticum,* 6.1a–b.

54. E.g., Plotinus, *Enneads* 5.3.17.11–14. Plotinus is echoing Plato, *Republic* 6.509B, a cryptic but influential passage in which Socrates characterizes the Form of the Good as "beyond being in dignity and power."

55. Plotinus, *Enneads* 1.4.4–5.

56. Proclus, *In Alcibiadem* 104.3–8.

BOETHIUS'S *CONSOLATIO PHILOSOPHIAE* AS A BRIDGE BETWEEN CLASSICAL AND CHRISTIAN CONCEPTIONS OF TRAGEDY

Christine Herold

Boethius's *Consolatio Philosophiae* holds a spectacular position in the transmission of classical ideas and modes of tragedy to the Middle Ages. While Boethius's role in the transmission of tragedy has received wide attention, little attention has been paid to the way in which the *Consolation* mediates Platonic views on tragedy and those of the late Roman tragedian, Seneca. As I shall argue in this essay, the *metra* of the *Consolation,* and their interaction with the *prosa,* serve as a vehicle for juxtaposing these distinct views on tragedy, and thereby provide an empirical demonstration of the inabilities of poetry to transcend its own rhetoric, and reason its formulations, in the philosopher-poet's request for a positive response to misfortune. In this sense, two aspects of Boethius come into conflict with one another in the *Consolation;* Boethius the poet, modeled on Seneca and represented by Boethius himself, comes into dialogue with Boethius the philosopher, modeled mainly on Plato and represented by Lady Philosophy. In his debate between poetry and philosophy, Boethius's model for philosophy provides an answer to Plato's theory of tragedy as "a just and good work" wrought by God,[1] whereas his view of poetry, though attractively human, never emerges from the level of question and debate, remaining, to the end, a less reliably transcendent view of life.[2] Boethius thus consciously bridges two world-views, and the element of Platonic idealism, added to the Senecan system, makes Boethius's treatise, though largely "pagan" in content, immediately recognizable to Christian writers and thinkers, without need of allegorization.

17

If we want fully to understand the elements that went into the distinctly paradoxical yet transcendently resolved medieval conception of tragedy, we must begin with Plato.[3] Plato is the source for the transcendence that is conspicuously lacking in the Roman sense of tragedy. Plato's theory of the goodness of God may be said to be the main theme of Boethius's *Consolation.* He expresses this view, for instance, in Book 4: "Since every kind of fortune, whether pleasing or hard, is granted for the purpose either of rewarding or exercising good men, or of punishing or correcting the bad, every kind is good, since it is agreed to be just or useful" (4 pr. 7, 4–8).[4]

Boethius refers to or borrows from several of Plato's works.[5] The *Republic,* however, offered Boethius the most extensive and well-developed evidence of Plato's views on tragedy. Lady Philosophy calls him "my Plato"; the bulk of the *prosae* in the *Consolation* are, in fact, dependent upon Plato. The *metra,* in contrast, are devoted largely to Senecan-style tragic lamentation. Indeed, the overall structure of the *Consolation* reflects the characteristic five-part structure of Seneca's plays. Within that structure, Boethius's verse-sections correspond to the choral sections of the plays: in their self-conscious metracization in comparison to the surrounding text; in their choral function as commentary on the preceding prose text; and even in their content, which employs imagery largely derived from Seneca.

Awareness of the Senecan influence on the *Consolation* long has informed Boethian studies. Henry Chadwick, for example, claims that Book 2 "is almost wholly Stoic in its inspiration, with many parallels in Seneca," and that Book 4 "concludes with a poem, full of echoes of Seneca's tragedies, concerning the struggles of Agamemnon, Odysseus, and Hercules."[6] Indeed, to miss the Senecan content of Boethius is to miss the Senecan element in medieval conceptions of tragedy. Lady Philosophy, one of the more influential admirers of the tragedian's martyrdom,[7] mentions Seneca several times in the *Consolatio* among her lessons on those brought down from the heights of fame by Fortune. Philosophy emphasizes Seneca's non-attachment to power and material goods, a claim made on his own behalf in his *De consolatione ad Helviam:*

> Never have I trusted Fortune, even when she seemed to be offering peace; the blessings she most fondly bestowed upon me—money, office, and influence—I stored all of them in a place from which she could take them back without dis-

turbing me. Between them and me I have kept a wide space; and so she has merely taken them, not torn them from me. No man is crushed by hostile Fortune who is not first deceived by her smiles. Those who love her gifts as if they were their very own and lasting, who desire to be esteemed on account of them, grovel and mourn when the false and fickle delights forsake their empty, childish minds, that are ignorant of every stable pleasure; but he who is not puffed up by happy fortune does not collapse when it is reversed. The man of long-tested constancy, when faced with either condition, keeps his mind unconquered; for in the very midst of prosperity he proves his strength to meet adversity. Consequently, I have always believed that there was no real good in the things that most men pray for; besides, I have always found that they were empty and, though painted over with showy and deceptive colours, have nothing within to match their outward show.[8]

Although Philosophy claims Seneca as one of her own, she implies a criticism of the Roman philosopher's ever having accepted Fortune's favors at all. It seems that she requires renunciation in deed as well as in spirit:

Well, need I say anything about the companions of kings, when I have shown that kingship itself is full of such weakness? For courtiers are cast down often both when kingly power is secure and when it is overthrown. Nero forced Seneca, his old companion and teacher, to choose the manner of his own death; Papinian had long been powerful at court, but Antonius threw himself to his soldier's swords. Yet both wanted to renounce their power; Seneca even tried to hand his wealth over to Nero and to retire. But while they stood on the brink and their very great-ness drew them down, neither achieved what he wished. What is this power, then, which those who have it greatly fear? While you want to possess it, you are not safe, and when you want to put it aside, you cannot get rid of it. (3 pr. 5, 25–38, 250–53)

Seneca, indeed, may fall short of Philosophy's requirements; he does, how-ever, make an apt companion for Boethius in exile. His several *consolati-ones,* in fact, may be models for Boethius's own *consolatio,* dealing as they do with the same theme of remedies for both good and bad fortune.

Boethius opens the *Consolation* with a portrait of himself as a tragedian:

Flebilis heu maestos cogor inire modos.
Ecce mihi lacerae dictant scribenda camenae
Et veris elegi fletibus ora rigant.

[Tearful, alas, sad songs must I begin.
See how the Muses grieftorn bid me write.
And with unfeigned tears these elegies drench my face.] (1 m. 2–4)

Although the tears are "real" [*veris fletibus*], the highly structured formal elegiac meter contradicts the claim of spontaneous lamentation. The elegies themselves, in fact, apart from the actual cause of Boethius's grief, are drenching his face in tears. The poet is making art of his grief, and the resulting artifact is affecting real emotions. We sense immediately that the poet luxuriates in his grief, even to the point of artificially stimulating that grief to increase his feelings of woe. There is something in this reminiscent of Plato's warning against making earnest of game.[9] All of the Senecan tragical paraphernalia are present: Herculean ("Oetaeus") grief at physical deterioration, calls for death ("Mors felix"), reminiscences of past joys (as in the *Troades*), the metaphor of the fall ("Qui cecidit"), and the familiar description of *fortuna* ("Nunc quia fallacem mutavit nubila vultum" [19]). Thus Philosophy's disgust at this stylized glamorization of suffering:

> "Quis," inquit, "has scenicas meretriculas ad hunc aegrum permisit accedere quae dolores eius non modo nullius remediis foverent, verum dulcibus insuper alerent venenis? Hae sunt enim quae infructuosis affectuum spinis uberem fructibus rationis segetem necant hominumque mentes assuefaciunt morbo, non liberant."

> [Who let these theatrical tarts in with this sick man? Not only have they no cure for his pain, but with their sweet poison they make it worse. Those are they who choke the rich harvest of the fruits of reason with the barren thorns of passion. They accustom a man's mind to his ills, not rid him of them.] (1 pr. 1, 28–34)

Despite Philosophy's Platonic position, Boethius's considerable skill as a metrician indicates that he does not take his poet self lightly; his *metra* are not merely interludes in a philosophical treatise. Not only do his poems display mastery of a variety of classical meters but they also exhibit a taste for experimentation. Moreover, Boethius manipulates meter as well as the flowers of rhetoric to produce his subtle but on-going narrative commentary that interacts with the prose text.[10] The debate between poetry and philosophy in Boethius concerns which of the two provides the more moral formula for human life and, more importantly, access to eternal truth. Boethius seems to have chosen his models carefully, since the works of both Seneca and Plato exhibit similar tensions between art and philosophy, and deal with the same question of truth. By following the progression of the debate between poetry (tragedy) and prose (philosophy) through the *Consolation,* we arrive at the solution Boethius achieved for himself. Recognition of the seriousness with which he engaged in poetry is necessary to our understanding of the reality and intensity of the issues at stake for Boethius in his *Consolation*, and the difficulty with which he leaves behind the tragic-poetic approach to life.[11]

Strangely enough, after her famous Platonic denunciation of poetry, Philosophy herself composes a formal complaint (1 m. 2); in a dactylic pentameter elegy with a profound and regular caesura, she laments her patient's sinking into poetic and irrational passions. She colors her complaint with Senecan sea-and-weather metaphors. It is as if, seeing the state Boethius is in, Philosophy realizes she must "speak his language" in order to communicate. Once she has gained his attention, however, she quickly drops poetic artifice to speak her own language of rational prose: "'Sed medicinae,' inquit, 'tempus est quam querelae'" ["But," she said, "now is the time for cure rather than complaint"] (1 pr. 2, 1). Boethius claims to see the light of reason: "Tunc me discussa liquerunt nocte tenebrae / Luminibusque prior rediit vigor / . . . Emicat ac subito vibratus lumine Phoebus / Mirantes oculos radiis ferit" [Then was the night dispersed, and darkness left me; / My eyes grew strong again / . . . So that the sparkling sunlight / Suddenly flashes on our wondering eyes] (1 m. 3, 1–10); yet he does so in a conceit of classical elegiac meters. Philosophy, aware that this will not be an easy "cure," continues to engage in poetic repartee with her patient, asking repeatedly, "Sentisne" [Am I getting through to you yet?] (1 pr. 4, 1). Philosophy's applications of poetry begin to resemble doses of serum for immunization. Boethius's *metra* continue to indulge in Senecan tragic misery:[12]

> O iam miseras respice terras
> Quisquis rerum foedera nectis,
> Operis tanti pars non vilis
> Homines quatimur fortunae salo.
> Rapidos rector comprime fluctus
> Et quo caelum regis immensum
> Firma stabiles foedere terras.

> [Look on this wretched earth,
> Whoever you are who bind the world with law!
> Of that great work far from the meanest part
> We men are buffeted by fortune's seas.
> Ruler, restrain their rushing waves and make the earth

Steady with that stability of law
By which you rule the vastness of the heavens.] (1 m. 5, 42–48)[13]

These *Musae saevientis* are criticized by Philosophy as being symptomatic of her patient's sickness (1 pr. 5, 36).[14]

When Boethius has "done thus baying" his "unabated grief" [*Haec ubi continuato dolore delatravi*] (1 pr. 5, 1), Philosophy, "with a calm expression" [*vultu placido*], unaffected by his complaints, responds with the argument that both good and bad fortune come from God:

> You grieve that you are an exile and stripped of your goods; since indeed you do not know the goal and end of all things, you think that evil and wicked men are fortunate and powerful; since indeed you have forgotten what sort of governance the world is guided by, you think these fluctuations of fortune uncontrolled. (1 pr. 6, 42–48)

Philosophy announces her attempt to engage in the one use of poetry authorized by Platonic thought; as Plato says, "rhetoric, like every other practice, is always to be used to serve the ends of justice, and for that alone."[15] Philosophy echoes this sentiment when she says:

> But now is the time for you to take some gentle and pleasant physic, which taken and absorbed will prepare you to take stronger medicines. So let us use the sweet persuasiveness of rhetoric, which can only be kept on the right path if it does not swerve from our precepts, and if it harmonizes, now in a lighter, now in a graver mood, with the music native to our halls. (2 pr. 1, 18–25)

The other music "native to our halls" is, of course, philosophy. Philosophy here risks rousing the "honeyed Muse," and personifies Fortuna. Indeed, Philosophy puts to the test Seneca's claim that "poetry is the cradle of philosophy."[16] This is Philosophy's "mild medicine," by which she hopes to begin the treatment of her patient:

> You are not yet ready for strong medicines, so we shall for a little use milder ones, so that by our gentler touch what was swollen hard under the influence of all these passions and worries may soften and become fit to be treated with a sharper, stronger physic. (1 pr. 5, 40–44)

Making something of a mockery of the attempt to harmonize poetry and philosophy, however, Fortune, as played by Philosophy, true to her dualistic nature puts together a poem of two nearly irreconcilable meters, alternating lines of Limping Iambic tetrameter (*choliambic*) and dactylic tetrameter. The Limping Iamb is especially well suited to her subject—the insatiable vices of men.[17] Fortune's *metrum* states overtly the inevitability of man's subjection to Fortune through his passions. And returning to Plato's theory of literary and human tragedy, Philosophy's Fortuna insists that misfortune is not to be bewailed but should be borne in patience by man.

Boethius's dramatic personification of Fortune is wholly consistent with that found in Seneca's plays, but is not found in Plato. Fortune's own disparagement of the function of tragedy, however, is a truncated version of the opinion explained at length by Plato:

> For this is my nature, this is my continual game: turning my wheel swiftly I delight to bring low what is on high, to raise high what is down. . . . What else is the cry of tragedy but a lament that happy states are overthrown by the indiscriminate blows of fortune? Did you not learn as a youth that on Jupiter's threshold there stands 'two jars, the evils in one, the blessings in the other'?[18]

Boethius is forced to admit, concerning the curative abilities of tragic poetry:

> Such arguments . . . have a specious sweetness, honeyed as they are with rhetoric and music. While a man listens to them, they please him, wretched though he is, but his sense of his wrongs lies deeper, so that once they cease to sound in his ears he is oppressed again by the grief deep in his heart.[19]

Philosophy agrees (2 pr. 3, 9–13).

We seem to have reached a stage in the contest at which philosophy begins to outstrip poetry in its ability to convey true wisdom and thus to effect a cure for the human condition. Nevertheless, Philosophy continues her mild fomentations of verse,[20] explaining:

> But it is not yet time for strong medicines. Men's minds are obviously such that when they lose true opinions they have to take up false ones, and then a fog arises from these false ideas, which obscures that true vision. So I shall try a while with gentle and moderate applications to lessen that fog, so that when the darkness of those deceptive ideas is removed, you may be able to recognize the glory of the light of truth. (2 pr. 6, 55–62)

When Boethius announces at the opening of Book 3 that he is ready for more potent medicines, we expect Philosophy to leave behind her sweet songs and to concentrate exclusively on the bitter remedies of philosophical prose. That she does not, she explains, is due to the fact that her patient's "sight" is "still too occupied with images" to see clearly what true happiness is (3 pr. 1, 17–20). She resumes, then, her poetic lessons in order that, recognizing these as "false goods," Boethius may turn his eyes on the opposite, "true blessedness" (3 pr. 1, 22–26). Philosophy, in this endeavor, even goes so far as to portray herself as a harp-plucking bard. The impression at this point is that it appears exceedingly difficult for Philosophy[21] (and thus for Boethius the poet) to reject poetry; in this she (and he) closely resembles Plato. Philosophy claims that true power consists of putting "complaining misery to flight," yet she praises and quotes the truths contained in the tragic laments of "her" Euripides (3 pr. 6, 1–4; 3 pr. 7, 16–18). Philosophy does not seem to be claiming that earthly pleasures, including those of poetry, are devoid of all happiness, however; they are merely the "by-ways" [*via devia*] that mislead by offering bits of truths and pleasures leading nowhere. In this they are akin to evil (3 pr. 9, 1–2).[22] These misleading pleasures she classifies as "false happiness" (3 pr. 9, 1–2). Curiously enough, having established poetry and other earthly pleasures as false or partial, Philosophy continues to praise in verse the tranquility and refuge from misfortune afforded by fixing one's mind on the perfect good alone. She goes so far as to compose a panegyric to God, in heroic meter.[23]

In Book 4, after some two hundred prose lines of reasoned Platonic argument on the subject of fate's subordination to divine providence, the impossibility of chance, and the disposition of all earthly things towards the good, Philosophy sees that her pupil, like a child, is restless and weary. His attention span exhausted, he is in need of a "sweet" to encourage him to go on. She offers him, then, another draught of verse (4 pr. 6, 206–10), a metered version of her preceding argument. "Every kind of fortune," she concludes, "is good" (4 pr. 7, 2–3). But her pupil is still unconvinced: "'Et qui id,' inquam, 'fieri potest?'" (4 pr. 7, 3–4). Philosophy's conclusion is most difficult for Boethius to understand, having shown himself to be a student of the tragical attitudes of Seneca. Ultimate, consistent divine goodness does not exist in Senecan thought; it is foreign to his characteristically

Roman tragic vision, which can posit the gods themselves as adversaries to man.

Book 4 concludes with a *metrum* in dactylic tetrameter in which Philosophy mentions the tragic stories of Agamemnon, Iphigenia, and Odysseus, but in which she concentrates mainly on the tragedy of Hercules. Hercules's great Labors are cataloged, as they invariably are in classical accounts of his demise. Significantly, the version retold in Philosophy's poem is not the unrelievedly miserable end of Sophocles's *Women of Trachis;* it is, rather, the triumphant end of Seneca's *Hercules Oetaeus.* I want to point out here the persistent attractiveness of certain of Seneca's views for Boethian (and Christian) interpretation. Despite Boethius's ultimate rejection of Senecan tragedy in favor of the Platonic ideal, the *Consolation* serves as a vehicle for the transmission and survival of Senecan attitudes towards tragedy. Indeed, although Seneca falls short of the Boethian ideal, Boethius pays homage to Seneca in many direct borrowings from Seneca's philosophical works, and from his artistic works as well. It is the defiantly self-immolating Senecan hero, rather than the Sophoclean or Euripidean, who will become a model for the Christian martyrs. Philosophy's poetic voice commands: "Ite nunc fortes ubi celsa magni / Ducit exempli via! Cur inertes / Terga nudatis?" [Go then, you brave ones, where the lofty way of this great example leads! Why in cowardice do you bare your backs?] (4 m. 7). These are nearly the words of Jocasta to her husband in Seneca's *Oedipus:*

> What boots it, husband, to make woe heavier by lamentation? This very thing, methinks, is regal—to face adversity and, the more dubious thy station and the more the greatness of empire totters to its fall, the more firm to stand, brave with unfaltering foot. 'Tis not a manly thing to [offer the back] to Fortune.[24]

This Jocasta is a very different woman from the fearful wife of Sophocles's play, who urges avoidance of Fate. Thus Seneca, through Boethius, offers material for the forging of a paradigm for Christian tragedy.

By Book 5, the weak but familiar stepping stones of verse have assisted Boethius to ever higher and more austere planes of philosophical thought. Neither the verses that had ceased to satisfy at the beginning of the *Consolation* nor the distracting muses of poetry that inspire such verses have been banished altogether. Rather, in Platonic fashion, they have been allowed to remain, on condition that the Sirens not flatter themselves with the name of truth but, instead, place themselves in the service of philosophy. Thus Seneca, while his tragic rhetoric has not been rejected outright, has been placed in a position of respect tempered by pity, since he has remained blinded by the fog of his belief that eloquence and passion lead to truth. Nevertheless, still utterly confused by his teacher's prose explanation of divine foreknowledge and freedom of choice, Boethius breaks into a pounding tetrameter *metrum* that consists almost entirely of demands for relief from the paradoxical situation. Philosophy's immediate answer is to remind her student of the limitations of human reasoning in these matters (4 m. 7). In a compromise made for the sake of communication, however, she reverts here to the Aristotelian conception of the tripartite soul in which reason holds the highest place, with imagination as a lower power of comprehension. Philosophy's Aristotelian argument is intended to show that reason, although limited, supersedes poetry as man's most appropriate means for contemplating divine truth.

In her final poem, Philosophy leaves behind poetry and thus rises above the imagination and the lower aspects of the soul. This *metrum* is filled with animal images that are poetic but at the same time illustrate the earthbound subjects man should shun. The irregular meter in this verse, so unlike the tight measures of the preceding *metra,* approaches a poetic realization of the conception, borne out in the preceding section, of the boundlessness of the divine mind:

> Now if just as we have a share in reason, so we could possess the judgement belonging to the divine mind, then just as we have judged that imagination and sense ought to give way to reason, so we should think it most just that human reason should submit to the divine mind. Wherefore let us be raised up, if we can, to the height of the highest intelligence; for there reason will see that which she cannot look at in herself, and that is, in what way even those things which have no certain occurrence a certain and definite foreknowledge yet does see, neither is that opinion, but rather the simplicity, shut in by no bounds, of the highest knowledge. (5 pr. 5, 46–56)

Thus, not only are sensory experience and poetic imagination left behind, but also human intellect and reason are transcended in favor of a Platonic leap of faith not available to Seneca, bound as he was by his confusion over the nature of God.

The final prose section of the *Consolation* contains a discussion of the eternal "present" of the mind of God in relation to the inviolability of the human will. True to her conclusions concerning the limitations of reason in the previous section, Philosophy's arguments here do not respond to reasoned examination but are, as she herself admits, a matter of faith and the guidance of theologians (5 pr. 6, esp. 94–139). In her not entirely successful attempt to distinguish between the two necessities—divine necessity and temporal necessity—Philosophy, perhaps unintentionally, proves her point concerning the need for faith. Appropriately, then, Boethius's *Consolation* closes with the air of an act of faith, ending with an exhortation:

> Nor vainly are our hopes placed in God, nor our prayers, which when they are right cannot be ineffectual. Turn away then from vices, cultivate virtues, lift up your mind to righteous hopes, offer up humble prayers to heaven. A great necessity is solemnly ordained for you if you do not want to deceive yourselves, to do good, when you act before the eyes of a judge who sees all things. (5 pr. 6, 1172–76)

Thus does Boethius still the swelling voice of tragedy. The visionary powers of the muses are reduced to mere *imaginandi,* picture-making (5 pr. 5, 37). And reason limps along after a glimpse of divine truth. Boethius consciously bridges two world-views: one, the unsuccessful classical pursuit, through art and philosophy, of a reasoned universe, exemplified by the proliferation of unanswered questions and contradictory answers of Seneca's moral essays and tragedies; the other, the certainties of Christian faith, its Platonic towers built upon the foundation of Roman inquiry, uncertainty, and defiance.

Notes

1. Plato finds fault with Aeschylus for saying, "God plants a fault in mortals / When he would ruin some house utterly" (Aeschylus, *Fragment* 160), and with tragic poets in general: "if poets write about the 'sorrows of Niobe'—in which these iambic lines of Aeschylus occur—or about the tale of the Pelopids, or the Trojan business or anything else of that sort, we must either forbid them to describe these events as the work of God, or else, if they do, they must find out some such explanation as we are looking for now—they must declare that God did a just and good work, and they gained benefit by being chastised. But to describe those who were punished as miserable, and to say that God made them so, is what the poet must not be suffered to do. Yet he may be suffered to say that the evil men were wretched because they needed chastisement, and that God did them good by punishing them"

(*Republic* 2.380 A–381D, quoted from *Great Dialogues,* trans. W. H. D. Rouse, ed. Eric H. Warmington and Philip G. Rouse [New York: New American Library, 1956], 1780). Augustine repeats these views in *De civitate dei.*

2. It must be noted that although Seneca does echo Plato on the spiritual benefits of tragedy, as in *De providentia,* his conception of the nature of God is much less stable than that of Plato, as the following excerpt from *De consolatione ad Helviam* shows:

> quisquis formator universi fuit, sive ille deus est potens omnium, sive incorpalis ratio ingentium operum artifex, sive divinus spiritus per omnia maxima ac minima aequali intentione diffusus, sive fatum et immutabilis causarum inter se cohaerentium series. . . .

> [the great creator of the universe, whoever he may be, whether an all-powerful God, or incorporeal Reason contriving vast works, or divine Spirit pervading all things from the smallest to the greatest with uniform energy, or Fate and an unalterable sequence of causes clinging one to the other. . . .] (*Seneca: Moral Essays*, vol. 2, trans. John W. Basore, Loeb Classical Library [1932; repr. Cambridge, Mass.: Harvard University Press, 1990], Book 8, verse 3, pp. 440–41).

Indeed, Seneca's gods at times enact a Greek-style rivalry or vindictiveness over the fates of men.

3. I begin with Plato (ca. 427–347 B.C.E.), whose pronouncements on the subject of tragedy have a traceable line of influence, through Boethius, whereas Aristotle's influence along these lines is nearly nonexistent.

4. This and all subsequent quotations from Boethius are taken from *The Consolation of Philosophy and the Theological Tractates,* trans. S. J. Tester, Loeb Classical Library (1918; repr. Cambridge, Mass.: Harvard University Press, 1978), 374–75.

5. The *Epinomis, Gorgias, Meno, Phaedo, Theaetetus, Timaeus,* and the *Republic* are among Boethius's sources.

6. Henry Chadwick, *Boethius: The Consolations of Music, Logic, Theology, and Philosophy* (1981; repr. New York: Oxford University Press, 1990), 228, 224. L. D. Reynolds, ed., *Texts and Transmission: A Survey of the Latin Classics* (1983; repr. Oxford: Clarendon Press, 1990), 378 n. 1, notes, though without documentation, that "many of the *metra* in Boethius's *Consolatio philosophiae* have obvious Senecan models." See also, for a discussion of the Senecan influence, Gerard O'Daly, *The Poetry of Boethius* (Chapel Hill: University of North Carolina Press, 1991).

7. Speaking of Canus (d. ca. 40 C.E.), Seneca, (d. 65 C.E.), and Soranus (d. 66 C.E.), "martyred" by the emperors Caligula and Nero, Philosophy says, "The only cause of their deaths was that they were brought up in my ways, so that their behaviour and pursuits were seen to be utterly different from those of wicked men" (*Consolation* 1 pr. 3, lines 35–37).

8. Seneca, *De consolatione ad Helviam* 5.2–6, 426–29:

> Numquam ego fortunae credidi, etiam cum videretur pacem agere; omnia illa, quae in me indulgentissime conferebat, pecuniam, honores, gratiam, eo loco posui, unde posset sine motu meo repetere. Intervallum inter illa et me magnum habui; itaque abstulit illa, non avulsit. Neminem adversa fortuna comminuit, nisi quem

secunda decepit. Illi qui munera eius velut sua et perpetua amaverunt, qui se
suspici propter illa voluerunt, iacent et maerent, cum vanos et pueriles animos,
omnis solidae voluptatis ignaros, falsa et mobilia oblectamenta destituunt; at ille,
qui se laetis rebus non inflavit, nec mutatis contrahit. Adversus utrumque statum
invictum animum tenet exploratae iam firmitatis; nam in ipsa felicitate, quid
contra infelicitatem valeret, expertus est. Itaque ego in illis, quae omnes optant,
existimavi semper nihil veri boni inesse, tum inania et specioso ac deceptorio fuco
circumlita inveni, intra nihil habentia fronti suae simile.

9. Speaking specifically about the mimesis of tragedy and the mimetic content of narrative
poetry, Plato reveals the dangers of imitation-forming habits of behavior. This tragic imitation is damaging both to the poet and to the audience, through its sympathy with the character portrayed by the poet. According to Plato, such internalization of fiction takes one
away from truth:

> imitative art is a long way from truth, and, as it seems, that is why it reproduces
> everything, because it touches only a little part of each, and even that an image.
> . . . All the poetic company from Homer onwards are imitators of images of virtue
> and whatever they put in their poems, but do not lay hold of truth. . . . The imitator
> will neither know nor have right opinion about what he imitates, as regards fine-
> ness or badness. . . . His imitation is a kind of play, not earnest; and those who
> take up tragedy in iambic or epic verse are imitators in the highest degree. . . .
> That which draws you to lamentation and brooding over past troubles incessantly,
> we will say is unreasoning and idle and the friend of cowardice. . . . The imitative
> poet . . . arouses and fosters and strengthens this part of the soul, and destroys the
> rational part . . . when the best of us hear Homer or any other of the makers of
> tragedy imitating one of the heroes, deep in mourning and making a long speech
> in his lamentations, when he shows them chanting and beating their breasts, you
> know we are delighted and yield ourselves; we go with him in sympathy, we take
> all in earnest and praise as a really good poet one who can make us feel most like
> that. . . . If you receive the honeyed Muse in lyric or epic, be sure that pleasure
> and pain will be kings in your city, instead of law and whatever reasoned argu-
> ment the community shall approve in each case to be best. . . . We must not take
> such poetry seriously, as if it were a serious thing that held fast to truth. (*The
> Republic* 10.595B, trans. Rouse, 394–408)

10. Chaucer appears to have perceived this narrative attitude toward literary tragedy and to
have emphasized it in his translation of Boethius's *Consolation*.

11. My position on the level of Boethius's poetic and philosophical engagement with his
sources differs from that of Gerard O'Daly, who believes the late Roman poetic tradition to
have had a major influence upon the work of Boethius only in terms of stylistics. O'Daly
writes, "Reference to those antecedents clarifies both Boethius's craftsmanship and his poetic
intentions. But that is not tantamount to an explicit comment on his antecedents. Part of the
pleasure to be derived from the reading of these poems [Boethius's *metra*] is due to a recognition of the tradition of which they are part. Yet that is not the same as intended explicit
dialogue with that tradition" (*The Poetry of Boethius,* 235).

12. Compare the opening image of 1 m. 5, for example, with that of Seneca's chorus in
Thyestes, lines 612–22; Boethius: "O stelliferi conditor orbis / Qui perpetuo nixus solio /

Rapido caelum turbine versas / Legemque pati sidera cogis" (1–4); Seneca: "Omne sub regno graviore regnum est / . . . res deus nostras celeri citatas turbine versat" (*Seneca in Nine Volumes,* IX, Tragedies II, trans. Frank Justus Miller, Loeb Classical Library [1917; repr. Cambridge, Mass.: Harvard University Press, 1987], pp. 89–181).

13. The desire of Chaucer's Dorigen to rid the coast of dangerous black rocks will remind one of Boethius's unenlightened plea.

14. Philosophy compares her efforts thus far to those of a sower who "sows his seed / In unreceiving furrows" [Tum qui larga negantibus / Sulcis semina credidit] (1 m. 6, 3–4). Chaucer's translation captures the Latin narrative edge by indicating that Boethius is not merely an unreceptive furrow but a field that refuses to receive the seed: "whoso yeveth thanne largely his seedes to the feeldes that refusen to resceyven hem" (*The Riverside Chaucer,* Larry D. Benson, gen. ed. [Boston: Houghton Mifflin, 1987], 406).

15. *Gorgias,* Part 3, in *The Dialogues of Plato,* trans. W. C. Helmbold (New York: Bantam, 1986), 340.

16. This would be a sticking point for Augustine throughout his career as a Christian theologian, and part of the incremental approach to virtue expounded by Horace, by which poetry is believed to be able to instruct while entertaining. Nicholas Trevet, in the preface to his commentary on Seneca's Tragedies, adheres to the same view.

17. According to Kenneth Quinn, "This metre, regarded by the Greeks as a deformed or mutilated version of the ordinary iambic line (hence its Greek name), seems to have been devised by Hipponax, to suggest by his halting lines the distorted subjects with which they dealt—the vices and perversions of humanity" (*Catullus: The Poems,* 2nd ed. [London: Macmillan, 1973], xxxiii). The Limping Iamb would be most appropriate to Machaut's vision of the tripping Fortune.

18. "Haec nostra vis est, hunc continuum ludum ludimus; rotam volubili orbe versamus, infima summis summa infimis mutare gaudemus. . . . Quid tragoediarum clamor aliud deflet nisi indiscreto ictu fortunam felicia regna vertentem? Nonne adulescentulus . . . in Iovis limine iacere didicisti?" (2 pr. 2, 28–42). We do not have in Plato, however, the extended personification of fortune that we find in Boethius. Also, although the disparaging attitude towards tragic mimesis remains the same, Boethius's Fortune appears to accept the Homeric depiction of Zeus's two jars containing evils and blessings, whereas Plato's Socrates reviles such a depiction as a grave "error" on the part of the poet, and a misrepresentation of the nature of God, which is all good. It is unclear whether we are to read Fortune's allusion to the Homeric image as a reflection of Boethius's differing (more Homeric) conception of God as presented by Fortune or as a misleading statement on the part of Fortune.

19. "Tum ego: 'Speciosa quidem ista sunt,' inquam, 'oblitaque Rhetoricae ac Musicae melle dulcedinis; tum tantum, cum audiuntur, oblectant. Sed miseris malorum altior sensus est. Itaque cum haec auribus insonare desierint, insitus animum maeror praegravat'" (2 pr. 3, 4–9).

20. Even Philosophy at times appears seduced by the sensations of poetry, as in 2 m. 6, which she intends as an exemplum that Good Fortune is not reserved for good men. She ends, however, with a passionate complaint against Bad Fortune, "Heu gravem sortem,

quotiens iniquus / Additur saevo gladius veneno!" (16–17), flying in the face of her own argument that wise men should be indifferent to all kinds of fortune.

21. And Augustine as well.

22. Philosophy reflects Plato's view of the fragmentary nature of poetry's mimetic "truths" (see n. 11 above).

23. This invocation of the perfect good that is the opposite of those false goods upon which Boethius had been casting his eyes is based largely upon Plato's *Timaeus* (3 pr. 3, 1–3).

24. Oedipus, trans. Miller, 434–35: "Quid iuvat, coniunx, mala gravare questu? Regium hoc ipsum reor—adversa capere, quoque sit dubius magis status et cadentis imperi moles labet, hoc stare certo pressius fortem gradu. Haud est virile terga Fortunae dare."

THIS IS COMFORTING?

BOETHIUS'S *CONSOLATION OF PHILOSOPHY,* RHETORIC, DIALECTIC, AND "UNICUM ILLUD INTER HOMINES DEUMQUE COMMERCIUM"

Krista Sue-Lo Twu

How does Philosophy console? Most scholars focus on the philosophy of the *Consolation,* but the philosophical arguments about Fortune and Providence in the *Consolation of Philosophy* are not necessarily a unified compendium of ideas and old standards derived from classical sources, and even if they were unified, it is not clear how they are consoling to a man waiting to be executed. For example, Henry Chadwick's extensive and exhaustive work helps us understand the historical and philosophical context in which the *Consolation* is situated, but if anything, his explanations of the philosophical moments in the text only show how little comfort the cold light of reason can provide. Chadwick comes close to identifying a moment of consolation in the Neoplatonic quest for the *summum bonum,* but the comfort of "an infinite first cause which is a simple undivided whole, free of the limitation resulting from division"[1] is at best theoretical, at worst hypothetical, and in any case, not experiential. That is to say, he indicates *why* philosophy ought to provide consolation, but not *how* it achieves this end. Seth Lerer begins to show us how by demonstrating the thematic and methodological coherence of this Neoplatonic progression toward the *summum bonum.*[2] But while he provides important insight into the work as a narrative, he stops just short of identifying the significance of the narrative as a story about conversion. Lerer's argument privileges the role of dialogue in the narrative progress. My argument takes his one step further in showing how the process of perfecting this dialogue produces the consolation of the *Consolation.*

From a Christian perspective,[3] consolation depends on the conversion of the imprisoned narrator, but as Chadwick notes, "the *Consolation* contains no sentence that looks like a confession of faith either in the gods of paganism or in Christian redemption."[4] This omission, however, does not necessarily lead us to conclude that it is "not a Christian work."[5] The Neoplatonic philosophy serves a Christian purpose, much like Augustine's use of Plotinus[6] in Book 7 of his *Confessions:* "Et inde admonitus redire ad memet ipsum" [By the Platonic books I was admonished to return into myself].[7] The philosophy of the *Consolation* functions as a pedagogical apparatus educating the prisoner in his proper identity and the nature of the *summum bonum*. Here consolation is experienced as a dialectical encounter with Philosophy through which the prisoner returns into himself to rediscover the right relationship with the *summum bonum*—God—in prayer.

The story of the *Consolation* encompasses the conversion of the prisoner's despair into hope. His despair takes the form of utter passivity and self-absorption in the guise of self-abnegation:

> Dum levibus male fida bonis fortuna faveret,
> Paene caput tristis merserat hora meum.
> Nunc quia fallacem mutavit nubila vultum,
> Protrahit ingratas impia vita moras.

> [Just at the time that in bad faith fortune favored me with worthless gifts, a sad hour has just about drowned me. Now because she has clouded her false face, my cursed life drags on as an unwelcome delay.] (1 m. 1)[8]

The very grammar of the passage shows the prisoner as only an object, with a body part standing in for the person, but objectified as the victim of cosmic indifference. He is so passive that even as he longs for death, which will eventually occur at his execution, he denies himself the agency to effect it. Lady Philosophy quickly determines that the cause of his despair is a failure of perspective and of self-identification. She finds him unable to see past the "stolidam . . . terram" [dull earth] (1 m. 2) of his mortal existence because "sui paulisper oblitus est" [he has forgotten himself a little] (1 pr. 2). Hence, his conversion must take the form of a re-identification of himself as an effective agent in a relationship with God rather than the world. Neoplatonic philosophy can help him rediscover himself and adjust his perspective to partake of God's, but the final consolation comes from the faith that "manet etiam spectator desuper cunctorum praescius deus visionisque eius praesens semper aeternitas cum nostrorum actuum futura qualitate concurrit bonis praemia malis supplicia dispensans. Nec frustra sunt in deo positae spes precesque" [God remains an observer up above, knowing all things, and the eternal presence of his vision runs through the character of our actions in the future, dispensing rewards to the good and humiliation to the evil. Nor are our hopes and prayers put to God in vain] (5 pr. 6). Philosophy herself cannot console, but she can enable the prisoner to find consolation in a right dialectical relationship with God. Hence, the effective power of Neoplatonic thought resides not in the philosophy itself but in its use of the dialectic as a directional method, which leads the soul toward a right relationship with God when internalized.

Boethius posits a barrier between human and divine understanding, which he figures as a mist [*caligio*] "cuius caliginis causa est, quod humanae ratiocinationis motus ad divinae praescientiae simplicitatem non potest admoveri, quae si ullo modo cogitari queat, nihil prorsus relinquetur ambigui" [the cause of which mist is that the process of human reasoning cannot be moved toward the simplicity of divine foreknowledge, which if at all comprehensible would leave nothing uncertain] (5 pr. 4). The "humanae ratiocinationis motus" creates "ambigui" such as language, which can never properly provide access to the "divinae . . . simplicitatem."[9] Initially the prisoner can see only from the perspective of the "humanae ratiocinationis motus"—or, rather, "stolidam . . . terram"—and concluding that he has been betrayed by fortune he responds with elegiac paralysis, wallowing in the comforts provided by the Muses of poetry. But elegiac poetry only can circumscribe his despair; it cannot provide consolation. Lady Philosophy, diagnosing his disease as despair, indicates the problem with his choice of nurses: "mentes assuefaciunt morbo, non liberant" [They accustom the mind to death, they do not free him] (1 pr. 1). In other words, they treat the symptoms but not the disease.

Likewise, his otherwise dazzling juridical performance is an utterly wrongheaded response to Philosophy's prompt. She asks him about his despair, "quid fles, quid lacrimis manas" [why are you crying? why do you hang onto your tears?] (1 pr. 4)—that is to say, she asks what is wrong with *him,* but he responds by telling her what is wrong with *the world.* His angry retort, "nihilne te ipsa loci facies movet?" [Does the appearance of this place not move you at all?] (1 pr. 4), indicates that he is unable to separate his perspective from the cell where he is imprisoned, which has become his world. Later in his speech the cosmic indifference of his elegiac lament reappears, tinged with malice, in his accusation that "nihil fortunam puduit si minus accusatae innocentiae, at accusantium vilitatis" [Fortune was not at all ashamed of the innocence of the accused and even less so of the villainy of the accusers] (1 pr. 4). Finally the metrical "prayer" concluding his speech of complaint highlights his misunderstanding of his problem from the perspective of the "stolidam . . . terram" (1 m. 2). He thinks that his problem is physical and external, and in his prayer he asks for a physical solution: "firma stabiles . . . terras" [make the earth stable] (1 m. 5).

From these answers Lady Philosophy diagnoses his problem as a methodological one. Both poetry and oratory are externally directed. Both seek to move others, but the prisoner's conversion depends on an internal adjustment. He needs to see that his jail cell itself is only a representation of his spiritual exile, the allegorical landscape of the "regio dissimilitudinis" [region of unlikeness][10] in which his mortal perspective traps him, and that by his error of perspective he "a patria non quidem pulsus es[t] sed aberra[t]" [has not been driven from his homeland, but has wandered away] (1 pr. 5). The misdirection of his speech acts is a symptom of his forgetfulness and further evidence that "sui paulisper oblitus est" (1 pr. 2). Philosophy compares his elegiac and rhetorical performances to sterile soil in her meter, implying a wrong methodology in the planting analogy through its use of the imagery of process:

> . . . qui larga negantibus
> Sulcis semina credidit,
> Elusis Cereris fide
> Quernas pergat ad arbores.
> . . . .
> Sic quod praecipiti via
> Certum deserit ordinem
> Laetos non habet exitus.

[He who plants his seed in unreceiving furrows must go look for acorns under trees, having been deserted by Ceres. . . . Thus whatever forsakes a certain order, rushing along the way, does not have a happy ending.] (1 m. 6.3–6, 20–22)

The poem indicates the fruitlessness of his efforts to reap spiritual nourishment through elegy or justification through empty oratory—he's been barking up the wrong tree, so to speak—while it invokes the importance of method in its use of the terms *via* and *ordo,* key terms in classical discussions of rhetoric.[11]

Hence his cure resides in his re-education in Neoplatonic dialectic. He must re-learn how to interpret a question in order to respond properly, and how to engage in active inquiry himself. His initial engagement in the process is limited at best. Philosophy begins with a classic, commonplace question of definition: "Quid igitur homo sit?" [What is a man?]. He responds with a classic, commonplace answer: "rationale animal atque mortale" [a rational animal and mortal] (1 pr. 6).[12] His answer betrays his failure to engage her question except on the most basic level. He fails to see her ulterior motive of prodding him into remembering himself, even with her additional prodding, "Nihilne aliud te esse novisti?" [You are sure that you are nothing more?]. "Nihil," he insists. His feeble response is symptomatic of his lost relationship with God, in that outside of a right relationship with God all he can ever be is a "rationale animal atque mortale." His perspective is temporally circumscribed by his mortality, and no matter how "rationale," the "humanae ratiocinationis motus ad divinae praescientae simplicitatem non potest admoveri" (5 pr. 4).

The meter following this discussion on the nature of man bound by the world addresses the limitations of a "rationale animal atque mortale" by urging the prisoner to let go of his animal passions:

> Gaudia pelle,
> Pelle timorem
> Spemque fugato
> Nec dolor adsit.
>
> [Cast off joy, cast off fear; fly from hope and sorrow.] (1 m. 7.25–28)

Acting upon these emotions even further abases man, depriving him of his reason such that "nubila mens est / vinctaque frenis" [The mind is clouded, conquered and bound] (1 m. 7.29–30). He is reduced to a mere animal governed by mortality rather than reason, much less God. Hence, from this perspective, the meter becomes a correction to the prisoner's complaint that

God has not been governing the world properly, neglecting to "hominum ... actus / merito rector cohibere modo" [rightly restrain the acts of men according to their desserts], along with his demand that God "firma stabiles ... terras" (1 m. 5.48). To the contrary, it asserts that the prisoner has let "haec ... regnant" [these (passions) govern] his experience of the world rather than God (1 m. 7.31).

Book 2 continues the prisoner's education in the dialectic by demonstrating how "rhetoricae suadela dulcedinis" [the sweet persuasion of rhetoric] is a dead-end street (2 pr. 1). Philosophy's diction here again emphasizes the importance of method, of being on the "recto calle" [the right path] (2 pr. 1), which the "rhetoricae suadela dulcedinis" turns out not to be. To demonstrate the problem with rhetorical persuasion, she employs various rhetorical strategies to convince the prisoner that he should not think of the world in terms of Fortune. Her performance makes use of hypothetical cases,[13] relativism,[14] and ontological[15] and epistemological[16] arguments to make a philosophical point about rhetoric as such. Rather than settling on any consistent system or definition, she performs all of the possibilities, displaying the multi-perspectival nature of the method. Her arguments against Fortune are all convincing, but they cannot all be simultaneously true. For example, she first asserts that his misfortune "tranquillitatis esse debuisset" [ought to be a reason for tranquility] because it ends the uncertainty associated with relying on fortune since "quam non relicturam nemo umquam poterit esse securus" [nobody can ever be sure that she will not leave] (2 pr. 1). Later, however, she contradicts her assertion that one is better off now that fortune "reliquit ... te" [has left you] (2 pr. 1) with her assertion that there are many "qui sese caelo proximos arbitrentur, si de fortunae tuae reliquiis pars eis minima contingat" [who would think themselves close to heaven if even the least part of your remaining fortune should rub off on them] (2 pr. 4). The one assertion dissociates happiness from fortune; the other connects them again. Both cannot be true.

As a measure of his progress, the prisoner's response to her performance addresses the inadequacy of rhetoric itself as an ephemeral distraction from rather than a lasting cure for his despair: "Speciosa quidem ista sunt ... oblitaque Rhetoricae ac Musicae melle dulcedinis; tum tantum, cum audiuntur, oblectant. Sed miseris malorum altior sensus est. Itaque cum haec auribus insonare desierint, insitus animum maeror praegravat" [Such arguments have a most specious beauty, dipped in the honeyed sweetness of Rhetoric and Music, such that they satisfy only when they are being heard. But those in misery feel their wrongs more deeply, and so when they cease to sound in his ears, the grief planted in his heart continues to oppress him] (2 pr. 3). The persuasion of persuasion reveals its emptiness. Lacking a truth-finding mechanism, persuasion in one way can just as easily yield to persuasion to the contrary. He no longer finds comfort in persuasive rhetoric since he sees that it does not get to the root of his despair.

Book 3 uses the prisoner's new understanding about the nature of his despair as a point of departure for their dialogue on the nature of the good. The first meter explains the methodological goals of replacing the honey of rhetoric and music—which masks the bitterness of his despair—with the new honey of true happiness: "Dulcior est apium mage labor, / Si malus ora prius sapor edat" [the work of the bees is far sweeter if a bitter taste first bites the mouth] (3 m. 1.5–6). Philosophy first points out the error informing his despair in sections three to eight. She explains to him that mourning the loss of earthly pleasures is a function of a purely mortal perspective, gently reminding him of his wish to "firma stabiles . . . terras" (1 m. 5) in her description of the "caeci" [blind men] who "quod stelliferum trans abiit polum, / Tellure demersi petunt" [seek buried in the earth that which passes beyond the starry pole] (3 m. 8.17–18). She contextualizes his new awareness of the transitory nature of rhetoric into the larger problem of how man, "mortale" and "tellure demersi," can establish a relationship with "divina praescienta," which "stelliferum strans abiit polum."

Having identified his despair as a perspectival problem, she then goes on to a discussion of the true and the good in prose nine: "Hactenus mendacis formam felicitatis ostendisse suffecerit; quam si perspicaciter intueris, ordo est dienceps, quae sit vera, monstrare" [Up to this point it has sufficed to have shown clearly enough the form of false happiness; if you have understood it well, the method to demonstrate what is the true follows] (3 pr. 9.1–3). Her use of the term *ordo* emphasizes the methodology behind the sequence of inquiry, reminding him about the methodological error of his elegiac lament and the work he needs to do in order to correct it. Whereas his lament "deserit ordinem" by planting "larga negantibus / sulcis

semina" (1 m. 6.21, 3–4), he now has the opportunity to "serere ingenuum
... agrum / ... ut nova fruge gravis Ceres eat" [to sow a fertile field ... so
that Ceres may come laden with new fruit] (3 m. 1.1, 3). Sowing the field
properly, however, requires effort in which the prisoner is not quite ready
to engage. He would rather passively listen than actively engage in the
method, displaying the remainder of his desperate sloth in his response,
even as he manifests the stirrings of insight: "Tenui quidem veluti rimula
mihi videor intueri, sed ex te apertius cognoscere malim" [I seem to be
seeing them as through a narrow crack, but I would prefer to learn them
more plainly from you] (3 pr. 9). While he is beginning to understand the
concept of demonstration as a truth-finding mechanism unlike rhetorical
persuasion, he has not yet started to engage actively in the process of dialectic inquiry—a process that requires independently gained insight.

The discussion that follows encourages him to become self-sufficient.
A dialectician does not rely on external proofs; therefore Lady Philosophy
bases her demonstration on the substance of the Good rather than its external trappings. Prose 10 opens then with a reformulation of the process in
terms of demonstration and active inquiry:

> Quoniam igitur, quae sit imperfecti, quae etiam perfecti boni forma, vidisti, nunc
> demonstrandum reor, quonam haec felicitatis perfectio constituta sit. In quo illud
> primum arbitror inquirendum, an aliquod huiusmodi bonum quale paulo ante
> definisti in rerum natura possit exsistere, ne nos praeter rei subiectae veratem
> cassa cognitationis imago decipiat.

> [Since you have seen the forms of the imperfect and perfect good, I think it should
> now be demonstrated what this perfection of happiness consists of. First we must
> ask whether a good of the kind you defined a little while ago can exist at all, so
> that we are not deceived by the appearance of thought and thus be prevented from
> reaching the truth of the problem.] (3 pr. 10)

The use of *inquirendum* here pointedly reminds the prisoner of the dialectical contract they made at the beginning of their dialogue.[17] Although
throughout prose 9 he does not engage in inquiry himself, but rather passively assents with an "inquam,"[18] in prose 10 he begins to qualify his assent based on the merits of the logic itself. Here he addresses the quality
of the argument itself rather than acting as the empty interlocutor: "Firmis-
sime ... verissimeque conclusum est" [the conclusion is most firmly and

truly drawn] (3 pr. 10.21–22) He even pipes in with a little "modo?" [how?] and "quid?" [what?] now and then, questioning the terms of the argument. But the measure of his progress stops when he actually interrupts Philosophy's demonstration to interject: "sed id quod restat exspecto" [but I am waiting for the rest] (3 pr. 10). His basic passivity still remains a barrier to his progress.

In prose 11, then, we see Lady Philosophy subtly urging him to read her statements for their truth-value instead of their logic. In this section she only acknowledges his responses when they reflect an objective understanding. When he reacts to the external logic governing her argument with subjective rejoinders such as "ita, inquam, videtur" [yes, so it seems], she presses him for a more active stance, forcing him to modify his answer to "ita est" [it is so] (3 pr. 11). The great turning point of this section happens when he begins to try actively to modify his understanding dialectically. *Considerem* yields to *dubito,* opening the way for a dialectic process through which he is able to "indubitato cernere" [see without doubt] (3 pr. 11.103). Hence, as he begins to internalize her method, he is able to respond to the truth-value of the argument, "verum est, inquam" [yes, it is true] (3 pr. 11), and let go of his previous rhetorical commitments. We see him anticipating her moves and becoming increasingly active in the dialogue. In the following section then, Lady Philosophy reiterates their dialectic contract, but with an emphasis on the confrontational nature of the method, specifically challenging him to "rationes ipsas invicem collid[ere]" [pit our arguments against each other] so that "forsitan ex huismodi conflictatione pulchra quaedam veritatis scintilla dissiliat" [perhaps from his kind of conflict some special truth may arise] (3 pr. 12). Through his dissent rather than assent, he comes to internalize the method. Compare with the *inquam* of his earlier assent: "Vehementer assentior . . . et id te paulo ante dicturam tenui licet suspicione prospexi" [I firmly agree . . . and I forsaw a little while ago, although only with a vague suspicion, what you were going to say] (3 pr. 12). He not only discovers the terms of his agreement but also begins to internalize them in such a way that he gains some amount of predictive control over the dialogue. Furthermore, he finally recognizes the internally driven structure of her proofs in prose 12: "haec nullis extrinsecus sumptis sed ex altero altero fidem trahente insitis domesticisque probationibus explicabas" [you proved all this without outside assumptions, but only from internal proofs drawing their force from one another] (3 pr. 12).

In the light of his progress then, the famous poem comparing the prisoner to Orpheus can be read as a warning against relapsing into his former "animal atque mortale" perspective:

> Nam qui Tartareum in specus
> Victus lumina flexerit,
> Quidquid praecipuum trahit
> Perdit, dum videt inferos.

> [For whoever is conquered and turns his eyes toward hell loses whatever excellence he takes with him when he looks on those below.] (3 m. 12.55–58)

Philosophy likens Boethius's former use of elegy and the persuasions of rhetoric to Orpheus's song to recover his lost earthly love. Both engage the animal passions but fail to transcend them, meeting their mortality in the "stolidam . . . terram" (1 m. 2). The poem is a reminder of where he has been, a marker of his progress, and a meditation on the attraction of the deathly, fallen passions of the world.

Book 4 opens with a demonstration of the prisoner's progress—and lack thereof as well. He takes the initiative in choosing a topic, fully participating in the dialectic method of inquiry, but his action here is circumscribed by his grief, still bound to worldly existence as he wonders about the existence of evil in a world supposedly governed by the *summum bonum*. However, he is finally answering her initial question about his despair, "quid fles?" by engaging the question on a slightly more metaphysical level. We recall that his first answer to this question involved his personal frustration over the immediate physical problem of his unjust incarceration. Now this concern has been converted to mankind's confrontation with the more general, abstract problem of evil: "ea ipsa est vel maxima nostri causa maeroris, quod, cum rerum bonus rector exsistat, vel esse omnino mala possint vel impunita praetereant" [this itself is the greatest cause of our grief, that while a good ruler of creation exists, evil can exist and goes unpunished] (4 pr. 1). On one hand, he now phrases his despair in terms of the human condition, referring to it as "nostri" [ours] rather than manifesting it in terms of self absorbed indignation. On the other hand, he still phrases the problem of "maeroris" in terms of the world—in terms of "rerum"—and as such, it is the task of Book 4 finally to rid him of this attachment.

Lady Philosophy offers him a solution to his despair, not in the world but in a right relationship to God. The meter that follows reiterates the key methodological terms, *via* and *ductus,* and moves these methodological concerns into the realm of the moral through the theme of spiritual exile recalled from 1 prose 5, where Philosophy first relates his despair to the state of exile: "Cum te . . . maestum lacrimantemque vidissem, ilico miserum exsulemque cognovi" [when I saw you weeping and full of grief, I knew at once that you were in a state of wretched exile]. Here the backward glance so deadly in the Orpheus poem can be recuperated in the completion of his Neoplatonic journey:

> Huc te si deducem referat via,
> Quam nunc requiris immemor:
> "Haec," dices, "memini, patria est mihi,
> Hinc ortus, hic sistam gradum."
> Quod si terrarum placeat tibi
> Noctem relictam visere,
> Quos miseri torvos populi timent
> Cernes tyrannos exules.

> [If the road leads you back to this place which you now seek, having once forgotten: "This," you will say, "I remember, is my homeland, here I was born, here I may halt my progress." But if it pleases you to look upon the night that you have left behind, you will see those tyrants whom wretched people feared as exiles.] (4 m. 1.23–30)

The "via" indicates process; the "gradum" marks progress, and at the end of the process, that which is left behind can be seen in the proper perspective.[19] No longer in exile himself, the prisoner will see his jailers as exiles instead.

And so in Book 4, the prisoner's resistance to Philosophy's assertions actually indicates his progress in the dialectical method. His new understanding of the method enables him to indicate which conclusions he finds problematic, rather than merely agreeing or demanding solutions. For instance, while he agrees with Philosophy's conclusion about the misery of the wicked, he qualifies it as a "mira quidem . . . et concessu difficilis inlatio" [a strange conclusion and difficult to concede], but recognizes and acknowledges that "his eam quae prius concessa sunt nimium convenire" [it follows from that which has already been conceded to be true] (4 pr. 4). Lady Philosophy not only approves of his implicit challenge but also instructs him in refining the technique:

> Recte . . . aestimas. Sed qui conclusioni accedere durum putat, aequum est vel falsum aliquid praecessisse demonstret vel collocationem propositionum non esse efficacem necessariae conclusionis ostendat; alioquin concessis praecedentibus nihil prorsus est quod de inlatione causetur.

> [You are right. But anyone who finds it hard to accept a conclusion should either demonstrate a false step has occurred earlier in the argument or show that the series of propositions does not indicate a necessary conclusion; otherwise, the premises having been granted, there is no reason why the conclusion should be disputed.] (4 pr. 4)

The form and the content of the argument are meant to jog the prisoner's memory of his proper homeland and his place in the society of philosophers such as Plato, on whose *Gorgias* the content of this section is modeled.[20] Hence the heroic verse that ends the book (4 m. 7.29–35) pictures the completion of the Neoplatonic ascent upward with only one "ultimus labor" left to go. The question of turning back now, "cur inertes / Terga nudatis?" [why slack off and turn your backs?] is almost out of the question as Lady Philosophy encourages him finally to turn his eyes from the "stolidam . . . terram" in order to align his vision with the "divina praescientia": "Superata tellus / Sidera donat" [earth overcome yields up the stars].

But it is not, apparently, completely out of the question, since the prisoner turns back one last time to the problem of the world in the question of Providence. Philosophy lets him know that his question is a detour from the "viam . . . qua patriam reveharis" [the way by which you may return to your homeland], but "paulisper aversa" [only a little bit out of the way] (5 pr. 1), and so lets him pursue it and fully demonstrate his command of the dialectic in prose 3. Probing the epistemological relationship between God and man in relationship to Providence, he arrives at the final answer to Philosophy's question about his despair. As a prisoner—both literally and metaphorically—he despairs that free will is an illusion and that "igitur nec sperandi aliquid nec deprecandi ulla ratio est" [therefore there is no reason to hope or pray for anything] (5 pr. 3). And his emphatic repetition of his belief that prayer is the "unicum illud inter homines deumque commercium" [the sole intercourse between men and God], the "solus modus . . . quo cum deo colloqui homines posse videantur" [the only way that men seem to be able to converse with God] (5 pr. 3), indicates that he finally understands what he stands to lose in his despair—his only link to God. So profound is his despair that he wonders if "cum mentem cerneret altam, / pariter summam et singula norat?" [when (the human mind) perceived the high mind (of God), did it know both the whole and all the parts?] (5 m. 3.20–21)—if man ever could be consoled with God. In light of his desperate situation, his final words provide a post-lapsarian answer to Lady Philosophy's initial question of "quid igitur homo sit?":

> Nunc membrorum condita nube
> Non in totum est oblita sui
> Summamque tenet singula perdens.
> Igitur quisquis vera requirit,
> Neutro est habitu; nam neque novit
> Nec penitus tamen omnia nescit,
> Sed quam retinens meminit summam
> Consulit alte visa retractans,
> Ut servatis queat oblitas
> Addere partes

> [Now buried in the cloud of its body, (the mind) has not wholly forgotten itself; although losing the particulars, it holds onto the general truth. Therefore whoever seeks the truth belongs to neither condition; for he neither knows nor is completely ignorant of everything, but holding onto the general truth that he remembers, he considers the things seen from above, so that he might be able to add the parts he has forgotten to those he has preserved.] (5 m. 3.22–31)

This account of man's nature goes well beyond the philosophically underdeveloped notion of man as "rationale animal atque mortale," such that it accounts for the potential of man's reason above and beyond the animal and mortal as the potential for redemption.

This despair and the potential for its conversion through the "humanae ratiocinationis motus" (5 pr. 4) then informs the final discussion on the nature of Providence. Its content rehearses the right doctrinal answer.[21] More important, it finds this answer through the dialectical process. Aristotle asserts that the speech act itself has persuasive force: "Of the pisteis provided through speech there are three species: for some are in the character [ethos] of the speaker, and some in disposing the listener in some way [pathos], and some in the argument [logos] itself, by showing or seeming to show something."[22] Lady Philosophy's speech succeeds by invoking logos itself as persuasion. She develops her character at the outset, through her allegorical markers; she establishes herself as a guide and intercessor between the prisoner and God; and she aligns herself with the "divina praescientia" through her ability to understand that which is beyond human comprehension. Given the combination of her ethos and the internal logic of the argument, it meets the success criteria set forth by Aristotle. But is this consoling?

If we consider the speech as an internal disputation proposed by Augustine in his *Soliloquia,* it can be read as a dialogue in which the question/answer exchange is subsumed under one voice, without further need for an interlocutor in the soul's conversation with God. By the end of prose 6, the speaker freely uses the future, more vivid, condition to hypothesize dialectic moves: "si inquies . . . respondebo . . ." [if you ask . . . I will respond . . .] (5 pr. 6). In this final speech, the author can leave behind the fictions of speaker and interlocutor, performing a sort of self-atonement. The consolation resides in the re-establishment of the soul's dialogue with God, such that once again it is possible for the prisoner—free now from his "animal atque mortale" perspective—to attain to the "divinae praescientiae simplicitatem" [simplicity of divine prescience] and "humiles preces in excelsa porrigite" [to offer up humble prayers to heaven]. As the prisoner atones with himself in the dialogue with Philosophy (an alienated part of himself), so is the soul made one with God and, hence, consoled.

Notes

1. Henry Chadwick, *Boethius, the Consolations of Music, Logic, Theology, and Philosophy* (New York: Oxford University Press, 1981), 236.

2. Seth Lerer, *Boethius and Dialogue: Literary Method in the Consolation of Philosophy* (Princeton: Princeton University Press, 1985).

3. Boethius confesses his faith and asserts his orthodoxy in *De fide catholica,* trans. Stewart, Rand, and Tester, Loeb Edition (Cambridge: Harvard University Press, 1973):
   Haec autem religio nostra, quae vocatur christiana atque catholica, his fundamentis principatliter nititur asserens: ex aeterno, id est ante mundi constitutionem, ante omne videlicet quod temporis potest retinere vocabulum, divinam patris et

filii ac spiritus sancti exstitisse substantiam, ita ut deum dicat patrem, deum filium, deum spiritum sanctum, nec tamen tres deos sed unum.

[Now this our religion, which is called Christian and Catholic, is supported chiefly
on these foundations which it asserts: From eternity, that is, before the establishment of the world, before all, that is, that can be given the name of time, there has
existed the divine substance of Father, Son, and Holy Spirit in such wise that our
religion calls the Father God, the Son God, and the Holy Spirit God, and yet not
three Gods but one.]

4. Chadwick, *Boethius,* 249.

5. Chadwick, *Boethius,* 249. Chadwick's conclusion here, however, seems to contradict his
prior assertion of "the presence of subtle biblical and perhaps even liturgical allusions in the
language of the *Consolation*" (248).

6. See Plotinus 5.1.1.

7. St. Augustine of Hippo, *Confessions* VII.x, Latin text ed. James J. O'Donnell (Oxford:
Clarendon Press, 1992), trans. Henry Chadwick (New York: Oxford University Press, 1991),
123.

8. All translations of the *Consolation* are my own.

9. Boethius also explores this problem of the inadequacy of human understanding and
language in *De fide catholica,* where he asserts that "qui sit tamen processionis [RE: the Holy
Trinity] istius modus ita non possumus evidenter dicere, quemadmodum generationem filii
ex paterna substantia non potest humanus animus aestimare. Haec autem ut credantur vetus
ac nova informat instructio" [yet what manner of that procession is we are not able to state
clearly just as the human mind is unable to understand the generation of the Son from the
substance of the Father. But these articles are laid down for our belief by the teaching of the
Old and New Testaments] (Loeb, 55). Here, too, the limits of intellection are met with faith.

10. See Augustine, *Confessions* VII.x; Plotinus I.8.13.15; and Plato, *Statesman* 273d.

11. See Quintilian, *Institutio oratoriae* II.xvii.41: "Ars est potestas via, id est ordine, effi-
ciens, esse certe viam atque ordinem in bene dicendo nemo dubitaverit" [An art is a power
working through a course, that is, by a method; no one will doubt that there is a certain
course and method in speaking well] (my translation). See also Seneca, *De beneficiis*
IV.xxxiii.2: "Omne hac via procedit officium" [everything serviceable comes through this
course] (my translation).

12. See Aristotle, Categories 1, *Nichomachaen Ethics* I.7, *Politics* I.2, *Parts of Animals* I.1;
and Porphyry, *Isagoge* 3, 11–12.

13. For example, Lady Philosophy speaks in the persona of Fortune to set up a hypothetical
argument: "Vellem autem pauca tecum fortunae ipsius verbis agitare. Tu igitur an ius potu-
let, animadverte" [Let me confront you with a few of Fortune's own words. See if she does
not appear to be right] (2 pr. 2).

14. Lady Philosophy also argues that, relatively speaking, the prisoner should still count his
blessings:

Nam si te hoc inane nomen fortuitae felicitatis movet, quam pluribus maximisque abundes mecum reputes licet. Igitur si quod in omni fortunae tuae censu pretiosissimum possidebas, id tibi divinitus inlaesum adhuc inviolatumque servatur, poterisne meliora quaeque retinens de infortunio iure causari?

[For if the empty notion of fortunate happiness moves you, then you should consider with me how you still prosper in many ways. Therefore if you still possess what was most precious in all your good fortune, saved for you by God unharmed and unhurt, can you still complain about your misfortune?] (2 pr. 4)

She also argues that he still retains a measure of good fortune relative to other people: "Quam multos esse coniectas qui sese caelo proximos arbitrentur, si de fortunae tuae reliquiis pars eis minima contingat?" [Think of how many people there are who would think themselves close to heaven if even the least part of your remaining fortune should rub off on them] (2 pr. 4).

15. Lady Philosophy argues that honor and power do not categorically belong to the good: Sic musica quidem musicos, medicina medicos, rhetorice rhetores facit. . . . Atqui nec opes inexpletam restinguere avaritiam queunt nec potestas sui compotem fecerit quem vitiosae libidines insolubilibus adstrictum retinent catenis, et collata improbis dignitas non modo non efficit dignos, sed prodit potius et ostentat indignos."

[Thus music makes musicians, medicine makes physicians, rhetoric makes rhetoriticians. . . . But riches cannot slake insatiable avarice nor can power give a man control over himself whose evil desires bind him with unbreakable chains, and honor bestowed upon wicked men does not make them honorable, but rather proclaims and exhibits their dishonor.] (2 pr. 6)

16. Lady Philosophy maintains that external manifestations of wealth, honor and power are reliable signs of their metaphysical existence: "Gaudetis enim res sese aliter habentes falsis compellare nominibus quae facile ipsarum rerum redarguuntur effectu; itaque nec illae divitiae nec illa potentia nec haec dignitas iure appellari potest" [You take pleasure in calling things having a different substance by false names, which are easily contradicted by the effect of the things themselves; and so this cannot rightly be called wealth nor this power, nor that honor] (2 pr. 6).

17. See 1 pr. 6: "Primum igitur paterisne me pauculis rogationibus . . . attingere?" "Tu vero arbitratu," inquam, "tuo quae voles ut responsurum rogato" ["First will you allow me to engage in a few questions?" "Ask what you will as you see fit," I replied, "and I will answer"].

18. His unqualified assent to Lady Philosophy's line of reasoning is meaningless in the context of a dialogue, adding nothing to the content of her argument: "minime, inquam," "ita est, inquam," "at hoc, inquam," "consequitur, inquam," "necesse est, inquam," "assentior, inquam," etc. He does at one point take a certain initiative in asking for clarification, "quonam, inquam, modo?" but overall the passage is marked by his passive acceptance of her assertions.

19. This passage is reminiscent of Augustine's dialogic vision of the *summum bonum* with Monica at Ostia: "perambulavimus gradatim cuncta corporalia et ipsum caelum. . . . et adhuc ascendebamus interius cogitando et loqueno et mirando opera tua" [Step by step we climbed beyond all corporeal objects and the heaven itself. . . . we ascended even further by internal

reflection and dialogue and wonder at you works, and we entered into our own minds] (*Confessions* IX.x, trans. Chadwick).

20. See Plato, *Gorgias* 472d–473a.

21. Chadwick provides a full account of the classic Christian explanations of providence, fate, divine foreknowledge, and free will set forth by Iamblicus and Proclus (*Boethius,* 242–47).

22. *On Rhetoric: A Theory of Civic Discourse* 1356a, trans. G. Kennedy (New York: Oxford University Press, 1991).

PART II

VERNACULAR TRANSLATIONS
OF THE *CONSOLATIO*

A *DIT CONTRE FORTUNE,* THE MEDIEVAL FRENCH BOETHIAN *CONSOLATIO* CONTAINED IN MS PARIS, BIBLIOTHÈQUE NATIONALE, FR. 25418

J. Keith Atkinson

MS fr. 25418 of the Bibliothèque nationale de France in Paris is a parchment manuscript from the turn of the fourteenth to fifteenth century. The pages are 220 x 145 mm. It consists of nineteen quires, most of them quaternions, a total of 140 folios protected by one flyleaf at the front and another at the back. Three different forms of signatures, three different hands (although all three are varieties of a *cursiva libraria*), and three large initials on a fili-greed background (fols. 1, 75, 103) clearly mark off the three major texts or collections in this codex.[1] It bears the ex-libris of the Abbey of St. Victor in Paris on folio 1; one might surmise that the manuscript was prepared, even written, by a devout Victorine for his abbey.[2] The success of the work must be judged as extremely limited, as we shall show. Folios 1–74 (quires 1–10) contain a French verse translation of Boethius's *Consolatio Philosophiae,* 4,615 verses, some 4,389 of them (95 percent) copied from the 7,914 line East Burgundian/Comtois verse adaptation of the *Consolatio,* the *Roman de Fortune et de Felicité,* written by Renaut de Louhans, a Dominican of the house of Poligny,[3] in 1337 (n.s.). Folios 75–102 contain a text of 1,578 verses selected from the 3,760 verse poem by Jehan Le Fèvre, *Le Respit de la Mort,* written in 1376. The editor of the *Respit de la Mort,* Geneviève Hasenohr, categorizes these extracts as follows: "une juxtaposition inco-hérente de groupes de vers du poème extraits de leur contexte."[4] The judg-ment on the third collection of texts is equally unfavorable. In 1927, J. Morawski published an article[5] on verses concerning the four human temper-aments, found on the back flyleaf of this manuscript. His characterization of the poems in honor of the Virgin which occupy folios 103–40 is as follows:

un chapelet inextricable de poèmes de différents rythmes, qui n'ont en commun que l'inspiration générale: la glorification de la Vierge. . . . Ajoutez que ces poèmes . . . ont été eux aussi remaniés et tronqués, de sorte qu'on ne sait pas trop où commence ni où finit chaque tronçon. (196–97)

My own interest in this article is to examine and assess, in more detail than previous scholarship has done, the abridgment of Renaut's *Roman de Fortune et de Felicité*.

Let us first review what earlier scholars have stated. Our starting point is the study of the manuscripts of the French translations of the *Consolatio* in the Bibliothèque nationale by L. Delisle in 1873.[6] Delisle numbers MS 25418 as his translation VI (Incipit: *Pour le tout poissant honnourer*); his VII is the *Roman* of Renaut de Louhans (Incipit: *Fortune mere de tristesse*) now known as translation IX, and his VIII is a later verse text (Incipit: *Celui qui bien bat les buissons*) now known as translation X, whose author claims to have undertaken the work to allay the grief of a young king, Charles, formerly dauphin. Subsequent scholarship has shown that the time of composition of this later version can safely be placed as 1380, the year of the accession of Charles VI.[7] In 1885, A. Molinier hypothesized a Benedictine as the author of X, based on a reading in an epilogue, unique to a Toulouse manuscript; a stronger case can be made for the author being, once again, like Renaut, a Dominican.[8] Delisle himself did not posit any influences amongst his texts VI, VII, and VIII, i.e., between 25418, Renaut's version, and the later version dating from 1380. It was Paul Meyer who, in a review of Delisle's essay, first claimed that Delisle's VI (MS 25418) should be eliminated from the count of Boethian French translations, as it was in his opinion an abridged and altered version of Delisle's VIII (= X).[9] In fact, our investigations[10] show that the Victorine borrows no more than twenty-six verses from the 11,084 verses of version X (Delisle's VIII). Of these, twelve are to be found in the opening verses of Book I, i,[11] the very verses chosen to illustrate the opening of the text proper by Delisle and picked up by Meyer. Meyer went on to claim that the parallels between 25418 and the text of 1380 (X) were even greater as the text proceeded. While technically this statement is not incorrect, the fact is that, apart from fourteen verses of the epilogue of X appearing in a sixteen-line stanza[12] as verses 9–22 of the introductory prologue of the Victorine text, plus the twelve verses of X appearing in I, i that seemed so conclusive to Meyer, there is not a single further verse that is not either an original creation of the Victorine (to a maximum of two hundred for the whole text) or a borrowing, with or without minor verbal adjustments, from the earlier text of Renaut de Louhans.[13] The unspecified parallels that Meyer believed were due to the Victorine borrowing from the translator of 1380 (X) must be attributed to the fact that both borrowed extensively from Renaut. The links suggesting that the version of 1380 was itself indebted to the text of Renaut had been noted by Paulin Paris in 1842 in his description of two manuscripts of the Bibliothèque royale,[14] now MSS fr. 577 (*Boece* X) and fr. 578 (*Boece* IX) of the Bibliothèque nationale. But it was only in the major study of A. Thomas on the medieval French tradition of translations of the *Consolatio Philosophiae,* partially completed by M. Roques and published in 1938,[15] that Paulin Paris's comment of 1842 was picked up and that the link between their IX and X (Delisle's VII and VIII) was acknowledged fully (488). Thomas died before his intended sections on his version X (the 1380 text) and his version XI (Paris 25418) were in anything other than embryonic form. This is acknowledged by Roques in the *Additions et corrections* to the 1938 publication (543–47), where 25418 is simply listed as a separate version (XI) and the earlier erroneous opinion of Meyer, which claimed that 25418 was a simple abridgment of X, is repeated. The authority of Meyer's comment continued unquestioned until 1976, when Richard Dwyer published his examination of the whole French Boethian tradition, *Boethian Fictions, Narratives in the Medieval French Versions of the Consolatio Philosophiae.*[16] While retaining 25418 as a separate version (XI) in his listing of French Boethian translations, he recognized its fundamental dependence on IX rather than on X. This article is both a confirmation and an expansion of the few comments that Dwyer makes about 25418. Let us begin by reviewing the points already made by him after his examination of a range of manuscripts:

> The translation in MS B.N. fr. 25418, from the end of the fourteenth century—the eleventh version to be noted here—has been mentioned in the surveys from Gröber to Roques as an abbreviation of the Benedictine's version (Delisle VI). It is nothing of the kind, sharing, in fact, only a few miscellaneous lines with that version. It is, rather, a skillful though anti-intellectual condensation of Renaut's translation, omitting, for example, all of the philosophical arguments of Book V. (16)

At another point Dwyer examines Renaut's treatment of I, ii and then the different treatments of the same meter by 25418 and the 1380 reviser. Of 25418 on this meter he writes:

> The abbreviation in MS B.N. 25418 . . . by cutting out alternate lines, managed to make of Renaut's version an almost exclusively morbid poem. And this effect is in keeping with the generally glum cast of this version, which also eliminates almost all of Philosophy's positive vision in Book V. Its author was more monk than *philosophe*. (71)

While my own option has been to regard 25418 simply as an abridgment of Renaut's work and not to classify it as a separate version at all,[17] the question of its classification as a separate version or not is perhaps a moot one. It is true that 95 percent of the 4,615 verses of 25418 can be traced to the Renaut tradition; 4.4 percent are original and 0.6 percent are borrowed from X. Nevertheless, the fact that its author omits Book V *in toto,* that he eliminates most of the mythological heroes, that the references to most of the philosophers and historical characters alluded to by Boethius are erased, that substantial and key sequences—such as III, ix, the cosmic hymn of creation—are reduced to some quite trite and dogmatic statements, does suggest that, while technically this is an abridgment of Renaut's work, the resulting text differs considerably in intention, tone, and effect from the earlier translation. One is led then to concur with the words Dwyer chose to describe the work, namely, *glum, morbid, monkish, anti-intellectual,* and one might add to the list adjectives such as *pious, devout, moralistic,* and, certainly, *anti-metaphysical.* Story-telling, whether biographical, historical, or mythological, and flights of the imagination are suspect. Whereas the title of *Roman de Fortune et de Felicité*[18] is aptly used for the work of Renaut, where the protagonist, by argument and progressive understanding, moves beyond the inconstancies of Fortune to some understanding of the true nature of an interior happiness centered on the stability and eternity of the divine,[19] this is more than can be said of 25418, which might best be called a *Dit contre Fortune.*

Of the two-hundred original verses of the Victorine, seven occur in the first octet of the prologue, and some thirty in the rather abrupt epilogue appearing at the end of Book IV, vii. It is instructive to read these two original passages together, since they do represent an honest statement of his purpose.

Pour le tout poissant honnourer
Et magnifïer son haut nom,
Et pour cuer humain conforter
Et hoster de toute turbacion,
Contre Fortune au cuer amer,
Mere de toute affliccion,
Dez dis Boëce vueil conter
C'om dit *de Consolacion.* (Prologue, 1r)

[In order to honor the all powerful and to magnify His great name, and to comfort
the human heart and remove all perturbation, I wish to relate the sayings of
Boethius, in the work called *de Consolacion,* against Fortune with the bitter heart,
and mother of all affliction.]

The rest of the brief prologue proceeds to praise Boethius for his continuing
faith in God, his virtues, and his teaching. The abrupt epilogue of thirty-four
verses at the end of IV, vii picks up similar themes.[20] It is an exhortation to
those engaged in the life battle against harsh Fortune to keep in mind the
lives and teachings of the saints, to pray to the Trinity and to God's Mother,
Holy Mary, that perfect felicity may be granted finally in heaven.

Given the above framework and statement of intention, many of the
considerable omissions and reductions wrought on the Renaldian text fall
into place. They are not accidental choices but, rather, a deliberate means
of trimming the source narrative adaptation into a more sober and restrained
moral work. Our task now is to categorize the omissions and major changes.
We will consider first certain technical changes, adjustments to poetic form
and changes brought about by dissatisfaction with certain Eastern rhymes.
In passing it will be instructive to show the alternative solutions to some of
the same issues made by the distinctively Picard reviser of 1380. The independence of the Victorine in these matters will be at once evident. We will
then turn our attention to some more substantial changes and omissions,
which may be categorized under headings such as the omission of mythological and historical stories, the removal of exempla and citations, the
removal of imagery and colorful vignettes, and a final major category, the
deletion of large portions of philosophical argument.

Poetic Form

One of the originalities of Renaut's text is a certain experimentation with poetic form. The prologue and Book I of Renaut's *Roman* is composed of octosyllabic octets, *ab ab ab ab*. In principle, the Victorine's prologue and abridgment of Book I are written in the same form. There are some occasional omissions of a verse from an octet, and, as already stated, the prologue contains one sixteen-line stanza of which fourteen verses are borrowed from the epilogue of X. The appearance of an additional six-line stanza in I, i serves only to confirm the Victorine's dependence on a particular branch of the Renaldian manuscript tradition, since these additional verses appear in the Renaut MS, New Haven, Yale University Library, 38.[21]

The exception to the octosyllabic couplets in the first part of Renaut's text is I, ii, which is composed of six twelve-line stanzas, *aab aab bba bba*. I, ii is Philosophy's lament to Boethius that care has dulled his previously alert mind. In the Victorine's abridged rewriting of I, ii (5r–v), the seventy-two verses of Renaut are reduced to thirty-two, which consist of three octosyllabic octets in rhyming couplets and one octet rhyming *aaba bbab*.[22] These verses are a clever patchwork of Renaut's text rearranged to create four new octets, which read as a new and coherent whole. The Victorine has appreciated the system of Renaut but rejected it in order to replace it with his own. This is more than can be said for the reviser of 1380; his revision of I, ii in forty-eight original verses follows a quite erratic and arbitrary series of rhymes that owes nothing to Renaut.

Renaut's Books II to V are written in octosyllabic rhyming couplets; Renaut justifies this shift by claiming that when the rhyme is "lighter" the sense is plainer: "Car quant la rime est plus legiere / La sentencë est plus entiere" (1600). The Victorine justifies the same shift in similar terms: "Quant rime est faite legiere, / La sentence en est plus clere" (18r). Within those books, two variations merit attention. In Renaut's II, i occurs a *Chantepleure* of thirty-eight verses. It is Music who speaks against the unruly and unharmonious movements of Fortune. Music claims that Fortune always sings falsely: "Mais tousjours trouveras / Qu'elle chante en fausset" (1892). Béatrice Atherton, editor of Renaut's text, correctly recognized the shape of the *Chantepleure:*

Strophe 1	12 octosyllables	*aab aab bba bba*	12/8
Strophe 2	6 octosyllables	*aab aab*	6/8
Strophe 3	8 hexasyllables	*ab cb db eb*	8/6
Strophe 4	12 hexasyllables	*aab aab bba bba*	12/6

Atherton suggests that Music, in her very form, imitates the lack of harmony, characteristic of Fortune.[23] The 1380 reviser has chosen to eliminate the *Chantepleure*. Not so the Victorine. He appears to have appreciated the novelty of the form and retained it,[24] with one exception: he has rewritten Strophe 3 with a more regular rhyme scheme: *ab ab cb cb*.

In Book II, vii, the Renaut manuscripts insert a poem on the theme of Death, consisting of between fourteen and twenty (maximum) stanzas of sextets of octosyllables, with the rhyme scheme of *aab aab*. In II, vii of the Boethian text, the severe limitations of the human goals of fame, glory, or reputation in life are revealed by a meditative consideration of the theme of Death as a leveler: "Mors spernit altam gloriam . . . / Aequatque summis infima" (12–14).[25]

The 1380 reviser, in his desire to give a more accurate rendition of the Latin source text than Renaut, has chosen to eliminate these stanzas as digressive. The Victorine again shows his independence from X by choosing to retain five of the sextets, those corresponding to stanzas 1, 8, 18, 19, and 20 in the edition of Renaut's version. In all this, the Victorine shows a clear dependence on the earlier translation of Renaut in terms of poetic form, while revealing, nevertheless, a certain skill in manipulating, adapting, and reducing in the direction of brevity and sobriety.

Rhymes

Another feature of the Renaldian text that undergoes certain modifications in both the rewrites under consideration is the rhymes. Renaut originates and spends his life in the territories of East Burgundy and the Franche-Comté. Certain of his rhymes reveal this dialectal coloring. The Dominican of 1380, originating in the Picard area around Beauvais, consistently eliminates the Eastern rhymes. The Victorine is more tolerant, and yet we catch him on more than one occasion rewriting or omitting verses in order to avoid an unacceptable rhyme. We will consider briefly the different treatments of three Eastern rhymes: (1) the rhyming of an open $e + r$ with $a + r$; (2) rhymes in which the result of a tonic closed o in a free position (virtually all examples derive from the generalized Latin suffix *-osu*) rhyme with the vowel deriving from the Latin diphthong *au* which had lowered to [u]—the words involved here are the participles *close(s), enclose(s),* and the substantive *chose(s);* and (3) rhymes where the loss of a vocalized *l* in the group *al,* allows such a vowel to rhyme with *a.*

1. Rhyme *ar* : *er*

There are some forty such rhymes in the *Roman de Fortune.* According to both Bourciez[26] and Pope,[27] an open $e + r$ (especially when the r is dental) may lower to a and rhyme with $a + r$. Such a phenomenon appears first in Eastern dialects but is quite common in less educated speech in Paris in the fifteenth and sixteenth centuries. Villon, for example, can rhyme *terme* with *arme.*[28] In Renaut's text, such rhymes most frequently involve a form of the verb *perdre,* which rhymes with forms of the verbs *garder, regarder,* or with substantives such as *part* or *depart.*

The reactions of the Picard reviser of 1380 and the Victorine to this phenomenon are quite different, revealing once again their fundamental independence. The Picard writer systematically removes all such rhymes, with one exception (an oversight no doubt), at X, 8847 *garde : perde* (cf. IX, 6653). As far as the Victorine is concerned, of the twenty-nine we have selected for relevant comparison, eleven occur in longer passages omitted; three are preserved as is with a retention of the etymological *a* and *e* spellings; thirteen are kept intact, but with a regularized *ar* spelling; and two are rewritten. Given the Victorine's ready acceptance of this semi-popular rhyme, there is no reason to suppose that the two verses rewritten are dictated by a need to change the rhyme. In the case of the two verses of 25418, "Si te afferme vrayement / Qu'aus biens mondains faillir couvient" (25v), which correspond in their positioning to IX, 2307–08 "Car en la fin, combien que tarde / Couvient tousjours que l'en les perde," they result from a need to rewrite a conclusion to a passage in which there has been an omission of some twenty verses rather than from an obvious need to replace the rhyme. Similarly in the case of the second rewrite:

Quant li montes a un musart	Ou monde sont aucun musart
Qui si folement se deporte	Qui moult folement se deportent:
Qu'il cuide que quant se depart	L'ame mourir, quant du cors part,
L'ame du corps qu'elle soit morte,	Cuident, et ce moult les confortent.
Li mondes l'atisë et art	Le monde les atise et art
D'acquerre les biens quë il porte;	De aquerre les biens qu'il portent;
Pour ce, aprés quant il les pert	Et quant aucun d'eulz les part,
Moult durement se desconforte.[29]	Moult durement s'en desconfortent.
Renaut 1417–24	(16r)

The reconstruction of the opening verse of this passage with a generalized plural "Ou monde sont aucun musart" leads to further syntactic changes and allows the Victorine to preserve the sense of the passage by the use of the verb *partir* [to separate], where Renaut had used the verb *perdre* [to lose]. The fool thinks that his soul is dead when it leaves the body; the result is that the fool is far more reliant on worldly goods. For Renaut, the fool is extremely disconsolate when he loses [*pert*] his worldly goods. For the reviser, the thrust of his logic leads him to attribute this extreme discomfort to that moment when someone separates [*part*] fools from their worldly goods.

2. Rhyme *ose* : *ouse/euse*

Rhymes in which the result of a tonic closed *o* in a free position rhymes with the vowel deriving from the Latin diphthong *au* that had lowered to [*u*] occur in Lorraine, East Burgundy, and the Comté.[30] The reviser of 1380 replaces all such rhymes by rewrites in which each rhyme is in either etymological -*ose* or -*euse;* if this proves not possible, then the verses are rewritten with an entirely different rhyme.[31] The procedure adopted by the Victorine is rather more ambiguous. Of the twelve groups of such rhymes chosen for comparative purposes, five mixtures of rhymes in *ose* : *euse* are retained,[32] one (IX, 5195) is quite deliberately omitted, and six are deliberately rewritten with a variety of different rhymes.[33] It would seem that this reviser became progressively sensitive to and dissatisfied with the Eastern rhyme, as all five of the mixed rhymes retained occur in Books I and II (along with some rewrites); in Books III and IV all such mixed rhymes are either omitted or rewritten.

3. Rhyme *aus* : *as*

There is, however, a set of Eastern rhymes used by Renaut that is consistently rejected and rewritten by the reviser of 1380 and by the Victorine. Rhymes where the loss of a vocalized *l* in the group *al* allows the remaining vowel to rhyme with *a* is a feature particularly characteristic of the Franche-Comté.[34] It is instructive to look at the different solutions proposed by both revisers to some of these rhymes. We have chosen six for the purposes of illustration. The following tables and commentary render some idea of the solutions proposed:

IX, 1457–63	X, 1429–35	25418 (16v)
desloyaulx	desloiaux	desloyaux
haulx	haulz	haux
faulx	faulx	faux
pas	mortaulx	haulx

IX, 1463 "Certes bieneurez n'est il pas" has been rewritten by the 1380 reviser as "Bieneürés n'est homs mortaulx" and by the Victorine as "Eüreux n'est mie ne haulx." Both revisers have found a way of rewriting the offending verse with a rhyme in *aux* to conform to the majority rhyme of the octet.

The rewrite of IX, 1433–40 involves both revisers changing one *aux* rhyme to *as,* again conforming to the majority rhyme in an octet. Their solutions, however, are different:

IX, 1433–40	X, 1421–28	25418 (16r)
as	as	as
principaulx	debas	cas
bas	bas	bas
las	las	mas

IX, 1435 "Une des causes principaulx" has been rewritten by the 1380 reviser as "La cause en principal debas" and by the Victorine as "Ung des plus principaux cas."

The Renaldian rhyme of 3913—"Les testes haultes met au bas, / Elle [Fortune] est a toutes gens egaulx"—is rewritten by 25418 as follows: "Les testes hautes met au bas / Et souvent fait dire 'Hélas'" (42r).

In two places, offending Renaldian couplets are simply omitted by the Victorine without any loss of meaning to the passages concerned.[35] On only one occasion has a "faulty" rhyme of this group evaded his attention or ingenuity. The sequence of rhymes is as follows:

IX, 1305–12	X, 1333–40	25418 (14r)
compas	compas	compas
gouvernaulx	postas	gouvernaux
faulx	cas	faux
pas	pas	maux

A similarly "culpable" rhyme, *casse* : *fausse* IX, 6659 leads once again to a rewrite with a new rhyme: the Renaldian couplet, "L'escu de pacïence casse; Et la doulce Fortune fausse" is replaced, with accompanying syntactic adjustments, by "Elle [Fortune] casse la pacïence, / Et la douce, par ignorance" (73v).

The above considerations reveal the clear rejection of significant Eastern rhymes by the reviser of 1380, who can be established on other criteria as Picard. In the case of the Victorine, he shows a clear awareness of Eastern rhymes, which he handles in various ways: rewrites, eliminations, or limited acceptances. His acceptance of the *ar* : *er* rhymes, taken in conjunction with other features, suggest a writer from the Parisian region of the early fifteenth century.

Omissions of Narrative, Allusions, and Images

We now turn our attention to the more substantial omissions alluded to earlier. The most obvious and dramatic of the story omissions are those of the mythological heroes, Orpheus in III, xii and the story of Hercules and Troy in IV, vii. In the case of Ulysses and Circe, IV, iii, the forty-six-verse narrative of Renaut is replaced by a ten-verse allusion to Ulysses as a man full of moral teaching [*doctrine*] and dependent on divine grace in his resistance to the charms of the flesh. This minimal ten-verse narrative leads on to the Renaldian conclusion, which contains a warning against those actions motivated by vice which will harm the soul, a harm far more serious than the metamorphosis into pigs, the result of Circe's enchantment of Ulysses's men.

But these are not the only narrative omissions. The omission or severe reduction of biographical details concerning Boethius in I, 4, part of his complaint to Philosophy, complaints and details picked up again in I, 5 and II, 3, is revealing. This shows a quite deliberate intention on the part of the Victorine not to obfuscate the general line of his moral exhortations with too much narrative. Thus the 336 verses of I, 4 in Renaut's version are reduced to 96 in 25418. All particular detail—of Boethius's defense of those overtaxed in Campania, of particular accusers with examples of their misdeeds—is omitted. The bitter but colorful comparison made by Boethius between the site of his exile, his current surroundings, and his clothing and those of his former state is omitted. The whole is reduced to a broad general statement in which, nevertheless, the thrust of the Boethian complaint is preserved. The same is true of similar passages in I, 5 and II, 3. A long biographical passage of 66 verses in II, 3, the story of the family success of Boethius in terms of his bond with his wife and the success of his two sons, is reduced to one verse: "Et [Fortune] t'en fist si grant homme" (25r). Of the other narratives omitted, we list the story of Croesus and Cyrus, which witnesses to the turns of Fortune's wheel and amply developed by Renaut (II, 2: IX, 2010–95). Again in II, 6, a prose showing the limitations of power and high office, Boethius makes reference to three stories: the first to Zeno (IX, 3379–98) who bit out his tongue rather than betray his companions; the second to the killer Egyptian king, Busiris (IX, 3433–40), himself killed by Hercules; and the third to the Roman Regulus (IX, 3445–86), who was finally placed in fetters by the Carthaginians. Not a trace of these narratives remains in the Victorine abridgment. While Nero is retained by name in II, vi, the narrative developments concerning his burning of Rome (IX, 3583–3604) and his violent inspection of his mother's body (IX, 3611–20) are removed. In II, vii, Renaut, drawing his information largely from the Latin commentary on the *Consolatio* by the English Dominican Nicholas Trevet,[36] expands to some 108 verses the two Latin verses: "Vbi nunc fidelis ossa Fabricii manent / quid Brutus aut rigidus Cato?" (vv. 15–16).[37] In this case, the Victorine's reduced references (12 verses) to loyal Fabricius, just Brutus, and virtuous Cato may seem to echo the succinctness of the Latin text. We may by now be reasonably certain that such is not his motivation but that, once again, it is his distaste for narrative addition or *exempla* or colorful, extended images that dictates the reductions or omissions.

One of the curious narrative additions to Renaut's text, in Book II, 4, is the so-called Fable of the Inconstant Scholar.[38] This 140-verse insertion in II, 4 (vv. 2555–2694), an amplification of the theme that the various gifts of Fortune, by definition unstable, can never lead to true happiness, is prompted by a passage of Trevet, who quotes the "filium inconstancie" of an Anglo-Latin text of circa 1235 entitled *De Disciplina Scholarium*, a text attributed at that time to Boethius himself. This inconstant son tries in turn the professions of clerk, merchant, gardener, knight, lawyer, husband, and astronomer before choosing to be transformed into an ass, in order to escape from his permanent dissatisfaction. This is an addition fully retained (vv. 2375–2544) by the reviser of 1380; indeed he acknowledges the source text as *De la discipline des estoilles et leur doctrine,* attributing it to Boethius, as did Trevet. Furthermore, he justifies the addition of this exemplum on three grounds: (1) its appropriateness; (2) the authority of the Latin commentator; and (3) the authority of Boethius, assumed to be the original author. The procedure of the Victorine at this point (27v–28v) is in an opposite direction. As we have seen, the majority of his omissions in the first four books relates to the disappearance of historical and mythological figures. It is perhaps surprising, then, that any part of the Inconstant Scholar has been preserved. And yet if we begin to see behind the Victorine a slightly dour but devout moralist, then we might understand that the retention of at least the skeletal outline of the fable is not in contradiction with his deletion of the stories of the pagan heroes. The narrative of the fable is, however, stripped of virtually all possible rhetorical coloring. The 140 verses of Renaut have been reduced to 43; of these 43, six introductory lines and the 6 concluding verses of Renaut are retained. Of the other 31, thirteen lines of linkage are new and the other eighteen are borrowed from Renaut in scattered sequences, single verses, or half verses. In an amazing feat of rewriting, the seven professions pursued and abandoned by the scholar have been preserved: introduction and the clerk—9 verses; merchant—3; gardener—3; knight—5; lawyer—5; husband—5; reclusive astronomer—5; and the ass and conclusion—8.

Similar in a sense to the narrative omissions is the suppression of small exempla, often based on a quotation; thus, for example, in III, 4 (IX, 4163–4622) Boethius quotes the verse of Catullus, who called Nonius a malignant growth, despite his high office; the Victorine deletes it. Other examples of such deletions include Philosophy's example of the rule of Athens (I, 5; IX, 1153–60); the allusion to Homer's story of the two jars at the door of the temple, one full of evil, and the other of good (II, 2; IX, 2101–16); the citation of Cicero concerning the failure of the fame of Rome to have reached the Caucasus (II, 7; IX, 3741–56); the Boethian exemplum of the philosopher who failed the test of patient silence (II, 7; IX, 3849–78); and an etymological digression by Renaut on the word *asylum* (III, x; 5557–66), derived from Trevet.

Before proceeding to a consideration of the excision of much of the philosophical argument, we note one further category of omissions that reveals a sober dislike of colorful imagery. Mentions of the sun, moon, or stars in poetic passages disappear. Neither Zephyrus (II, iii; IX, 2355–58) nor the morning star Lucifer (III, i; IX, 4359–62) retain their place in the appropriate meters. In I, vii (IX, 1529–68), all the cloud, star, and storm imagery is deleted. The moral conclusion of I, vii which recommends the abandonment of "fausse joye, tristessse demesuree, fole esperance" [false joy, excessive sadness, misplaced hope], is, however, retained. Similar reductions occur in the opening passage of I, iii and III, vi. In II, vii, the majority of the rhetorical questions of the type, "Who looks on vines for precious jewels?" disappear.

Among other images omitted are those of a colorful or homely nature, for example: in I, 2 (IX, 441–64) the picture of Philosophy at the bedside of Boethius gently placing her hand on his chest, encouraging him to move out of his temporary lethargy of spirit; again, at the end of the same prose, the touching image of Philosophy wiping away the tears of Boethius with the edge of her garment (IX, 481–88); the gentle image at the opening of I, 3 in which Boethius finally recognizes Philosophy as his former nurse at whose breasts he had suckled (IX, 505–20); and the long descriptive section of II, v (IX, 3201–30) on the idyllic age of happy innocence, reduced to a three-verse summary.[39] And then, finally, let us consider the fate of III, ix, that pæan of joy to the unchanging Mover who, through a series of descending but harmonious energies, creates. The first fifty-six verses (5383–5438) of Renaut's eighty-six-verse treatment of this meter preserve and represent well enough the Latin text; the Victorine reduced those fifty-six verses to the following rather trite and colorless summary:

> Pere qui toute puissance as
> Et qui toutez choses creas,
> Sire, qui trestoutes les choses
> Es cieux et en terre encloses
> As ordonnees par ta franchise. . . . (60v)
>
> [Father Who has all power and Who created all things, Lord Who has ordered all things included in earth and in heaven by Your freedom. . . .]

The Victorine's omission of so many narrative elements (biographical and narrative), as well as his distaste for colorful imagery, reveals a desire to convert his source text, the *Roman* of Renaut, from a poetic narrative into a treatise of sober moral admonition and exhortation. His text is a *dit moral* rather than a *roman*.

Omissions of Philosophical Argument

It is more precisely towards the end of Book III that the anti-intellectual or anti-metaphysical tendencies of the Victorine become all too apparent. Under the impetus provided by the meter III, ix, III, 10 looks forward to the more challenging metaphysical arguments to be opened up in Books IV and V and begins with a series of questions and demonstrations to explore where perfected happiness is to be found. The argument moves in a series of ascending connections to the conclusion that since both happiness and God are supreme goodness, then it follows that happiness is identical with supreme divinity. Renaut does make an effort to present this progressive argument in the opening sixty-three verses of III, 10 (IX, 5467–5529). The Victorine, perhaps impatient with the exploratory nature of the metaphysical argument, undercuts the whole process and sums up his pious view of the matter as a confession of faith:

> Or te vueil monstrer clerement
> Que Dieu est le commencement,

Moien, fin, en verité,
De parfaite felicité,
Qui a tout cree et tout fait
Et qui de tout bien est parfait.
Qui veult felicité trouver
Jusqu'a Dieu la couvient chacier. . . . (61r)

[Now I wish to show clearly that God is the beginning, middle, and end, in truth, of perfect happiness, He Who created and made everything and Who is perfected in every good. Whoever wishes to find happiness must pursue it up to God . . . .]

III, 11 provides arguments showing that all things have an instinctive desire to preserve life and to avoid destruction, and that the goal of unity that all things reach for is identical with goodness, which is the end of all things. It is at this point that we can see most clearly the Victorine's rejection of the logical arguments based on previous demonstrations, which are to form the basis of the metaphysical explorations in Book V into the apparent contradictions between the course of Fate and the simplicity of Providence, between the freedom of the will and divine foreknowledge, between discursive reasoning and divine insight, between time and eternity. The reviser does not choose to open up any of these vistas. His work will remain at the level of a *Dit moral contre Fortune*. His way for man to escape the chains of change, misfortune, and injustice is not by an interior knowing or by an exploration of hierarchies of knowing. Rather, he advocates realization of perfect happiness in heaven through trust in the Trinitarian God, through the good offices of the Virgin and the saints.[40]

His abbreviated prologue had already established that conclusion as his particular agenda; he holds to it, progressively reducing the arguments at the end of Book III and in Book IV, to the point at which his work ends suddenly, at the end of Book IV, obliterating the positive and hopeful contemplative ascent to that still center of eternity proposed in Book V. In so doing he has severely truncated, if not destroyed, the powerful intellectual and metaphysical thrust of the original Latin text, a process of reduction already partially begun in Renaut's popular adaptation of the work. But then too, he has eliminated so much of the colorful narrative retained or developed by Renaut in his work. We are left with a text that reveals a rather narrow-minded and dogmatic piety, in which, against the backdrop of the injustice and misery of this life, the only way to find happiness is to throw oneself on the mercy of God, trusting in the intercession of the Virgin and the saints. Such is the nature of this little *Dit moral contre Fortune.*

Notes

1. A fuller description of the manuscript is to be found in B. M. Atherton and J. K. Atkinson, "Les manuscrits du *Roman de Fortune et de Felicité*," *Revue d'Histoire des Textes* 22 (1992), 169–251, esp. 221–22.

2. While this can in no way be proved, we shall refer to the translator throughout this article, simply as a matter of convenience, as the Victorine.

3. Louhans is in the department of Saône-et-Loire, East Burgundy, and Poligny (Jura), further to the east, was in the Franche-Comté.

4. G. Esnos-Hasenohr, ed., *Le Respit de la Mort par Jehan Le Fèvre* (Paris: SATF, 1969), xcv. Her description of the MS covers pp. xcii–xcvii.

5. J. Morawski, "Le manuscrit fr. 25418 de la Bibliothèque nationale et les Vers sur les quatre tempéraments humains," *Neuphilologische Mitteilungen* 28 (1927), 195–208.

6. L. Delisle, *Anciennes traductions françaises de la Consolation de Boëce conservées à la Bibliothèque nationale, in Inventaire général et méthodique des manuscrits français de la Bibliothèque Nationale* (Paris, 1876–78), 2:317–46; originally in *Bibliothèque de l'École des chartes* 34 (1873), 5–32.

7. It was Delisle who established beyond any doubt, in the study already quoted, that, by reason of the dating of certain manuscripts, this translation (his VIII) could not possibly be attributed to Charles d'Orléans as some had earlier surmised. The attribution of this same text to a Jehan de Langres, an error most recently relayed by G. Hasenohr in her edition of *Le Respit de la Mort,* is without foundation. A report on the origin of this latter error is to be found on p. 292 of the study by Ch. V. Langlois on these texts (see note 8).

8. A. Molinier, in his description of MS Toulouse, Bibliothèque municipale, 822, *Catalogue général des manuscrits des bibliothèques publiques des départements* (Paris, 1885), 7: 469–72, esp. 470, interpreted the following verse, "Blans est mon corps, noirs ses habis" (85r), in the epilogue unique to that MS, as indicating an author who was a Benedictine. This opinion has been accepted at its face value since then.

    Ch. V. Langlois gives a succinct summary of the information contained in that epilogue in his study of 1928, "La *Consolation* de Boëce d'après Jean de Meun et plusieurs autres," in *La Vie en France au moyen âge de la fin du xiie au milieu du xive siècle,* vol. 4, *La Vie spirituelle* (1928; Geneva: Slatkine, 1970), 269–326: "Cet épilogue confirme la date de 1380 pour la composition du poème, et désigne clairement celui qui l'a composé: un Bénédictin anonyme. Ce personnage paraît avoir eu une carrière assez agitée, car, né à Beauvais, il avait été prieur du côté de la Savoie; il passa ensuite au service de Louis II de Bourbon, comte de Clermont en Beauvaisis de son chef, et comte de Forez du chef de sa femme en 1372" (293).

M. Noest, whose doctoral thesis is a critical edition of this text (see note 10), makes a strong case for considering the author to have been a Dominican. I summarize his arguments (17, n. 79) briefly, with some additional reflections of my own in passing: a black robe, the scapula, over a white body gown characterizes the Dominican habit from the inception of the Order, as anyone familiar with medieval representations of Dominican saints is aware (they were nevertheless known, and still are, as Blackfriars); the Toulouse epilogue speaks of the author as a *prieur* in Savoy, at one stage of his career—there is nothing in this title that contradicts the possibility of a Dominican; Noest further notes that in a number of miniatures in MS Paris, Bibl. nat, fr. 12459, Boethius is shown wearing what resembles the habit of a Dominican. I add the following reflections: (1) the text was written with the young King Charles VI in mind—the Dominicans played a crucial role as confessors and advisers to at least the male members of the royal family throughout the fourteenth century and beyond; (2) it is interesting to note that the French source text, that of Renaut, is that of a Dominican, and that the author has consulted the Latin commentary of the English Dominican Nicholas Trevet on the *Consolatio* quite independently of Renaut's consultation of the same commentary. While not conclusive, all these factors point us in one direction.

9. P. Meyer, review of Delisle's *Anciennes traductions françaises de la Consolation de Boëce, Romania* 2 (1873), 271–73: "je crois donc que le ms. 25418 n'est qu'une copie altérée (et par places abrégée) de la version que M.D. [décrit] sous le no VIII" (272).

10. The investigations have been greatly facilitated by the completion recently of two doctoral theses at the University of Queensland, which consist of critical editions of the text of (1) Renaut and (2) of the 1380 revision and expansion: B. M. Atherton, ed., *Edition critique de la version longue du "Roman de Fortune et de Felicité" de Renaut de Louhans, traduction en vers de la "Consolatio philosophiae" de Boèce,* 2 vols. (Brisbane: The University of Queensland, 1994); and M. Noest, ed., *A Critical Edition of a Late Fourteenth Century French Verse Translation of Boethius' "De Consolatione philosophiae": Boëce de Confort* (Brisbane: The University of Queensland, 1997) [published as "A Critical Edition of a Late Fourteenth Century French Verse Translation of Boethius' 'De Consolatione Philosophiae': The Böece de Confort," *Carmina Philosophiae* (1999/2000)].

11. The texts have been divided by the editors into divisions based on the books, proses, and meters of the *Consolatio.* Books are numbered in large Roman numerals, proses with Arabic numerals, and meters with small Roman numerals.

12. In the final analysis, these fourteen verses must be seen as borrowed from the epilogue of version X; nevertheless eight of them appear as one of the octets in the prologue to Renaut's *Roman,* see n. 19. The parallels between the following fourteen verses of the prologue of 25418 (with the exception of verse 8, taken from Renaut) and the verses of the epilogue of X, make it clear that for these verses X is the primary source.

Cilz qui bien estudieroit	Cilz qui bien estudieroit
De ce livre cy la substance,	Cestui livre a grant diligence,
Fortune point ne priseroit	Fortune point ne priseroit
N'en luy n'aroit point d'esperance	N'en en lui ne mettroit son esperance
Quant d'umains biens habonderoit;	Quant d'umains bien habunderoit;
Toudiz vivroit en grant doubtance,	Touzdiz vivroit en grant doubtance,

Et quant souffreteux en seroit	Et quant souffreteux en seroit
Point ne lairoit perseveranc;	Tout porteroit en pacience.
Son cuer en Dieu reposeroit	Son cuer en Dieu reposeroit
En qui ne puet estre muance,	En qui ne puet estre muance,
Et toudis en luy trouveroit	Et tousdiz en luy trouveroit
Plenté de biens et habondance	Planté de biens et habundance
Ainsy que mestier li seroit	Ainssi que mestier luy seroit
Selon la divine ordenance,	Selon la divine ordonnance;
Car en Dieu servant gaigneroit	Et ja de biens ne defaulroit
En ce siecle sa suffisance.	Mais en auroit grant pourveance. (1r)
Epilogue of X: 11063–78	Prologue of 25418: 9–24

13. One other echo of X might be detected in the verse of 25418 corresponding to IX, 295–96. The couplet in question in Renaut's text reads: "Raison d'omme et entendement / Ne se doit pas envers leur traire"; X, 291–92 reads: "Par leur espineux sentement / Le fruit de raison font retraire"; and 25418 reads (4r), "Pour leur serieux sentement / Hommes font de rayson retraire."

14. *Les manuscrits françois de la Bibliothèque du roi* (Paris, 1842), 5:55–56.

15. A. Thomas and M. Roques, "Traductions françaises de la *Consolatio Philosophiae* de Boèce," *Histoire littéraire de la France* 37 (1938), 419–88, 543–47.

16. Cambridge, Mass.: The Medieval Academy of America.

17. See my "Manuscript Context as a Guide to Generic Shift: Some Middle French Consolations," in *Medieval Codicology, Iconography, Literature, and Translation: Studies for Keith Val Sinclair,* ed. P. R. Monks and D. D. R. Owen (Leiden: Brill, 1994), 321–32, esp. 322, n. 8.

18. For a discussion of the use of this title, see B. M. Atherton, *Edition critique,* 1:1. Ultimately it is taken from the following rubric on fol. 1r of the MS Glasgow University, Hunterian Museum, 439: "C'est le prologue du romans de fortune et de felicité sus Boëce de consolacion."

19. Et pour ce qui estudiroit	Son cuer en Dieu reposeroit
Ce livrë a grant diligence,	En qui ne puet estre muance,
Fortune point ne doubteroit	Et tousjours en lui trouveroit
N'en lui ne mettroit s'esperance; 100	Planté de biens et habondance.

[And for this reason, whoever would study this book diligently, would not fear Fortune nor put their hope in her. Such a person would rest the heart in God in Whom there can be no change, and would always find in Him plenty and abundance of goods.]

20. Three verses only of this epilogue are borrowed from Renaut's V, 6, those printed in italics. The coincidence of the verse "Qui toutes choses scet et voit" with X, 11060 is just that, a coincidence.

... Et especial les vies

Des glorieux sains et doctrines

Qui ont tout desprisé le monde

Qui plus ordoie qu'il ne monde.

Pour la grace de Dieu querir,

C'on puet par bien faire aquerir,

Ayés tous cuers de vous deffendre

Car bons vassaux ne puet emprendre

Chose que il ne la parface;

Quant veult bien quiert et bien chace.

Alés doncques la droite voye

Qui vers le ciel tout droit a voye;

Ne fuiez pas sans faire guerre; (74r)

Cilz a le ciel qui vaint la terre;

Ceste guerre est fuir les vices.

Lessiez donquez mauvese vie;

Amez bonté et sainte vie,

Et fuiez toute vanité.

Vos prieres en haut dreciez

A Dieu le Seigneur tout puissant,

En unité trinité regnant,

Qui toutes choses scet et voit,

Et tout tres justement pourvoit,

Qui toutez chossez a en baillie,

Et qui sur tout a seignourie;

Et a sa glorieuse mere,

Saincte Maire, non amere,

Qui tant est bonne, belle et sage,

Que rien a li ne s'aparage;

Et a touz les sainctifiez,

Pour estre ou ciel glorifiez

En felicité perfaicte,

En joye de touz biens perfaicte.

Amen. Explicit Boece de Consolacion

[. . . and especially the lives and teachings of the glorious saints who have all contemned the world which sullies more than it cleans. In order to seek God's grace, which one can acquire through doing good, take courage all, to defend yourselves, for a good vassal cannot undertake anything that he does not bring to completion; when he wants good, he seeks and pursues good. So take the straight path which leads directly to heaven; do not flee away without making a struggle; he has heaven who conquers on earth; this war involves fleeing vices. Leave then to one side evil ways of life, love goodness and holy life, and flee all vanity. Raise your prayers on high to God the all powerful Lord, reigning Trinity in Unity, Who knows and sees all, and Who foresees all very justly, Who has all things in His power; and to His glorious mother, Holy Mary, not bitter, who is so good, beautiful and wise that nothing can compare with her; and to all the saints in order to be glorified in perfected happiness, perfected in the joy of all goods. Amen.]

21. The Newhaven MS in fact has an additional octet; 25418 retains six verses of that octet: "'P' signifie vie active / Que on dit laborieuse / Et 'T' vie contemplative / Que on puet dire glorieuse / On vient a la contemplative / De ce fu elle bien songneuse" (3v). This passage does not appear in version X.

22. Dwyer's comment (quoted on p. 52 above) that the process is one of "cutting out alternate lines" (71) is not correct.

23. Atherton, *Edition Critique,* 1:106.

24. Nevertheless, one verse has been omitted from the first strophe and one from the fourth, thus destroying the game of patterned numbers in Renaut.

25. "But leveler Death despising glory's pride . . . the mighty to the humble equal made." Translation of V. E. Watts, *The Consolation of Philosophy* (Baltimore: Penguin , 1969), 75. The Latin edition consulted is that of L. Bieler, *Anicii Manlii Severini Boethii "Philosophiae Consolatio,"* Corpus Christianorum, Series Latina 94 (Turnholt: Brepols, 1957).

26. E. and J. Bourciez, *Phonétique française: Étude historique* (Paris: Klincksieck, 1967), §47, II.

27. M. K. Pope, *From Latin to Modern French* (Manchester: Manchester University Press, 1934), §496.

28. Cf. Renaut's rhymes *lermes : termes : armes* 3963.

29. Renaut: "When there is a fool in the world who acts so mistakenly that he believes that the soul is dead when it leaves the body, then the world stirs and moves him to acquire the goods it provides; for this reason, afterwards, when he loses them, he is desperately disconsolate." 25418: "In the world are some fools who act mistakenly; they believe the soul dies when it leaves the body, and this provides them with a strong sense of comfort. The world stirs and moves them to acquire its goods, which they take to themselves. And when anyone separates them from them, they are desperately disconsolate."

30. E. Philipon, "Les parlers du duché de Bourgogne aux XIIIe et XIVe siècles," *Romania* 39 (1910), §§ 28, 29, 30, 33bis, 36; E. Philipon, "Les parlers de la Comté de Bourgogne aux XIIIᵉ et XIVᵉ siècles," *Romania* 43 (1914), §§ 28, 29, 30, 33bis, 36; and Pope, *From Latin to Modern French,* 495, E §xxiv and 499, SC §xiv.

31. Hence, for example, IX, 235 *chose: vigoreuse* > X, 231 *vertueuse: viguereuse*; IX, 3285 *precieuses : encloses* > X, 3101 *precieuses : tenebreuses*; and IX, 2987 *precieuse : chose* > X, 2865 *nouvelle : belle.*

32. IX, 1314 *chose : melencoulieuse : enclose : perilleuse*; 1362 *gracieuse : chose*; 3105 *choses : preciousos*; 3285 *precieuses : encloses*; 4281 *precieuse : chose.*

33. Thus IX, 2531 *delicieuse : chose* > *delicieux : courouceux* (27v); IX, 3359 *precieuse : chose* > *chose : chose* (37r); IX, 4355 *nuiseuses : choses* > *grevables : agreables* (45v); IX, 5065 *chose : gracieuse* > *plaisant : avenant* (56r); IX, 5437 *choses : preciouses* > *choses : encloses* (60v); IX, 6627 *choses : merveilloses* > *verras : cuideras* (73r).

34. Philipon, "Les parlers de la Comté de Bourgogne," 495–559, §§ 16bis et 38.

35. The rhymes of IX involved are those at vv. 5155 and 6379, rhymes that are replaced by new ones in X at vv. 5245 and 8279.

36. The commentary, dating from ca. 1300, *Exposicio Fratris Nicolai Treveth Anglici Ordinis Predicatorum super Boecio de Consolacione,* is available to scholars in the unpublished edition of E. T. Silk, kindly provided to me by Yale University Library with the authorization of Mrs E. T. Silk.

37. "Where now the bones of staunch Fabricius? Where lies unbending Cato, Brutus where?" (Watts, *The Consolation of Philosophy,* 75).

38. The text of the Inconstant Scholar appears independently of the *Roman de Fortune* in MS Genève, Bibliothèque publique et universitaire, 179bis. It was published under the title of *Des Estats du Siecle* by A. De Montaiglon and G. Raynaud, in *Recueil général et complet des fabliaux* (Paris, 1872–90), 2:264–68.

39. "Le glan du boscage mengoient / Claré ne pyment ne buvoient/ Draps ne savoient coulourer" (35v) [They ate acorns from the woods, they drank neither claret nor aromatic wine, nor did the have the knowledge of dying cloth].

40. See note 20.

AN ITALIAN TRANSLATION OF
LE LIVRE DE BOECE DE CONSOLACION

Glynnis M. Cropp

Translations of translations might seem unjustified, but they illustrate the cultural interchange within Europe during the Middle Ages. Recent research has shown that the most widely known of the medieval French translations of Boethius's *Consolatio Philosophiae, Le Livre de Boece de Consolacion,*[1] was translated into both Middle Dutch[2] and Italian in the fifteenth century.[3] While the first of these "re-translations" was based on the glossed version of *Le Livre de Boece,* the second was based, as we shall see, on the unglossed version, of which the oldest known manuscript (Dijon, Bibliothèque municipale, MS 525, fols. 201r–221r) is dated 1362.

E. G. Parodi published the Italian translation in 1898 in a collection of documents that form the basis for a descriptive study of Ligurian/Genoese dialectal forms of Gallo-Italian.[4] It is found in a parchment manuscript (275 x 190mm) of the first half of the fifteenth century, containing various historical and religious texts. The manuscript lacks the first folio and some folios at the end. The text of the translation "De le questioim de Boecio" (fols. 357r–386r), written in two columns with Latin rubrics introducing verse and prose sections, is incomplete, lacking Book 5 meter 1, prose 2, and meter 2 and breaking off at the end of prose 4. The manuscript, which then belonged to the Congregazione delle Missioni Urbane, Genoa (MS 46), was thought to have been amongst the two thirds of this collection destroyed in a fire in 1944, during wartime shelling of the city. It has now been established that the manuscript still exists and is manuscript 56 in the Biblioteca Franzoniana, Genoa, which obtained the remaining manuscripts from the Missioni Urbane collection.[5]

In the second oldest known manuscript of *Le Livre de Boece de Consolacion* (Paris, Bibliothèque nationale de France, MS fr. 1728, fols. 221r–270v), the verse–prose translation is introduced by Jean de Meun's prologue from his prose translation of the *Consolatio Philosophiae*. This prologue, which consists of the dedication of his work to Philippe le Bel, king of France, and a translator's preface, joined to a translation of the prologue preceding William of Aragon's thirteenth-century Latin commentary, became an integral part of *Le Livre de Boece* and explains the long-standing erroneous attribution of this translation to Jean de Meun. The Italian translator turned Jean de Meun's dedication into verse and translated into prose, with some abridgement, the prologue and *vita* Jean de Meun had derived from the prologue attributed to William of Aragon.[6] The Italian translator tended to skim over text and meaning, sometimes omitting details and subtleties, even at times a passage of text. This style is already evident in the prologue, where he adopted the verse–prose alternation characteristic of Boethius's *Consolatio Philosophiae*.

The first twenty lines of the prologue, which are the translator's own contribution, it seems, are of interest, for they situate Boethius and the *Consolatio Philosophiae* in an explicitly Christian context, as is characteristic of the Italian tradition:[7]

> A lo nome de lo nostro Segnor ueraxe
> e de la gram corte de cel
> e de la uergem Maria,
> chi uoia esser nostra guia
> 5   in lo so sancto reame:
> chaum chi ode diga amen.
> Questo libero in Pauia,
> ornao de phillossoffia,
> fe Boecio in prexom
> 10   per soa conssollaciom;
> unde ello fo descapitao
> e sam Seuerim fo apellao,
> per la uita uirtuossa,
> che cum Elpes soa spossa
> 15   fe, e imperso che ello porta
> la soa testa [e] pressenta
> sum lo otar, poy che tagia
> si fo fora in lo piassar;

        si como expoxiciom
20   a faito Ioham de Meom,
        chi lo uosse translatar
        per la maiste real
        de Fillipo quarto de Franssa.[8]

The exordium (lines 1–6) places the work under the aegis of Christ, Heaven, and the Virgin Mary. Boethius's imprisonment, execution, and virtuous married life justify his sainthood: "sam Seuerim" (line 12) and representation as a martyr saint, carrying his head (lines 15–18). The author then inserted Jean de Meun's dedication (lines 19–23) and list of works (lines 24–33), from which his translation of the letters of Héloïse and Abelard is missing. Jean de Meun's preface on translation has been omitted, the translator simply introducing the prose section in the final lines of verse: "Aora trateremo de Boecio, / de che ello a preisso la fior / de la sentencia de l'aotor" (lines 34–36).

Boethius is presented in dialogue not with Philosophy but with Proffeta/ Propheta, to whom are attributed in 1 prose 1 Philosophy's ascending categories of practical and theoretical knowledge (said here to be designated by Greek words, not included in the text), and without mention of the tears in the gown Philosophy had herself made, the books and sceptre she held.[9] Despite the masculine form of her name, Proffeta is clearly a woman with healing powers (1 pr. 2 and m. 3);[10] in 1 prose 3, "Phillossoffia" momentarily replaces "Proffeta /Propheta."[11]

In 2 meter 6, the translator amplified the text, first adding allusion to the emperor Nero's execution of the apostles, Saint Peter and Saint Paul: "E sam Pero fe crucifficar, / e la testa a sam Poro (fe) tagiar";[12] and then outlining Nero's own fate after he set fire to Rome, with comment from a Christian perspective:

        Che quando Roma bruxa,
        si forte se spauenta
35   de um gram bruzo che ello oi,
        che for de la citae fuzi,
        e de um par che ello troua
        in lo uentre se imspea,
        unde tuto spauentao
40   fo da loui rozigiao(r),
        e, si como e scripto in lo querno,

fo uisto inter lo infferno,
batuo e tormentao
e d'oro caodo abeuerao;
45   e uerra cum Anticriste
a contrar la fe de Criste,
contra Nohe e Ellia,
chi de li boim seram guia.[13]

Is it possible that this amplification owes something to the gloss on Nero accompanying 3 prose 5, 10 in the glossed version of *Le Livre de Boece?* Compare the following:

et cestui Neron dit Claudius qui occist Senecque et les appostres saint Pierre et saint Pol, et depuis mourut il moult chetivement, car les senateurs de Romme se rebellerent contre lui, pour ce qu'il avoit fait bouter le feu en la cité, et pluseurs Rommains avoit fait mourir, et le firent batre de verges de fer; et ne pot trouver en la fin amy ne ennemy, amy qui lui voulsist aidier, ennemy qui le voulsist tost faire mourir pour eschever les paines qu'il souffroit et en la fin s'occist de sa main.[14]

The Italian translator strongly affirmed Christian theology illustrated by Old Testament examples, Noah and the prophet Elijah, and Christ of the New Testament.

The Italian translation evinces some of the distinctive lexical features of *Le Livre de Boece:*

	Consolatio Philosophiae	Le Livre de Boece	Italian translation
2 pr. 2, 12	tragoediarum clamor[15]	les chançons des jugleurs[16] (fol. 202va)	le canssoim de li iugollai (p. 60, lines 18–19)
2 m. 7, 15	Vbi nunc fidelis ossa Fabricii manent?	Ou sont les osses de Platon? (fol. 205va)	Unde e lo corpo de Platom? (p. 66, line 37)
3 pr. 6, 1	ϖ δοξα, δοξα, μυρισισι δπ βροτϖυ ουδευ γεγϖσι βιστου ωγκωσαζ μεγαυ. Euripides, *Andromache,* 319–20	O vaine gloire espandue es miliers des gens Tu n'es autre chose fors enfleure d'oreilles. (fol. 207vb)	O uanna gloria spandua in li milli[a]r de li homi, chi no e aotro cha inffiaura de oregie (p. 72, lines 1–2)

	Consolatio Philosophiae	Le Livre de Boece	Italian translation
	[O glory, glory, myriads of mortals, / Born nothings, thou hast blown their lives up big.]		
4 m. 5, 1	Arcturi	. . . septentrion / Qu'on clame le char saint Martin (fol. 214va)[17]	. . . septentriom / so e lo carro sam Martim (p. 87, lines 2–3)

Further sign of the close correspondence occurs in 4 meter 7, in which the author of *Le Livre de Boece* stopped enumerating Hercules' achievements after the victory over Cerberus, thus omitting lines 20–30 of the Latin text, which he simply summed up in the couplet: "Et tant ot de fors aventures / Que plainnes sont les escriptures" (fol. 216va). The Italian translator followed suit, omitting also lines 17–19 (feats of the golden apples and Cerberus), thus reducing the total number of labors to three. In this way he perpetuated the tradition of the entire corpus of known manuscripts of *Le Livre de Boece:* "Tante aue de forte auenture, / como cointam le scripture" (p. 91, lines 21–22).

In preparing his edition, Parodi had comparison made for him between the Italian text and the glossed version of *Le Livre de Boece* contained in the manuscript Turin, Biblioteca nazionale universitaria, MS L.IV.9, which was subsequently badly damaged by fire in 1904. As a result of this comparison, Parodi occasionally modified the Italian text. For example, in 3 meter 9, line 18, following the Turin manuscript reading, "en perfaitte paix se deuise," Parodi unnecessarily corrected the Italian *parea* to *paxe* ("e in compia paxe diuissa").[18] Most manuscripts of *Le Livre de Boece* here render the Latin *paribus* correctly: "En parfaictes *pars* se devise."[19] In 4 prose 7, 18, Parodi corrected *martirio* to *materia* on the basis of the Turin manuscript reading, which in this instance conforms with that of the majority of manuscripts: *matiere,* and with the Latin *materia*.[20] However, the two oldest manuscripts containing the unglossed version of *Le Livre de Boece,* those of Dijon and Paris mentioned above, have the reading *martire*.[21] Renderings close to those of these two manuscripts occur elsewhere in the Italian translation, for example in 4 prose 6, 18 "per fructo chi rendem" corresponds to their *rendent,*[22] rather than to the more frequent reading *portent,* and in sentence 33 of the same prose *a chaum,* resembles their *a chascun,*[23] which is itself an erroneous rendering of the Latin *Catoni,* translated correctly in most manuscripts as *a Cathon.* The evidence is sufficient to propose that the Italian translation is based on the unglossed version of *Le Livre de Boece.*

Book 5 of the Italian translation diverges from the general character of Books 1–4. Besides the Latin rubrics, it has Latin lemmata that connect the translation to specific passages of the *Consolatio.* The alternation of verse and prose has been replaced by prose only, but with meter 1, prose 2, and meter 2 missing and the text ending with prose 4, this difference is not particularly apparent. No longer a translation of *Le Livre de Boece,* the text seems more probably derived directly from a Latin text with commentary and reads increasingly like a summary commentary rather than a translation of the Latin text of the *Consolatio.*[24]

This comparison is sufficient to show that Books 1–4 of the Italian translation are a translation of the unglossed version of *Le Livre de Boece,* evincing the translator's tendency to abridge and omit passages, rather than to amplify. The few additions noted emphasize Christian implications of the dialogue. Parodi described the state of the Italian text as "disgraziatissimo" and drew attention to its inaccuracies;[25] it certainly lacks the rhetoric and the force of Boethius's voice calling for pity and help, and its incompleteness is a serious defect. Nevertheless, "De le questioim de Boecio" is a valuable piece in the mosaic of the medieval Italian translations[26] and their connections with the French translations of the *Consolatio Philosophiae.* Furthermore, as a translation of a translation, it strengthens the vernacular textual tradition and marks the tendency to displace the Latin source tradition of the *Consolatio Philosophiae* in favor of recent translations. For, despite its inaccuracies, incompleteness, and unusual linguistic features, the greater part of this Italian translation can be considered a palimpsest of *Le Livre de Boece de Consolacion.*

Notes

1. Glynnis M. Cropp, "Les Manuscrits du *Livre de Boece de Consolacion,*" *Revue d'histoire des textes* 12–13 (1982–83), 263–352; Glynnis M. Cropp, *"Le Livre de Boece de Consolacion:* From Translation to Glossed Text," in *The Medieval Boethius: Studies in the Vernacular Translations of "De Consolatione Philosophiae,"* ed. A. J. Minnis (Cambridge: Brewer,

1987), 63–88; and Glynnis M. Cropp, "The Medieval French Tradition," in *Boethius in the Middle Ages: Latin and Vernacular Traditions of the "Consolatio Philosophiae,"* ed. Maarten J. F. M. Hoenen and Lodi Nauta (Leiden: Brill, 1997), 243–65, esp. 249–50.

2. Mariken Goris and Wilma Wissink, "The Medieval Dutch Tradition of Boethius' *Consolatio philosophiae,"* in *Boethius in the Middle Ages,* ed. Hoenen and Nauta, 121–65 and pl. 1.

3. Thomas Ricklin, ". . . *Quello non conosciuto da molti libro di Boezio.* Hinweise zur *Consolatio philosophiae* in Norditalien," in *Boethius in the Middle Ages,* ed. Hoenen and Nauta, 267–86, esp. 272–80, 286.

4. E. G. Parodi, "Studi liguri," *Archivio glottologico italiano* 14 (1898), 1–110, esp. 37, 49–97 for the edition. It is referred to in the notes as "Parodi, *Ed.*" I am very grateful to Dr. Thomas Ricklin, Université Miséricorde, Fribourg, who sent me a photocopy of the edition.

5. Paul Oskar Kristeller, *Iter Italicum: A Finding List of Uncatalogued or Incompletely Catalogued Humanistic Manuscripts of the Renaissance in Italian and Other Libraries,* vol. 1 (London: Warburg Institute, 1965), 241. Kristeller does not mention this manuscript. I am grateful to the Institut de Recherche et d'Histoire des Textes, Paris; the Biblioteca Universitaria, Genoa; Professor L. Obertello, Chiavari; Dr. C. de Hamel, formerly of Sotheby's, London, and now Parker Library, Corpus Christi College, Cambridge; Professor A. M. Babbi, Università di Verona; and Mr. Jose Vincenzo Molle, Università di Genova, who helped me trace the fate of the manuscript. Mr. Molle is preparing a critical edition of this translation of the *Consolatio.*

6. Roberto Crespo, "Il prologo alla traduzione della 'Consolatio Philosophiae' di Jean de Meun e il commento di Guglielmo d'Aragona," in *Romanitas et Christianitas. Studia I. H. Waszink* (Amsterdam and London: North-Holland Publishing Co., 1973), 55–70; and Glynnis M. Cropp, "Le Prologue de Jean de Meun et *Le Livre de Boece de Consolacion,"* *Romania* 103 (1982), 279–83. The text of Jean de Meun's prologue is found in V.-L. Dedeck-Héry, ed., "Boethius' *De Consolatione* by Jean de Meun," *Mediaeval Studies* 14 (1952), 165–275, esp. 168–71.

7. Ricklin, ". . . *Quello non,"* 278–81.

8. Parodi, *Ed.,* p. 50, lines 1–23. The precise meaning of lines 17–18 is difficult to interpret. I am grateful for the light Dr. Bruno Ferraro, University of Auckland, shed on the problem. Boethius's stand for public justice and the torture and death sentence imposed by the emperor Theodoric, an Arian, made him acclaimed a martyr. He was worshipped in Pavia from the thirteenth century and his cult confirmed in 1883 for the diocese of Pavia, where his relics are enshrined in the church of S. Pietro in Ciel d'Oro. The supposed date of his death, 23 October, is the feast day of Saint Severinus Boethius. "Elpes soa spossa" (line 14) reflects a very doubtful tradition according to which Boethius married Helpis, a native of Sicily. Her epitaph is found, for example, in Cambridge, University Library, MS Dd.vi.6 (fol. 67v) and Cambridge, Trinity College Library, MS O.3.7 (fol. 52v), which contain, respectively, text and commentary on the *Consolatio.* But rightly the epitaph refers to a different Boethius (John R. Martindale, *Prosopography of the Later Roman Empire,* vol. 2 [Cambridge: Cambridge University Press, 1980], 537–38). The wife of the author of the *Consolatio* was Rusticiana, daughter of Q. Aurelius Memmius Symmachus, patrician and head of the senate 521, executed 525.

9. Parodi, *Ed.,* p. 52.

10. Parodi, *Ed.,* p. 53.

11. Parodi, *Ed.,* p. 53, line 43.

12. Parodi, *Ed.,* p. 65, lines 29–30.

13. Parodi, *Ed.,* p. 65, lines 33–48.

14. Glynnis M. Cropp, ed., *Le Livre de Boece de Consolacion* (Geneva: Droz, 2006), 163.

15. *Philosophiae Consolatio,* ed. Ludovicus Bieler, Corpus Christianorum Series Latina, 94 (Turnhout: Brepols, 1984). All references to the Latin text are to this edition.

16. These examples are quoted from Dijon, Bibliothèque municipale, MS 525, where *Le Livre de Boece,* unglossed and without prologue, occupies folios 201r–217ra, the text from 5 pr. 3 onwards being the prose translation of Jean de Meun (fols. 217rb–221rb).

17. Glynnis M. Cropp, "Le Char saint Martin: désignation de la Grande Ourse," *Zeitschrift für romanische Philologie* 118 (2002), 173–81.

18. Parodi, *Ed.,* p. 74, line 43 and n. 9.

19. Dijon, Bibliothèque municipale, MS 525, fol. 209ra.

20. Parodi, *Ed.,* p. 90, line 38 and n. 10.

21. For example, Dijon, Bibliothèque municipale, MS 525, fol. 216rb.

22. Parodi, *Ed.,* p. 88, line 13; and Dijon, Bibliothèque municipale, MS 525, fol. 215ra.

23. Parodi, *Ed.,* p. 88, line 38; and Dijon, Bibliothèque municipale, MS 525, fol. 215va.

24. Ricklin, ". . . *Quello non,*" 278.

25. Parodi, *Ed.,* p. 50.

26. For an account of the Italian translations, see Helmuth-Wilhelm Heinz, *Grazia di Meo: Il Libro di Boeçio de chonsolazione (1343)* (Frankfurt-am-Main: P. Lang, 1984), 10–12; and Ricklin, ". . . *Quello non,*" 280, n. 76. The known medieval Italian translations number eleven, with the recent acquisition by Columbia University Library, New York, of a manuscript (now Lodge MS 24) containing a hitherto unknown and seemingly independent Italian translation, written towards the end of the fifteenth century and almost certainly in Umbria, as Dr. Consuelo Dutschke, Curator, has identified from the language of the text.

SOME VERNACULAR VERSIONS OF BOETHIUS'S *DE CONSOLATIONE PHILOSOPHIAE* IN MEDIEVAL SPAIN

NOTES ON THEIR RELATIONSHIP WITH THE COMMENTARY TRADITION

Francesca Ziino

Boethius's *De Consolatione Philosophiae* was one of the most popular books of the Middle Ages. In Spain, as in many other European countries, we find the traces of its diffusion and lasting influence.[1] We do not as yet have a comprehensive conspectus of the Latin and vernacular manuscript tradition of *De Consolatione* in Spain, such as exists for other countries;[2] but, according to the extant evidence, the two earliest Latin manuscripts are of English and Italian provenance (Real Biblioteca del Escorial, MS E.II.1, eleventh century; Madrid, Biblioteca Nacional, MS 10109, late twelfth to early thirteenth century).[3]

Apart from the surviving manuscripts (most of which date from the fourteenth and fifteenth centuries), we have documentary evidence (from inventories, letters, testaments, etc.) of many copies now lost. Unfortunately, often the references are so vague that we cannot say whether the *Consolatio* mentioned was in Latin or in the vernacular, or if it was accompanied by glosses. We find copies and translations of *De Consolatione* in the libraries of monasteries and cathedrals: for example, in the thirteenth century, the monastery of Santo Domingo de Silos owned a copy of *De Consolatione* and an unidentified *Liber Boecii,* while a copy of *De Consolatione* and a copy of the Boethius commentary on the Aristotelian *Categories* are mentioned in a list of books borrowed from King Alfonso X by the monastery of Santa Maria de Najera.

From the fourteenth century onwards, the *Consolatio* became increasingly popular among lay people, who appreciated it not only as a philosophical masterpiece but also, above all, for its ethical and didactic value: the *Consolatio* could give moral advice as well as answers to such important questions as the nature of evil and divine providence. Boethius's *Consolatio* fully complied with the needs of readers who, as Jeremy N. H. Lawrance has observed,[4] were seeking "exemplos"—and "consolación" in particular—in what they read or, as J. Keith Atkinson has remarked,[5] were seeking "a set of recipes for the good life."

There also may be a link between the growing popularity of *De Consolatione,* as a sort of manual for spiritual guidance, and the difficult historical situation of the Spanish regions in the late fourteenth century, with the spread of plague and famine. Nevertheless, despite my stressing a moral reading of the *Consolatio,* I should mention that in Spain, as in the rest of Europe, the *fortuna* of Boethius's work developed in many different ways. It also was considered as a source book for mythological *fabulae* and for the allegorical symbolism; it was used to teach Latin grammar in the schools, and it was quoted and drawn upon by several writers. Boethius's work was translated into the vernacular for a new audience of laymen: between the fourteenth and fifteenth centuries, four distinct vernacular versions circulated in medieval Spain, along with a Castilian translation of Trevet's commentary on *De Consolatione.*[6]

We are quite far from the twelve extant French translations of the *Consolatio;* nevertheless, as Glynnis M. Cropp recently has written, "in no other country than France, in no other language than French [. . .] did so many vernacular translations of the *Consolatio* exist in the Middle Ages."[7] I must add that the first French translation dates from as early as the beginning of the thirteenth century.[8] In contrast, the Hispanic translations all date from the second half of the fourteenth century to the first half of the fifteenth, a period characterized by a growing tendency to translate and adapt the Latin classics, since new readers, who were not familiar with Latin language, were turning their attention to the literature that had for a long time been the cultural heritage of the clergy alone. First in Catalonia, and then in Castile, there was an increasing demand for translations, especially at the royal courts and in the cultivated circles close to the courts and the royal chancelleries.

Kings such as Alfonso the Magnanimous and Martin I of Aragon, and noblemen such as the Marquis of Santillana and the Constable Peter of Portugal, possessed copies of vernacular versions of the *Consolatio,* as did physicians, lawyers, and merchants. Most copies mentioned in private collections are made of paper, as was usual for the manuscripts circulating in late medieval Spain.[9] However, given their structure and the purpose for which they were intended, the Hispanic renderings cannot be defined as "humanistic translations": for example, most translators were concerned not with respecting the text translated but with making it comprehensible to its readers, often by interpolating glosses.

In this essay I will examine some aspects of two of the four Hispanic translations of Boethius's *De Consolatione Philosophiae.* I shall call the two translations version α and version β. First I will briefly describe α and β; then I will give some evidence of a Catalan source for a Castilian translation of β; and finally, I will discuss the relationship among α, β, and the tradition of Latin commentary on *De Consolatione.*

The first translation (α) exists in seven manuscripts and an edition:

A: Barcelona, Biblioteca Universitària, MS 77, 117 fols., sec. XV

B: Barcelona, Biblioteca de Catalunya, MS 68, 121 fols., sec. XV

G: Madrid, Biblioteca Nacional, MS 18396, 156 fols., sec. XV

P: Paris, Bibliothèque nationale de France, MS fonds esp. 474, 119 fols., sec. XV

Be: Berkeley, Bancroft Library, MS UCB 160, 109 fols., (ca. 1470–80)[10]

V: Avignon, Archive du Département de Vaucluse, MS fonds Requin 177, sec. XV (23 fols. with fragments from Books 1–5)

Ce: Cervera, Arxiu Històric de la Ciutat, MS 1, 90 fols., sec. XV (missing the beginning)

C: *editio princeps,* Lleida (Lérida), Heinric Botel, 2 June 1489, 116 fols.

An eighth manuscript (Barcelona, Arxiu del Palau, MS XII, 37 fols., sec. XV) is now missing.[11] The α translation is a Catalan prose version, in five books, divided into proses and meters that follow the corresponding *prosae* and *metra* of Boethius's *De Consolatione.* It is attributed to Antoni Ginebreda, a Dominican friar who was prior of Santa Catalina in Barcelona and preacher at the Royal Chapel. He came into frequent contact with the kings of the Aragon Crown, Peter IV and John I; Peter IV charged him with completing the Catalan translation of *Compendium historiale* begun by another Dominican, Jaume Domènech.[12] The name of Antoni Ginebreda as author of the translation occurs in the rubric and in the dedicatory preface that precede the prologue and the actual text of the translation. In the dedicatory preface, surviving in its Catalan form only in the Berkeley manuscript, Ginebreda says that others before him translated the *Consolatio* into Catalan, among whom was one who addressed his work to a Prince of Majorca. But as his translation was incomplete, lacking the history of Theodoric and some sections of Book 5, Antoni Ginebreda accepted the task of completing and revising it. Let me quote only the first lines:

> Per ço com lo libre de Consolació de Boeci es fort necessari a **<ricrear>** los hòmens **qui són en tribulació e a exercitar-los a devoció e a entendre la altesa dels sacrets divinals**, per ço alguns han ffet tot lur poder de aromansar lo dit libre **a instrucció dels qui no saben sciència**, e entre los altres hun lo qual lo endreçà al inffant de Mallorqua.[13]

> [Since the book of Boethius's *Consolatio* is very necessary to **<rekindle the spirit of>** those **who live in suffering and to stimulate them to devotion and a full comprehension of the divine secrets**, for this reason some people have done their best to translate this book **so that it could teach those who do not possess "knowledge."** Among these translators, there was one who addressed his version to the Prince of Majorca.]

In this passage, you again will notice the idea that the *Consolatio* is a book leading to devotion and to the comprehension of divine secrets, as well as the assertion that a translation is needed for people who are not able to understand Latin. Ginebreda's version can be dated to the late fourteenth century.[14] It became very popular and was later translated into Castilian.[15]

What then of the version revised by Ginebreda? We know that the library of the monastery of Montserrat possessed a manuscript of a Catalan version of the *Consolatio* addressed to the Prince James IV of Majorca. The manuscript was lost when Montserrat was sacked by Napoleon's troops in 1811. According to a description made before its disappearance, the work was a prose version of the *Consolatio,* in five books divided into meters and proses, interpolated with glosses and preceded by a dedicatory preface.[16] In this preface, the author (a Dominican friar, Pere Saplana from Tarragona) dedicated the version to Prince James of Majorca while the latter was in prison at the command of King Peter IV of Aragon at Barcelona (1358–62), after the death of his father James III. Saplana said he used a commentary on the *Consolatio* by Thomas Aquinas. The general consensus is that Ginebreda revised Saplana's version; any further speculation is invalidated by the loss of the Montserrat manuscript.[17]

The second translation that we will discuss (β) exists, in its Catalan form, only in a fragmentary text. It is in manuscript **R**, Barcelona, Arxiu de la Corona d'Aragó, MS Ripoll 113, 5 fols., sec. XIV. **R** forms part of a miscellaneous volume that contains also some hagiographical texts.[18] The Boethian fragment occupies the last five leaves of the codex; it begins with a prologue and ends in Book 1, meter 4. The text is divided into chapters that comprise one meter and one prose of the Latin original; the prologue constitutes the first chapter.[19]

We have a complete Castilian translation of the text transmitted fragmentarily by **R**, that exists in manuscript **N**, Madrid, Biblioteca Nacional, MS 10193, 82 fols., 21 September 1436. The colophon of **N** reads as follows:

> Este libro fizo Pedro de Valladolid, criado del señor Rey de Navarra e oficial suyo de pararle su tabla en que comiese e las cortinas en que oya missa, e fizolo en la villa de Alcañiz en el año de mill e quatroçientos e treynta e seys años en el mes de setienbre ha veynte e un dia andados. (fol. 82v)

> [Pedro de Valladolid made this book, servant of the King of Navarre, as well as official assigned to lay the table and arrange the curtains where the King hears Mass. He made it in the town of Alcañiz on the 21st of September 1436.]

The king of Navarre is John, who was crowned John II of Aragon in 1425 after he married Blanca, daughter and heir of King Charles III of Navarre. The mention of the town of Alcañiz is a reference to a long stay by the king in Alcañiz where he was presiding over the *Cortes generales* of the kingdom of Aragon (1436). As for Pedro de Valladolid, I have found some documentary evidence about a man of that name who was "repostero" of King John in 1435–36, but this does not tell us anything about his role (was he translator or copyist of the translation?).[20]

Indeed, apart from the colophon, we have no information about the sources of the Castilian translation; however, some facts confirm that **N** makes use of a Catalan source, that is, a former Catalan translation of the *Consolatio*.[21] First, we find in **N** many lexical and grammatical Catalanisms. This short list shows on the left the "Catalanized" form; on the right the genuine Castilian form:

cogitaçiones, fol.10v	[< cogitacions]	vs.	pensamientos, fol. 10v
enpachar, fol. 20r	[< empatxar]	vs.	enbargar, fol. 20v
fuerte, fol. 11r	[< fort]	vs.	mucho, muy, fol. 1r
guardar, fol. 11r	[< guardar]	vs.	mirar, fol. 11v
ya se sea que, fol. 7v	[< jatsia que]	vs.	aunque, fol. 14r
més, fol. 47r	[< més]	vs.	más, fol. 2v
pro, fol. 14r	[< prou]	vs.	asaz, fol. 14r
senblant, fol. 13v	[< semblant]	vs.	semejante, fol. 9r
sinse, fol. 13v	[< sense]	vs.	sin, fol. 9v
tancar, fol. 65r	[< tancar]	vs.	çerrar, fol. 7r
todos tienpos, fol. 3v	[< tots temps]	vs.	sienpre, fol. 12v
toste, fol. 9v	[< tost]	vs.	luego, fol. 12v
tantoste, fol. 7r	[< tantost]	vs.	luego, fol. 12v

Second, we find in **N** many mistakes that can be explained only by assuming that the translator misunderstood a Catalan source:

Example 1

Si . . . nemorum gratas viderit umbras (*De Cons.* 3 m. 2. 22–23)[22]
las aves . . . fuyen a los *omnes* de los árboles. (fol. 39r)

[los ocells . . . fugen a les ombres dels albres]

[the translator read the Catalan term *ombres* "shadows" as if it were the Castilian term *[h]ombres* "men," and so he translated it with *omnes,* another Castilian form for "men."]

Example 2

las gentes se maravillan mucho de algunas cosas . . . ansý como es del *cuerpo* de la estrella llamada Poetes . . . que se mueve entorno de la tramontana. (fol. 64v)

[the translator read the Catalan form *córs* "course" (of a star) as if it were *còrs,* a homograph that means "body."][23]

Third, if we compare **N** with **R** we find a strong similarity between the two texts; I should say that the Castilian is almost a word-for-word translation of the Catalan text. In addition, **N** is divided into chapters that correspond exactly with those in **R**. An example from the prologue with the stories of Theodoric and Boethius follows:

α: En aquest temps lo dit Theodorich amave e loave fort lo dit Boeci; mas per tal com lo dit Theodorich axí com a treydor tenia Roma, duptant-se que los romans no li rebellassen fenyé que los romans scrivien a l'emperador contra ell, e per ço com lo principal era Boeci imposà-li crim de lesa magestad e exelà.l e tramès-lo en un càrçer a Pavia. (**A**, fol. 3v)

R [*missing the beginning*]: la qual cosa en breu los vendria en ajuda contra lo dit Theodorich e.l desposseyria del regne; posant falçament títol de tració al dit Boheci per ço cor era major e pus virtuós e pus poderós que.ls altres; emperò era innocent en la cosa. E en absència del dit Boeci fo promulgada sentència contra ell que fos exiylat e mes en presó en la ciutat de Pavia, on per colpa malament fenta fo malmenat. (fol. 141r)

N: Aqueste Theodorico era tirano e erege seguiendo la error de los arrianos, e por tal que el dicho Theodorico falsamente fazía su poderío de destroyr las f[r]anquezas e libertades de la çibdat e el dicho Boeçio con buenas maneras le contrastava, onde quando el di[c]ho Theodorico vio que Boeçio le enpachava que non pudía conplir su coraçón en muchas malvestades que se pensava contra la dicha comunidat, buscó manera con la quale pudiese matar al dicho Boeçio. E como non pudiese fallar justas razones por tal que el dicho Boeçio era verdaderamente bueno, <e> fazía letras de parte del enperador de Gresçia [las] quales dichas letras enbiase al dicho Boeçio e a los otros senadores e cónsoles de Roma, respondiendo ha ellos como avía resçebidas sus letras e entendidas, *por la qual cosa en breve les vendrie en ayuda contra el dicho Theodorico e le desposearie del regno; e poniendo falsamente título de trayçión al dicho Boeçio e a los otros senadores, mas prynçipalmente a Boeçio por tal que era mayor e más virtuoso e más poderoso que los otros, enpero ynoçente en la cosa. E en absençia del dicho Boeçio fue provulgada la sentençia que fuese desterrado e metido en prisión en la çibdat de Pavía; onde por culpa malamente fecha fue maltrabtado.* (fol. 7rv)

We therefore can be reasonably confident that the Castilian translation of MS Madrid, Biblioteca Nacional, 10193 (**N**) derives from a lost copy of the Catalan version of the *Consolatio* now represented fragmentarily by the Ripoll MS. That is to say, the Castilian text is a translation of the Catalan version now surviving only in the Ripoll MS; but it is not a translation from that particular Ripoll MS.[24] So, I shall call version β the translation represented by **R** + **N**.

The interest of scholars recently has focused on the relationship between version α and version β. Indeed, as one will see from the following examples, there is a strong similarity between them. We can exclude the possibility of version β being the translation made by Pere Saplana and later revised by Ginebreda, because it presents none of the characteristics Ginebreda ascribes to that version (namely, the absence of a historical *accessus* and some sections of Book 5). I agree with other scholars, such as Jaume Riera i Sans, that α and β are two distinct versions of one basic text, that is, two distinct versions of the Catalan translation of the *Consolatio,* now lost, attributed to Pere Saplana. Some differences between them make me exclude the possibility that α is a "remake" or adaptation of β, or vice versa.[25] Leaving aside philological problems, I would prefer to discuss here some results of my current research, that is, the relationship among α, β, and the tradition of Latin commentary on the *Consolatio.*

Rather than translations in the current meaning of the word, both α and β can be considered to be examples of "translation-commentary," that is, what has been defined by J. Keith Atkinson as "a genre combining the vernacular translation of an *auctor* with vernacular commentary."[26] In our versions, the translation of the Boethian text is followed by the translation of material that derives from Latin commentaries on the *Consolatio,* with no clear distinction between text and gloss. We do not find rubrics such as *Texte* and *Glose* to mark the alternation (as happens in the *Livre de Boece de Consolacion,* a French glossed translation dating from the second half of the fourteenth century).[27] The result is something that must be read as a continuous work, although at some points in the text we find "key-phrases," such as "on és notadora cosa, ço és," etc., that introduce a gloss.[28] Most of the explanatory material derives from the Latin commentary on the *Consolatio* attributed to William of Aragon (alias Guillelmus de Aragonia, de Hispania, Hispalensis),[29] which is dated to the late thirteenth century and which now survives, as far as we know, in five manuscripts, none of them in Spain (but we have at least one inventory giving evidence of its diffusion in Catalonia).[30] Those five manuscripts are:

1. Erfurt, Bibliotheca Amplonensis, MS F 358, fols. 1–25 (dated 1335)

2. Paris, Bibliothèque nationale de France, MS lat. 11856, fols. 9–130 (sec. XIV *ex.*)

3. Wroclaw, Bibliotheka Universitecka, MS I. F. 135, fols. 82–139 (*t. ante quem* 1372)
4. Cambridge, Gonville and Caius College MS 309/707, fols. 89–170v (sec. XIV *ex.*)
5. Cambridge, University Library, MS Ii. 3. 21, part II, fols. 9–119v (sec. XIV–XV).

It should be noted that in the Paris manuscript, the commentary of William of Aragon is attributed to Thomas Aquinas (the rubrics say: "Explicit prologus sancti Thome; glosa sancti Thome"). The false attribution could explain why Pere Saplana, the possible author of the first Catalan translation of the *Consolatio,* said in the preface to his work that he used a commentary on the *Consolatio* by Thomas Aquinas: it might be that he found a manuscript in the library of his monastery, which, like the Paris manuscript, transmitted the incorrect attribution.

We have little data about William. In the colophon of some manuscripts of his works we read that he was "medicus de dicione Regis Aragonie" [master of medicine of the domain of the King of Aragon].[31] He wrote also a *Liber de nobilitate* (where he discusses the nature of true nobility),[32] a commentary on Pseudo Aristotle's *Physionomia* (ante 1310),[33] a *Liber de pronosticatione sompniorum,*[34] and a commentary on Pseudo Ptolemy's *Centiloquium.*[35] His commentary on the *Consolatio* has been described as "rare and hightly distinctive"[36] because on many occasions it differs from the common tradition of glossing, providing explanations about specific points of the *Consolatio* in a very distinctive manner. It seems that William of Aragon's commentary enjoyed quite a good diffusion in the fourteenth century. Apart from the Hispanic versions, three more translations owe some of their glosses to William of Aragon's commentary: Jean de Meun's *Livre de Confort de Philosophie,* a prose translation in the dialect of Hainaut, and a Picard verse translation. Both the translation from Hainaut and the Picard translation are anonymous.[37] The Hispanic versions, nevertheless, use the whole of William's commentary, showing remarkable similarities with it from the prologue to the end of the fifth book.

What can we say about how the Hispanic versions use William's commentary? Do they follow it in a pedestrian way or do they select some particular glosses? If so, which ones? Do they use only William's commentary, or do they insert material obtained from different sources? In other words, can α and β be seen to be the result of a conscious and active application of a technique (the "translation-commentary" technique)?

Before offering some concrete examples, let me provide some general insights. As far as I have observed until now, it seems to me that version α and version β follow William's commentary quite closely. However, they adapt the commentary in three fundamental ways: first, they eliminate or abridge some glosses, selecting only what they need; second, they change the order the glosses follow in William's commentary; and third, they have details not present in William's commentary.

To deal with the first type of adaptation: α and β reveal a tendency to eliminate those glosses that are felt to be irrelevant or too technical for a lay audience—most likely, those glosses that did not belong to the cultural ambit of the public for whom the translations were intended. For example, William of Aragon offers full information about the "studia eleatica et academica" made by the young Boethius:[38]

> Intelligendum autem sicut studia achademica atque eleatica sunt dicta a locis ubi Plato et Aristoteles studuerunt docentes: Plato iuxta portam Achademicam, quae sic dicebatur Athenis sicut porta Sancti Dionysii Parisius; Aristoteles vero iuxta portam Eleaticam, a regione Elinum, id est Macedonum, dicta. Per illas enim portas ibatur ad loca unde nomen habebant. (MS CUL Ii.3.21, fol. 14r)

Both α and β remove this note.[39] We do not find, in α or β, any trace of those sections where William explains grammatical and rhetorical points, or provides information about the metrical structure of Boethius's *metra*. Little space is given to etymological questions. Some geographical notes have been retained, but the majority of those referring to astronomical and meteorological details have been left out. Often names such as Boreas, Auster, Phoebus, etc. have been translated simply as "wind" or "sun" and so on. However, α and β are particularly concerned with the mythological and historical glosses: they dwell upon those figures who might be un-familiar to the readers or whose lives and stories could provide useful moral advice. So we have narrative digressions about Socrates, Seneca, Cato, Brutus, and so forth, as well as Hercules, Ulysses, and Orpheus. Sometimes the names have been translated so that they reveal the Latin source behind the vernacular rendering: for example, we find forms such as *Gay Cesar fill de Germanici* (α) and *Gai fiio de Grimani* (β); or *Cani* (for *Canius*) that correspond to *Germanici filius; CANIOS id est Canii sequaces,*[40] and so on in William's commentary, with the vernacular versions retaining the inflected forms of Latin names (in these cases, genitive). The exposition of relevant philosophical points is often simplified, since the main function of the translations is to give essential information in order to clarify Boethius's text, not to analyze his thought closely. See, for example, the passage of William's commentary on the lemma SUPRA VERTICEM VISA EST MULIER: it is the beginning of the first book, first prose, the portrait of Lady Philosophy.

William of Aragon: SUPRA VERTICEM VISA EST MULIER. Sed est intelligendum quod philosophia uno modo accipitur antonomasice pro scientia causarum universalissimarum primarum [. . .] accipitur etiam alio modo philosophia pro scientiis realibus [. . .] tertio modo accipitur philosophia large, secundum quod est comprehensiva et regulativa omnis habitus scientifici et hoc modo communiter accipitur nomen philosophiae [. . .] est sub forma mulieris descripta. Mulier enim est ad hoc naturaliter ordinata, ut virum pariat et nutriat. Istud est opus suum proprium et perfectum, et <quia> sola philosophia virum facit perfectum munde nutriendo et suaviter informando, secundum quod legitur Libello de vita philosophorum Demostenem et Platonem dixisse. Quilibet enim eorum dixit se duas habuisse matres, scilicet naturam et philosophiam, et quod natura primo fecerat quasi rudes et materiales eos; philosophia vero a vitiis eos mundans, [virtutibus et scientiis nutriens], divinis bonitatibus informavit.[41]

α: Aquesta dona era Philosophia, e és dita dona per ço car axí com a la dona se pertany, segons la sua condició, de infantar l'om e de nudrir-lo, e a açò és ordonada naturalment, axí la philosophia fa l'om perfet e acabat nodrint e informant aquell nedeament e bella [. . .] Aquesta dona fo mare dels philòsophs e dels savis; per que Plato e Demostenes dixeren que havien haudes dues mares, ço és, natura e philosophia, e deyen que natura los havia fets materials, mas natura los havia denejats de vicis, e la saviesa informats de virtuts. (**A**, fol. 14v)

β: Aquesta dueña era la Filosofía, la qual es dicha dueña por esto que ansí como a la dueña o mujer perteneçe según la sua condición de parir e de criar al omne, e por aquesto es naturalmente ordenada, ansí la filosofía faze al omne perfecto e acabado, naçido e criado aquél linpiamente e bella [. . .] Aquesta mujer fue madre de los sabios antiguos, por lo qual Platon e Demostranes dixeron que avien avidas dos madres, conviene saber, natura e filosofía, e dezien que natura los avía fechos materiales, e la filosofía los avía linpiados de viçios e informados de virtudes. (**N**, fol. 9r)

William gives three definitions of philosophy (*methaphysica, physica,* and *moralis*); the vernacular versions dismiss all the philosophical material, keeping only the nice parallel between Lady Philosophy and the woman who takes care of her children and turns them into men. Otherwise, the vernacular versions select William's gloss and adapt it not by condensing it (as in the example just seen) but by paraphrasing it.

The abridgement and simplification of Boethius's text is more evident in the meters, which usually have been paraphrased and deprived of those elements that are characteristic of the poetry of the *Consolatio* (such as the frequent metaphors, detailed descriptions of the natural world, poetic language, etc.). We should notice that the parallels among α, β, and William's commentary are more marked in the case of the meters: the vernacular versions often follow the arrangement of the verses provided by William, and in many passages they ignore Boethius's verses and translate only William's glosses.

But the process of abridgement at times affects the commentary itself. See, for example, the treatment of *De Cons.* 3 meter 3:[42]

William of Aragon: Deinde cum dicit QUAMVIS FLUENTE etc. ostendit quid ex divitiis hominibus contingat qui summum bonum appetunt in ipsis quos rationabiliter divites avaros hic appellat sicut patet ex dictis. Dicit igitur QUAMVIS DIVES AVARUS COGAT id est coagat vel coacervet OPES FLUENTE GURGITE AURI id est habundantissime OPES dico NON EXPLETURAS indigentiam ut dictum est QUE id est et QUAMVIS HONORET BACHIS [*sic*] id est vinis diversis COLLA id est portus RUBRI LITORIS id est mari aegyptiaci QUE id est et GRAVIS SCINDAT id est aret OPIMA RURA id est campos fertiles CENTENO BOVE id est quinquaginta paribus boum NEC CURA MORDAX DESERIT SUPERSTITEM id est ipsum avarum viventem quod dicit propter laborem in aggregando et timorem in custodiendo QUE id est et; ipsum dico divitem avarum DEFUNCTUM LEVES OPES id est leviter transeuntes NON COMITANTUR quod est contra rationem summi boni quod facit sufficientem in vita et in morte non derelinquit habentem. Notandum quod de isto metro.[43]

α: E jassia que la persona avara ajusta moltes e sobre abundants riqueses, emperò la sua ànsia que.l remort no.l desempara per axò; ans quant més ha, més lo remort, e fa-li crexer lo treball en ajustar, e la pahor en ben guardar, e la ànsia en conservar; e lo pus mal que és contrari del sobiran ben, que aprés la mort no.l volen seguir, car sobiran ben no desempara ne en vida ne en mort. (**A**, fol. 56v)

β: E ya se sea que la persona avrá allegado muchas e superfluas riquezas, enpero non le desanpara el remordimiento de cuidado que ha de aquéllas, antes quanto más ha, mayor cuidado le cresçe, e mayor trabajo ha en ayuntar, e mayor pavor en guardar, e cuidado en conservar. E el más mal contrario del soberano bien es que después de la muerte no.l quieren seguir; e el soberano bien no desanpara en vida ni en muerte. (**N**, fol. 40r)

In this case, α and β follow the commentary ("habundantissime opes," "propter laborem in aggregando," etc.) in leaving out any allusion to the Egyptian sea, the oxen and the "wines" of William's gloss. They provide only the essential idea: not only does wealth fail to dispel cares, it even produces troubles of its own. It must be noted that William reads *Bacchis*— from BACCUS—and therefore explains "wines" while the *Consolatio* reads *bacis, pearls*—from BACA, AE. Again we must stress that the vernacular renderings give priority to a didactic and moral interpretation: translating the *Consolatio* means also to interpret and offer a work of particular ethical value. Many meters are defined, such as *exemples* or *semblançes:*[44] even when the translations borrow the term from William's commentary—which has *similitudo* or *simile*—we get the impression that the translations are referring mostly to the didactic genre of "exempla homiletica" rather than to the rhetorical meaning or function of the term.[45]

A different use of William's commentary is shown when α and β do not follow William's *divisiones textus,* displacing his *sententias.* For example, William provides a gloss for each element of Boethius's description of Philosophy, following Boethius's text: first, the site where Philosophy appears (SUPRA VERTICEM), then MULIER, then REVERENDI VULTUS, etc. And α and β change the order of the glosses, giving first a general description of Lady Philosophy, then an allegorical interpretation of each element of the description. Or, William quotes from Ovid to gloss the lemma QUID IGITUR O MAGISTRA in 1 prose 4; the translations include the same quotation but at the beginning of 1 prose 5 (cap. 12 in β). We might think here that the vernacular renderings are displacing the glosses according to a particular plan: nevertheless, we cannot exclude the possibility that the different setting of the material in α and β depends on the particular copy of William's commentary that was used.

Sometimes we find, in α and β, details that do not come from the commentary of William of Aragon, but these are not numerous. It seems to me that the translator who produced the lost translation from which α and β later derived (the translator who, as I said before, has been identified with the Dominican Pere Saplana) limited his work to translating and adapting William's glosses, without having recourse to other sources. I even wonder if α and β would be better defined as translations of William's commentary on the *Consolatio,* rather than translations of the *Consolatio!* Nevertheless, we can detect in α and β some elements that do not derive from William's commentary. Let us now consider some examples:

1. William of Aragon: SED ABITE POTIUS SIRENES USQUE IN EXITIUM DULCES Appellat eas Sirenes metaphorice quia sicut quaedam pericula marina dulciter cantantia naves attrahunt et immergunt, ita istae musae pulchre et ornate loquendo fructum rationis immergunt, ad passiones trahendo.[46]

α: car sots axí com a serenes qui cantant dolçament matan los hòmens. Serenes són en la mar e diu-se que *són en forma de fembres* les quals cantan molt dolçament e tiren les naus, e *fan adormir los mariners* per la dolçor del cant, *e com dormen ocien-los tots* e.ls offeguen. Axí aytals arts paren plasents mas puys crexen la dolor e la tristor en tant que porten la persona tribulada a desesperació si molt las atura ab si, car no la garexen perfetament. (**A**, fol. 16r–v)

β: ca soys ansí como las serenas del mar que cantan dulçemente e matan las gentes. E dízese *en las fablas* que las dichas serenas *son en forma de fenbras,* las quales cantan muy dulçemente e tiran las naos contra sí *faziendo adormir los marineros* por el dulçor del su cantar, e desí mátanlos; e ansí atales cogitaçiones paresçen plazientes, mas fazen cresçer el dolor en tanto que fazen al omne venir en desesperaçión si mucho las atura consigo. (**N**, fol. 10v)

[*De Cons.,* 3 m. 12: Orpheus]

2. William of Aragon: per cervam et leones et leporem et canem intellegimus diversos tam in moribus quam in natura qui diversis passionibus dediti ad convivere non sunt apti; deducti tamen ad medium virtutis convivere bene possunt.[47]

α: Per los cervos són enteses *les persones leugeres de seny.* Per los lehons, *persones qui han massa rigor e crueltat.* Per les lebres, *persones pahorugues.* E per los cans, *persones iroses.* Tots demunts dits e semblants quant lo savi e bon parler volen ascoltar, poden covinentment concordar ab si mateys, e ab los altres estar, e poden covinentment viure ensemps. (**A**, fol. 80r)

β: Por los çiervos son entendidas *las personas ligeras de seso;* por los leones *las personas mucho rigurosas e crueles;* por las liebres *las personas medrosas allá donde no cal;* por los canes *personas yradas.* Todos los susos dichos, e semejantes, quando quieren escuchar e entender los buenos consejos del sabio e buen fablador conveniemente pueden concordar en bevir entre sí mesmo[s] e con los otros estar en uno. (**N**, fol. 55v)

3. William of Aragon: Advertendum quod Ixion fuit secretarius Iovis et Iunonis.[48]

α: Car segons que recompten los poetes, Ixio fo secretari o cambrer de na Juno *qui és deessa de les dones qui prenen marit e que infanten.* (**A**, fol. 80v)

β: Segund que ponen los poetas, Husio fue secretario e camarero de Junno *que es deesa de las mugeres que toman marido o que son paridas.* (**N**, fol. 56r)

4. William of Aragon: Tertium quod tangit est quod Tantalus amplius non sitivit. Abstulerat enim sitim bonitas melodiae Orphei. Bonitate enim virtutis omnes excessus avaritiae et cuiuslibet cupiditatis tolluntur.[49]

α: Lo segon peccat diu que és avaricia, quant diu que Tantulus moria de fam e de set, e quant vench Orpheu no hac fam ni set. *Tantulus fo molt avar, axí que no.s gosava sadollar e feya morir sa companya de fam e de set, per que fon posat en infern en aygua tro a la barba e no podia beure, e dessús li penjava un pom molt excel.lent de odor e de sabor, e estava prop de la bocha, e no podia menjar, per que havia gran fam e gran set;* e lavores per la melodia de Orpheu no hac fam ni set, car per la bocha virtuosa tot desig desordonat per avarícia és tolt e reffrenat. (**A**, fols. 80v–81r)

β: El segundo pecado es avarisçia, que dize que *Tantalus fue mui avaro en tanto que no se osava fartar, enpero avía conplimiento; mas no osava despender por gran mesquindad que avía de corasçón. Por la qual cosa fue puesto en el infierno en agua fasta la barva e non puede tomar del agua que beva, e desuso d'él está bianda mui presçiosa e non puede d'ella comer.* Aquéste por la melodía de Orfeo se le olvidó la fanbre: que por la dotrina de la persona sabia todos deseos desordenados de las cosas terrenales son refrenados e quitados pensando en las riquezas espirituales, que pueden seer olvidadas todas las terrenales corruptibles. (**N**, fol. 56v)

5. William of Aragon: Quartum quod tangit est quod vultur, saturatus modiis seu melodiis Orphei, cessavit trahere Titii iecur. Ad hanc poenam fuerat traditus Titius apud infernos eo quod pro incestu interpellaverat Latonam; in quo luxuriosos ad omnem libidinem denotamus. Et licet ista vitia tamquam principaliora in fabula exprimantur.[50]

α: Lo terç és peccat de carnalitat, quant diu que lo voltor cessà de tirar lo fetge de Tici. *Aquest fo gigant molt luxuriós* qui per la sua gran viltat volch corrompre na Letona *qui fo mare de na Diana, la qual Diana fo feta deessa de castedat; e axí mateix fo mare de Apollo, lo qual fo fet déu:* per la qual cosa fon condempnat en los inferns que un voltor pesqués tostemps lo seu fetge. Per lo qual Tici són entesos tots los luxuriosos. E jassia que aquests tres pecats axí com principals sien declarats en aquesta faula. (**A**, fol. 81r) β: El tercero es pecado de carnalidad que es entendido por Tiçi. *Aquéste según que dizen los poetas fue gigante muy luxurioso* el qual por la su gran viltad quiso asayar de corronper ha Latona *que fue madre de Diana, la qual Diana fue fecha diesa de castidat;* e por aqueste pecado qu'el dicho Tiçi quiso asayar de fazer con *tan casta e buena dueña* él fue condepnado a los infiernos por los dioses, e que uno [voltor] bolviendo le tirase todos tienpos por el fígado, *por tanto como el fígado es comen-çamiento de la calor corporal donde salen los deseos desordenados de carnalidat.* E por aquéste son entendidos todos los loxuriosos. E ya se sea que aquestos tres pecados suso dichos sean posados desuso claramente, enpero. (**N**, fol. 56v)

As one can see from the examples, it is a question of brief *amplificationes:*

1. The vernacular renderings add that the Sirens have women's bodies and send sailors to sleep with their sweets songs before killing them (William of Aragon: "maritime monsters"); the Sirens seem pleasant but cause grief and pain, leading man to desperation (William of Aragon: "they use their ornate eloquence to drown the fruit of reason").

2. The vernacular versions expand William's interpretation: harts represent men of little wisdom; lions, men who are excessively cruel and severe; hares, fearful men; and dogs, men easily aroused to anger.

3. The vernacular versions add that Juno is the goddess of women who get married or have children.

4. The translations add that Tantalus was so miserly that he made his companions starve, so he was punished in the underworld: he was plunged in water up to his chin without being able to drink and at the same time was prevented from eating the fruit that hung over him (see *Myth.* I, 12; *Myth.* II, 124; *Myth.* III, 6, 21; *Remigius*).[51]

5. The translations add the detail that Tityus was a giant and tell of his attempt to rape Latona, mother of Apollo and Diana, goddess of chastity (see *Myth.* I, 13; *Remigius; Myth.* III, 6.5 [only for the detail of liver]. It has been pointed out that mentioning Diana together with Apollo punishing Tityus is unusual and is perhaps an addition made by Remigius and then borrowed by Myth I).[52] It should be noted that the Castilian version adds that the liver is the seat of lust, "the beginning of the bodily heat from which arise the disordered desires of flesh" (an element that we read in *Myth.* III).

We might speculate about the possibility of another Latin commentary being used; nevertheless, the origin of these brief *amplificationes* could be "standard" interlinear or marginal glosses in Latin manuscripts of the *Consolatio*. For example, in Cambridge, Gonville and Caius College, MS 309/707, William of Aragon's commentary on Boethius is preceded by a *Consolatio* with a marginal gloss based upon Remigius' commentary, which provides additional information about the punishments of Tityus, Tantalus, etc. This leads us to another question: can we identify a manuscript of William's commentary that might have represented the Latin source for the Catalan translator, even the one used by the Catalan translator when making his translation? I am at present comparing the vernacular versions with the five manuscripts of William's commentary, in order to discover, if possible, textual elements that might indicate a relationship between the translations and one specific manuscript of William's commentary (or, better to say, a specific branch of the tradition of William's commentary). Of course, *lacunae, amplificationes,* and details of the Hispanic translations may well have originated in the text of the *Consolatio* and of William's commentary the translator had at his disposal.[53]

Finally, we have to draw our attention to something concerning only α, the version revised by Antoni Ginebreda. Some passages of the α version with all probability depend upon the commentary on the *Consolatio* composed by the Dominican Nicholas Trevet at the beginning of the fourteenth century.[54] Trevet's glosses occasionally appear in α, replacing the corresponding glosses of William's commentary—which we find translated in β.[55] For example, the prologue of Ginebreda's version is a translation from Trevet's prologue to his commentary,[56] giving an account not only of Boethius's life and death but also of the life of Theodoric, king of Goths, his successful political career, and his military campaign against Odoacer. In contrast, version β follows William of Aragon's prologue.[57] Also, in a digression on the history of Croesus (*De Cons.* 2 pr. 2), version β adheres to William's commentary, reproducing its brief account of the anecdote.[58] Croesus, king of Lydia, dreams he is on a tree, warmed by the sun, drenched by rain and pecked at by birds. He relates the dream to his daughter Phania, who is gifted for interpreting dreams. She warns her father that he should not carry on with the war against King Cyrus, on pain of death by hanging.

Croesus ignores Phania's words and is hanged after being defeated by Cyrus. Version α adds a detail: Croesus does not pay attention to the warning because he has made sacrifices to idols, consulting them about his campaign against Cyrus. He misunderstands the idols' answer, being deceived by a *diable* [devil]: "Cressus perdet Alim transgressus plurima regna" [If Croesus crosses the Alys, many kingdoms will fall]. The king crosses the river and many kingdoms do fall, his own. Version α could have borrowed the anecdote from Trevet's commentary, where the prophecy about the river Alys is attributed to Apollo. I have to say that Trevet himself derives the anecdote from William of Conches,[59] but it would be more economical for version α to consult Trevet alone; besides, we do not find any other evidence of its use of William of Conches. In order to explain the presence of material deriving from Trevet in version α, I would suggest that Ginebreda used Trevet's commentary while revising his version of the *Consolatio.* What leaves me perplexed is that, so far as I can see, there is no clear or systematic plan in Ginebreda's use of Trevet. I cannot say, for example, that version α differs from version β in replacing William of Aragon with Trevet every time that William of Aragon offers one of his very distinctive and personal glosses. Perhaps Ginebreda intended to update his version by interpolating in it glosses deriving from Trevet's commentary, which was one of the most popular and influential commentaries on the *Consolatio.* Or perhaps he was not satisfied with the treatment given to some passages of the *Consolatio* in William's commentary (the historical background, for example).

Let me end by drawing some conclusions from this discussion. From the comparison between version α and version β (that is, what I believe are two distinct versions of a same Catalan translation of the *Consolatio* by the Dominican friar Pere Saplana) and the commentary on the *Consolatio* by William of Aragon, it is possible to obtain some clues as to how Saplana used the commentary. He shows himself inclined to abridge the commentary, and he shows himself most interested in the mythological and historical glosses, or, what we could define as the narrative digressions of the commentary. In doing so, Saplana acts like the majority of the medieval translators of the *Consolatio.* For example, the glossator of *Le Livre de Boece de Consolacion,* the most popular of the French translations of Boethius (before 1383), made use of the compilation of William of Conches's commentary known as *Commentum domini linconiensis* and selected just the glosses about ancient history and mythology, as well as anecdotes about the names of places and peoples.[60] But, as far as I can now see, Saplana limited himself to a single commentary. So we cannot say that he made a really active use of the tradition of Latin commentary on Boethius—by active use I mean the process of "selecting from multiples sources." Saplana is simply a translator, not a commentator *cum inteprete* like the author of the Picard "translation-commentary" of the *Consolatio,* who constructed an original vernacular commentary using many distinct sources according to his needs; or like the author of the first known French translation, who used not only William of Conches's commentary but also Ovid, Virgil, and the Vatican Mythographers.[61]

Saplana's lost translation, as we can deduce from the versions derived from it (α and β), was quite a successful rendering of the *Consolatio:* I have so far not found any serious misunderstandings of the Latin text. It was intended to be an aid for the comprehension and appreciation of the *Consolatio* aimed at readers who were cultivated but unable to understand either Latin or the philosophical subtleties of Boethius's work.

Addenda

In a short note published in *Carmina Philosophiae* 10 (2001), 31–38, I exposed a new hypothesis about the Catalan tradition of the *Consolatio,* by examining the Hebrew version of the *Consolatio* composed by Samuel Benveniste in 1412 at Asentiu near Balaguer in Catalonia.[62] In fact, a perusal of the Hebrew text shows that, in general, it follows Saplana's text as we read it in the fragment of Ripoll and in the Madrid, Biblioteca Nacional, MS 10193; but, here and there, it completes Saplana with passages taken from Ginebreda. The data recollected in my note suggest that Benveniste used for his translation a manuscript that constituted one of the first stages in the development of Ginebreda's text and, at the same time, they show that the Madrid and Ripoll text are to be considered not only mere revisions but also quite faithful witnesses of Saplana's translation.

The note includes a tentative stemma of the Catalan tradition of the *Consolatio.* See also Francesca Ziino, "Una traduzione latina del *Boezio*

catalano," *Romania* 119 (2001), 465–82, where I examined a Latin translation of the Catalan version of Antoni Ginebreda, probably dating from the
fifteenth century. Further data about the presence of the Catalan versions in
medieval libraries are in Orland Grapí and Glòria Sabaté, "Traducciones de
Boecio en la Corona de Aragón," *Euphrosyne* 29 (2001), 211–20. A passage of Willam of Aragon's commentary has been published by Carmen
Olmedilla Herrero in *L'Orphée de Boèce au Moyen Age. Traductions françaises et commentaires latins (XIIe–Xve siècles)*, ed. Anna Maria Babbi and
J. Keith Atkinson (Verona: Fiorini, 2000), 181–96.

Notes

1. On the reception of Boethius's works in Medieval Spain, see the classical studies of
Marcelino Menéndez y Pelayo, *Bibliografía hispano-latina clásica*, in *Edición Nacional de
las Obras Completas de Menéndez Pelayo*, vol. 44 (Madrid: CSIC, 1950), 274–353; and
Mario Schiff, *La Bibliothèque du Marquis de Santillane* (Paris: Bouillon, 1905), 174–86.
More recent essays (with further bibliography) are Jaume Riera i Sans, "Sobre la difusió
hispànica de la *Consolació* de Boeci," *El Crotalón. Anuario de Filología Española* 1 (1984),
297–327; Ronald G. Keightley, "Boethius in Spain: A Classified Checklist of Early Translations," in *The Medieval Boethius: Studies in the Vernacular Translations of "De consolatione Philosophiae,"* ed. A. J. Minnis (Cambridge: Brewer, 1987), 169–87; and D. Briese-
meister, "The *Consolatio Philosophiae* of Boethius in Medieval Spain," *Journal of the
Warburg and Courtauld Institutes* 53 (1990), 61–70.

2. See M. T. Gibson and Lesley Smith, eds., *Codices Boethiani: A Conspectus of Manuscripts of the Works of Boethius* (London: The Warburg Institute), Part 1: Great Britain and
the Republic of Ireland, 1995; Part 2: Austria, Belgium, Denmark, Luxembourg, The Nether-
lands, Sweden and Switzerland, 2001; Part 3: Italy and the Vatican City, 2001.

3. The MSS are described in Fabio Troncarelli, *'Boethiana aetas'. Modelli grafici e fortuna
manoscritta della 'Consolatio Philosophiae' tra IX e XII secolo* (Alessandria: Edizioni
dell'orso, 1987), 241–42. See also Nolasc Rebull, "Un manuscrit del *De consolatione* de
Boeci a Banyoles," *Estudios franciscanos* 73 (1972), 244–54.

4. Jeremy N. H. Lawrance, "The Spread of Lay Literacy in Late Medieval Castile," *Bulletin
of Hispanic Studies* 62 (1985), 79–94.

5. J. Keith Atkinson, "Manuscript Context as a Guide to Generic Shift: Some Middle French
Consolations," in *Medieval Codicology, Iconography, Literature and Translation: Studies
for Keith Val Sinclair*, ed. Peter Rolfe Monks and Douglas David Roy Owen (Leiden, New
York, and Cologne: Brill, 1994), 321–32, esp. 332.

6. For the Castilian translation of Trevet's commentary on *De Consolatione*, see Miguel
Pérez Rosado, *La versión castellana medieval de los 'Comentarios' a Boecio de Nicolás
Trevet (tesis doctoral)*, 2 vols. (Ph.D. diss., Universidad Complutense de Madrid, Facultad

de Filología, Departamento de Filología Española, Editorial de la Universidad, servicio de reprografía, Madrid, 1992), colección Tesis Doctorales n. 263/92; and Carmen Olmedilla Herrero, "Comentarios a la *Consolatio Philosophiae* de Boecio: Guillermo de Aragón y la versión castellana anónima del comentario de Nicolas de Trevet," *Cuadernos de filología clásica. Estudios latinos* 2 (1992), 266–88.

7. Glynnis M. Cropp, "The Medieval French Tradition," in *Boethius in the Middle Ages: Latin and Vernacular Traditions of the "Consolatio Philosophiae,"* ed. Maarten J. F. M. Hoenen and Lodi Nauta (Leiden: Brill, 1997), 243–65, esp. 245.

8. It is a prose translation datable to 1230, in south Burgundian dialect, contained in the MS Wien, Österreichische Nationalbibliothek, 264, fols. 1–92 (*Li confortement de Sapience*). It is 1 according to the classification proposed by Antoine Thomas and Mario Roques, "Traductions françaises de la *Consolatio Philosophiae* de Boèce," in *Histoire littéraire de la France* 37 (1938), 419–88. See also the classification proposed by Richard A. Dwyer, *Boethian Fictions: Narratives in Medieval French Versions of the Consolatio Philosophiae* (Cambridge Mass.: Medieval Academy of America, 1976), 129–31.

9. See Lawrance, "The Spread of Lay Literacy," 82.

10. I would like to thank Prof. Lola Badia, who informed me of the existence of this MS and sent me a copy of it.

11. See Ignaci Casanovas, "Còdecs de l'Arxiu del Palau," *Revista de Bibliografia Catalana* 6 (1906), 5–42, esp. 31–32 (the MS was clearly incomplete). Lluís Cifuentes, "La promoció intel·lectual i social dels barbers-cirurgians a la Barcelona medieval: L'obrador, la biblioteca i els béns de Joan Vicenç (fl. 1421–1464)," *Arxiu de textos catalans antics* 19 (2000), 429–79, esp. 458, adds the existence of another fragment of Ginebreda's translation in Sevilla, Biblioteca Colombina, MS 5-5-26, fols. 121–32, sec. XIV.

12. Biographical information (with further bibliography) on Antoni Ginebreda can be found in Riera i Sans, "Sobre la difusió hispànica," 313–14; and Jaume de Puig i Oliver, "Alguns documents sobre Antoni Ginebreda, O.P. (1340?–1395)," *Arxiu de textos catalans antics* 19 (2000), 511–24.

13. See MS **Be**, fol. 1. I correct the MS reading *retirar* on the basis of the Castilian translations of Ginebreda's version, that read *recrear* (see *infra,* note 15).

14. Antoni Ginebreda died in 1394. We have an edition of Ginebreda's version, by B. Muntaner, who did not use all the manuscripts (*Libre de consolació de Philosophia lo qual féu en latí lo gloriós doctor Boeci, transladat en romanç catalanesch* . . . a cura de don Bartomeu Muntaner ab algunes notes bibliogràfiques del Angel Aguiló [Barcelona: Llibreria d'Alvar Verdaguer, 1873]).

15. Madrid, Biblioteca del Palacio Real, MS II–589; printed editions: Toulouse 1488; Sevilla 1497 and 1499; and Toledo 1511.

16. For this description, which includes fragments of Saplana's version, see Anselm M. Albareda, "L'Arxiu antic de Montserrat (intent de reconstrucció)," *Analecta Montserratensia* 3 (1919), 77–216, esp. 198–200; and Cebrià Baraut, "Els manuscrits de l'antiga bib-

lioteca del Monestir de Montserrat (segles XI–XVIII)," *Analecta Montserratensia* 8 (1954–55), 339–96, esp. 360–61.

17. For biographical information and further bibliography on Pere Saplana (d. 1365), who was preacher of the Dominican order and prior of the convent at Játiva (1352–53), see Riera i Sans, "Sobre la difusió hispànica." Riera i Sans (p. 300) gives documentary evidence about copies of Saplana's version—copies now lost (see also J. N. Hillgarth, *Readers and Books in Majorca, 1229–1550,* 2 vols. [Paris: CNRS, 1991], vol. 2, nn. 345.9, 349.13, giving the name of Saplana: *Comença: Prolech de Frare Pere Saplana*).

18. On this hagiographical section of the MS, see Jaume Vives i Gatell, "Un llegendari hagiogràfic català," *Estudis Romanics* 10 (1962), 255–71.

19. The Boethian fragment has been transcribed in Prospero Bofarull y Mascaró, *Colección de documentos inéditos del Archivo General de la Corona de Aragón,* vol. 13 (*Documentos literarios en antigua llengua catalana*) (Barcelona: Eusebio Monfort, 1857), 395–413, but for a more recent edition, see Francesca Ziino, *Una versione castigliana del 'De consolatione Philosophiae' (MS Madrid, Biblioteca Nacional, 10193),* 2 vols. (Ph.D. diss., Università degli Studi di Napoli, Filologia Romanza e Linguistica, VIII ciclo, 1997), 2:176–97.

20. Receipts of payments for Pedro de Valladolid can be found in F. Idoate, *Archivo General de Navarra. Catálogo de la sección de comptos. Documentos, t. XLII (años 1435–36). Adiciones: 1331–1434* (Pamplona: Aramburu, 1966), n° 383, 472, 690. The *repostero* was the official responsible for "los objetos personales del monarca, tanto referentes al vestido, calzado, alhajas o armas, como a las dependencias de palacio y alimentos [. . .] fue también el encargado de las compras de ropa, tapices, tejidos, alimentos, etc." (see José Trenchs Odena, *Casa, Corte y Cancilleria de Pedro el Grande (1276–1285)* [Rome: Bulzoni, 1991], 65–66).

21. The connection between **R** and **N** has been pointed out by Riera i Sans, who confirmed an intuition of Menéndez y Pelayo, *Bibliografía hispano-latina,* 298, 300. On the relationships between **N** and **R**, see also Ziino, *Una versione castigliana del 'De consolatione,'* 1:59–71.

22. *De Cons.* 3 m. 2.17–23: "Quae canit altis garrula ramis / Ales caveae clauditur antro [. . .] Si tamen arto saliens texto / Nemorum gratas viderit umbras" [The tree-top loving, chirruping bird / Is shut in a coop like a cavern [. . .] Yet if she sees, hopping in her narrow cage, / The beloved shade of trees]; translation by S. J. Tester in Boethius, *Consolatio,* Loeb Classical Library (Cambridge, Mass.: Harvard University Press, 1973). All the quotations of the Castilian text are from my edition of **N**.

23. See *De Cons.* 4 m. 5.1–6: "If a man know not how Arcturus' stars / Glide next the pole of heaven / Or why Bootes follows slow the Wain, / and sinks his fires so late into the sea / While he so quickly rises, / He will be astounded at high heaven's law" (trans. Tester).

24. See Ziino, *Una versione castigliana del 'De consolatione,'* 1:69–71.

25. Indeed, as **N** contains those sections which, according to the Ginebreda's prologue, were not to be found in the original translation sent by Saplana to the Prince of Majorca, I incline to believe that Saplana's translation did contain those sections; perhaps they were missing only in the copy of the translation used by Ginebreda.

26. See J. Keith Atkinson, "A Fourteenth-Century Picard Translation-Commentary of the *Consolatio Philosophiae*," in *The Medieval Boethius*, ed. Minnis, 31–62, esp. 32.

27. Thomas-Roques VI (Dwyer, *Boethian Fictions*, 7).

28. Note that the majority of the medieval Catalan translations of Latin classics do not distinguish the text from the gloss; see Josep Pujol, "Expondre, traslladar i reescriure clàssics llatins en la literatura catalana del segle XV," *Quaderns. Revista de traducció* 7 (2002), 9–32, esp. 13.

29. The first to point out the connection with William of Aragon's commentary were Tomás González Rolán and Pilar Saquero Suárez Somonte, "Boecio en el Medioevo Hispánico," in *Humanitas in honorem Antonio Fontán* (Madrid: Gredos, 1992), 319–37.

30. See Josep Hernando, *Llibres i lectors a la Barcelona del s. XIV*, 2 vols. (Barcelona: Fondació Noguera, 1995), vol. 1, n°179.55: between the books owned by Ramon Vinader, *doctor en lleis i ciutadà de Barcelona*, there was a *Scriptum super Boecium de consolacione, qui incipit "Sicut dicit Philosophus primo Politicorum etc. "* (the same incipit of William of Aragon's commentary). Vinader owned also a *textus Boecii De consolacione* (n. 95). The inventory of his books is dated November 8, 1356.

31. The commentary is partially edited by Charles Ignatius Terbille, *William of Aragon's Commentary on Boethius's De Consolatione Philosophiae*, 2 vols (Ph.D. diss., University of Michigan, 1972). Terbille reminds that "the term which is translated 'domain,' *dicio*, indicates not geographical origin but political allegiance" (1: 6).

32. Ed. by Marvin L. Colker, "De nobilitate animi," *Medieval Studies* 23 (1961), 47–49.

33. See Jole Agrimi, "La ricezione della *Fisiognomica* pseudoaristotelica nella facoltà delle arti," *Archives d'Histoire Doctrinale et Littéraire du Moyen Age* 64 (1997), 127–88.

34. See the edition by Roger A. Pack, "De pronosticatione sompniorum libellus Guillelmus de Aragonia adscriptus," *Archives d'histoire doctrinale et littéraire du Moyen Age* 33 (1966), 237–93; see also Roger A. Pack, "Addenda to an Article on William of Aragon," ibid., 35 (1968), 297–99.

35. Lynn Thorndike and Pearl Kibre, *A Catalogue of Incipits of Mediaeval Scientific Writings in Latin* (London and Cambridge, Mass.: Medieval Academy of America, 1963), col. 1489.

36. See A. J. Minnis, "'Glosynge is a glorious thing': Chaucer at Work on the *Boece*," in *The Medieval Boethius*, ed. Minnis, 111.

37. Jean de Meun's *Livre de Confort de Philosophie* (Thomas-Roques III) and the Hainaut translation (Thomas-Roques II) only derive part of their prologues from the Latin prologue to William's commentary; the Picard translation (Thomas-Roques VII) makes use of William's commentary on the twelve labors of Hercules in 4 m. 7. See Roberto Crespo, "Il prologo alla traduzione della *Consolatio Philosophiae* di Jean de Meun e il commento di Guglielmo d'Aragona," in *Romanitas et Christianitas. Studia. Iano Henrico Waszink oblata*, ed. W. den Boer et al. (Amsterdam and London: North Holland, 1973), 55–70; Rolf Schroth, *Eine altfranzosische Übersetzung der "Consolatio philosophiae" des Boethius (Handschrift Troyes Nr. 898). Edition und Kommentar* (Bern and Frankfurt: Peter Lang, 1976); and

Atkinson, "A Fourteenth-Century Picard Translation-Commentary of the *Consolatio Philosophiae*," in *The Medieval Boethius*, ed. Minnis, 32–62. Further study is required for the Hainaut translation: see G. M. Cropp, "The Medieval French Tradition," in *Boethius in the Middle Ages*, ed. Hoenen and Nauta, 243–265, esp. 246 on 3 m. 12 and 4 m. 3].

38. "At si quem profanum, uti vulgo solitum vobis, blanditiae vestrae detraherent, minus moleste ferendum putarem; nihil quippe in eo nostrae operae laederentur. Hunc vero Eleaticis atque Academicis studiis innutritum?" (*De Cons.*, 1 pr. 1).

39. I have collated the MS CUL, Ii. 3.21 (= **Cu**) with the MS Cambridge, Gonville and Caius, 309/707 (= **C**). MS **Cu** omits *dicta* and the gloss on Musae Camenae (1 m. 1). Sometimes it is a matter of replacing rather than removing: for example, the Goodness of Abundance [*Abondantia*] becomes the Goddess Fortuna (2 m. 2).

40. For *Canii sequaces*, see C. I. Terbille, *William of Aragon's Commentary*, 1:48 on *De Cons.* 1 pr. 3; for *a Gaio Caesare Germanici filio*, see *De Cons.* 1 pr. 4 (the anecdote about Canius being charged of conspiracy against Caligula, Germanicus' son).

41. Text from MS Cambridge, University Library, Ii.3.21 (**Cu**), fol. 11, collated with Cambridge, Gonville and Caius College, MS 309/707 (**C**). **Cu** omits *virtutibus et scientiis nutriens*.

42. *De Cons.*, 3 m. 3: "Quamvis fluente dives auri gurgite / Non expleturas cogat avarus opes / Oneretque bacis colla rubris litoris / Ruraque centeno scindat opima bove, / Nec cura mordax deseret superstitem, / Defunctumque leves non concomitantur opes."

43. **Cu**, fol. 50r. **Cu** omits [HONORET . . . GRAVIS].

44. In **N** they are presented as *enxienplos* and *semejanças*. See in α: 1 m. 6; 2 m. 3; 2 m. 6; and 3 m. 1 (in **N** corresponding to chapters I, 12; II, 3; II, 6; and III, 1).

45. See Peter von Moos, "Sulla retorica dell'*exemplum* nel Medioevo," in *Retorica e poetica tra i secoli XII e XIV. Atti del secondo Convegno internazionale di studi dell'Associazione per il Medioevo e l'Umanesimo latini (AMUL) in onore e memoria di Ezio Franceschini, Trento e Rovereto 3–5 ottobre 1985*, ed. Claudio Leonardi and Enrico Menestò (Florence: Sismel, 1988), 53–77.

46. **Cu**, fol. 14r.

47. **Cu**, fol. 72r. **C** omits *tam in moribus quam in natura*.

48. **Cu**, fol. 72r.

49. **Cu**, fol. 72v.

50. **Cu**, fol. 72v.

51. For the first and the second Vatican Mythographers, I refer to the edition by Peter Kulcsár, *Mythographi Vaticani I et II, Corpus Christianorum, S.L., XCI c* (Turnhout: Brepols, 1987); for the third Vatican Mythographer, see the edition by Georg Heinrich Bode, *Scriptores rerum mythicarum latini tres Romae nuper reperti* (1834; repr. Hildesheim: G. Olms, 1968); and for the Remigian glosses on *De Consolatione*, see Diane K. Bolton, "The Study of the

Consolation of Philosophy in Anglo-Saxon England," *Archives d'Histoire Doctrinale et Littéraire du Moyen Age* 44 (1977), 33–78.

52. *Le premier Mythographe du Vatican,* ed. Nevio Zorzetti and trans. Jacques Berlioz (Paris: Les Belles Lettres, 1995), 8, n. 35.

53. We could also suppose he had at his disposal an abridged text of William's commentary, for example.

54. The bibliography on Nicholas Trevet is quite wide. See the articles collected in the volumes I quoted in the notes above: Gibson, *Boethius: His Life, Thought, and Influence; The Medieval Boethius,* ed. Minnis; Minnis, *Chaucer's "Boece";* and *Boethius in the Middle Ages,* ed. Hoenen and Nauta.

55. A list of all passages where version α replaces William's glosses with Trevet's can be found in Ziino, *Una versione castigliana del 'De consolatione,'* 1:90 ff.

56. Ginebreda translates only part of Trevet's prologue, omitting some elements (for example, Trevet's gloss on Psalm 93).

57. Version β translates William of Aragon's exposition of *vita auctoris, intentio, utilitas,* and *modus tractandi* of Boethius's *Consolatio.* See Riera i Sans, "Sobre la difusió hispànica," 316; Keightley, "Boethius in Spain," 181; and Rolán and Saquero Suárez, "Boecio en el Medioevo hispánico," 331–32.

58. See MS **N,** fol. 23r (version β) and MS **A** of Ginebreda's version (version α), fol. 34r (64 in Muntaner's edition).

59. For more details about the gloss on Croesus in the commentary tradition, see Alastair J. Minnis, "Aspects of the Medieval French and English Traditions of *De consolatione Philosophiae,*" in Gibson, *Boethius: His Life, Thought and Influence,* 312–61, esp. 329–37.

60. See Glynnis M. Cropp, "Les Gloses du *Livre de Boece de Consolacion,*" *Le Moyen Age* 92 (1986), 367–81; and "Le *Livre de Boece de Consolacion:* From Translation to Glossed Text," in *The Medieval Boethius,* ed. Minnis, 63–85.

61. Cropp, "The Medieval French Tradition," 246, referring to the Burgundian translation (*Del Confortement de Philosofie,* ca. 1230) in MS Wien, Österreichische Nationalbibliothek, 2642, ed. Margaret Bolton-Hall in *Carmina Philosophiae. Journal of The International Boethius Society,* special double issue, vols. 5 and 6 (1996–97).

62. Mauro Zonta, "Le origini letterarie e filosofiche delle versioni ebraiche del *De consolatione philosophiae* di Boezio," in *Hebraica. Miscellanea di studi in onore di Sergio J. Sierra per il suo 75° compleanno,* ed. Felice Israel, Alfredo Mordecai Rabello, and Alberto M. Somekh (Turin Istituto di Studi Ebraici-Scuola Rabbinica S. H. Margulies-D. Disegni, 5759/1998), 571–604.

PART III

BOETHIUS IN ART AND LITERARY HISTORY

VISUALIZING BOETHIUS'S *CONSOLATION* AS ROMANCE

Ann W. Astell

Beginning in the thirteenth century with Jean de Meun's *Roman de la Rose,* medieval poets frequently parodied Boethius's sixth-century *Consolation of Philosophy* in the form of an amatory romance in which a worldly wise go-between, substituting for Lady Philosophy, helps to secure erotic remedies, rather than philosophical ones, for a lovesick hero.[1] Among these parodies, Chaucer's *Troilus and Criseyde* stands as a prime example.[2] The indebtedness to Boethius in each case is overt; frequently the poems acknowledge him explicitly by allusion and/or verbal echoes of his consolatory dialogue.

The question, however, remains: why did Boethius's work inspire a tradition of amatory imitations? As Donald W. Rowe once remarked to me, the phrase "Boethian lovers" is practically an oxymoron, and the combination of Boethian and Ovidian themes seems, at first glance, unlikely if not absurd. The *Consolation* offers no explicit treatment of *amour;* relates no love-story, with the important exception of the myth of Orpheus and Eurydice (3 m. 12);[3] and only mentions sexual love in passing in Book 3, prose 2, in a discussion of the goods of Fortune: wealth, honor, power, glory, and pleasure. While John V. Fleming finds the "literary possibility"[4] for the *Roman de la Rose* and the entire tradition of Boethian romance precisely in this brief passage, it seems to me that a better solution to the puzzle lies in the auditor's visualization of the opening scene of the *Consolation,* a visualization reflected in manuscript illuminations of the *incipit.*

To speak of the visualization of a medieval text is, of course, to evoke a complex, interlocking tradition with epistemological, rhetorical, moral, and pedagogical dimensions. As the magisterial work of scholars such as

Frances Yates, V. A. Kolve, and Mary J. Carruthers has demonstrated, the ancient and medieval arts of memory from Aristotle to Petrarch were based on the "idea that the memory stores, sorts, and retrieves material through the use of some kind of mental image"—an idea that was "not attacked until the eighteenth century" and which has gained new support in our time from empirical studies.[5] Even as writing itself was perceived as a mnemonic aid for recalling the spoken word, the memory had its "impressed" or "engraven" images of sensory experience, which the "eye of the mind" beheld.

Memorizing a text—especially in the sense of *memoria ad res* (as opposed to *memoria ad verbum*)—meant therefore, in the words of Saint Augustine, retaining:

> illa quae putamus ita se habuisse vel ita se habere, velut cum disserendi gratia quaedam ipsi fingimus nequaquam impedientia veritatem, vel qualia figuramus cum legimus historias, et cum fabulosa vel audimus vel componimus vel suspicamur.

> [the images of things we imagine to have been so or to be so, as when, for the sake of an argument, we build up a certain case not repugnant to truth, or when we picture a situation to ourselves while a narrative is being read, or while we hear or compose or conjecture some fabulous tale.][6]

As Saint Thomas Aquinas was to insist, the more striking and vivid the mental image, the easier it was to retain, recall, and use as a source of invention; the more, too, it affected one's emotions, moral choices, and actions.[7] Thus, Kolve observes:

> Not only were medieval readers asked to respond to literature in this way—to "see" what they heard described—but the act of literary composition itself was often represented as an act of visual imagining: the author at his desk sees the subject of his work, often a personified idea, standing before him.[8]

Boethius's *Consolation of Philosophy* is, of course, a prime example and arguably the principle model for this visual and visionary literature in the Middle Ages.

My aim in this essay is not, however, simply to relate Boethius's text to the pictoral images used to represent or illustrate his work; rather, I am attempting to go the opposite route: to discover the mental image and the related iconography that connect the *Consolation* with its erotic literary parodies, especially Jean de Meun's *Roman de la Rose* and Chaucer's *Troilus and Criseyde.* I argue that the dialogue between the suffering prisoner and his sapiential lady could be, and often was, associated with conversations between lovesick heroes and their amatory physicians, not because Boethius's philosophical work explicitly warns against pleasure-seeking but as a result of the way readers visualized the opening scene of the *Consolation.* This primary, visual connection inspired all the subsequent, intricate, erotic parodies.

Alcuin Blamires and Gail C. Holian remark in their study of illuminated manuscripts of the *Roman de la Rose:* "It was the presence and impact of the *incipit* miniature on the first page (the manuscript frontispiece, as it were) which fulfilled the function of today's book jacket."[9] The image on the page helped to make the text memorable, outstanding, noteworthy, desirable to read, even at the cost of popularizing and reducing its content. "The craft in which medieval illuminators were steeped was not a craft of literary criticism, and their working practices were probably not conducive to extended textual analysis," Blamires and Holian insist.[10] In the case of Boethius's *Consolation,* many illuminators chose to represent the opening scene in a way that resembled a bedroom scene in a courtly romance.

To what extent did this depiction and visualization misrepresent Boethius's *Consolation?* Let us begin by asking some fundamental questions: How are we to imagine the opening scene of the *Consolation?* What does Boethius's text present to the mind's eye? And, finally, how does that mental image, in turn, gloss or interpret the text in a way that allows for its parody? The confusion about the place where we find Boethius initially— library, prison, or bedchamber; in exile or at home—and the resultant problem of visualization is a deliberate textual strategy of the *Consolation,* aimed at involving the reader or auditor in the pedagogical process of the dialogue. We are challenged to discover the *loci facies:* the appearance of the place, even as the sufferer enters into a process of recall.

The description given to us by Boethius definitely makes visualization difficult. The opening meter identifies the speaker as a weeping poet, compelled by the Muses to begin sad songs. The first line of the first prose describes him writing his complaint with a stilus—a tool and a task that suggests that he is sitting, perhaps at a desk, or standing at a podium. While he is writing, a bright-eyed woman appears above him, standing over his head. His description of her abounds in contradictions: her complexion has a youthful bloom, yet she seems ancient. Her stature is indeterminate [*statura discretionis ambiguae*]—sometimes shrinking to an ordinary human height, sometimes growing so tall that she touches the very heavens with her head and even disappears into them (1 pr. 1.1). The cloth of her garment is fine and imperishable, but darkened as if by age or soot, and torn. The lower and upper borders of her dress are embroidered with the emblematic Greek letters Pi and Theta, respectively, with a seven-rung ladder connecting them. In her right hand she carries a book; in her left, a scepter.

When the woman appears, we see the scene a second time through her eyes. She looks and finds the poetical Muses standing by Boethius's bed [*nostro toro*] and cries out, in Chaucer's translation, "Who hath suffred aprochen to this sike man thise comune strompettis of swich a place that men clepen the theatre?"[11] Her angry dismissal of the meretricious Muses, who leave the scene blushing and hanging their heads, leaves Philosophia alone with the man who, blinded by his own tears, dimly sees her approach and sit down on the end of his bed [*in extrema lectuli mei parte;* 1 pr. 1.14]. After bemoaning his condition, she asks him whether he recognizes her. Then finding him in a lethargy and unable to answer, she places her hand gently on his breast, promises his recovery, and wipes his eyes tenderly with her garment to restore his sight.

How are we to picture this scene, which has been related to us by a witness who was, according to his own testimony, at least part of the time half-blind and in a stupor? Is the speaker a bemused poet, alone and writing at a desk? Or is he a sick man in bed, surrounded by a bevy of sirens? Is the mysterious woman above his head, or is she seated cozily on his bed? Carruthers notes that the various postures attributed to the Boethian dreamer serve to characterize him in an almost encyclopedic way as an archetypal man of melancholy meditation:

> He is lying in bed because that physical attitude was among the postures that were commonly thought to induce the mental concentration necessary for "memory work," recollective, memorative composition. It was not the only such posture possible: sitting or standing at a lectern pensively, head in hand or staring into

space, eyes open or closed, with or without a book, are also common postures of meditative memory work.[12]

While Carruthers is no doubt right about the metaphoricity of these postures, it is nonetheless difficult to imagine the suffering, assuming them either all at once or in a temporal sequence. Indeed, the reader's initial confusion concerning space, movement, and time is a metonymic extension of, and a pedagogical participation in, the sufferer's own loss of location, both in himself and in the universe.

These issues are complicated by further details as the actual dialogue between them begins. When Lady Philosophy asks her patient to lay bare his wound, he points first of all to his surroundings:

> Ne moeveth it nat the to seen the face or manere of this place [*loci facies*]? Is this the librarye which that thou haddest chosen for a ryght certein sege to the in myn hous, ther as thow disputedest ofte with me of the sciences of thynges touchynge dyvinyte and touchynge mankynde?[13]

He complains that his library has been exchanged for (or turned into?) a prison cell, and that he has been persecuted and condemned to death, like many other lovers of wisdom, such as Socrates and Seneca. After he has related the story of his fall from favor at the court of Theodoric the Ostrogoth, Lady Philosophy replies to his initial question, saying that she is less moved by the condition of the place than by his mental state. She is concerned not about the walls of his fine library, "apparayled and wrought with yvory and with glas," but, rather, about "the sete" of his thought, in which she once placed not books, but what makes books precious and valuable, their "sentence."[14]

According to Lady Philosophy's diagnosis, he has forgotten who and where he is. He cannot locate and access the philosophical sentences stored in the library of his mind. As Carruthers notes, the memory-as-library metaphor, used here by Lady Philosophy, is one of several medieval commonplaces with striking and definite implications:

> It is apparent from the metaphors they chose to model the processes of memory and perception that the *imagines* [i.e., mental images] were thought in some way to occupy physical space. . . . The words *topos, sedes,* and *locus,* used in writing

on logic and rhetoric as well as mnemonics, refer fundamentally to physical locations in the brain, which were made accessible by means of an ordering system."[15]

For the narrator of the *Consolation,* remembering is synonymous with relocating himself, with finding himself no longer in worldly exile but at home in the true fatherland of the soul. Similarly, for the reader of the *Consolation,* remembering its *res,* its moral teaching or *sententia,* requires a process of location in which one first creates and then fixes in the mind a memorial image or images. The opening scene or frontispiece of the *Consolation*—primarily as one imagines it, but also as an artist represents it as an example for such imaging—is particularly apt to serve as a mnemonic aid for the work as a whole with all of its *propria.*

The opening scene is, however, refractory to representation if we hope to achieve an identity between the textual and pictorial images. Because, as we have noticed, the text abounds in contradictions, the reader and the artist must make choices about what is imaged. In so doing, as Stephen G. Nichols has remarked in a different context, a "dual system" is created,

> in which the illumination stands in relation to the text as its symbolic other. The illumination profits from its status outside of language less to illustrate the text . . . than to demetaphorize it. That is, it confronts the rhetorical image of the text with a literal image, thereby graphically showing the difference between them.[16]

The selection of one pictorial image out of several possible images to represent the scene calls attention to verbal/visual difference; it simultaneously creates a space or potential for textual parody, which by definition entails, as Linda Hutcheon has shown, "repetition with . . . a critical difference."[17]

To return to our dilemma, we could choose to imagine the *incipit* of Boethius's work by isolating the details given us in the first meter and first part of prose 1 and stopping there. If we do so, we see the suffering narrator as a poet, writing at a desk, with a larger-than-life Lady Philosophy appearing in the air above his head, as, for example, in this hieratic Romanesque illustration (Figure 1). There is nothing in this image to inspire an erotic, Ovidian parody.

Figure 1. Oxford, Bodleian Library, University of Oxford, MS Auct. F. 6. 5, fol. 1v. Reproduced by permission. Twelfth century.

Another possibility would be to combine the images of the book-writing and the bedridden Boethius through a split-screen technique, as in a beautiful fifteenth-century French illumination. The author literally would visualize himself in a framed picture hanging on a wall and then would use the image of a sick man attended by Philosophia as a topic of invention for himself as he writes, translating into words what he first sees.[18] A third possibility would be to try to represent as many of the contradictory details as possible, as we find in several late illuminations reproduced by Courcelle (Plates 60, 61, 83, 84, 95, and 96), where Boethius is chained like a prisoner and either sitting up in bed or lying there uncomfortably, fully clothed. A fourth option would be to focus narrowly on the confrontation between Lady Philosophy and the strumpet Muses. (For illustrations of this kind, see Plates 50–61 in Courcelle.)

Yet another possibility would be to forget the image of Boethius the writer and focus exclusively on the solitary encounter between the sick man, naked in his bed, and the woman who lovingly nurses him, as in Figure 2. Figure 3, which parallels Figure 2 in significant ways, corresponds to a possible mental image of the opening of the *Consolation;* it is not, however, an illustration of Boethius. It represents instead a biblical scene, the ravishment of Thamar by her half-brother Ammon who, sick with desire for her, took the advice of his "very wise" friend, Jonadab, feigned illness, and went to bed in order to seduce her when she, at King David's request, came alone to nurse him (2 Kings 13:1–18).[19] The story, as Charles Muscatine and D. W. Robertson, Jr., noted long ago, is the scriptural *locus classicus* that inspired Chaucerian scenes like Damyan's seduction of his "nurse," May, and the lovesick Troilus's meeting with Criseyde in the house of Deiphobus.[20]

To visualize the opening scene of the *Consolation* with an image like this would "locate" the work as a whole in a topical "commonplace"—that of the "lover's malady," its symptoms, and amatory cures. As Mary Carruthers has shown, in a "textual community" constituted by a specific, institutionalized literary canon, readings and interpretations held in common are "the sources of a group's memory" and provide an organizational matrix for its associations and reenactments.[21] The mental images that arise from imagining particular narratives—in this case, the *incipit* of the *Consolation*—tend to cluster in the mind with "larger images" possessing "public meanings

Figure 2. Utrecht, Biblioteck der Rijksuniversiteit, MS 1335, fol. 86bis, v. Reproduced by permission.

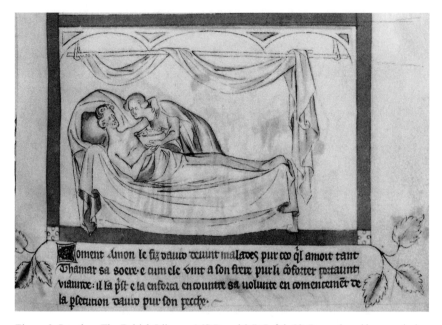

Figure 3. London, The British Library, MS Royal 2.B.7, fol. 58. Reproduced by permission of The British Library.

independent of the narrative" that discloses them.[22] In these "memorial centers," to use Kolve's phrase, the mind's estimative faculty recognizes the mental image "as being *like*—as being 'in approximate register' with—symbolic images known from other medieval contexts, both literary and visual,"[23] such as the Bible and Ovid. The moral and affective meaning that arises from such associative clusterings is what scholastic philosophers called the *intentio* of the image, that is, the power of the image as we perceive it to *affect* us, to attract or repel us, to move us to good or evil.[24]

Did medieval readers of the *Consolation,* like Jean de Meun and Chaucer, visualize the opening scene in a way that associated it with the biblical story of Thamar and Ovidian *remedia?* The very existence of amatory Boethian parody and its iconography attest that they did. The *incipit* illustration for the *Roman* in almost all the illuminated manuscripts shows a lovesick man, an alter-Boethius, in a canopied bed, falling asleep to dream a dialogic dream in which a series of allegorical guides instruct and admonish him. (See, for example, Figure 4.)

Figure 4. Oxford, Bodleian Library, University of Oxford, MS Douce 332, fol. iii recto.

Both the text and the illustrations for Chaucer's *Troilus* repeatedly show the lovesick protagonist in bed, weeping, often in the company of his friend and counsellor, Pandarus, who parodies Lady Philosophy in his words of advice about how to deal with blind love, fickle Fortune, and Criseyde. Figure 5, reproduced from a fifteenth-century French manuscript of *Le Roman de Troyle,* typifies this scene.

More, of course, could be said. I have only briefly opened the topic. As Kolve notes, "we are only beginning to understand the issues involved in using pictures as a means of recovering the meaning of literary texts" and "the grounds upon which we may appropriately employ images from the visual arts in thinking about a work of medieval literature."[25] Literary critics have by and large left the work of studying illustrations to art historians, and art historians have frequently failed to correlate patterns of literary and iconographic influence. The illustrations of the *Consolation* and the *Roman*

mſi eſſant
tropte Amus
Jour ſeuſſet
en ſachābre

Dıff troyſe · queſſe fortune
vous a Jry aðmené pour
moy Veon· ſanguır· Je bo
pzie que vous en parteꝛ

Figure 5. Oxford, Bodleian Library, University of Oxford, MS Douce 331, fol. 8r.

de la Rose have, for instance, each been studied separately, by Pierre Courcelle and Alfred Kuhn, respectively,[26] but virtually no attempt has been
made to connect the two large sets of illustrations or to explore their
mutual influence, even though, as Fleming emphasizes, "the great bulk of
the *Roman* is an earlier version of Jean [de Meun]'s *Boèce.*"[27] Such studies
would, doubtless, show common iconographic features that would help us
to understand why and how medieval readers grouped together—and
closely associated the moral teaching of—works as diverse as Boethius's
Consolation, Dante's *Commedia,* Chaucer's *Troilus,* and de Meun's *Roman.*
Even more fundamentally, a radically imagistic approach may help us to
understand the associational patterns that underlie literary *imitatio* and,
thus, the reading and translative rewriting of Boethius's *Consolation* in the
parodic form of romance.[28]

Notes

1. See Katherine Heinrichs, "Lovers' 'Consolations of Philosophy' in Boccaccio, Machaut, and Chaucer," *SAC* 11 (1989), 93–115; and Ann W. Astell, "Boethian Lovers," in Astell, *Job, Boethius, and Epic Truth* (Ithaca: Cornell University Press, 1994), 127–58 .

2. See John P. McCall, "Five-Book Structure in Chaucer's *Troilus,*" *Modern Language Quarterly* 23.4 (1962), 297–308; Theodore Stroud, "Boethius's Influence on Chaucer's *Troilus,*" *Modern Philology* 49.1 (1951), 1–9; and Martin Camargo, "The Consolation of Pandarus," *Chaucer Review* 25.3 (1991), 214–28.

3. On the importance of this meter to the tradition of medieval romance, see John Block Friedman, *Orpheus in the Middle Ages* (Cambridge, Mass.: Harvard University Press, 1970); and Ann W. Astell, "Orpheus, Eurydice, and the 'Double Sorwe' of Chaucer's Troilus," *Chaucer Review* 23.4 (1989), 283–99.

4. John V. Fleming, "Jean de Meun and the Ancient Poets," in *Rethinking the Romance of the Rose: Text, Image, and Reception,* ed. Kevin Brownlee and Sylvia Huot (Philadelphia: University of Pennsylvania Press, 1992), 81–100, esp. 89.

5. Mary J. Carruthers, *The Book of Memory: A Study of Memory in Medieval Culture* (Cambridge: Cambridge University Press, 1990), 17.

6. Saint Augustine, "Nebridio Augustinus," *Epistolae* 1.7, PL 33, col. 69; quoted in V. A. Kolve, *Chaucer and the Imagery of Narrative: The First Five Books of the Canterbury Tales* (Stanford: Stanford University Press, 1984), 10. Kolve uses Augustine's *Letters* in Sister Wilfrid Parson's translation.

7. Saint Thomas Aquinas, *Summa theologica,* Blackfriars edition (Latin and English), 61 vols. (New York: McGraw-Hill, 1964–81), 1a.Q.78. art.4; Carruthers, *Book of Memory,* 51–60; and Frances A. Yates, *The Art of Memory* (Chicago: University of Chicago Press, 1966), 61–94.

8. Kolve, *Chaucer and the Imagery of Narrative,* 32.

9. Alcuin Blamires and Gail C. Holian, *The "Romance of the Rose" Illuminated,* Medieval and Renaissance Texts and Studies 223 (Tempe: Arizona Center for Medieval and Renaissance Studies, 2002), xxix.

10. Blamires and Holian, *"Romance of the Rose" Illuminated,* xxvii.

11. Chaucer, *Boece,* pp. 395–469 in *The Riverside Chaucer,* 3rd. ed., gen. ed. Larry D. Benson (Boston: Houghton Mifflin, 1987), 1 pr. 1, lines 47–50.

12. Mary J. Carruthers, *The Craft of Thought: Meditation, Rhetoric, and the Making of Images, 400–1200,* Cambridge Studies in Medieval Literature 34 (Cambridge: Cambridge University Press, 2000), 174.

13. Chaucer, *Boece* 1 pr. 4, lines 12–18.

14. Chaucer, *Boece* 1 pr. 5, lines 36–45.

15. Carruthers, *Book of Memory,* 27, 29.

16. Stephen G. Nichols, "Ekphrasis, Iconoclasm, and Desire," in *Rethinking the Romance of the Rose: Text, Image, and Reception,* ed. Kevin Brownlee and Sylvia Huot (Philadelphia: University of Pennsylvania Press, 1992), 133–60, esp. 151.

17. Linda Hutcheon, *A Theory of Parody: The Teachings of Twentieth-Century Art Forms* (New York: Methuen, 1985), 32.

18. See Plate 44 in Pierre Courcelle, *La Consolation de Philosophie dans la Tradition Littéraire* (Paris: Études Augustiniennes, 1967).

19. MS 1335, fol. 86bis, v (here Figure 2) appears as Plate 40 in Courcelle, *La Consolation.*

20. See D. W. Robertson, Jr., *A Preface to Chaucer: Studies in Medieval Perspectives* (1962; repr. Princeton: Princeton University Press, 1969), 259–60 and Plate 108; and Charles Muscatine, "The Feigned Illness in Chaucer's *Troilus and Criseyde,*" *MLN* 63 (1948), 372–77.

21. Carruthers, *Book of Memory,* 9–12, 156–88.

22. Kolve, *Chaucer and the Imagery of Narrative,* 2.

23. Kolve, *Chaucer and the Imagery of Narrative,* 61.

24. On the *intentio,* see Yates, *Art of Memory,* 64, 225–26, 290–92, 299, 314, 371; Carruthers, *Book of Memory,* 53–54; and Kolve, *Chaucer and the Imagery of Narrative,* 45, 58.

25. Kolve, *Chaucer and the Imagery of Narrative,* 3.

26. Courcelle, *La Consolation de Philosophie Dans La Tradition Littéraire* (Paris: Études Augustiniennes, 1967); Alfred Kuhn, *Die Illustration des Rosenromans* (Freiburg i.B.: Wagner, 1911) and "Die Illustration des *Rosenromans,*" *Jahrbuch der Kunsthistorischen Sammlungen der allerhöchsten Kaiserhauses* 31.3 (1912), 1–66. Courcelle's main interest is the shift from hieratic to more realistic depictions of Boethius in the later Middle Ages. (See Diane Bolton's commentary on Courcelle's work in "Illustrations in Manuscripts of Boethius's Works," in *Boethius: His Life, Thought and Influence,* ed. Margaret Gibson [Oxford: Basil Blackwell, 1981], 428–37.) Kuhn, by contrast, emphasizes how "the predominantly religious iconography of the thirteenth century impressed itself upon the illustrations of the *Roman de la Rose*" (John V. Fleming, *The Roman de la Rose: A Study in Allegory and Iconography* [Princeton: Princeton University Press, 1969], 36). See also Charles Dahlberg, "The Illustrations," in Jean de Meun, *The Romance of the Rose,* trans. Dahlberg (Princeton: Princeton University Press, 1971), 22–26. Dahlberg, like Kuhn and Fleming, argues that the illustrations of the *Roman* give evidence of perceived irony, of an awareness of a "double point of view," especially through iconographic parallels between the opening miniatures of the *Roman* and contemporary Nativity representations.

27. Fleming, *Roman de la Rose,* 111.

28. Earlier versions of this essay were given as papers at the November 1993 "Text, Image and Technology" conference at George Mason University and at the May 1994 International Congress on Medieval Studies, held in Kalamazoo, Michigan.

THE ETERNAL TRIANGLE OF WRITER, PATRON, AND FORTUNE IN LATE MEDIEVAL LITERATURE

Christoph Houswitschka

In late medieval literature, three different attitudes can be distinguished towards the Boethian question of whether man can oppose Fortune, who might level a destabilizing blow at any time. Many authors advise their readers not to fight the inevitable but, rather, to accept misfortune, reminding them of the transitoriness of all worldly goods. Other writers deny that Fortune, as God's instrument, acts in an arbitrary fashion and instead argue that Fortune punishes sinful deeds and rewards good deeds according to God's providential plans. A third group of writers takes up a voluntaristic position, suggesting that man can, within a narrowly circumscribed sphere, shape Fortune to his own end. These various positions on Fortune carry with them profound intellectual, philosophical, and theological consequences and are central to academic debate in the later Middle Ages. At the same time, however, there is a very practical dimension to this problem: a given writer's position on Fortune also can be understood within the context of the writer's social and economic situation and the relationship the writer wishes to establish and maintain with his or her patron. In the fourteenth and fifteenth centuries, the author's position was still defined by his exclusive relationship to his patron. Only in later centuries could the latent tension between the patron and the printer's or the readers' expectations be mediated, rejected, or used to reverse "the power relationship between patron and client."[1] Benefitting from the socio-cultural status Sir Philip Sidney had achieved, Ben Jonson instructed "his social superior in his duty and challenges him to live up to the ideal image presented in the rhetoric of praise."[2] Before the printing press, the author's intellectual and cultural authority towards his/her patron/patroness could not be improved by selling one's books. For this reason, the fatalistic, providential, and voluntaristic attitudes toward Fortune prior to the sixteenth century are inextricably tied not only to notions of governance and the proper comportment of a ruler but also to the author's social and economic position. According to conventional wisdom, the prince should be ever mindful of his impending fall, and in this sense his dealings with Fortune are seen in fatalistic or providential terms. The prince is counseled either to align his rule with the providential design of God or to renounce the things of this world that his power as ruler might bring him. The welfare of the state, however, justifies the high esteem of earthly happiness, since it is regarded as a state of the worldly order in which man can fulfill God's will. On this premise, Fortune's power is abandoned in favor of a secularized concept of public welfare that no longer emphasizes the *contemptus mundi* but is legitimated by the idea of the "common good." This position holds that the prince should actively struggle against the vicissitudes of Fortune in order to fulfill his duty as the preserver and defender of the public welfare.

One way to account for these attitudes toward Fortune is to see them as part of a progression of thinking that connects the Middle Ages to the modern era. According to this view, man moves from a fatalistic or providential view of himself and his capacities in the Middle Ages to a more voluntaristic view in the modern era, placing greater faith in the efficacy of individual actions. The voluntaristic elements of late medieval nominalism would seem to support this interpretation. But there are also significant problems with such a progressive view of Fortune. First, it is by no means clear that all writers—or even a sizeable portion of them—pursued the kind of active interest in philosophical issues that this interpretation assumes. Even more important, writers of the late Middle Ages do not fit into the tidy chronological series that the progressive view posits. Thus, for example, I would argue that in such works as The Knight's Tale and The Nun's Priest's Tale, Chaucer, writing in the fourteenth century, presents a less fatalistic view of Fortune than do either Thomas Hoccleve and John Lydgate in the fifteenth century.[3]

This article aims, then, to show that a particular writer's account of Fortune is as much a consequence of his or her social and economic position as it is the result of broad intellectual movements. The writings of political authors in particular are dependent on the specific local authority they manage to establish for themselves on questions concerning the political order.[4] Part of their writing, therefore, serves to establish this authority within the framework of their commitment to a patron. In this essay, I shall attempt to show that Fortune's power is weaker in proportion to the strength of the author's social position and that, consequently, it is relatively easy for such an author to establish himself as a political authority. Conversely, the more an author must gain his patron's benevolence and patronage, the more emphatically he praises his prince's power. But the author also warns him to remember Fortune's power. In this case, Fortune's mutability reflects the author's dependence on the prince's benevolence.[5]

If, however, the author wants to gain a status that makes him independent, he will not emphasize the prince's power but, rather, will describe it in a more objective and impersonal way. Whereas the prince's praise is combined with a warning of Fortune's mutability, the concept of the prince's obligation to the public welfare reduces both Fortune's power and the author's dependence. The more forcefully the author raises his voice in the name of the public welfare, the more he is able to free himself from the necessity of praising his patron and of emphasizing his dependence. Thus a complex triangle between author, patron, and Fortune develops in which Fortune loses her relevance to the same extent that the writer gains authority and independence.[6]

An author whose authority is founded on the basis of his services will play the role of someone who warns and admonishes the prince to not abuse his power to his people's disadvantage. He will stress the fact that God rewards good works and punishes sins. The author reminds the prince of many *De Casibus* stories. In this way he claims a position as an advisor, which naturally helps not only his patron but also the author himself. Among the authors considered here, only Hoccleve clearly fits this type. Christine de Pisan and Lydgate, in contrast, are also dependent on their patrons, but they try to justify their political writings with a different kind of authority.

The other type of author legitimates his authority to speak about the political order in a completely different manner. He emphasizes the prince's obligation to the public welfare and God and regards the prince's power as limited. Thus Fortune loses power over man's fate and the author obtains influence and authority at the same time. Alain Chartier, William of Worcester, and Sir John Fortescue belong to this group of authors.

Fortune's power is one of the most frequently discussed topics in the writings of Christine de Pisan.[7] It is mainly in her early works, such as *Le Livre de la mutacion de Fortune* (1403), that she makes Fortune's instability responsible for man's fate. In this article I would like to draw attention to Fortune's character in the *Le Livre du corps de policie* (1405),[8] which was translated into English in the last third of the fifteenth century. In this book Christine sees hardly any chance for man to influence Fortune's decisions.[9] This is due at least in part to Christine's attempts to achieve a respected position as an advisor by writing and arguing in a certain way.[10] She recommends that the king show humility and modesty and warns him "that by pryde a man is not enhaunced to good fortune" (p. 79). Christine deplores the misery that Fortune brings into the world and reminds the reader to remember the "variaunce of fortune."[11] It is, however, not the goddess of Fortune alone who is to blame. It is also man's sins that cause misfortune.[12]

Christine's work describes the order of the body politic and how this ideal order can be destroyed by the king's mistakes. Significantly enough, Christine considers man's free will only as a virtue for resisting the temptations of sin, not for changing one's fortune with regard to the future.[13] Christine writes from a ruler's point of view, and it is therefore important to remember that she depends upon a ruler to support her endeavors as a writer. Being a woman and a writer in a patron's service, her influence on the secular hierarchy could not be very substantial.[14] This fact is evident in her fatalistic way of judging human beings' influence on Fortune's power, which judgment cannot be understood without taking into account her difficulties of being accepted in a male world. Forhan sees one of the steps to an understanding of the "paradox of Christine de Pizan" in her vulnerability:

> Christine always wrote from a deeply rooted sense of her own vulnerability, and thus of the contingent nature of life. The crises, both personal and political, that she faced fostered the major themes of her work. Central to her concern was the nature of the political community itself.[15]

In her book *Le Livre de la Mutacion de Fortune,* Christine calls Fortune a power that changes history. In the same book, however, she defends her profession, maintaining that she was turned into a man by Fortune's grace when she was left alone with her family after her husband's death.[16]

Christine's interpretation of Fortune can be understood as a means of opposing her male critics and, even more so, of claiming authority as a female author.[17] On the one hand, she confirms their traditional arguments by admitting that it is unusual for a woman to write and by excusing herself through references to Fortune's mutability and the world's instability. On the other hand, these words are only a rhetorical *captatio benevolentiae* for which she does not want to be esteemed. She wants instead to establish her reputation as a writer who has an excellent knowledge of ancient historians. With this she hopes to achieve an independent authority that would allow her to be accepted as an author.[18] At the same time, she insisted on what Elshtain calls "the medieval sex complementarity argument."[19] So her particular position in the social order remains a literary one that allows her to enter the political field with words, but certainly does not allow her to conquer it as a critical advisor. This, of course, is due also to the fact that Christine was "intensely loyal" to her employers.[20] Christine's description of Fortune makes it clear that she does not want to cross the borders that she found in the late medieval Parisian milieu in which she lived and worked as a female author. By rejecting gender as an earthly trapping and "accepting that a change of gender would not help improve her moral and spiritual lot, Christine indicates that gender ceases to be a defining factor as regards how she must actually respond to Philosophie's teachings."[21] However, the tension between the authority she claimed and the authority she gained remains, in spite of her literary achievements. Her treatment of Fortune's power is a revealing illustration of this fact.

Nevertheless, her authority as an author is more convincing than that of Hoccleve. In his *Regement of Princes,* Hoccleve refers to Boethius in the course of his argument that it is useless to fight Fortune:

> best is I stryuë nat
> Agayne e pays of fortunës balaunce;
> ffor wele I wote, at hir brotel constaunce,
> A wyght no whilë suffer can soiourne
> In a plyt; us nat wiste I how to torne.[22]

Hoccleve plays the role of a modest and humble man who is at the same time a paragon of wisdom. Thus he wants to gain the authority of a writer. He presents himself as a virtuous man who is in a position to speak of good government because he has the moral qualification to do so. At the same time, however, he confirms his patron's power. The virtue and authority he claims are legitimated by his poverty rather than his knowledge of the literary tradition.[23] It is this simple, traditional, and rhetorical way of justifying his authority that makes him less convincing than Christine.

Hoccleve reflects upon Fortune's power for two reasons. He wishes first to justify his own position and second to remind his patron of the world's instability. The writer counts on the prince's personal interest in keeping his power. Hoccleve, however, does not try to establish an authority that would furnish him with the equal right to speak about politics. His argument is based on the prince's superiority and his own dependence on him. The only common basis they have is their respect for Fortune's power.

In contrast to Christine de Pisan and Hoccleve, Lydgate writes as a churchman. Lydgate is not interested primarily in the maintenance of the prince's power but instead is concerned with the preservation of the public welfare, which he considers a prerequisite for stable government. Even though Lydgate did not significantly change his source for *The Fall of Princes,* the most prominent alterations reveal a highly political and Christian perspective. Derek Pearsall is certainly right in stating that Lydgate did not develop a political philosophy of his own; it becomes clear that he does not want to write only about the prince's good or bad fortune but that he intends to promote the political idea of a "common weale" that accomplishes God's providence. Lydgate warns the prince to not be inconstant and to not listen to false advisors.[24] He refers to his authority as a churchman by pointing out that Fortune is subject to God's "souereynte" (Book 6, 295–301). According to Lydgate, Fortune follows the "fatal purueiaunce" that brings happiness or ruin to the prince depending on his good works or sins (Book 1, 4971–79). The same applies to the prince who wants to rise to power and abhors the idea of his downfall (Book 2, 526–32 and 568–81). Lydgate reminds the powerful: "noble vertu off feithful obeiaunce, / Establisshid vpon humylite . . . Causeth weelfare, ioie and prosperite" (Book 2, 547–51). The prince who is obedient to God can expect obedience from his subjects (Book 2, 610–16).

But Lydgate does not speak only as a churchman. He also stresses his concept of good government by referring to the ideal of a "prudent policie"

(Book 2, 602, and Book 6, 353). Lydgate outlines the rather practical interests of the prince and promises a long government within the limits of the transitoriness of all worldly things. Thus the virtue of prudence reconciles the worldly interests of the prince with God's power. Whereas Fortune is treated in a traditional way in the numerous *De Casibus* stories that follow the concept of providential retribution, Lydgate develops quite an original approach in his interpolation of John of Salisbury.

Lydgate introduces the metaphor of the body politic and uses John of Salisbury's ideas to explain why the people's welfare is the fundamental prerequisite of the ruler's happiness and why the writer acts as a mediator between both: "Rekne up all, and first the worthy nyne . . . Ther marcial actis . . . Be low labour off comouns was first reised" (Book 2, 883–89). He comes to the conclusion that it is always the subjects themselves who enthrone a prince (Book 2, 820–26). Lydgate underlines his position as a churchman and thus legitimates his important position as a writer within the body politic. The body politic has "membris with gostli mociouns, / Which shal be maad off folk contemplatiff" (Book 2, 877–78). Lydgate is not the nation's voice in a desperate situation, like Chartier is, but he associates his political writing with the nation's welfare and consequently claims to have a more responsible position than Hoccleve, who is content with his role as a begging writer.

Lydgate claims to be a preserver of the country's welfare and therefore does not emphasize Fortune's mutability; rather, he outlines the common profit to be gained in defying her. The interpolation of John of Salisbury reveals, more than the remainder of the work (which is more directly dependent upon Boccaccio), the interdependence between the idea of the public welfare and the control of Fortune. Nowhere else in *The Fall of Princes* does Lydgate define his position as a mediator between the ruler and his subjects: "First out off labour al lordshepe dede arise" (Book 2, 917). Here Lydgate goes beyond the simplistic concept of providential retribution. Although he writes in the service of a nobleman and although *The Fall of Princes* proves that his state of dependence determines his choice of topics and even words,[25] his striving for an independent authority as a writer is shown by his interpretation of Fortune's power over man's life within the political system.

Christine de Pisan compromises as a woman, Lydgate as a churchman. Whereas Christine does not go beyond literary tradition in establishing her authority as a political writer, Lydgate claims for himself a political authority as a member of the body politic. Consequently, he believes that man can oppose Fortune's mutability. In the *De Casibus* stories, however, the concept of providential retribution is dominant due to the fact that it is the individual ruler's perspective that prevails and that changes the author's authority to address the ruler.

These reservations do not apply to Chartier, who raises his voice as a Frenchman worried about the "common weale." Chartier does not write in a ruler's service. He is independent and legitimates his writing neither by falling back upon the authority of the literary tradition nor by appealing to an aristocratic or clerical perspective.

In *The Quadrilogue Invectif,* Chartier rejects a fatalistic interpretation of Fortune's mutability. Man's inability to recognize God's will in events seems to prove Fortune's power. Chartier criticizes people who blame Fortune and thus give her a power over their lives she does not have. She is "a thing veyne and voide." It is God's just retribution of man's sins "that our Lorde taketh on vs for our defaultes." This is considered true even if man cannot see God's decision behind an event, since it might take longer than man would think and hit harder than expected.[26] This is a very important statement, especially when compared with Lydgate, because it defends the concept of providential retribution against the fatalistic objections of those who claim that man is lost in "diepe derkenes which no man may clerely vndirstonde."

Chartier, however, does not confine himself to warnings but makes his compatriots and the nobility in particular responsible for the misery into which France has fallen. The nobility was not diligent and far-sighted enough.[27] In *The Quadrilogue* Chartier regards the individual's virtuous living, i.e., the ability to live according to reason [*reson*], as a prerequisite of maintaining the public welfare.[28] This shows that Chartier has a concept of providential retribution very different from that of Lydgate. Acting in a far-sighted manner as a precondition for public welfare is recommended not just to the ruler but to everyone. Fortune's antagonist is not Philosophy as in the *De Consolatione,* but the personification of France who discloses the reasons for the nation's downfall in the wars against England.[29] Chartier speaks as a patriot. He is not dependent on the king's services. His authority as someone who speaks for the entire country also determines his Boethian interpretation of Fortune.

In the opening chapters of *The Treatise of Hope,* Chartier plays the Boethian role of a man who suffers injustice.[30] Although he had worked for the public welfare, he was always cheated out of his reward by malevolent people; in a clear reference to his own experiences, Chartier has the character *Indygnacion* say, "the liff of courte is of the nature of folis."[31] Thus he distinguishes himself from authors who write in the nobility's service. His way of using the "common weale" to justify his authority as a political writer is different from that of Christine and Lydgate. He claims to have suffered for the public welfare.[32]

Chartier is concerned about the decay of the "common weale" and its strongest pillar, justice.[33] As in *De Consolatione,* Chartier describes the hopeless situation at the beginning of *The Treatise of Hope.*[34] At the point of his deepest despair, the author even considers suicide as a possible remedy for his misfortunes (19). Chartier's despair can be seen as parallel to the state of affairs of his country. His growing hope and confidence in God's help create the vision of a renewal of France. *Vndrestondynge* and *Feythe* warn him that God does not do anything without a reason.[35] Due to his intention to speak for all those who work for the public welfare, Chartier does not reduce his words to a warning of sin: "the yate through which men passe into perdicion is large and opyn . . . of which the one yate is working of synne and [thorn]e other omission of good dedis" (22). Chartier reminds people that they might gain God's grace in return for good works. His readers are not the king and the nobility but all those who work to improve the situation in a "tyme of tribulacion." Thus he allows to man more influence in changing and determining his own fate than do authors who write for only one patron.

Even though he refers to the concept of providential retribution several times and therefore does not seem to write about Fortune in a way that distinguishes him from other authors, Chartier sees a direct interaction between man and God.[36] Man's free will could be expressed by prayer. *Hoope*'s principal characteristic is to ban fatalism: "So may thou know that

if prayers and deseruynges shuld not haue profited and God had so or-
deigned thingis that the fre wille of man war constreyned by necessite, I had
be create for nought."[37] Thus, Chartier draws the conclusion that "vertu
maketh vs parteneres and folowers of the godhede."[38] In contrast to Christine and Lydgate, Chartier is a providentialist who not only warns of the
consequences of sin but also calls for the rescue of France. He does not,
however, define "common weale" in a secularized manner. Man's influence
on his fate and that of his country cannot be understood without God's
grace.[39] Chartier speaks as an independent author who feels responsibility
for his nation. It is not Fortune but God, through his providence, who can
realize the public welfare of France.

Both Christine and Chartier are recommended to the young reader
whom William of Worcester addresses in his *Boke of Noblesse*.[40] This nobleman claims authority in a completely different way from the authors previously discussed. On the one hand, William of Worcester writes in the service
of Sir John Fastolf and for the "most hyghe and myghety prince Kynge
Edward iiij for the avauncyng and preferryng the comyn publique of the
Royaumes of England and of Fraunce."[41] On the other hand, he belongs to
the nobility himself and writes from an equal's point of view. He is quite
explicit about this from the very beginning, where he quotes a Roman senator on the duty of the "nobilitas genus" to preserve the "res publica."[42] His
book is not a treatise on political or theological questions like the writings
of Chartier and Lydgate; rather, it relies on his own knowledge of history.[43]
In contrast to Chartier and Lydgate, then, William can appeal to the nobility's honor in order to remind them of their historical responsibility.

More than any other author discussed here, William of Worcester secu-
larizes the question of whether man can determine his destiny and control
Fortune's power. He does not associate prudent and far-sighted actions with
a virtuous life that will be rewarded by God. And man's free will is able to
achieve more than simply resistance to the temptations of sin. William refuses to believe that man descends into misery "be casuelte of fortune, by
prophesies, orellis thoroughe influence and constellacions of sterris of
hevyn."[44] Granting man qualities like responsibility and foresight, he ada-
mantly rejects, for instance, the fatalistic belief in astrology. Even if something happened in accordance with the constellation of stars, it would be

"contingent and of no necessite, that is to sey, as likely to be not as to be." Each prophesy is "dispositiflie," since the opposite would imply that the stars had power over God.[45]

William criticizes the nobility's negligence and goes into detail more than do Lydgate, Chartier, or Christine. He attacks the military planning that he thinks insufficient and that made "the whele of fortune" turn to England's disadvantage.[46] England's misfortune had been brought about by the crown and the nobility "for synne and wrecchidnes, and for lak of prudence and politique governaunce . . . and havyng no consideracion to the comen wele, but rathir to magnifie and enriche oure silfe by singler covetise."[47] The "divine providence" cannot be completely understood by man, but one knows from the Bible "that nothing fallithe or risithe on the erthe without a cause."[48]

It is his independent standing that allows William to take this practical and sensible view of Fortune and human responsibility; such an attitude would be virtually unthinkable for a writer who is in the service of the nobility and who cannot claim his own social authority. William does not have to develop an authority as a churchman, a historian, or a patriot. He appeals to the nobility's honor. This has an impact on his definition of God's part in actions through which Fortune is controlled.

William is convinced that God does not have the "souvereynte" to determine man's fate without man's consent. God has laid this power into man's soul "that he, havyng a clene soule, may turne the contrarie disposicion that jugement of constellacion or prophesies signified." Being invested with a soul, man is closely connected with God and thus has the chance to accomplish God's providence. William's writings thus convey an attitude toward Fortune that is consonant with voluntaristic interpretations of Boethius.[49] William is not more modern than his contemporaries, nor does he possess a more extensive knowledge of philosophy. But his social background makes it easier for him than for other writers to speak about the actual problems of the nobility. William goes beyond the concept of providential retribution, and in this sense his writings remind one of the didactic and providential historiography of the fifteenth and sixteenth centuries, which tries to explain the causes for the rise and fall of kings and countries.[50]

Sir John Fortescue answers from a lawyer's point of view the question that Boethius left to all those who want to accomplish a stable government, namely, whether there is a way to deal with Fortune's mutability. Fortescue quotes Boethius in *De Laudibus Legum* and *The Governance of England.*[51] In only a few words he combines Boethian thoughts on the nature of evil and misfortune with his own political and legal ideas by adopting a sentence from *De Consolatione:* "Quia, ut dixit Boicius, *Potencia non est nisi ad bonum,* quod posse male agere ut potest rex regaliter regnans liberius quam rex politice dominans populo suo, pocius eius potestatem minuit quant augmentat."[52]

In this way, Fortescue explains why a despotic ruler cannot gain power.[53] His explanation does not depend upon the concept of providential retribution, nor does he admonish rulers for their misdeeds with this sentence; rather, he formulates his basic thesis that a good government is the prerequisite of power. In this sentence, Fortescue justifies the superiority of the *dominium regale et politicum* over the *dominium regale,* and he describes the political order promised to England, which is comparable to the government of God described in the Old Testament (112 ff.). The "good governance" and the "common weale" are guaranteed by the *dominium regale et politicum.*

While Fortescue is a nobleman and a lawyer in the king's services, his social rank gives him the authority to speak about and to describe the political and legal order in such a way that Fortune's mutability is ignored. The concept of the providential retribution of an individual's sins is replaced by an impersonal legal structure. Through this means, he is able to overcome the traditional method of discussing the rise and fall of a king from an individual point of view. The legal order of the *dominium regale et politicum* constitutes a secularized equivalent to God's providence.

The political writers discussed here offer a wide variety of answers to the question of whether man's fate is in Fortune's hands. The more independent an author is from an individual patron, the more Fortune loses power and the greater is man's authority as someone who takes part in political decisions. It is clear, moreover, that authors who belong to the nobility, even when they are in the service of the powerful, can easily bridge the gap between the theory and the reality of politics. Authors who do not belong to the nobility, in contrast, must establish an authority to speak. In order to achieve this they must refer to an authority that is also accepted by their patrons—either God or country.

Almost all of these writers rely on their knowledge of the written tradition of literature and history. Christine, as a woman, tries to establish her authority to write about political topics exclusively through her knowledge of the ancient authors. Her dependence upon literary tradition means that Fortune remains quite powerful in her works. Her social position in relation to her patrons is too weak to allow more confidence. The interdependence between social position and the treatment of Fortune is also demonstrated in the case of Hoccleve, who emphasizes his patron's power and his dependence on his grace. He surrenders to his patron just as he surrenders to the powers of Fortune and, thus, reminds his patron of a danger that could precipitate both of them into misery.

As a daily experienced limitation, the social position—or, in the case of Christine, the gender—of an author necessarily affects the means by which the author defends his or her authority and independence. The question of what a human being's free will can achieve in the predestined world he was born into cannot be discussed without also discussing the social situation of the late medieval author and his need to gain for himself both authority and respect.

Notes

1. All quotations from Arthur F. Marotti, "Patronage, Poetry, and Print," in *Patronage, Politics and Literary Traditions in England, 1558–1658,* ed. Cedric C. Brown (Detroit: Wayne State University Press, 1993), 42.

2. Ibid.

3. For the epic tradition, see Ann W. Astell, *Job, Boethius, and Epic Truth* (Ithaca and London: Cornell University Press, 1994), 213, who suggests a typological rather than a historical distinction. According to her assessment, there are two complementary perspectives of stasis and kinesis, the "sinless steadfastness" of Job and growth in self-knowledge in the tradition of "Boethius' heroism": "These differences help to distinguish, and establish a relationship of creative tension between, two opposed poles in medieval romance, whose narratives indicate both stability and movement."

4. For a theoretical approach to the question of how authority is created by authors, see *Discourses of Authority in Medieval and Renaissance Literature,* ed. Kevin Brownlee and Walter Stephens (Hanover and London: University Press of New England, 1989).

5. For this problem compare Richard Firth Green, *Poets and Princepleasers. Literature and the English Court in the Late Middle Ages* (Toronto, Buffalo, and London: University of Toronto Press, 1980), 10: "Unfortunately, there is very little evidence that the enlightened

attitude towards literature implied by the very word 'patronage' was commonly to be met with medieval courts. . . ."

6. Marotti, "Patronage, Poetry, and Print," 43, described the final step of such an early emancipation of the author for Jonson's relationship to Pembroke: "Jonson instructs his social superior in his duty and challenges him to live up to the ideal image presented in the rhetoric of praise. [. . .] The would-be morally superior poet thus patronizes patrons."

7. Christine reported that she had plunged into the lecture of the *Consolatio* on the evening of October 5, 1402, and that she had meditated quite a long time about the evils of the world. See Gilbert Ouy and Christine M. Reno, "Où mène le Chemin de long estude? Christine de Pizan, Ambrogio Migli, et les ambitions impériales de Louis d'Orléans," in *Christine de Pizan 2000. Studies on Christine de Pizan in Honour of Angus J. Kennedy,* ed. John Campbell and Nadia Margolis (Amsterdam: Rodopi, 2000), 188.

8. The dates are taken from Kate Langdon Forhan, *The Political Theory of Christine de Pizan* (Aldershot: Ashgate, 2002), xiii–xiv. For the relationship to the most influential source of this book, *Polycraticus,* see Kate Langdon Forhan, "Polycracy, Obligation, and Revolt: The Body Politic in John of Salisbury and Christine de Pizan," in *Politics, Gender, and Genre: The Political Thought of Christine de Pizan,* ed. Margaret Brabant (Boulder, Colo.: Westview Press, 1992), 33–52.

9. "For a man shulde thynke that fortune distribueth ofte tyme aftir hir wille and geueth victorie to a man at on tyme and at an othir tyme turneth the whele," *The Middle English Translation of Christine de Pisan's Livre du corps de policie,* ed. from MS C.U.L. Kk. 1.5. by Diane Bornstein (Heidelberg: Carl Winter, 1977), 79.

10. "the prynce or the prynces holden the highe place of the hede, for as moche as they shulde and ought to be soveraynes . . . in like wyse the exercise of prynces and nobles ought to retourne to the comon wele," *Livre du corps de policie,* 40.

11. *Livre du corps de policie,* 80. Christine also speaks of the "grete freelte of fortune, whiche is neuer stable" (80). Christine's fatalism is compared with Chartier's attitude in Janet M. Ferrier, "The Theme of Fortune in the Writings of Alain Chartier," in *Medieval Miscellany Presented to Eugène Vinaver by Pupils, Colleagues, and Friends,* ed. Frederick Whitehead, Armel H. Diverres, and F. E. Sutcliffe (Manchester: Manchester University Press, 1965), 124.

12. "Tragedie, Valere seithe, it is a maner of a ditee that blameth thyngis that be euyll done in ordre of policie of the comonte or of prynces" (Valerius Maximus Bk. III, Ch. 7), *Livre du corps de policie,* 64.

13. Christine explains why she is writing this work as a woman and concludes her book with a *captatio benevolentiae* in 39 ff. and 193.

14. See Ursula Liebertz-Grün, "Autorinnen im Umkreis der Höfe," in *Frauen Literatur Geschichte. Schreibende Frauen vom Mittelalter bis zur Gegenwart,* ed. Hiltrud Gnüg and Renate Möhrmann (Stuttgart: Metzler, 1985), 31 ff. Forhan, *The Political Theory of Christine de Pizan,* 42, points out that Christine constructs herself as an educator and used her authority to recommend three principles of good rule.

15. Forhan, *The Political Theory,* 45.

16. See Christine Moneera Laennec, "Christine *antygrafe:* Authorship and Self in Prose Works of Christine de Pizan with an Edition of B.N. Ms. 603 Le Livre des Fais d'Armes et de Chevallerie" (Ph.D. diss., Yale University, 1988, summarized in *Dissertation Abstracts,* 50, 11 [1990], 3581-A): "She must establish an authoritative position in contradiction to them, but she does so by adopting their own methods of argumentation, thus raising the question of how she can avoid conforming to the discourse of her opponents." Charity Cannon Willard, "Christine de Pizan: From Poet to Political Commentator," in *Politics, Gender, and Genre,* ed. Brabant, 26, emphasizes that this experience helped Christine to begin "a program of self-education."

17. See Nadia Margolis, "Christine de Pizan: The Poetess as Historian," *Journal of the History of Ideas* 47/3 (1986), 366 and 374, who believes that Christine was more independent than other authors, such as Froissart, due to her humanistic ideas. Also see Eric Hicks, "Discours de la toilette, toilette du discours: De l'idéologie du vêtement dans quelques écrits didactiques de Christine de Pizan," *Revue des Langues Romanes* 92/2 (1988), 328.

18. See Blanchard, "Christine de Pizan: les raisons de l'histoire," *Le Moyen Age* 92 (1986), 436: "la destinée poétique la [Christine] conduit naturellement à s'introduire dans le champ politique et à faire l'épreuve de sa pratique philosophique sous la forme d'une libre interpollation de la vie du prince. . . ."

19. Jean Bethke Elshtain, "Introduction," in *Politics, Gender, and Genre,* ed. Brabant, 4.

20. See Sheila Delany, "'Mothers to Think Back Through': Who Are They? The Ambiguous Example of Christine de Pizan," in *Medieval Texts and Contemporary Readers,* ed. Laurie Finke and Martin B. Shichtman (Ithaca and London: Cornell University Press, 1987), 177–99, who argues that Christine was not the rebel some critics would like her to have been. Delany claims that in the *Livre du corps de policie* Christine "praises her corrupt and fratricidal patrons as the most benign and humane nobility in the world" (195).

21. Rosalind Brown-Grant, *Christine de Pizan and the Moral Defence of Women: Reading beyond Gender* (Cambridge: Cambridge University Press, 1999), 121.

22. *Hoccleve's Works. III. The Regement of Princes and Fourteen of Hoccleve's Minor Poems,* Early English Text Society 72, ed. Frederick J. Furnivall (London: Kegan Paul, Trench, Trübner, 1897), 3 and 59–63.

23. Derek Pearsall, *John Lydgate* (London: Routledge and Kegan Paul, 1970), 243–45.

24. John Lydgate, *The Fall of Princes,* Early English Text Society, e.s. 121–24, ed. Henry Bergen (London: Oxford University Press, 1918–19), Book 1, 4817–44.

25. See E. Hammond, "Poet and Patron in the *Fall of Princes,*" *Anglia* 38 (1914), 120–36.

26. *Fifteenth-Century English Translations of Alain Chartier's "Le Traité de l'Espérance" and "Le Quadrilogue Invectif,"* Early English Text Society, ed. Margaret S. Blayney (London, New York, and Toronto: Oxford University Press, 1974), 138/140 (Rawlinson MS) and 139/141 (Univ. MS).

27. See also Edward Joseph Hoffman, *Alain Chartier: His Work and Reputation* (1942; repr. Genève: Slatkine Reprints, 1975), 192.

28. Chartier, *Fifteenth-Century English Translations,* 142: "the derknes of our lyuyng and corrupte manerys blindith in vs the iugementes of reason and our parciall desiers maken colde thaffections of the comon wele."

29. See also Hoffman, *Alain Chartier,* 148 ff.

30. Chartier, *Fifteenth-Century English Translations,* 11. For information on Chartier's knowledge of Boethius in *Traité de l'Espérance,* see Hoffman, *Alain Chartier,* 185.

31. Chartier, *Fifteenth-Century English Translations,* 8.

32. *Indygnacion:* "O thou infortunat man, which hast passid the daungerous wayes and anoyeng watchis, and othir also which haue borne vpon their shuldirs the hevynes of theire exile and travailed in pouerte for the wele publike . . ." (Chartier, *Fifteenth-Century English Translations,* 11).

33. Chartier, *Fifteenth-Century English Translations,* 12.

34. Chartier, *Fifteenth-Century English Translations,* 15.

35. "the high Maister of werkis, whose prouidence makith nothing in vayne" (Chartier, *Fifteenth-Century English Translations,* 21).

36. See, for example, "The Treatise of Hope," in Chartier, *Fifteenth-Century English Translations,* 36.

37. See Chartier, *Fifteenth-Century English Translations,* 121, who has *Hope* say in a different place about God: "For though be it He knoweth thingis for to come necessarily in Himself as they shal be, yett He may theym lordely chaunge in them as it pleasith Him by our preyers, by His mercye or by our deservingis" (121).

38. *A Familiar Dialogue of the Friend and the Fellow. A Translation of Alain Chartier's Dialogus Familiaris Amici et Sodalis,* Early English Text Society, o.s. 295, ed. Margaret S. Blayney (London, New York, and Toronto: Oxford University Press, 1989), 2.

39. Hoffman, *Alain Chartier,* 197.

40. William of Worcester, *The Boke of Noblesse. Adressed to King Edward the Fourth on His Invasion of France in 1475,* ed. John Gough Nichols (1869; repr. New York: Burt Franklin, 1972), 25, 27, and 30. For the question of to whom William dedicated his book, see Kenneth Bruce McFarlane, "William Worcester: A Preliminary Survey," in *Studies Presented to Sir Hilary Jenkinson,* ed. James Conway Davies (London: Oxford University Press, 1957), 210–15.

41. William of Worcester, *The Boke of Noblesse,* 1.

42. See William of Worcester's definition of "the terme of Res publica, whiche is in Englisshe tong clepid a comyn profit" (68).

43. See, for instance, William of Worcester, *The Boke of Noblesse,* 22.

44. William of Worcester, *The Boke of Noblesse,* 50. In contrast to this, Arcite complains in The Knight's Tale, ll. 1090 ff.: "So stood the hevene whan that we were born / We moste endure it. . . ."

45. William of Worcester, *The Boke of Noblesse,* 50.

46. William of Worcester, *The Boke of Noblesse,* 48.

47. William of Worcester, *The Boke of Noblesse,* 51.

48. William of Worcester, *The Boke of Noblesse,* 52.

49. William regards Boethius as the epitome of someone who serves the "comyn wele." See William of Worcester, *The Boke of Noblesse,* 52.

50. See Henry Ansgar Kelly, *Divine Providence in the England of Shakespeare's Histories* (Cambridge, Mass.: Harvard University Press, 1970), 36 for the Lancaster, 64 for the York historiographs, and 299 for a comment on the changing attitude towards a moral definition of guilt and punishment.

51. Fortescue either quotes Boethius from Vincent of Beauvais (Chrimes) or he may have known Boethius's book (Plummer). See John Fortescue, *The Governance of England. Otherwise Called the Difference Between an Absolute and a Limited Monarchy,* ed. Charles Plummer (1885; repr. Oxford: Oxford University Press, 1926); and John Fortescue, *De Laudibus Legum Anglie,* ed. and trans. S. B. Chrimes (Cambridge: Cambridge University Press, 1942), xc.

52. *De Laudibus Legum Anglie,* 34; Chrimes translates: "For, as Boethius said, *There is no power unless for, good, so* that to be able to do evil, as the king reigning regally can more freely do than the king ruling his people politically, diminishes rather than increases his power." Also compare *The Governance of England,* 121: "As it is no poiar to mowe synne, and to do ylle, [. . .] Ffor all thes poiars comen of impotencie" and *De Consolatione Philosophiae,* 4, pr. 11, 2.

53. *De Laudibus Legum Anglie,* 35, and *The Governance of England,* 121.

BOETHIUS, THE WIFE OF BATH, AND THE DIALECTIC OF PARADOX

† Michael Masi

The most philosophical mind among all of Chaucer's characters in the *Canterbury Tales* belongs, interestingly enough, not to a cleric but to the Wife of Bath. In the Wife of Bath, Chaucer has created a personality that, among all the characters of medieval literature, is certainly one of the most complex that modern readers will encounter. By examining her intensively self-analytical prologue, we may see that she not only understands herself but also is able to represent accurately to others her own mind and personality. She tells us that she is rough and lecherous, and on that account she has been much castigated by modern critics. At the same time, however, she also gives considerable evidence of an intense intellectual interest, one certainly as great as that of any male on that pilgrimage.[1]

Her claim to have been schooled by five husbands is a clever reference not only to marital and sexual learning, "For she koude of that art the olde daunce" (I. 476)[2] but also is an allusion to the liberal arts curriculum wherein she particularly excelled in logic and rhetoric. Her best teacher was the blond, curly haired ex-cleric, Jankyn, who instructed her not only in hard knocks but also in the love of learning and of books. This fifth husband was an endless source of fascination for her, because he was young and attractive, and because he was schooled in literature and philosophy. It was he, doubtless, who taught her to cite author and title as example in arguments. Unfortunately, however, that learning also was directed against her as a woman, and so their relationship was clouded in conflict.

Nevertheless, her association with the Oxford cleric had a considerable influence on her way of thought. Certainly she was not "trained" in any formal sense as he was. But the scholastic bent of her thought, derived in some way through discourse with Jankyn, is evident from the opening of her prologue where she marshals evidence for her arguments in true scholastic fashion. The position *contra* her argument is presented first, then answered and followed by arguments in support of her opinion. An appeal is made in turn to authority (Old Testament, New Testament, as well as the ancients) and to logic.[3]

There is, however, one particular aspect of the Wife's logical method that thus far has attracted little attention. In many instances, her method of argumentation advances in the form of contrasting opposites; it is a logical process that may be observed with particular clarity and masterly effectiveness in Boethius's *Consolation of Philosophy,* which was singularly important in almost everything Chaucer wrote during the middle part of his career. This argument of the Wife of Bath from apparent contradiction appears elsewhere in medieval thought, but since it is such an integral part of the *Consolation,* and since Chaucer's interest in that work is of far-reaching significance, I should like to train my focus primarily on the *Consolation* and Chaucer's use of it.[4]

In the footnotes to his *Oppositions in Chaucer,* Peter Elbow identifies a number of other critical discussions of oppositions in Chaucer, but these appear to be even more remote from my approach. See, for example, Charles Muscatine, *Chaucer and the French Tradition* (Berkeley, 1957), 132, 153; Dorothy Everett, *Essays on Middle English Literature* (Oxford, 1955), 85; Robert Payne, "Chaucer and the Art of Rhetoric" in *Companion to Chaucer Studies,* ed. Beryl Rowland (Toronto, 1968), 55; and Ida Gordon, *The Double Sorrow of Troilus: A Study of Ambiguities in "Troilus and Criseyde"* (Oxford, 1970), 138, 142.

Boethius's influence on medieval thought is well evidenced by the steady stream of new studies, which, despite their volume, have not exhausted this rich subject. His commentaries on Aristotle, as well as his translation of Greek works on arithmetic and music, supplied both the textbooks and the structure for the liberal arts curriculum in medieval universities.[5] The training of students in the curriculum of the liberal arts was directed toward philosophical studies, which were considered the culmination of the arts program. The Boethian *Consolation* summarizes in a particularly integral fashion the study of the arts, in terms both of their ethical preoccupations and their logical development.

The *Consolation of Philosophy* is important not only for its philosophical content but also for its logical process. Those who are familiar with the total corpus of Boethius's writing are aware that, given the sheer bulk of his works on logic, he must be considered primarily as a logician.[6] His translations and commentaries on the logical works of Aristotle were only the beginning of a much more ambitious program to translate and comment on all the works of the Stagirite. But as it is, he has left us mostly with logical treatises. The Boethian preoccupation with logic is evident in the *Consolation,* and a particular method of proceeding by paradox is especially worthy of mention. It is not a method that he discusses in his logical writings, but method it is nonetheless. I have chosen to call this method the "Dialectic of Paradox," for reasons that I will explain shortly.

Any attempt to trace the logic of paradox to its source must eventually arrive at the works of Zeno of Elea in the fifth century B.C.E. Zeno is especially recognized, now as in ancient times, for his arguments against plurality and against motion. In his demonstrations of these topics he uses the argument of paradox with considerable skill and with devastatingly effective results. His most famous example is that of Achilles and the tortoise. If Achilles and a tortoise were to run a race on the course A–Z but the tortoise were to begin slightly ahead of Achilles at B, Achilles would never win the race. This must be, since the distance from A to B, from Achilles to the tortoise, also can be broken into an infinite number of parts. But it would take an infinite amount of time to traverse an infinite number of spaces. Therefore, Achilles will never pass the tortoise.[7]

Zeno directed his arguments to epistemological problems, because he was concerned with the validity of the evidence derived from sense perception, and after that perhaps showed some interest in metaphysical applications. Boethius doubtless read of Zeno's proofs in Aristotle's *Physics,* where the Stagirite undertook their refutation. In writing the *Consolation,* however, Boethius was much more interested in ethical demonstration than he was in either epistemology or metaphysics. Whether he directly drew upon the arguments of Zeno cannot be determined, but we can see in the *Consolation* the basic approach of Zeno adapted for the purpose of moral paradox. It is this process in the Boethian ethical argument that I have chosen to call the Dialectic of Paradox. This logical process may be simply explained: The effect a person thinks he will achieve through a given action or decision is not the effect he truly desires, but in fact will prove to be an effect directly opposite to his desire. This process of proceeding by contraries is used by Boethius to prepare the way for acceptance of the *summum bonum,* the highest good, in which there is no illusion of opposites or any frustration of legitimate desire.

Discourse in the *Consolation of Philosophy* takes the form of exposition alternating with plentiful example (as in the Wife of Bath's Prologue). Lady Philosophy undertakes, in the first book, to console the victim of evil fortune—one who is rather the victim of his own misunderstanding of the nature of fortune—by disposing of illusory happiness. Men have striven after happiness, she explains, by endeavoring to acquire material possessions, power, honor, or fame. In Books 2 and 3, Lady Philosophy patiently demonstrates that the acquisition of these illusory goods does not bring happiness at all. On the contrary, acquiring them achieves an effect precisely the opposite of that desired by those who aspire to their possession. To achieve wealth, power, honor, or fame is, in reality, to achieve a state that is worse than remaining without them. Neither Croesus nor Nero, for all their riches, died happy men. The possession of wealth creates insecurity, fears of theft, and ignorance about the identity of one's true friends. Lady Philosophy makes this point when she asks, "If riches cannot eliminate need, but on the contrary create new demands, what makes you suppose that they can provide satisfaction?" (3 pr. 3).[8] Nor can power give real happiness. Regulus, Roman consul during the first Punic War, had bound many of his African captives in chains; but before long he was himself chained by his captors. Again, Philosophy asks, "What kind of power is this then which is found incapable even of preserving itself! And though political power is a cause of happiness, is it not also a cause of misery when it diminishes?" (3 pr. 5). The same may be seen in those who desire fame and honor.

The underlying reason for the failure of these attractive earthly means to happiness is that they are given to many by Fortune. Therefore they are transitory, empty, and unpredictable. Their coming and their passing is beyond the control of those who desire them or possess them. Their loss or acquisition is at the whim of *Fortuna,* whose only constant and necessary attribute is continual change. To rely on Fortune for happiness is to rely on an inconstant woman, on a prostitute, as Philosophy makes clear when she tells Boethius:

> You have put yourself in Fortune's power; now you must be content with the ways of your mistress. If you try to stop the force of her turning wheel, you are the most foolish man alive. If it should stop turning, it would cease to be Fortune's wheel. (2 pr. 1)

After she has logically demonstrated the inherent failure of transitory happiness, Lady Philosophy continues to develop her argument through the Dialectic of Paradox. By means of an elaborate discourse from apparent contradiction, she moves from the discussion of transitory goods to the definition of the unchanging good. This transition proceeds by an examination of the external or apparent success of evil in a world created and ruled by a good God. In such a world, one must believe firmly that good men in reality do prosper. Those who are misled by the evil that men do into believing that these vile men do prosper are clearly and fundamentally mistaken about the nature of good and evil in relation to the sovereignty of God. Evil men do not in fact exist, because evil itself has no substantial existence. Boethius here appeals to a type of moral existentialism in which existence depends on the good and in which evil, the lack of existence, renders a person as "non-existent." Lady Philosophy concludes her discussion of illusory existence by relegating evil men to the same position as the illusory happiness disposed of in an earlier book. This conclusion culminates in a closely woven paradox:

> Therefore, since he who can only do good can do all things, and those who can do evil cannot do all things, it is obvious that those who can do evil are less powerful. Moreover, we have already shown that every kind of power is included among the things that men desire, and that all objects of human desire are related to the good as the goal of their natures. But the ability to commit crime is not related to the good, and so it is not desirable. And, since every power should be desired, it follows the power to do evil is not a power at all. From all this it is clear that good men have power, but evil men are weak. (4 pr. 1)

The concluding portions of the *Consolation* take up the problems of chance in God's providence and, especially, free will and God's foreknowledge. Paradox rests at the bases of these questions as well, but the Boethian paradox works expertly to demonstrate the co-existence of God's knowledge, which does not at the same time effect what it knows, with man's free will. God's infinite knowledge includes in it, as part of a master plan for the universe, the free will of men who make their decisions in the context of divine providence.

Among those who knew and read seriously the works of Boethius were Chaucer and Jean de Meun. Both translated the *Consolation* into their vernaculars, and Chaucer made it one of his youthful tasks to translate Jean de Meun's *Roman de la Rose* into English. Jean de Meun's *Romance,* as well as that portion of the work written by Guillaume de Lorris, held a lifelong fascination for Chaucer. The *Consolation* and the *Romance* may be considered the warp and woof of his intellectual fabric. Chaucer read and used ideas from both Boethius and Jean de Meun throughout his poetry, and Jean's thought was itself thoroughly impregnated with Boethian ideas. Interestingly enough, while both read Boethius seriously, the two poets also made comic, and at times even satirical, use of what is rather straightlaced philosophical discourse in the *Consolation.* Most notably, Jean makes comic use of Boethius in the encounter between the Lover and Reason, as does Chaucer in his portrayal of Pandarus as a figure for Lady Philosophy in *Troilus.*[9]

This is not the place for a full-scale analysis of what could be considered Boethian paradox in the *Roman de la Rose,* but its possible existence there is worthy of note. For example, paradox plays an important role in the catalogue of contrarious passions in the lover that Jean adapts from Alain de Lille's *De planctu naturae.* Here, love is defined cumulatively through a recitation of its paradoxes:

> Love is a troubled peace, an amorous war—
> A treasonous loyalty, disloyal faith—
> A fear that's full of hope, a desperate trust—
> A madman's logic, reasoned foolishness—
> A pleasant peril on which one may drown—
> A heavy burden that is light to bear—
> Charybdis gracious, threatening overthrow—
> A healthy sickness and most languorous health—
> A famine swallowed up in gluttony—
> A miserly sufficiency of gold—
> A drunken thirst, a thirsty drunkenness—
> A sadness gay, a frolicsomeness sad—

Contentment that is full of vain complaints—
A soft malignity, softness malign—
A bitter sweetness, a sweet-tasting gall—
A sinful pardon, and a pardoned sin—
A joyful pain—a pious felony—
A game of hazard, ne'er dependable—
A state at once too movable, too firm—
An infirm strength, a mighty feebleness
Which in its struggles moves the very world—
A foolish wisdom, a wise foolishness . . .   4272–4293[10]

The catalogue of a lover's contrarious passions lived an independent life of its own in courtly literature. We hear it from the love-stricken hero in the first book of Chaucer's *Troilus* and in the translations and adaptations of Petrarch's sonnets that proliferated during the Renaissance in England. The Dialectic of Paradox, however, is a particular application of paradox to a mode of argumentation; in the Wife of Bath's Prologue and Tale it takes on a carefully conceived artistic function.

Chaucer's adaptation of clerical logic for such an exuberant affirmation of sexual vitality is striking and original. It is, however, appropriate that the Wife should deploy this scholastic form of logic in the indirect argument she carries on with her fellow pilgrim, the Clerk, over the nature of marriage. For in the end, the Clerk is beaten at his own game: the Clerk's logic, which he presumably has learned through years of study, is used with mastery against male domination and against celibacy by a woman who is excluded from clerical culture by both her gender and her personal predilections. The Friar recognizes the Wife's incursion into clerical territory after her tale, but he is hardly in a position to rebut her. Instead, he pursues a course of bitter satirical diatribe directed against the Summoner, whose very presence on the pilgrimage seems to bother him more than any of these arguments about the nature of marriage.

The Wife's discourse on marriage is laced with concessions to the clerical establishment but is, at the same time, persistently irreverent and self-serving. So, while she is a wooden vessel in her master's house, and does not envy the golden vessels of celibacy, the Wife will grant that "Virginitee is greet perfeccion / And continence eek with devocion" (III. 105–06). But her argument is structured so as to give the victory to marriage, by which she clearly means sexual indulgence, and thereby to undermine the argument in favor of virginity. In the Wife's view of things, not only is marriage inherently superior to virginity, but virginity is in fact dependent upon marriage. This paradox is implicit in the compact argument of the Wife's question: "And certes, if ther were no seed ysowe, / Virginitee, thanne wherof sholde it growe?" (III. 71–72).[11] That is, if a given couple were to content themselves with a vow of chastity, the world would have but two more virgins. Should they, however, bear four children, two of whom would marry and two remain celibate, and should this process continue for three or four generations, three or four times as many virgins would result. Thus, paradoxically, is virginity dependent upon marriage, and thus is marriage superior to virginity.

The argument from paradox appears again further on in the Wife of Bath's Prologue, when she appeals to the stereotypical idea that women are not as rational as men. Since this is so, the Wife suggests, men should make concessions to women, who clearly are not able to understand rational processes:

Oon of us two moste bowen, doutelees,
And sith a man is moore resonable
Than womman is, ye moste been suffrable.
What eyleth yow to grucche thus and grone? (III. 440–43)

The paradox here comes of the fact that it is a woman who is making this rational and self-serving argument.

The Wife's mastery of the Dialectic of Paradox is not confined to her Prologue but informs her tale as well, where it is adapted fittingly to the theme and characters of her narrative. The Wife has set out to show in her Prologue that female domination is ideal in marriage and that she had the personality and intellect to achieve this dominance over five consecutive husbands. Strangely enough, a certain measure of acceptance is evident on the part of the males she had dominated. But if this masculine acceptance is not always clear in her life, it is the central theme and preoccupation of her tale.

Her tale begins, ironically enough, with a rape, which is a physical assertion of masculine sexual domination. By the end of the tale, one wonders which way the irony has cut. Before long, the reader's sympathies have shifted to the young rapist, who must, in a year and a day, discover what women most desire. It should be noted that this task is imposed by King Arthur's wife, whose will supercedes her husband's original (and unimaginative) command that the knight be beheaded. The tale thereby illustrates the theme of domination by the wife over her husband. The queen's intervention also gives the knight an unrecognized clue to the answer to the difficult question she poses.

At the end of the tale, Boethian paradox comes into full play. The foul old woman assumes a relationship to the wretched knight that is reminiscent of the opening scene in the *Consolation*. There Lady Philosophy comes to the bed of the disconsolate Boethius and initiates a teacher-pupil relationship with her charge. In the tale, the forlorn knight, who appears as a mild satire of the Boethian seeker of knowledge, is instructed by the wife who comes to his bed. In seeking a remedy to his existential sickness, the knight agrees with the wife's diagnosis of the nature of his unhappiness: he is wed to a woman who is ugly, old, poor, and of low degree. Like Boethius, in the initial stages of his despair, the knight longs for the goods of this world; he wants a wife who is beautiful, young and noble.

Having identified the source of the knight's despair, the old wife undertakes a lengthy demonstration, reinforced by logic and example, of the folly of the knight's desires. A young and beautiful wife will surely be untrue to her husband; an old and ugly wife, by contrast, will be faithful:

> Now ther ye seye that I am foul and old,
> Than drede you noght to been a cokewold;
> For filthe and eelde, also moot I thee,
> Been grete wardeyns upon chastitee. (III. 1213–16)

Paradoxically, then, a desirable wife may be of less worth than an apparently undesirable one and may ultimately be the source of great unhappiness. Like Lady Philosophy, the loathly lady suggests that true *gentilesse* comes not from high birth but from noble deeds. To understand this, she tells the knight, he should read Seneca and Boethius. She likewise argues, with Boethius's instructor, that wealth is not the source of true happiness; poverty is freedom and allows a man to know God and himself. Furthermore, poverty functions as a seeing-glass through which a man may perceive his true friends. But most of all, the lady tells her student, the knight is fortunate that his wife is foul and old, because ugliness and age are the wardens of chastity. As in the attacks of Lady Philosophy on wealth, power, and fame, the loathly lady presents the knight with the paradoxical argument that a pleasing beauty could ultimately be the cause of his undoing.

At this point, Chaucer's narrative departs from the pattern of consolation that has shaped the tale. The Wife's narrative, after all, is not meant for consolation; it is instead designed to show that men must submit to their wives. Accordingly, the old woman winds up her argument and poses the alternatives, after carefully structuring the case so as to render the knight impotent to make a decision:

> "Chese now," quod she, "oon of thise thynges tweye:
> To ban me foul and old til that I deye,
> And be to yow a trewe, humble wyf,
> And nevere yow displese in al my lyf,
> Or elles ye wol ban me yong and fair,
> And take youre aventure of the repair
> That shal be to youre hous by cause of me,
> Or in som oother place, may wel be." (III. 1219–26)

The husband submits; the paradox is not for him to reconcile. The old woman has brought to this reformed rapist the knowledge to save him from the king's sword. The knight considers it best that she keep the mastery of him and that she resolve the dilemma as it suits her.

In response to the knight's submission, the old woman announces that she will be both fair and true. She not only has the knowledge to save the knight but also is a shapeshifter who is able to make herself young and beautiful. She has already made operative her knowledge in saving the knight's life; now she is able to shape their marriage according to her knowledge that women most want to have sovereignty over their husbands and this sovereignty is for the ultimate good of the husbands. The knight turns to find beside him a beautiful young creature whom he takes into his arms as his lawful wife, and "His herte bathed in a bath of blisse" (1253). Paradoxically, the lascivious knight received what he wanted by accepting what he thought he did not want. And thus, in the final demonstration of the Wife's thesis, the knight's wife has attained true and providential mastery in the marriage.

As we turn from this closing scene of happiness, we know that abstract knowledge and a thoroughly palpable sensuality have achieved that higher synthesis which is so characteristically the Wife of Bath's, from the very opening of her Prologue.

Notes

1. The Wife of Bath's intellectual abilities have been recognized by a number of critics. Patrick Gallacher, in his essay "Dame Alice and the Nobility of Pleasure," *Viator* 13 (1982), 276–93, also has a useful discussion of how Aristotle's practical syllogism may be applied to the Wife of Bath's Prologue. Mary Carruthers, in "The Wife of Bath and the Painting of Lions," *PMLA* 94 (1979), 209–22, recognizes the satirical use of Jerome's works in a very perceptive discussion about the Wife's citation of the *Adversus Jovinianum.* Neither critic, however, refers specifically to the use of paradox in Chaucer's technique.

2. All quotations from Chaucer are taken from *The Riverside Chaucer,* gen. ed. Larry Benson, 3rd ed. (New York: Houghton Mifflin, 1987).

3. This method of argumentation may be found throughout the works of Aquinas, but one may point out as a particular example, in the *Summa Theologica,* the Question of the External Causes of Sin, Question LXXIX: Whether God is a cause of sin? It seems that God is in fact a cause of sin, for the Apostle says of certain people (Rom.i.28) "God delivered them up to a reprobate sense, to do those things which are not right." He also cites Wisdom, xiv.II and Isaiah, xlv.7. But, he says, On the Contrary, It is written (*Wis.* xi.25): "Thou . . . hatest none of the things which Thou has made." Now God hates sin, according to Wisdom xiv.9: "To God the wicked and his wickedness are hateful." Therefore God is not a cause of sin. Aquinas then replies with quotations from Ezech. iii.28 and from St. Augustine, *De Gratia et Libero Arbitrio,* XXI, and so demonstrates that God cannot be a cause of sin (see *Basic Writings of Saint Thomas Aquinas,* vol. 2, ed. and annotated, with an Introduction by Anton C. Pegis [New York: Random House, 1945], 651–53).

4. Professor Peter Elbow, in *Oppositions in Chaucer* (Middletown, Conn.: Wesleyan University Press, 1975) has developed a similar concept and has certainly addressed himself to the identical technique in both Chaucer and Boethius. His approach, however, differs considerably from my own, and, though he uses the terms *dialectic* and *paradox,* he does not use the two terms together, as I have in this essay. In addition, Elbow has taken a more literary approach to paradox and opposition, while I am concerned with a procedure based more on assumptions of logical discourse. Elbow does not address the passages in Boethius that concern me here, including the arguments against power, wealth, pleasure and fame as avenues of happiness. And finally, although Elbow's discussions of *Troilus* and The Knight's Tale are of great interest, he does not refer at all to The Wife of Bath's Tale. I look upon my essay, therefore, as an extension of the work of Elbow, carried out with the understanding of a process of thought common to Chaucer and Boethius.

5. A very extensive bibliography of commentary on the works of Boethius may be found at the end of the article "Boezio," in the *Dizionario Biografico degli Italiani,* vol. 11 (Rome:

Istituto della Enciclopedia italiana, 1969), 142–65. See also the collection of essays, *Boethius and the Liberal Arts,* ed. M. Masi (Berne: Peter Lange, 1981).

6. A list of Boethius's works includes two commentaries on the *Isagoge* of Porphyry, one on the translation by Marius Victorious, another on a translation undertaken by Boethius himself; a translation of Aristotle's *Perihermeneias* (*De Interpretatione*), with two commentaries, one for beginners and another for advanced readers; a translation of Aristotle's *Prior Analytics, Posterior Analytics, Sophistic Arguments,* and *Topics.* In addition to these logical works, Boethius wrote a *De Arithmetica,* a *De Musica,* and a *De Geometrica* (this last now extant only in fragments). Finally, there is *The Consolation of Philosophy,* the work best known to modern readers, and several short theological treatises: *De Sancta Trinitate, Utrum Pater et Filius et Spiritus Sanctus de Divinitate substantialiter Praedicentur, De Persona et Duabus Naturis in Christo, Quomodo Substantiae, in eo quod sint, bonae sint cum non sint substantialia bona* (also called the *De Hebdomadibus*). See Etienne Gilson, *History of Christian Philosophy in the Middle Ages* (New York: Random House, 1955), 603–06.

7. This brief summary does not do justice to the subtleties of Zeno's thought. His argument has received considerable attention in modem times, notwithstanding Aristotle's well-known attempts to refute it. As an introduction to Zeno's work, one may consult the article by Kurt von Fritz under Zeno in the *Dictionary of Scientific Biography,* ed. Charles Coulston Gillispie (New York: Scribners, 1976), 14: 607–12. That same article is followed by a useful bibliography, the more relevant items of which are: H. Frankel, "Zeno of Elea's Attacks on Plurality," *American Journal of Philology* 63 (1942), 1–25, 192–206; Adolf Grünbaum, "A Consistent Conception of the Extended Linear Continuum as an Aggregate of Unextended Elements," in *Philosophy of Science* 19 (1952), 288–305; and his book, *Modern Science and Zeno's Paradoxes* (Middletown, Conn.: Wesleyan University Press, 1967). See also G. Vlastos, "Zeno's Race Course," *Journal of the History of Philosophy* 4 (1966), 95–108. Aristotle's discussion of Zeno may be found in his *Physics,* VI. 9, 239b. For Aristotle and Zeno, see *Zeno's Paradoxes,* ed. Wesley C. Salmon (Indianapolis: Bobbs-Merrill, 1970), 48–55.

8. All translated passages from Boethius are taken from Richard Green's *Consolation of Philosophy* (Indianapolis: Bobbs-Merrill, 1962).

9. For a discussion of the satirical element in Jean de Meun and Chaucer's use of the *Consolation,* see F. Anne Payne's *Chaucer and Menippean Satire* (Madison: University of Wisconsin Press, 1981). See also Alan Gaylord's "Uncle Pandarus as Lady Philosophy," *Michigan Academy of Sciences, Arts, and Letters* 47 (1961), 574–95.

10. The translation of *The Romance of the Rose* used here is by Harry W. Robbins (New York: Dutton, 1962), 95–96.

11. This argument is derived from St. Jerome's statement, "Laudo nuptias . . . sed quia mini virgines generant," in *Epistola xxii, ad Eustochium* (PL [col], xxii, 406). See F. N. Robinson's edition of Chaucer's *Works* (Boston: Houghton Mifflin, 1957), 699) or *Riverside Chaucer,* 866.

PART IV

BOETHIUS IN RELIGION AND MYTHOGRAPHY

BOETHIUS, CHRIST, AND THE NEW ORDER

Romanus Cessario

In his *Intellectual History of Europe,* the distinguished German historian Friedreich Heer refers to Boethius as one of the "first Europeans."[1] Professor Heer gives the adjective *European* a secular meaning. He argues that Boethius, both by his resolve to translate the best of ancient thought from the available works of classical pagan philosophers and by his failure to include Greek ecclesiastical writers among the authors that he made available to the Latin world, consciously established a norm to guide the formation of the Western intellectual tradition. In other words, by his choices as well as by his omissions, Boethius's literary production reflects his deliberate and personal views about what kinds of works should comprise the canon of Western liberal studies. Professor Heer invites us, then, to consider Boethius as prototypical of those members of the higher education community whom Roger Kimball once christened the "tenured radicals."[2] These academicians, albeit for diverse reasons, are still influential in promoting substantially extrinsic and, so it appears, politically inspired criteria for determining the basic curricula used in the nation's institutions of higher education. On the account of Heer and others, Boethius represents a model for those who would endorse a thoroughly secular canon of higher studies and, at the same time, remain indifferent to or even antagonistic toward the importance of religious beliefs in supplying a rounded education. Are we to accept the view that, like certain ensconced members of today's North American academic community, Boethius made judgments about what texts a good liberal education should incorporate into its program, not on the basis of the intrinsic merits of the choices available to him but, rather, on some *a priori* conviction of a highly ideological kind, namely, that only non-Christian philosophy merited translation? This essay demonstrates that we should not.

Other intellectual historians have advanced the view that Boethius was not friendly to things Christian, and they have done this even to the point of wondering aloud whether Boethius seriously embraced the Christian faith. Emile Bréhier, to cite but a single example, has found significance in the fact that Boethius's most influential work, the *Consolation,* lacks any apparent reference to explicitly Christian themes, and some distinguished Boethian scholars maintain that this well-noted omission signals at least Boethius's profound disillusionment at the end of his life with Christianity.[3] This point of view, whose lineage reaches back at least to the beginning of the modern period, fails to take into account the things that Boethius actually accomplished to develop a consensus about what is normative for the instruction of an educated Christian man or woman.

I contend that Boethius made a significant contribution toward laying the foundation for the development of the European community, and that this contribution would be unthinkable apart from his Christian belief. I further contend that both Boethius's life and his intellectual labors perfectly illustrate the conviction that European culture cannot be understood without reference to Christianity. For while there may be little in Boethius's philosophical works to confirm his Catholic fervor, his theological tractates unequivocally reveal the hand of a Christian theologian. In these frequently overlooked compositions, we find Boethius seeking to inform with Catholic doctrine issues of lasting importance for the development of Western civilization. Boethius, I propose, achieves this objective especially in his *Contra Eutychen et Nestorivm,* where he elaborates the basis for comprehending the most fundamental of all Christian doctrines, the doctrine of Jesus Christ, true God and true man, and unravels some of the major implications that are contained in orthodox christological formulations about the person and natures of Jesus Christ.

In addition to what is contained in the specifically christological *opusculum,* there is much in the other theological writings of Boethius to support the view that he was more than tangentially related to the Christian faith.[4] And what is more, current practices of piety closely associate him with the Catholic Church. There exists the living tradition that Boethius died as a witness to the value of authentic, undivided Christian *communio;* in 1883, Pope Leo XIII even officially recognized the practice of venerating Boethius as a Christian martyr.[5] We know too that Italian folklore continues to circulate the notion that Theodoric, whom historians generally credit as the person ultimately responsible for Boethius's grisly execution, was condemned to hellfire for perpetrating the judicial execution of an innocent man.[6] It should come as no surprise, then, to learn that a number of Christian theologians and philosophers have recognized Boethius as a mediator or channel whereby what might be called a vision of integral humanism was transmitted to the West. Instead of reconstructing Boethius as a founding spirit of modernity, with its preference for secular approaches to knowledge, these scholars recognize the true achievement of Europe's first schoolmaster. Boethius, while remaining "a man positive to the values of great literature and philosophy wherever found," clearly shows himself also to embody a man of the Church, that is, one whose concern for the unity and integrity of the Christian community undergirds and directs his life's work.[7]

Before we consider his written work, however, it is important to recall that there are certain features of Boethius's biography that may explain why he was able to appreciate profoundly that the Christian Church with its orthodox christological doctrine offered an appropriate matrix for the burgeoning of the new socio-cultural order.[8] First, Boethius was a member of an old and noble Roman family, one that had been Christian for four generations; indeed, the Anicii were among the first Roman families to take advantage of the conversion of Constantine in order to embrace publicly the Christian religion. Next, although there were heretical deviations among the Goths who had been influenced by Arian Christians, the fact remains that by the early sixth century, Christianity had become the established and dominant religion of the Western empire; and it was within this milieu that Boethius's own education took place.[9] Finally, Boethius was a member of the Senate, which during his tenure continued to play an active role in promoting Nicene orthodoxy and its creed against the encroachments of a repristinated and heterodox Arianism; this last Roman, then, surely was accustomed to hearing about the importance that the unity of Christian faith held for the commonweal. Much as Goethe (1749–1832) would opine that Europe was born on pilgrimage and that Christianity is its mother tongue, so Boethius perceived in his period that a distinctive feature of European culture resulted from its centuries-old dialogue with the Christian Gospel.

In his specifically christological deliberations, Boethius confronted a problem whose roots sink back to the pre-Constantinian period. Toward the end of the third century, the shape of the Church's christological doctrine reflects as much the shadows as the brightness of a theological twilight. Some general features of the christological development during this era derive from Origen's two-sided theological heritage, which affirmed, on the one hand, the full reality of Christ's rational soul or psyche, thereby fully providing for the humanity of Christ, and, on the other hand, the existence of a "second God," thereby suggesting a subordinationist view of Christ's divinity. Indeed, before the Council of Nicea, the posing of the Trinitarian problem more than favored the emergence of subordinationism, to the extent that a general ambiguity concerning the origins of the Logos marks even orthodox writers of this period. We see this, for example, not only in the terminological ambiguity stemming from the orthographic similarity between *gennētos* [begotten] and *genētos* [created] but also in the emergence of a strict Logos Sarx model, in which the divine Logos serves as the *kinetikon* or the natural executive principle of the body. Both the technical language and the anthropological paradigm favor a theological construal of the Incarnation that diminishes the fully divine status of the second person in God. It is from within blurry conceptions such as these that a figure like Eusebius of Caesarea, the last "non-heretical subordinationist," attempts to explain the divinity of the Logos by reference to "the second" or "a second God." Even though Eusebius's explicit christological witness opposes Paul of Samosata's adoptionist view of Christ as a "mere man," the former's technical language still fails to convey and ensure sufficiently the divine character of the Logos.

The Arian controversy issues from this welter of Trinitarian misunderstandings. The theological project of Arius, which dominates the late third and early fourth centuries, requires that one possess a comprehensive view of its philosophical and cultural context, especially, the Middle Platonist opinion about divine mediation in the cosmos. Arius's Trinitarian doctrine considers the Father as an incommunicable divine principle and the Logos-Son as a first and pre-eminent participant. But on a more general level, Arianism represents the dangers that a purely rational, common-sense explanation can pose to the uniqueness of Christian revelation. And today, some accounts of the conflict in fact argue that the Arian explanation gained popularity precisely because it was easy for the common people to grasp the content of a preaching that presented the incarnate Son as almost divine, instead of as a full member of the Trinity of divine Persons.[10] This easy-to-comprehend language may supply one reason why a newly converted Goth found subordinationism a satisfactory account of the Christian mysteries, whereas an educated Roman, who was better able to understand the significance of the Nicene *homoousion*—namely, that Christ is consubstantial with the Father—proved more difficult to persuade.

Arius held that Christ was "God" only in the broad sense. For Arius, radical transcendence can belong only to the Father, even though the generation of the Logos by grace results in the creaturely superiority of the Logos-Son. Arianism does not so much intensify the subordinationism of the Origenist doctrine of the Logos as replace the divine Logos with the Origenist psyche, which is understood to be the created soul of Christ. For this reason, Arianism, judged by the standards of the Gospel, clearly signals a questionable christology. Arius identifies a created psyche as the Logos and argues that this life-principle serves as the sole factor to explain Christ's ontic integration and operations, with the added result that, according to the Arian model of Christ, the Logos-Son remains intrinsically susceptible to change and sin. While such a view admittedly offers an attractive picture of a savior who is able to sympathize with the weaknesses of those whom he saves, it accomplishes this only at the cost of renouncing that belief upon which the Christian faith bases its claim for the definitiveness and universal character of Christian salvation. This central belief of Christian faith confesses the transcendence and divinity of the incarnate Logos-Son, whom Christians call Jesus of Nazareth. When the Church upholds the divinity of Christ, she at the same time affirms the human person's capacity for transcendence, for only a savior who is fully divine can open up human time to the dimension of eternity, and bring creatures otherwise confined to their creaturely existence to share in God's own life.

The theological tractates offer some good evidence that even if Boethius, while awaiting his execution, chose to limit himself to using philosophical categories, recognized throughout his career that the development of European culture requires a Christian theology that accurately interprets the

Incarnation of the divine Logos.[11] Arianism itself had created a problem for the ecumenical Church. The Council of Nicea solved this problem. But after Nicea authoritatively affirmed the divinity of the Logos as a constitutive part and interpretation of the Christian creed, the Church still had to explain how one of the Trinity became consubstantial with us who are human and lived a fully human existence, even up to the point of his submitting to death by crucifixion.

After the resolution of Nicea, there remained for the Church the task of affirming the true humanity of Christ. In 451, the Council of Chalcedon formulated an authoritative document that still forms the basis for the Church's belief in the Incarnation. This ecclesial resolution struck a balance between the exaggerated positions of two particular schools of ancient Eastern theology, one centered around Antioch and the other in Alexandria, for which Nestorius and Eutyches, respectively, have come to serve as repreentatives. Nestorius championed a divisive christology, that is, one which failed to give a full account of the substantial union of the two natures in Christ. The monk Eutyches encouraged a right-wing reaction to the Arian position that emphasized the divinity of Christ in a way that reduced his human nature to the status of a luminous though inanimate physical body. In his preface to the André-Jean Festugière edition of the *Actes du Concile de Chalcedoine,* Henry Chadwick explains what he considers to be the main theological achievement of the fifth-century Council of Chalcedon:

> In contending for the affirmation that Christ is both God and man the Council of Chalcedon was contending for that without which the shape of the Christian faith would be utterly changed. The Definition's merit is to mark a sign of impasse against pathways which either so devalue nature and creation as to disparage man's capacity for God and aspiration for perfection, or so stress the human perfection of Christ as to discover in an individual man, and not in God, the crown towards which all creation moves.[12]

If Chadwick is correct, and a general consensus agrees that he is, then the christological definition agreed upon at Chalcedon affects not only abstract speculation about the ontology of Christ but also the way that the Church presents the Gospel message as part of its dialogue with secular learning and culture. Chalcedon sets the stage for Boethius's achievement.

According to the Chalcedonian dogmatic formula, Christ is said to possess two natures, one divine and the other human, which he acquires at the Incarnation. Moreover, these two complete and distinct natures subsist in the one divine person of the Logos-Son. Once the definition of Chalcedon began to be examined in the local churches of the West, difficulties surfaced about the meaning of the central notions used to explain the substantial personal unity of a Christ who possesses two complete and distinct natures. The query that arose is simple to state: What is a person? What is nature? Anyone given to propose that Boethius may not even have been a Christian surely ignores how Boethius shows his Christianity with great conviction when he addresses these foundational questions for Christian belief and life.

We know that Boethius composed the treatise *De duabus naturis contra Eutychen et Nestorivm* in circumstances that clearly indicate his impatience with confusion in doctrinal matters and with muddled thinking in theology.[13] In the prologue to this treatise, Boethius describes the otherwise unknown assembly that prompted this theological tractate as follows:

> On that occasion all loudly protested that the difference [between person and nature] was evident, that there was no obscurity, confusion or perplexity, and in the general storm and tumult there was no one who really touched the edge of the problem, much less anyone who solved it.[14]

Concern for clarity in Church doctrine motivated Boethius to consider an issue that, strictly speaking, belongs to the discipline of philosophy but, as a matter of historical fact, enters into philosophical reflection only as a result of the distinctively Christian revelation that is the Incarnation. For this reason, Etienne Gilson contends that the question about the metaphysical constitutives of created personhood remains one of those philosophical issues that exemplifies what he calls Christian philosophy.[15] But why did Boethius consider this question of such particular importance for the life of the Church?

Boethius himself tells us that his analysis aims at finding an expression of Catholic truth that avoids a Nestorian Scylla and an Eutychian Charybdis when speaking about the Hypostatic Union.[16] This resolve leads Boethius in the *Contra Eutychen et Nestorivm* to analyze several definitions of nature. He considers, for example, whether nature is best understood as that which is capable of being grasped by the intellect, or as that which is the subject for either an action or passion, or as a principle of self-movement, or, lastly, as a principle of logical differentiation.[17] These definitions reflect some of the different applications that Aristotle draws from the polyvalent notion of *natura* (*physis, ousia*). Boethius continues by pondering the various kinds of natures that exist in the world, observing the substance of each type of nature. He concludes this dialectical inquiry by defining person as "rationabilis naturae individua substantia," that is, "an individual substance of a rational nature."[18] Although some intellectual historians contend that the doctrinal influence of Boethius reached its acme in the twelfth century—especially in the commentatorial tradition associated with the school of Chartres, represented by writers such as Gilbert de la Porrée, Thierry of Chartres, and Clarenbald of Arras—Boethius's definition of person continued to influence the high scholasticism of the thirteenth century.[19] His definition, moreover, continues to serve as a starting point for theological reflection on the Trinity and the Incarnation, especially to the extent that these mysteries of the Christian faith carry consequences for the development of human culture.[20]

The success of Boethius's definition of person in the later scholastic discussions that were held in monasteries, in cathedral schools, and especially at the universities does not force one to conclude that this definition provides the only approach to the question of personhood. In fact, some contemporary authors have remarked on the tentativeness of Boethius's proposed solution.[21] It should nevertheless be underscored that the Boethian definition has become a classical one in Western theology. Subsequent theological reflection, especially in the period of Renaissance scholasticism, continued to expand on the definition, with the result that a variety of commentatorial traditions shaped later theological debates about created personhood, especially during the Leonine Thomist revival. What is more important, however, is that Christian personalist thinkers still refer back to Boethius's original definition of person, even if only indirectly, as when spiritual writers assert that the human person loses the right way when his or her time spent on earth is no longer illumined by the eternal light of Christ. And these sorts of reminders bring us back to the original intuition with which Boethius undertook the project of talking about person and nature. Boethius wishes to serve as a witness to the importance that a clarified account of doctrinal positions, especially those concerning the Savior himself, holds for the life of the human community, whose development, he believed, depends on adherence to Christian faith.

Boethius dedicated his second theological tractate to a certain Deacon John, who, it is argued, would become in the summer of 523 the Roman pontiff.[22] Boethius in fact closes the *De duabus naturis* by affirming to this John that the author has written the work as an expression of his faith: "So much have I written to you concerning what I believe should be believed."[23] Christian faith recognizes a certain kind of personal intimacy as a pathway to the divine. In the divine person of Christ, the intimacy of God and man come face to face. Because of this encounter with the divine intimacy, Christian believers hope to adorn their souls with those interior forms of wisdom and sanctity that comprise the virtuous life. Christians also hold that without virtuous men and women, no society or culture can long survive.

The unique kind of intimacy that the Incarnation makes available to each human person develops into the call to form a new assembly [*ecclesia*], the union of Christian believers in the Church.[24] Neither the Christ of Nestorius nor that of Eutyches could establish the bridge that needs to be built up within the community of men and women, and of peoples and nations, for each of these opposing images of Christ falls short of expressing the completeness of the divine intimacy that the Incarnation effects with the real and historical condition of our human family. Recall that it is only Christ, so the Church upholds, who fully reveals mankind to itself: "Reapse nonnisi in mysterio Verbi incarnati mysterium hominis vere clarescit."[25] Boethius's professional theological analysis helped those responsible for setting the new order on the right path to realize that only the orthodox faith about Christ points men and women to their true identity and destiny. On account of this orthodoxy, we can cherish the hope that some future historian will hail Boethius not only as one of the first Europeans but also as one of the first citizens of a world community in which the personal dignity of each woman and man would be fully respected.

Notes

An earlier version of this article appeared in French: "Boèce, le Christ et la civilisation européenne," *Pierre d'Angle* 1 (1995), 51–60.

1. Friedreich Heer, *The Intellectual History of Europe,* trans. Jonathan Steinberg (Cleveland: World Publishing Co., 1966), 28.

2. See Roger Kimball, *Tenured Radicals: How Politics Has Corrupted Higher Education* (New York: Harper & Row, 1990).

3. Emile Bréhier, *The History of Philosophy: The Middle Ages and the Renaissance,* trans. Wade Baskin (Chicago: University of Chicago Press, 1965), 7.

4. Ralph M. McInerny, *Boethius and Aquinas* (Washington, D.C.: Catholic University of America Press, 1990), states: "There is little in his other writings that suggests what a fervent Catholic Boethius was, but in the [theological] tractates he is unequivocally a Christian theologian seeking to apply close analysis to the dogmas of the faith and to refute heresies" (97). McInerny's chapter 3 discusses the importance of the theological tractates and analyzes Aquinas's commentary on two of them, namely, the *De trinitate* and the *De hebdomadibus.* For another recent discussion of the five tractates, see Henry Chadwick, *Boethius, the Consolations of Music, Logic, Theology, and Philosophy* (Oxford: Clarendon Press, 1981), chapter 4, "Christian Theology and the Philosophers," 174–222.

5. For the approval in 1882 by the Sacred Congregation for Rites of the practice at Pavia of venerating Boethius as a martyr, see *Papiensis confirmandum cultus ab immemorabili tempore praestiti Servi Dei Severino Boethio Philosopho martyro sancto nuncupato* (Rome, 1883).

6. See H. R. Patch, *The Tradition of Boethius: A Study of His Importance in Medieval Culture* (New York: Oxford University Press, 1935), 122, and "The Beginning of the Legend of Boethius," *Speculum* 22 (1947), 443–45.

7. The phrase comes from Chadwick, *Boethius,* 251. Authors who readily accept Boethius as the first schoolman include F. C. Copleston, *Medieval Philosophy* (New York: Harper, 1961), 35; and Josef Pieper, *Scholasticism: Personalities and Problems of Medieval Philosophy,* trans. Richard and Clara Winston (New York: McGraw-Hill, 1964), 29.

8. J. G. Suttner, in his nineteenth-century study *Boëthius der letzte Römer* (Eichstatt, 1852), argues against the rationalist notion that Boethius represents an epitome in secular learning. For a more recent biographical essay, see John Matthews, "Anicius Manlius Severinus Boethius," in Margaret Gibson, ed., *Boethius: His Life, Thought and Influence* (Oxford: Basil Blackwell, 1981), 15–43.

9. Chadwick, *Boethius,* 247–53, argues that it is difficult today to maintain that even the *Consolation* is without its own sort of resonances with Christian culture. He claims, for example, that "much of the vocabulary in Boethius' two passages about prayer . . . can also be found in early Latin collects of the ancient sacramentaries." Chadwick also thinks that the *Consolation* is "a work written with the consciousness of Augustine standing behind the author's shoulder, so to speak." Earlier, in the preface to his edition of the *De Conso-*

latione Philosophiae (London: Burns Oates & Washbourne, 1925), Adrian Fortescue made a similar case: "Nempe de *Philosophiae Consolatione* hoc est opus; revelatam igitur doctrinam ibi invenire ne postulaveris, sed philosophiam satis habens tradi christianam. Sed illa quaenam? An Platonis, an Aristotelis, an Neoplatonicorum? Nullius, inquam, jurat Christianus nisi in Christi verba magistri. . . . Neque enim quae pagani recte dixerunt et vere, illa facere sua Christiani erubescunt, nam sanae philosophiae revelata doctrina contraria esse nequit . . ." (xlviii).

10. For a defense of this view, see Robert C. Gregg and Dennis E. Groh, *Early Arianism: A View of Salvation* (Philadelphia: Fortress Press, 1981); and for more information about the Arian controversy, see R. P. C. Hanson, *The Search for the Christian Doctrine of God: The Arian Controversy 318–381* (Edinburgh: T&T Clark, 1988).

11. In *Boethius,* 174, Chadwick points out that even in the early Middle Ages it was customary to conjecture an authorship other than Boethius for the Christian *opusucla,* but that the tenth-century literary critic Bovo of Corbie discredited the theory on the grounds of a stylistic comparison with Boethius's other works, even though Bovo used this evidence to dissuade people from the Boethian *corpus.*

12. Chadwick writes this in the Preface to André-Jean Festugière, O.P., *Actes du Concile de Chalcedoine* (Geneva: P. Cramer, 1983), 16.

13. For both the Latin and the English translations of Boethius's theological works, I am using the Loeb Classical Library edition, *Boethius: The Theological Tractates,* ed. E. K. Rand, 2nd ed., trans. H. F. Stewart, E. K. Rand, and S. J. Tester (Cambridge, Mass.: Harvard University Press, 1973), 1–129. For a textual study, see John Mair, "The Text of the *Opuscula Sacra,"* in Gibson, ed., *Boethius,* 206–13.

14. "Hic omnes apertam esse differentiam nec quicquam in eo esse caliginis inconditum confusumque strepere nec ullus in tanto tumultu qui leuiter attingeret quaestionem, nedum qui expediret inuentus est" (17–21).

15. See his *The Spirit of Mediæval Philosophy* (Gifford Lectures 1931–32), trans. A. H. C. Downes (New York: C. Scribner's Sons, 1940), 189–208, esp. at 204: "It is Boethius' *De duabus naturis,* that is to say in a treatise on the two natures in Christ, that there occurs that definition of the person that inspired the whole Middle Ages, and weighs so heavily on the development of modern ethics."

16. See the Prologue, 55–61: "prius extremi sibique contrarii Nestorii atque Eutychis summoveantur errores; post vero adjuvante deo, Christianae medietatem fidei temperabo. Quoniam vero in tota questione contrarium sibimet de personis dubitatur atque naturis, haec primitus definienda sunt et propriis differentiis segreganda."

17. I, 1–60 (passim): "earum rerum quae, cum sint, quoquo modo intellectu capi possunt"; "vel quod facere vel quod pati possit"; "motus principium per se non per accidens"; "unamquamque rem informans specifica differentia."

18. IV, 5–9: "Hoc interim constet quod inter naturam personamque differre praediximus, quoniam natura est cuiuslibet substantiae specificata proprietas, persona vero rationabilis naturae individua substantiae."

19. For further information, see G. R. Evans, "*Speculatio* and *Speculativus:* Boethius and the Speculative Theology of the 12th Century," *Classical Folia* 32 (1978), 69–78; and Margaret Gibson, "The *Opuscula Sacra* in the Middle Ages," in Gibson, ed., *Boethius,* 214–34.

20. For example, theologians must confront texts in Saint Thomas Aquinas that adopt Boethius's definition, e.g., "Nihil aliud est persona quam rationalis naturae individua substantia" (*Summa theologiae* III q. 2, a. 2) and "hoc nomen 'personae' communiter sumpta nihil aliud significat quam: substantiam individuam rationalis naturae" (*Quaestiones disputatae de potentia* q. 9, a. 4).

21. For example, see Maurice Nedoncelle, "Prosopon et persona dans l'antiquité classique," *Revue des Sciences Religieuses* 22 (1935), 477–99; and M. Elsaesser, *Das Person-Verständnis des Boethius* (Würzburg, 1973). In the twelfth century, Richard of St.-Victor, in his *De trinitate,* Book IV flatly rejects Boethius's definition of person and proceeds to develop one that was inspired by the patristic doctrine of Trinitarian relations.

22. See Chadwick, *Boethius,* 248.

23. VIII, 94–97: "Haec sunt quae ad te de fidei meae credulitate scripsi."

24. I am here following certain observations that Kenneth L. Schmitz makes in "The Geography of the Human Person," *Communio* 13 (1986), 27–48.

25. Second Vatican Council, "Pastoral Constitution on the Church in the Modern World," *Gaudium et spes,* ed. Norman P. Tanner, S.J.: "In fact, it is only in the mystery of the Word incarnate that light is shed on the mystery of humankind" (no. 22).

THE MUSES IN THE *CONSOLATION*
THE LATE MEDIEVAL MYTHOGRAPHIC TRADITION

Graham N. Drake

At the beginning of the *Consolation,* Boethius is lying in sickbed, bemoaning the misfortune that constitutes his disease: his misery, his exile, and his premature old age. His only companions are the Muses [*Camenae*], who faithfully remain with him but also force him to write elegies, only increase his sorrow. Into this doleful chamber enters the figure of Philosophy. Scandalized by the presence of the Muses, she denounces them with powerful invective, not scrupling to avoid calling them "sluts" [*meretriculae*]. She says that she will replace these Muses of poetry with her own philosophical Muses. Visibly ashamed, the Muses leave Boethius's bedside.

While Boethius speaks about "the Muses," he never specifies them as the nine Muses of classical mythology. The Muses who force him to write elegies in Book 1, meter 1 do have a name frequently given to the classical Muses—"Camenae"—yet Boethius never gives them familiar, individual names such as Calliope or Euterpe. Nor does he identify his Muses as the nine sisters, born to Jupiter and Memory, who lived together on Mount Helicon. Nor does he stake out any individual functions for his Muses—inspiring poets and historians, or presiding over nine different subjects such as comedy, tragedy, astronomy, geometry, etc. They are simply "lacerating Muses" who make him miserable.[1]

For his own times, Boethius's omission is not standard. Early Christian poets may protest, as does Paulinus of Nola, against pagan usage by deliberately replacing the traditional invocation to the Muses and Apollo with an invocation to Christ.[2] Or, like Fortunatus, they may embrace the nine Muses wholeheartedly without any sense of contradiction between pagan and

Christian.[3] One might invoke the Muses, make them conspicuously absent—or, as we shall soon see, create clusters of nine-fold allegories. But few poets who speak of the Muses present so little of their classical embodiment as does Boethius.

Yet of course, even as Philosophy will denounce and vilify these Muses, she calls for her own to replace them. And even though these new, philosophical Muses set the stage for a philosophical remedy to Boethius's problems, Philosophy herself will compose and perform most of the meters that follow in the *Consolation,* flaunting a dazzling virtuosity in many different meters—asclepiads, Sapphics, heroic hexameters, glyconics, and even elegiacs. Her meters always have a philosophical point, and Philosophy always subordinates them to the prose arguments in her dialogue with Boethius. Nevertheless, it may seem paradoxical that the Muses who inspired poetry are banished only to be replaced by Philosophy's own singing career. This tension parallels, perhaps, the deportation of the poets in Plato's *Republic,* in which Plato suspects both the form and content of verse-making.[4]

Even without direct knowledge of Plato, medieval commentators find that they must do business with Boethius's paradoxical setup. What to make of the Muses in Boethius—whether to rehabilitate them or connect them in some way to the nine Muses of classical tradition—becomes a problem for which commentators provide a number of solutions in commentaries between 1150 and 1500.[5] A few of the commentators will adhere to Boethius's vague delineation of the Muses of poetry (as opposed to the Muses of philosophy, who never appear except as an image created by Philosophy, the only Muse for the rest of the *Consolation*). But the widely available tradition of the classical Muses transmitted through a variety of mythographical sources —through Ovid, Martianus Capella, Macrobius, Fulgentius, and the Vatican Mythographers—leads the commentators to correct Boethius's apparent omission. Boethian commentators of later medieval tradition move collectively towards restoring the "classical" vision of the Muses to greater or lesser degrees.

"Classical" should be understood here as shorthand for what the commentators understand as the pagan myths of ancient Greece and Rome, known through the mythographic tradition and surviving Latin texts. Except for the later part of the period under discussion, Boethian mythographers are not exactly Renaissance humanists. If they restore the names and number of the Muses, with some of their biography, these mythographers still are liable sometimes to allegorize them; and some late medieval commentators, regardless of chronology, do not move much further than Boethius in depicting the classical Muses. Still, there is continuity between these mythographers and the humanists.

In considering the historical changes in responses to Boethius's Muses, we might note how Alastair Minnis's *Medieval Theory of Authorship* sheds light on the general tendency towards the literal in the prologues to late medieval commentaries on the Bible and, eventually, on classical texts. With the introduction of Aristotle and the development of scholastic methods that favored him over the Neoplatonic approaches to myth in Macrobius and Martianus Capella, commentaries on myth in the later Middle Ages became somewhat less attracted to allegory, though not completely uninterested; allegorical interpretations continued to appear in commentaries. Yet new literary approaches, derived from scriptural exegesis, were helping to make the study of "poetic lies" more acceptable.

This tendency, which Minnis calls "Aristotelian," is apparent in the prologues to the commentaries. Earlier commentary prologues, for instance, whether on myth or on Scripture, had been arranged according to a loose series of topics ("titulus libri," "nomen auctoris," "intentio auctoris," "materia libri," etc., is just one example of such a series).[6] These topics did not disappear completely in the thirteenth century but were subordinated to Aristotle's four causes (material, formal, efficient, and final), and within the discussion of the efficient cause there arose a new emphasis on the author and on the literal sense of a text.[7] The renewed emphasis on the literal sense moved mythography at least partly away from the complicated allegories that had been a feature of Boethian commentaries since the ninth century.[8]

Commentary became increasingly a matter of amplification of the original text rather than the construction of an allegory whose structure competed with the original text for attention. More frequently, the commentator preferred to explain difficult points of grammar, historical allusions, and the bare sequence of events from a mythological story. In Courcelle's opinion, by the fourteenth and fifteenth centuries this trend led to longer, less interesting, less original commentaries, with less influence than their predecessors; they were more like school texts.[9] By no means were all of them dull:

the commentary of the "classicizing friar," Nicholas Trevet, includes some fascinating new explanations of the labors of Hercules and, more to our purposes here, of the Muses.[10]

The following examination of late medieval Boethian commentators, then, will focus on certain textual aspects of Book 1, meter 1 and prose 1: that the Muses are called "Camene lacere"; that they were the glory of Boethius's youth and will not now abandon him; that Philosophy calls them "scenice meretricule," the "thorns" who destroy the fruits of reason, and "Sirens"; and that the Muses depart blushing from Boethius's bedchamber. We then will consider some more elaborate interpretations of the Muses from the commentaries. The first of these is the "classicizing" of the Muses, i.e., providing details of earlier classical accounts of them, especially from Ovid, which Boethius omits. Next, there are two types of allegorizing (often applied to these classicized Muses, though not always): "naturalizing," which makes them represent aspects of the physical universe; and "psychologizing," which turns the Muses into an allegory set that corresponds to specific components of human reasoning.[11] Finally, Denis de Ryckel's method of interpreting the Muses differs significantly from the practice of his colleagues; hence he deserves separate attention. Taken together, these commentators present one diachronic view of reading the Muses in late medieval Europe, specifically as *Boethian* mythography, as opposed to the better-known mythography on the works of Ovid and Virgil. A complete list of commentators and their manuscripts is found in the Appendix to this essay; references to their works in the text include only commentator name and folio.

Camene lacere

Ecce mihi lacerate dictant scribenda Camenae.

[See how the Muses grieftorn bid me write.]

(Tester, 131, 1.3)[12]

Guillaume de Conches (*fl.* ca. 1140) sets the stage for later commentators with his simple glosses on the second line of the *Consolation:*

They are called "Camene," which is to say they sing beautifully of any sort of thought or idea [*sentencie*]. But some are whole and complete [*integre*]: others are

lacerating. The complete ones are philosophical thoughts, which by the unbroken-
ness of reason and constancy strengthen a person. The lacerating ones are called
poetic thoughts—that is, the knowledge of composing and describing things in
verse, for they tear apart the hearts of men and render them inconstant by bringing
pleasure or sorrow to the memory, yet neither instructing nor consoling it. These
lacerating Muses dictated words that Boethius must write, because they disposed
him to describe his sorrow metrically rather than provide him with philosophical
consolation.[13]

By showing no concern for the Muses' classical narrative, as one might
find in Ovid, Guillaume follows Philosophy's lead.[14] Guillaume extends his
author's implications to make the point that philosophy, not poetry, will
keep a person in reason and constancy. We may infer from Guillaume that
it is not rational to make things up or to describe things metrically; these are
not philosophical consolations. This position soon becomes troubling to us,
of course, because Philosophy herself will use meter as part of the therapy
for her patient, Boethius. Guillaume and many other later commentators
will flog "poeticas sentencias" and yet go on to comment on the content of
the remaining thirty-eight meters in the *Consolation*.

Between Guillaume and his famous follower, Nicholas Trevet, comes
a brief commentary found mainly in the Vatican manuscripts, the so-called
Anonymous of the Reginenses. Courcelle places it in the twelfth century.
This commentator calls the Muses "seculares scientie" in both, 1 meter 1
and 1 prose 1.

Nicholas Trevet's commentary appears almost a century and a half
later.[15] Like Guillaume, Trevet interprets "Camene" as "singing beautifully," adding that it was the poets who invented the Muses. He sets *integre*
and *lacere* in opposition, as Guillaume does, refining these terms a bit.
There are some arts and sciences, Trevet says, which amuse the mind the
way a song does. But there are others, like "physical arts and sciences,"
which keep a person in the "integrity of reason and constancy of soul."[16]

Typically, Pierre de Paris tells us very little about the Muses: in
meter 1, they are only "sciences depeciees" [dismembered knowledge].[17] In
prose 1, they are "sciences versifiees" [versified knowledge] as opposed to
the "sciences pratiques" [practical knowledge] of Philosophy; and they are
also called "veilles pucerelles . . . proce que les sciences versefiees est la
premiere science que sen seut aprendre as enfans" [old girls, since verse-

skills are the first that one teaches to children] (Pierre de Paris, fols. 3v–6r). One might argue that Pierre sees an infantilizing quality in the making of verses, implying that real grown-ups leave metrical nonsense in order to pursue more appropriate knowledge.

For William of Aragon, the Camene are not only "lacere" but also "dissute" [untied, loose, detached]. The Camene are so described because "it is the property of unleashed sorrow to touch on various matters."[18] Meanwhile, Wheteley's "Camene lacere" break Boethius's heart and urge on his misery. They remind the commentator of a Psalm: "De die et de nocte interius penetrantes / Cor meum sicut lacerantes" (Wheteley, fols. 15r–v). To the already mentioned contrast between poetry and philosophy, Wheteley adds a matter of rhetoric:

> As the poet and the philosopher are different kinds of makers [*artifices diuersi*], they must each have a different mode of expression [*modum dictandi*]. For the poet must contrive things and so must have a lamenting and complaining mode of expression. But the philosopher must tell the truth and have a weighty [*compendiosum*] mode of expression; and this mode of expression must certainly confer solace on the writer [*dictanti*].[19]

Giovanni Travesio stresses the musical aspect of poetry. His Camenae are "science musica dictantes" (fol. 24). Yet, whether they are called arts or sciences, they are not like Philosophy's Muses, which differ from the others because they are useful forms of knowledge.[20]

A guiding theme for the Anonymous of the Erfurtensis is that of writing elegies of exile, which "cannot dictate [one to write] about exile without sobs." Or, they may be lacerating in the sense that Boethius has had his possessions torn away from him while in prison. The Anonymous almost seems to draw our attention away from the Muses somewhat and more towards Boethius's sorrowful condition.[21]

By the fifteenth century, Reinerus van Sankt-Truiden (Regnier de Saint-Trond) constructs a composite of a number of earlier commentators, and this method is a trademark of his mythography. Of particular note is the way he combines the oppositions of true and false tears, lacerating and integrating Muses, and poetical fiction as opposed to philosophical truth:

Behold, the Pierides—the poetical Muses—are with me, singing beautifully; they often give me words which I must write, words suitable to my sorrows; and the Muses move me so that I bathe my face with tears—and real ones, not false. It should be noted that the Camene are any delightful teachings [*sentencie*], as if they were singing beautifully. Hence some are whole and complete, others lacerating [*lacere*]. The complete ones are known as the teachings [*sentencie*] of the philosophers and the theologians, woven together [*contexte*] with the most efficacious reason and with the indissoluble bands of truth. And this is what true consolation is made of. But other Muses are lacerating; that is, they are poetic fictions in which truth is torn apart by falsehood, and in them true consolation is not to be found, only a seeming consolation, as will appear later.[22]

If the judgment on the Muses seems harsh by now, we must recognize that several commentators argue to varying degrees that not all the Muses are to be considered useless. For example, Tolomeo Asinari (1307) initially admits that the Muses are lacerating because they treat of diverse and varied things, one after another—as if ripping the focus of the mind into little bits (Tolomeo, fol. 6r).[23] This recalls a similar theme in William of Aragon (*supra*). The Muses also tear men apart by separating them from the *summum bonum*. With respect to their subjects, the Muses are vain indeed and are meant merely for bodily delights; they distract men from the knowledge of the *summum bonum* and from supreme and noble philosophy; they are "vile and obscure" (fol. 6v). In spite of these vices, the Muses are neither bad in every way nor entirely useless. For one thing, knowledge comes from God, as St. James tells us, "Every good endowment and every perfect gift is from above, coming down from the Father of lights" (James 1.17). The commentator now proposes that the Muses are not bad in themselves; rather, it is their improper use that is harmful, and their skills, consequently, can be put to good purposes. The art of music, for example, can help others to sing the praises of the Creator (fol. 6v).

Clearly, Tolomeo seems to be implying a distinction between the worthy classical Muses (and what they may stand for; see *infra*) and the Camenae of the text at hand. But even if those Camenae are pernicious in a literal sense, Tolomeo suggests that they are quite wholesome, allegorically speaking. In the passage on "Has saltem," for example, the Camenae stand for good knowledge that will not abandon a person (Tolomeo, fol. 7v). Nevertheless, Tolomeo will add the caveat that these Camenae of Boethius's also represent the "whisperings" [*susurrones*] that advise him to write in a variable way at different times, to glory in prosperity or to weep in adversity. Pietro da Moglio presents a similar defense of the Muses (with reservations).[24]

Guglielmo da Cortimiglia approaches the difference between the Camenae and their classical heritage by showing how their name has an equivocal meaning, "for it sometimes signifies sexual delights [*veneream delectationem*]." Sometimes they stand for poetical knowledge [*scientiam*]. But at other times, they are in fact the nine Muses. The poetical Muses "scatter [people] about into diverse affections: now with tears, now with laughter, now by honest or dishonest means" (fol. 96). In contrast, "natural knowledge" [*sciencie naturales*], implicitly identified with the nine classical Muses, is either political or mathematical. These kinds of knowledge do not lacerate the human mind "but compose and adorn it."[25]

In the opinion of Josse Bade d'Assche, meanwhile, the Camenae are "inventrices carminum"—almost an echo of many handbooks on rhetoric. In his commentary on 1 prose 1, Bade d'Assche tells us that Philosophy does not teach that the poetical Muses must be driven out no matter what. Nor does she condemn all Muses—only poetical ones. Afterwards, she resolves to cure Boethius with her own Muses.[26] We will soon see more of how Bade d'Assche (together with Trevet, and even more so Tolomeo), elaborates on just who the good Muses are, as well as several different methods of rehabilitation which these commentators deploy.

Has saltem

Has saltem nullus potuit peruincere
Ne nostrum comites prosequerentur iter. (1 m. 1)

[But them at least my fear that friends might tread my path
Companions still
Could not keep silent.]
(Tester, 131, lines 5–6)

Like Boethius, Guillaume shows how the Muses are in a sense faithful: "But terror could not conquer these Muses: for a person's wisdom always follows him wherever and however distant he may be displaced."[27] Trevet also acknowledges that the Muses retain a degree of loyalty to Boethius.

That the Muses would not leave Boethius means that the art of poetry—a consolation to Boethius—could not be taken away, since it was not a material good [*bonum corporale*].[28]

At this point in 1 meter 1, William of Aragon narrates a good portion of Boethius's sad history, especially how Boethius was captured and sent into exile by Theodoric. Yet no matter how dreadful the circumstances or how great the tyranny, the Camenae would not stop following this exile. It was only they who could help him unravel the complexity of his sorrows. But William reminds us that there are other Muses:

> who pertain to virtue and other kinds of knowledge, and these [attempt to] bury sorrow; [but] memories were veiled by the confusion of sorrow—although, strictly speaking, every art and science follows the knower. It is just as Cato says: "Learn something; for when [good] Fortune suddenly withdraws, art remains and will not desert a person."[29]

In a literal sense, Boethius has said that, for better or for worse, the lacerating Muses will not leave him. In the allegorical sense, these Muses are transformed; the commentator remembers only the whole and complete Muses [*Muse integre*] who steadfastly accompany the person endowed with knowledge. These Muses are equivalent to Philosophy's own, who will replace the ones who have caused Boethius so much grief and harm.

In his comments on this passage, Wheteley commends *ars,* especially any art that is called liberal. Yet he seems to ignore the meaning of *has,* which should refer to the Muses, not the liberal arts.[30] At any rate, it is clear that the Camenae themselves are the "prosperity of the life I was used to in Rome and the beautiful sweetness I was used to in the Athenian schools," and that they are the "'arts which I learned in my youthful state.' Now they comfort him in the time of trouble from gloomy fate" (fol. 15v). In Boethius's present condition, however, they do not actually mitigate pain; in his comments on 1 prose 1, Wheteley reminds us that the "poetical Muses incite sadness."[31]

Reinerus concedes faithfulness to the Muses without any grammatical mix-up. They may tear Boethius apart with elegies; "nevertheless, they are commendable because they faithfully remain with Boethius." Further, his allegorical sense of *Musa* nearly matches William of Aragon's comments.

"The Muse is connected with the activities of the understanding or the mind when genius continually accompanies a man" [*Musa ad industrias intellectus vel ingenij referatur quando ingenium semper hominem concomitatur*].

Gloria felicis

Gloria felicis olim uiridisque iuuentae
Solantur maesti nunc mea fata senis (1 m. 1)

[they were once my green youth's glory;
now in my sad old age they comfort me]

(Tester, 131, lines 7–8)

Commentators vary in their attention to Boethius's days of youthful poetic glory. Guillaume simply states that, in Boethius's prosperity, he reveled in "meter and rhythm" [*metro et ritmis*] (fol. 3v). The Camenae now console him in the bad fortune of his old age.[32] But Trevet plays with the notion of "green youth" a bit more when he says that youths used to be "pruned" in their tender years in order to learn poetic knowledge. Travesio, meanwhile, would rather say that these Muses were the beauty of Boethius's youth.[33]

Similarly, Reinerus tells how the presence of the Muses in Boethius's youth was commendable, as it is even now, when they console him in his miserable old age. Or so it appears, for their consolation is only temporary, and like the wind blows away. Such transience reminds Philosophy of what Job said to his comforters: "Miserable comforters are you all. Shall windy words have an end?" (Job 16:2b–3a).[34]

Scenice meretricule

Quis, inquit, has scenicas meretriculas ad hunc aegrum
permisit accedere . . . ? (1 pr. 1)

[Who let these theatrical tarts in with this sick man?]

(Tester, 135)

The Muses appear next in 1 prose 1. After Boethius introduces Philosophy, describing her stature and her unusual clothing, Philosophy becomes outraged that the Muses are at Boethius's bedside and condemns them.[35] She calls them "scenice meretricule," a pejorative phrase best translated as "theatrical sluts." Guillaume and his followers make observations about each of these words; we will take a look at *scenice* first.

Scenice

> They are called "scenice" as if to say "theatrical." For the "scena" was that part of the theater in which characters [*persone*] hid themselves and [from which] they exited; and there they recited the works of the poets. On account of this, therefore, the poetical Muses were called "scenice," that is, "theatrical." For their whole intention was bent on this, that their works might be recited in theaters. Or one might say "scenice" in the sense of "shadowy." For the "scena" is called a "shadow." Thus the poetical Muses are called "scenice," which is "shadowy," for they are the shadows of knowledge, not real knowledge; or they might be thus because they shadow or cloud over the hearts of men.[36]

Guillaume's first explanation is tame enough: *scenice* means theatrical, and the Muses take on this name because they recited their works in theaters. That their intention was bent on performance may indicate something excessive about their character. But the next possible meaning is more telling, and clearly damning. *Scena* means shadow; the Muses are shadows of true knowledge. They have already lacerated human hearts: now they darken them.

But Trevet's source for explaining *scena* is Isidore's *Etymologiae*. The chapter of Isidore's encyclopedia entitled "De ludo scenice" provides a few more details of a theater's physical structure. The *scena* is a place below the theater, in the ship of a house, and equipped with a platform" (Trevet, 35). From what Trevet tells us, this construction with a stage still hid the players—or, more acceptably, reciters—from the audience.[37]

Tolomeo's interpretation is a little less hard on the Muses' reputation: *scenes* are the places where *ludibria* [derision, sport, mockery] are carried out. In fact, in such places the Muses teach song and the playing of the psaltery and other musical instruments (fol. 12r).[38]

The Muses are theatrical for any of five reasons in Giovanni Travesio:

> "theatrical" . . . from that place in which people congregated for dictating things, or because for the most part there are six-part structures in poems [*seni*], that is, he wrote poems in sixers. "Scena" is a dark place, or it is the recitation [of a work]. Or a "scena" is material which occupies itself, so to speak, in the art of versifying."[39]

Meretricule

Next, Guillaume's consideration of *meretricule* is seminal for later commentators:

> And note that the poetical Muses are called "prostitutes": they attract a man themselves by delighting him, conferring little or nothing of use, and they bring a great deal of penance or poverty after he has been sated. Also, just as prostitutes have relations with a man not for love but for the hope of money, so poets write not for the love of knowledge but so that they can extort some sort of praise or reward.[40]

What Guillaume does not explain is why these *meretricule* should have any connection with theaters (whatever theaters were for him).[41] Later commentators, as we will see, do make some kind of connection.

Tolomeo continues his theme of the *summum bonum* here. The Muses affect the mind the way prostitutes attract customers, all the while pulling the human mind away from the highest good. They are "momentary inclinations" [*predelectationes momentaneas*]. Reinerus's remarks are likewise largely negative. The poets are like prostitutes, and the works of such poets are recited in "scenis." The poetic Muses similarly cloud men with "false fantasies," and their poems attract in the same way that prostitutes do with their make-up.[42]

Venenis

quae dolores eius non modo nullis remediis foverent,
verum dulcibus insuper alerent uenenis? (1 pr. 1)

[Not only have they no cures for his pain
but with their sweet poison they make it worse]
(Tester, 135)

Philosophy then accuses the Camenae of giving Boethius no cure for his troubles, only "sweet poison." Composing verses about sorrow is neither remedy nor consolation, Guillaume declares. On the contrary, doing so provokes even more sorrow. The sweet poisons actually harm because a recollection of pain inevitably follows the writing of elegies.[43] The Anonymous of the Erfurtensis identifies these poisons as "secular songs or desires; such desires are sweet for the time being, but immediately after-wards become bitter."[44]

Tolomeo observes a similar contrast. The Muses' "dulce uenenum" is still disreputable, and quite sneaky: "it is sweet poison to the taste: never-theless, once tasted, it kills. This knowledge is delightful, but it draws the intellect away from the real good.[45]

Fructibus rationis

Hae sunt enim quae infructuosis affectum spinis uberem fructibus rationis segetem necant hominumque mentes adsuefaciunt morbo, non liberant. (1 pr. 1)

[These are they who choke the rich harvest of the fruits of reason with the barren thorn of passion. They accustom a man's mind to his ills, not rid him of them] (Tester, 135)

Guillaume calls the fruits of reason "the perfection of the soul." A crop grows with increase "ex agricultura" [through tending of the fields, agricul-ture]: so knowledge [*sciencia*] and the virtues of the soul grow through "learning" [*doctrina*]. The fruit of reason is both "to know well and to act well" [*bene cognoscere et bene operari*]: "For what is the fruit of man per-fected in knowledge, except to know well? And what is the fruit of a man perfect in virtues, except to act well?" [*Quis enim est fructus hominis per-fecti in sciencijs nisi bene cognoscere? Et quis est fructus hominis perfecti in uirtutibus nisi bene operari?*].[46]

For the fruitless thorns of the affections themselves, which Philosophy ascribes, Guillaume presents "the affections of the soul," a commonplace in Stoic as well as Scholastic thought: "joy, which concerns present good; anger, which concerns present evil; hope, which concerns future good; fear, which concerns future evil. The fruitless thorns influence these affections: "just as thorns prick and extract blood from anyone who dares touch them, so these affections make one anxious."[47]

It can also be said that the fruit of reason resides in "good studies and pleasures" (Anonymous of the Erfurtensis), but the Muses accustom the mind to wicked studies and do not liberate it from earthly pleasures. Several centuries later, the fruits of reason can still be connected in a similar fashion to Travesio's concern for useful knowledge.[48]

While much of Tolomeo's discussion resembles the Anonymous of the Erfurtensis, Tolomeo is the first to allude to the parable of the sower in the Gospels. The seed that "fell on thorny ground" chokes the growing plant of reason. The thorns are bodily delights and earthly affections. Minds given to such forms of knowledge can hardly tend towards other, better forms: the study of pleasure or emotion only breeds more delight in them.[49]

Finally, William of Aragon's Muses are thorns because they "arrange it so that the human capacity for conceiving [things in the mind] undergoes diverse experiences—of hope, sadness, or the sharpness of sorrow." The Muses harm because they "cloud and impede for the sake of moving the passions."[50] Now the images of cloud and darkness seem earlier in the glosses on "science meretricule" become associated with Boethius's image of thorns. Anxiety is both pain and darkness.[51]

Sirenes

Sed abite potius, Sirenes usque in exilium dulces. (1 pr. 1)

[Get out, you Sirens, beguiling men straight to their destruction!]
(Tester, 135)

The final name Philosophy has for the Muses is "Sirens." Guillaume readily explains that:

> The Sirens are sea monsters, by whose singing many are deceived. But at one time they were the daughters of Achelous, who were picking the flowers with Proserpina when she was kidnapped by Pluto; as they were mourning the seizure of Proserpina their comrade, the gods took pity on them and made them goddesses of the sea. And they are marine monsters: part animals, part maidens. They have wings and talons; they are said to put sailors to sleep by their sweet song, and to cause shipwrecks. And one of them makes music with her voice, another plays the flute, and the third plays the harp.[52]

Most of these literal details can be found in Ovid, Isidore, and the Vatican Mythographers, and some of them tend to demythologize the image of the Sirens.[53] The First Vatican Mythographer says that the Sirens actually were three prostitutes [*meretrices*] who drove men to poverty. In Guillaume's view, they were three sisters who used their beauty not only to deprive their lovers of their goods but also to lead them into eternal damnation. The Third Vatican Mythographer also observes that the Sirens are winged [*volatiles*] because they change the mind of their lovers, and they have "bird feet" because "through the impulse of lust certain [acceptable] possessions are scattered [*affectu libidinis quaequae habita sparguntur*]." This allegorical observation manifested no obvious parallel with the literal details other than [*ungulas*] that "love deserts and wounds" [*amor transit et uulnerat*]. The Muses come by such a name because they lure and tempt with poetic meter [*quia metro alliciunt*].[54]

Trevet invokes Isidore again (*Etymologiae* 11.4, "De portentis") when he speaks about the Muses. Again, he derives most of his other information from Guillaume except that the Sirens are now half-bird, half-woman (in contrast to Guillaume's less specific half-beast, half-woman). Trevet also leaves out the allegories that Guillaume provides for details such as *alas ungulas,* merely setting the literal characteristics of the Sirens in comparison with the Muses.[55]

The list of epithets for the Sirens grows longer with another original contribution from Wheteley: they now become dangerous fish (Wheteley, fol. 20r):

> such fish who sing sweetly in the water as they attract sailors even to destruction. . . . For there are fish that are very dangerous to men. For when it rains and there is a great storm in the sea, a shipwreck is soon to follow.[56]

It is not true, as the common people think, "that the Sirens weep when there is bad weather; for after bad weather they hope to have good weather. Thus they cry when the weather is pleasant and beautiful, because after that time they expect it to be wretched."[57]

Bade d'Assche concludes his remarks about the Muses with his own explanations of the Sirens. He offers a brief etymology: *Siren* comes from the Greek *herein,* meaning "to connect and to retain." Bade d'Assche retells the story of the Sirens and Proserpina, whose details do not match Guillaume's version. For the later commentator, the sirens are the daughters of Achelous and Calliope, living on Pelorus "between Sicily and Italy." Bade d'Assche introduces the story of names for the first time: Parthenope (named after the city that is now called Naples), Leucosia, and Ligia.

Bade d'Assche then refers to Claudian, who mentions many details about the Sirens, as does Virgil; but it is Homer who gives the Sirens their fullest representation in the twelfth chapter of his *Odyssey*. The recovery of the *Odyssey* is something entirely new and striking among late medieval commentators, though Bade d'Assche only mentions it in passing. In any event, the exhaustive coverage of the Sirens here pushes the Muses so far away as to nearly make us forget how useless they may have been to Boethius in his time of adversity.[58]

Rubor

His ille chorus increpitus deieci humi maestior uultum, confessusque rubore uerecundiam limen tristis excessit (1 pr. 1)

[Thus upbraided, that company of the Muses dejectedly hung their heads, confessing their shame by their blushes, and dismally left my room] (Tester, 135)

When the Muses leave Boethius, their faces are red from blushing. Guillaume simply explains that *rubor* is a sign of modesty (fol. 10r). Trevet, however, pays more attention to Boethius's words and transfers the shame to him. It is *Boethius's* face which is gloomier, "for one accustomed to poetical Muses relinquishes them with difficulty" (Trevet, 39). It is his face that reddens with shame: "For the wise man is ashamed when looking on something disgraceful among himself. Trevet supposedly wrote a *Commentum super predicamenta;* in the chapter "On quality and quantity," he explains that when the face is in the state of modesty, the blood comes out [to the surface]: just as it is about to hide a transgression, the blood comes rushing forth.[59]

Tolomeo's physiology of *rubor* adds psychological depth to Trevet's:

Note that a blushing face indicates modesty; pallor indicates fear. The reason for this is that the blood is drawn to the face on account of modesty, but with fear the blood is drawn to the heart. And thus the face pales.[60]

Classicizing

So far, we have seen how commentators name the Muses, gauging their worth for Boethius as he writes sorrowful verses, and then explicating Philosophy's renamings of the Muses—as prostitutes, as thorns, or with an allegorical adjustment that makes them something like the useful Muses of philosophical knowledge. Beyond these common remarks, several commentators make some reference to the nine classical Muses. The Muses are subject to reinterpretation that adds the explicit classical connection lacking in Boethius's text.

The first mythographical connection we get between Boethian and classical Muses comes quite early in the period under consideration. The Anonymous of the Erfurtensis speaks of the Muses invoked by secular writers such as Horace and Virgil, who pretended that the nine Muses were nine goddesses, whose aid people might invoke when needed.[61]

Trevet's contribution here appears in his comments on *scenica meretriculis,* and they require some explanation. Having compared poets to prostitutes, Trevet reminds us of the prologue to one of Persius' satires:

> Quod si dolosi spes refulgeat nummi
> Comas poetas et poeticas picas
> Credas cantare Pegaseum melos.
>
> [But if cunning coins should reflect hopes, you may believe poets are crows and poetic magpies sing a Pegasean melody.][62]

Trevet does not comment further here: Persius' words are scathing enough, for, through a type of guilt-by-association, he turns the poets into crows (crows and magpies are, of course, legendary in their attraction to shiny objects such as coins). Moreover, *picas* reminds us of the well-known story in Ovid's *Metamorphoses,* Book 5, of the song-contest between the Pierides and the Muses, after which the Pierides were turned into magpies. Pegasus, meanwhile, would have been known through Ovid (*Metamorphoses,* 5.257) and through the Vatican Mythographers for opening a fountain sacred to the Muses with a kick of his hoof.[63] The selection from Persius is both appropriate and quite dense, for it deftly combines the subjects of mercenary money (which we saw above), poetry, and the Muses; Trevet is also making a tenuous identification here between Boethian and classical Muses.

Much more explicitly classicizing are Tolomeo's remarks. The Muses, he says, were the nine daughters of Jupiter and Memory. They were supposed to have lived on Mount Helicon. When a poet wanted to write, he would go to that mountain, call on the Muse responsible for the general subject of his writing, and she would come to his assistance. Alternatively, it is supposed by some that both Apollo and the Muses ministered to the poets.[64]

At this point, Tolomeo lists the Muses and their functions:

> The first is Euterpe, who discovered trumpets and other tubed instruments—in other words, instruments which are sounded with the breath. The second is Melpomene: she composed tragedies. The third is Terpsicore, [who invented] the psaltery, or stringed instruments. The fourth is Calliope: [she invented] feigned or fictional writings, and "figures," or the knowledge of letters. The fifth was Clio: she composed histories. The sixth was Erato: she invented the art of geometry. The seventh was Pollimia [*sic*], [who invented] rhetoric. The eighth was Thalia, [who invented] "comedies," or the art of singing. The ninth was Urania: she invented . . . astronomy.[65]

While Trevet's quotation from Persius only hints at it, Reinerus van St. Truiden (Regnier de Saint-Trond) calls the Camenae by their classical nickname "Pierides" for the first time. In his commentary on 1 prose 1, Reinerus explains that there were nine Muses near the fountain of Mount Helicon, the daughters of Love and Memory; others know them as the daughters of Memnonis (which, Reinerus seems not to know, also means "Memory") and Testes.[66]

Additional information about the nine Muses comes in the commentary on 1 prose 1 by Guglielmo da Cortimiglia (fol. 100r). According to Isidore, he says, the Muses were nymphs, goddesses of the waters—for the motion of water creates music. The word *Muse* itself comes from *moys,* which means "water" (fol. 100r). Guiglielmo then explains the meanings of their names[67] and lists several kinds of Muses according to their habitat: "The Oriades are the Muses of the mountains, Diadee of the woods, the Amadriades of fountains, the Maides [for Naiads] of fields, and the Marides [for Nereids] of the sea."[68]

Bade d'Assche quotes a metrical list of the Muses that appears in the Vatican Mythographers.[69] He then offers a typical explanation of the Muses' names, as well as Fulgentius's "naturalization" (see *infra*) of the Muses. A list of authorities now develops. Anaximander (according to Landino) believes the poets were under the protection of Apollo and the Muses. Plato called the Muse the music of the spheres. Virgil says they are the daughters of Jove. Alcineon [*sic*] makes them the daughters of heaven and earth, and Theodontius says they were descended from Thespia and Menno [*sic*]. To Diodorus Siculus, they were eight girls whom Osiris led in a band throughout the world.[70]

Naturalizing

Another method of interpreting the Muses is "naturalizing"—taking poetic figures and interpreting them as a system belonging to the natural world. Boethian commentators who naturalize the Muses in this way generally see them in anatomical or astronomical terms.

"In truth," says the Anonymous of the Erfurtensis, "the Muses are nine instruments of the voice: four teeth, two lips, the tongue [*plectrum linguae*], the palate [*repercussion palate*] and the lungs [*anhelitus pulmonis*]. Even if only one of these instruments were lacking, the voice would be incomplete. This list is similar to the one Fulgentius (55) provides.[71] Tolomeo agrees with this nature of the Muses, refining his explanation of the teeth as *dentes anteriores.*

For Guglielmo da Cortimiglia as well (fol. 100v), the Muses form the voice; but, he notes, according to Varro, there are only three Muses of voice, breath, and beat [*voce, flatu, pulsu*]. They pertain to sound and form the "material of old songs" [*material cantilenarum*].[72]

Naturalizing the Muses invokes the macrocosm as well as the human microcosm. Tolomeo calls them the nine planets:

Others say that the aforementioned Muses represent nine celestial harmonies, of which seven are formed by the revolution of the seven planetary spheres, that is, of the moon, Mercury, Venus, the sun, Mars, Jupiter, and Saturn. The eighth is formed by the revolution of the firmament. The ninth, however, is composed from the others. And Macrobius discusses this in *On the Dream of Scipio.*[73]

Psychologizing

Yet another interpretive method among the commentators is "psychologizing," whereby the Muses become the components of human mental processes. In Tolomeo's case, the Muses can stand for the nine steps towards the accomplishment of a given area of knowledge [*ix gradus ad perfectionem*]:

> First, to will something. Second, to delight in what is willed. Third, to meditate on it. Fourth, to hold the meditation in the understanding. Fifth, to give it over to memory. Sixth, to find something that is similar. Seventh, to make a judgment about what is found. Eighth, to choose something good from what is judged. Ninth, to advance that good.[74]

Following Fulgentius, Tolomeo explains how each of these categories applies to a particular Muse:

> Euterpe acts first: for she moves the will, or the appetite, towards something useful or delightful, towards which all human appetite bends its efforts. Moreover, we arrive at these things best through knowledge. Thus, all desire knowledge, just as the Philosopher says in the first book of the *Metaphysics,* that men by nature desire to know; hence, [Euterpe] is interpreted is "good delight." Second, Terpsichore makes one delight in the things willed; her name is interpreted as "delighting in instruction;" for we delight in what we want to know. Third, Clio, whose name means "reflection on things," causes one to reflect. Fourth, Melpomene, who makes the things reflected on to be perceived in the understanding, means, "causing reflection"; for reflection is perfected when it is perceived by the understanding; that is what reflection is. Fifth, Polyhymnia makes one remember, since her name is interpreted as "causing memory." Sixth, Erato causes one to discover things that are similar to one another, since her name means "finding analogies." Seventh, Thalia means, "subtle and capable" because she causes one to make judgments about the things found, that is, to determine whether it is well that the things are found or not. For one is thought to be subtle and capable of knowledge when one knows how to judge about things. Eighth, Urania makes one choose the good both among the things found and the things judged; her name means "heavenly," for it is heavenly to choose good and reject evil. Ninth, Calliope, who makes one proceed melodiously or with good sound, is translated as "good sound," for she is provided for producing sound and for speaking with a sweet tone. And thus through these steps we arrive at perfection.[75]

Theologians say that the Muses are nine "causes of knowledge" [*scientales causas*] by which the soul of man is perfected, "quantum ad bene esse":

But afterwards it [the soul] is perfected by these processes of mind—that is, by imagination, understanding, memory, knowledge, skill, study, exertion, wisdom, and virtue. For in the first place the imagination perceives the forms of things. Then the understanding takes hold of them and makes judgments about them. Third, the memory stores up the things judged and seldom from the understanding and keeps them. Knowledge leads the things that reside in the memory into habit; and when this is led forth into action, it is called skill. For skill [*ars*] is nothing other than knowledge in action: after this, increase of knowledge [*ad sciencie conseruationem et augmentum*] and for the safekeeping of mind [*ingenium*] lest it grow meager [or, perhaps, "go loitering about"—*ingrassetur*].[76]

Next, Tolomeo offers an alternative set of the steps of completion [*imperfectio*] or achievement that is "not according to the theologians":

For, in the first instance, the senses perceive something and present this to the imagination. The imagination presents this in turn to thinking, which forms [a thought from] this material. The "mind" [*ingenium*], however, investigates it; reason judges it, memory preserves it; understanding comprehends it and leads it towards contemplation. But contemplation joins it to God, and thus the soul is perfected.[77]

Finally, the Muses may be nine properties, which are said to distinguish humanity from the beasts:

The first is to distinguish between the honest and the disgraceful. For it is only proper for humans to pursue nothing except what is useful or delightful. The second is to order the passions according to the limits imposed by reason. The third is to elevate the understanding: just as [people] walk erect in body, so they may be lifted up in his mind, as it is said in the second book, Chapter Three [of Aristotle?]. For if one should make oneself inferior through clinging too much to earthly matters, one undergoes a change in the understanding: as it is said also in the tenth book, at the end of the second chapter. The fourth point is to have friendship, according to the proper kind of friendship that differs from the animals, who have natural friendship but that which has its origin in delight and change and things of this kind. The fifth is to blush when something disgraceful has been perpetrated; because of which they [presumably, "bestial" persons] are said to be incapable of correction for modesty, because they are changed from the order of reason, taking on a bestial nature. The sixth is that there should be conjugal perfection, to the extent that if they contract marriages, they make laws and customs and other ordinances of the state. The seventh is that the human [person] be a civic animal who observes laws and customs. Eighth, that such an animal should be able to perceive doctrine according to the use of his reason. Ninth, that he be a domesticated animal; for in such ways he differs from beasts, because beasts cannot be tamed.

These nine properties make human beings complete.[78]

Denis de Ryckel

Denis de Ryckel's (or Dionysius Carthusianus's) commentary on 1 meter 1 and prose 1 focuses less on the Muses and more on the anatomy of misery and consolation. Normally, he does not pay much attention to the Muses except to give us clusters of epithets. "The Muses sing beautifully [*canens amene*]: That is, 'sounding pleasant.'" "'Poetical Muses': the reflections, cajolings, and consolations of flattery" (Denis, 39).

Denis is interested in the nature of knowledge, and in this context we learn about the Muses: they are the "natural modes of knowledge [*scientie naturales philosophice,* whether poetical or philosophical, which are delightful in themselves and which delight the knower." Yet of course they are "'lacerated'—and we might say, 'gone to pieces,' 'unfastened' [*quasi dissute*]; they are heaping up the mournful condition of shattered or imperfect knowledge into Boethius's inward ears. . . ." To be sure, the natural modes of knowledge and the teachings [*sententiae*] of the poets are imperfect and weak (23–24). Denis seems to put human endeavor, whether natural knowledge or poetry, in the same category: because it is human, it is imperfect.[79]

Yet there is some usefulness in this knowledge, at least to make a point, which accompanies Denis's comments on "Has saltem nullus":

> Although my persecutor deprived me of homeland and friends, riches, dignity, honor, and earthly prosperity, yet he could not take away that knowledge and consoling teachings [*sententiis*] which I have mentioned, nor could he prevent them from enduring in my heart: and thus they continue with me everywhere I go. (25)

Denis bolsters his argument with several examples, including that of the philosopher Seneca. Though he lost his material goods in a fire, he calmly asserted, "I have my possessions with me." If pagans can have such contempt for worldly things, Denis wonders, "what shall carnal and greedy Christians answer to God when they stand before Him?" [*quid carnales et cupidi Christiani coram Deo sunt responsuri?*] (25).

Unlike his colleagues in the Boethian mythographical tradition, Denis takes no interest in theaters or Sirens.[80]

Conclusion

In this survey of mythography on the Muses, we see that some commentators will only consider the Muses in the same way Boethius appears to. They find poetical Muses (who sometimes constitute the Muses) harmful, and make no reference to their classical counterparts. We might refer to these in a very general way as forming the "conservative" tradition of approaches to the Muses. Other commentators recognize the harmful possibilities of these Muses, yet at the same time include common classical knowledge about the uses or about the allegories of their functions, copied from such sources as the Vatican Mythographers. We may refer to this tradition as "moderate."[81]

Among these commentators, Tolomeo is one who stands back and makes an issue of the fact that the Muses may elicit a number of possible interpretations. After all, Boethius himself gives them various names: "Camenae," "poeticae Musae," "scenicae meretriculae," and "Syrenes dulces" (fol. 6r). Yet Tolomeo's work, which compiles the opinions of earlier mythographers including Macrobius and Fulgentius, takes on dimensions to which the sparer text of his *auctores* gives no clue. Tolomeo's exhaustive discussion that considers the Muses from the standpoint of classical poetry, natural science, and psychology indicates further that Tolomeo's main underlying methodology is polyvalence.

Considered as a whole, the variegated tradition of late medieval Boethian commentators presents a textual context that diverges from the more closely studied Ovidian mythographical tradition.[82] The very existence of the Boethian commentaries reminds us that mythological knowledge was available through the particular literary context of the *Consolation*—presented in sequential, marginal, or interlinear form. For a compiler, preacher, student, or scholar in the late Middle Ages, reading Trevet's commentary on Boethius's Muses, for example, may mean something very different from reading an Ovidian commentary where the Muses are not necessarily being opposed to philosophy or compared to Sirens. Indeed, the execrations of Philosophy against the Muses and the ways that commentators elucidate them provide yet another contribution to the medieval antifeminist tradition, with elaborations on prostitution and make-up and the collocation of these with theaters (in the sense that Isidore and others understood theaters). The Boethian mythographers, then, provide their own slant on the Muses, and their perspective should be valued as another contribution to the rich weave of medieval responses to pagan mythology.

Appendix: The Commentators

This list of commentators and chief manuscripts, arranged by century, is based on Courcelle's chronology of commentators in his *Consolation de philosophie dans la tradition littéraire* and includes information from the catalogues of the collections that hold the manuscripts. As Troncarelli[1] notes, however, the state of flux in which commentaries find themselves makes Courcelle's findings only tentative, and there may well be other commentaries to discover. Until such discoveries are made, however, and until critical editions become available to sort out the manuscript tradition of each commentator, Courcelle's list stands as the most useful available. This usefulness has been confirmed to me as I have worked with catalogues of manuscript collections at many European libraries.

Twelfth-Century

Guillaume de Conches. London, British Library, Royal MS 15.B.III. Vellum, 143 fols., fourteenth century. May have belonged to King's College, Cambridge; then to John Thayer (fol. 75, "Liber Iohannis de Coupershill iuxta Gloucester," 1633 C.E.).
————. Munich, Bayerische Staatsbibliothek MS 4603. Boethius commentary in late Carolingian hand; 177 fols. Fol. 1, Aristotle, *Liber de anima de nova translatione;* fol. 23, Aristotle, *Topics;* fol. 60, Aristotle, *De Sophisticis elenchis;* fol. 71, excerpts from the grammars of Donatus, Priscian, Remigius, and others; fol. 85, Donatus, "edition prima

---

1. Fabio Troncarelli, "Per una ricerca sui commenti altomedievali al *De Consolatione di Boezio,*" in *Miscelanea in memoria di Giorgio Concetti* (Rome: Università degli Studi di Roma, Scuola Speciale per Archivisti e Bibliotecari; Turin: Bottega d'Erasmo, 1973).

(vel minor), with commentary of Remigius; fol. 109, Sallust, *Catilina et Jugurtha;* fol. 130, anonymous commentary on Geoffrey of Vinsauf's *Poetria Nova;* fol. 136, anonymous commentary on Horace, *De arte poetica;* fol. 142, anonymous commentary on Boethius, *Consolatio philosophiae;* fol. 176v, "varietas metrorum Boetii"; fol. 177v, humorous verses; parchment, twelfth to fourteenth century.

Anonymous of the Reginenses 72 and 244. Vatican Library, MSS Reginensis 72 and 244. Similar manuscripts; both in tight, highly abbreviated Carolingian hand; both on parchment, both twelfth century. Mythographical commentary in MS 72, fols. 110r–123r; in MS 244, fols. 43r–62r.

————. Paris, Bibliothèque de l'Arsenal 910; similar to Vatican Reginenses 72 and 244, in tight, highly abbreviated Carolingian hand, on parchment, 34 fols., twelfth century; commentary of Guillaume de Conches interpolated on fols. 174–224v.

Anonymous of the *Erfurtensis.* MS Q.5. In *Saeculi nonis auctoris in Boetium consolationem philosophiae commentarius.* Ed. E. T. Silk. Rome: Papers and Monographs of the American Academy in Rome, vol. 9, 1935.

Anonymous of the Vaticanus latinus 919. In Vatican Library, MS Lat. 919 (fragment; includes 3 m. 12). Late Carolingian hand, twelfth century.

Thirteenth-Century

No additional commentators known (Courcelle, 317).

Fourteenth-Century

Trevet, Nicholas. Unpublished critical edition by E. T. Silk (microfilm).

Tolomeo Asinari. Vienna, Österreichische Nationalbibliothek Cod. 53. Large, readable, rounded Gothic hand, with a few interpolations in what appears to be a later hand; on parchment, 162 fols., fourteenth century.

————. Paris, Bibliothèque Nationale de France MS Latin 6410. Late Gothic hand, on parchment, 171 fols., fourteenth century (September 1307, according to colophon).

Pierre de Paris. Vatican MS Lat. 4788. Contains Old French translations and glosses. Hand includes lobed "a," always dotted; on parchment, 88 fols., fourteenth–fifteenth centuries.

William of Aragon. Cambridge University Library MS Ii.3.21. Vellum, 298 fols., fourteenth century. Contents: Boethius, *De Consolatione philosophiae,* with Chaucer's *Boece,* fol. 1; William of Aragon, *Commentary on Boethius's Consolation,* fol. 1814; commentary colophon indicates that the manuscript was prepared by Johannes Theutonicus, June 1306.

———. Cambridge, Gonville and Caius College MS 309/707. Various hands, on vellum, 176 fols., twelfth–fourteenth centuries. Contents: Boethius, *De Trinitate,* fol. 1; Boethius, *Tractatus . . . ad Iohannem diaconum de eo utrum pater et Filius et Spiritus Sanctus substantiter predicetur de Deo,* fol. 10; Boethius, *Contra Nestorium et Euticen,* fol. 15; Boethius, *De consolatione philosophiae,* fol. 28v; William of Aragon, *Commentary on Boethius, Consolation,* fol. 89; further notes on Boethius, fol. 171; Boethius commentary has anonymous interlinear and marginal notes in Carolingian and Anglicana hands.

Wheteley, William, Oxford, New College MS 264. Boethius commentary in large, slightly cursive Gothic bookhand with thick pen strokes that sometimes obscure reading. On parchment, 261 fols., fourteenth century. Includes some letters from Wheteley to his colleagues and relatives; fragments of his notes on philosophical questions; short exposition on two hymns by Hugh of Lincoln. Owned by one William Reed; later owned by New College.

———. Oxford, Exeter College MS 28. Commentary in close Gothic secretary hand, on parchment, 307 fols., fourteenth century. Contents: Wheteley, commentary on Boethius, *De Disciplina Scholarium,* fol. 2; Wheteley commentary on Boethius, *Consolatio Philosophiae,* fol. 68; anonymous questions on the same work, fol. 206; miscellaneous sermons, fol. 250; St Augustine, sermon on patience, fol. 289; anonymous sermon on the nativity of St. Mary Magdalene, fol. 293; Robert Grosseteste, *De veritate,* 294v; Robert Grosseteste, *De libero arbitrio,* fol. 297; Robert Grosseteste, *De Dei scientia, voluntate, misericordia, et justitia et praesentia,* fol. 306.

———. Cambridge, Pembroke College MS 155. *Boethius cum commento.* Vellum manuscript, in an often illegible hand (though described by cataloguer as "very pretty hand") with red and blue initials, fifteenth century. Fols. 1a–86a: *Boecii de disciplina scolarium cum exposicione de Whetelay;* fols. 86b–259b: *Boethius de consolatione philosophiae cum commento eiusdem.* . . .

Anonymous of St. Gall. St. Gall MS 824. Cursive interlinear and marginal glosses, in Latin and German, 519 fols., fifteenth century.

Pierre d'Ailly. Paris, Bibliothèque Nationale de France MS Latin 3122. Angular late Gothic hand, fifteenth century. (Consulted; no specific information on the Muses.)

Reinerus van St. Truiden [Regnier de Saint-Trond]. Liège, Bibliothèque Universitaire MS 348. Gothic secretary hand, on paper, 166 fols., fifteenth century. With illustrated initials featuring grotesques of Boethius and Philosophy, marginal sketches of small animals.

———. Paris, Bibliothèque Mazarine MS 3589. Early fifteenth-century hand, parchment, fols. 14–222v.

Pietro da Moglio. Poppi, Italy. Biblioteca Riminale MS 45. Current (not cursive) Gothic bookhand; on paper, fourteenth century.

Travesio, Giovanni. Turin, Biblioteca Nazionale, MS G IV 2. Gothic bookhand to fol. 43; obscure cursive hand beyond; on paper, 174 fols., fourteenth century.

Fifteenth-Century

Guglielmo da Cortimiglia (Guillermus de Cortumelia). Paris, Bibliothèque Nationale de France MS Latin 6773. Gothic cursive, on parchment, fifteenth century. Text of the *Consolation,* fols. 1r–84r; penitential prayer, "Heu cur peccaui quod non decuit faciendo," fols. 84v–85r; Boethius commentary, fols. 85v–197v.

———. Vatican, MS Chig. EVII 229. Late Gothic cursive hand, on paper, fifteenth century (1446, according to colophon). Also contains Robert Holcot's glosses on the Apocalypse and a list of Holcot's works. First pages give notes in what appears to be a late eighteenth-century hand on the life of "Guielmo [*sic*] da Cortimiglia."

Denis de Ryckel (also known as Dionysius Carthusianus, Denis de Leeuwis), *Opera,* vol. 26. Tomaci, 1906.

Greban, Arnoul. Paris, Bibliothèque nationale de France MS Lat 9323. Fine French humanist script; paper, 151 fols., fifteenth century. With colored illustration of Boethius in bed surrounded by Philosophy and the Muses, with a view of the outer cloister garden attached to a church. On bottom of fol. 1r in sixteenth-century hand: "Ex bibliotheca Jo. Huralti Bois-tallerij Roberti Huralti patrui demo."

————. Reims, Bibliothèque Municipale MS 896. Late Gothic cursive hand on paper, fifteenth century.

Bade d'Assche, Josse [Jodocus Badius Ascensius] and Pseudo-Thomas Aquinas. *Commentum duplex in Boetium de Consolatione Philosophiae cum utriusque tabula. Item commentum in eundem de disciplina scholarium cum commento in Quintilianum de officio discipulorum diligenter annotate.* Lyon: Iohannis de Vingle, 1498.

Notes

1. Classical uses of the term *Camenae* that late classical and medieval readers could easily have seen include Horace, *Carm. Saec.* 62 ("acceptus novem Camenis"); Virgil, *Eclogues* 3.59 ("amant alterna Camenae"); and Ovid, *Metamorphoses* 14.434, 15.482.

2. Ernst Curtius, *Europäische Literatur und lateinisches Mittelalter* (Bern: Francke, 1948), 242.

3. Curtius, *Europäische Literatur,* 243: "er hat eine metrische Martinsvita verfaßt. Aber in seiner weitlichen Dichtung hat er gegen die Musen nichts einzuwenden. In der Vorrede zu seiner Gedichtsammlung schildert er, wie er auf beschwerlicher Reise durch die Donauländer, Germanien und Gallien, von einer—freilich mehr kalten als trunkenen—Muse begeistert, als neuer Orpheus die Wälder angesungen habe.... Weltliche und kirchliche Dichtung bei ihm gehen nebeneinander her."

4. For a very thoughtful speculative analysis of Plato's objections, see Eric Havelock, *A Preface to Plato* (Cambridge, Mass.: Belknap, Harvard University Press, 1963).

5. For a chronology of commentators and major manuscripts, see the Appendix.

6. Alastair J. Minnis, *Medieval Theory of Authorship: Scholastic Attitudes in the Later Middle Ages,* 2nd ed. (Philadelphia: University of Pennsylvania Press, 1988), 118.

7. R. W. Hunt was the first to classify the elements of the medieval prologues and showed that commentaries could be dated according to prologue type. See R. W. Hunt, "The Introduction to the 'Artes' in the Twelfth Century," in *Studia Medievalia in honorem admodum reverendi patris Raymundi Josephi Martin Ordinis Praedicatorum: theologiae magistri LXXum natalem diem agentis* (Bruges: De Templ, 1948), 85–112. Minnis expands Hunt's

findings and observes within them medieval attitudes towards the nature of authorship and fiction in *Medieval Theory of Authorship.*

8. For a discussion of Remigius, the Anonymous of St. Gall, Adabold of Utrecht, and others, see Pierre Courcelle, *La Consolation de Philosophie dans la tradition littéraire: Antecedents et posterité de Boèce* (Paris: Études Augustiniennes, 1967), 275–99.

9. Courcelle, *La Consolation,* 306, 337.

10. Beryl Smalley, *English Friars and Antiquity in the Early Fourteenth Century* (Oxford: Basil Blackwell, 1988).

11. Boethian mythographers allegorize their ancient materials in ways that continue into the Renaissance. See Jean Seznec, *The Survival of the Pagan Gods: The Mythological Tradition and Its Place in Renaissance Humanism and Art,* trans. Barbara F. Sessions (Princeton: Princeton University Press, 1953).

12. Standard Latin quotations of Boethius are taken from Adrian Fortescue, *De Consolatione Philosophiae,* re-edited by George D. Smith (New York: Georg Olms, 1976). Other quotations come from individual commentators, as the context will make clear. English quotations are taken from Boethius, *The Theological Tractates,* with English translations by K. F. Stewart, E. K. Rand, S. J. Tester, and (in the same volume) *The Consolation of Philosophy,* trans. S. J. Tester, Loeb Classical Library (Cambridge, Mass.: Harvard University Press; London: William Heinemann, 1973).

13. Guillaume, fol. 3v:
> Camene dicuntur quasi canentes amene quelibet sentencie. Sed sunt alie integre, alie lacere. Integre sunt philosophice sentencie, quia integritate racionis et constancia firmant hominem. Lacere dicuntur poetice sentencie: id est, sciencie fingendi et describendi metrice, quia lacerant corda hominum et inconstancia reddunt, reducendo ad memoriam uel uoluptatem uel dolorem, non instruendo uel consolando. Lacere iste dictabant Boecio scribenda, quia metrice dolorem suum disponebant describere, non philosophice consolationem.

Quoted from British Library Royal MS 15.B.III. All quotations from Guillaume de Conches's commentary will come from this manuscript; I will sometimes consult Munich MS 4603.

14. Curtius reminds us that the Muses "besaßen keine ausgeprägte Persönlichkeit wie die Olympier. . . . Sie verkörpern ein rein geistiges Prinzip, das sich vom griechisch-römischen Pantheon loslösen ließ." This does not suggest that there is any personality for Guillaume to ignore; there are features of the Muses, such as the stories of their song-contest with the Pierides in Ovid's *Metamorphoses* or the more individuating account of their separate provinces of knowledge, that belong to a literal sense that does not interest Guillaume. See as well Klaus Heitmann, "Boethius' Verdamnung der Musen im Mittelalter," in Klaus Heitmann and Eckart Schroeder, eds., *Renatae Litterae: Studien zum Nachleben der Antike und zur europäischen Renaissance, August Buck zum 60. Geburtstag am 3.12.1971 dargebracht von Freunden und Schülern* (Frankfurt-am-Main: Athenäum, 1973), 30–34.

15. For these and subsequent quotations from Trevet's commentary, I use the late E. T. Silk's edition. At the time of this writing, only a typescript of the edition was available. Mrs. Eleanor Silk graciously furnished me with a microfilm of the edition.

16. Trevet, 16: "CAMENE LACERE. Camene dicuntur Muse quas poete deas carminum fingebant, et dicebantur Camene quasi 'canentes amene' et designant quascumque artes uel sciencias, quia ad modum cantus oblectant animum. Arcium autem et scienciarum quedam sunt integre sicut artes et sciencie physice que in integritate racionis et constancia animi conseruant hominem. Quedam dicuntur lacere a 'lacerando' quia lacerant cor hominis et a constancia detrahunt."

17. See Richard Dwyer, *Boethian Fictions: Narratives in the Medieval French Versions of the Consolatio Philosophiae* (Cambridge, Mass.: Medieval Academy of America, 1976). Despite his mythographical mistakes, Pierre de Paris's insights (fol. 3v) are sometimes quite interesting, as in his discussion of Boethius's sadness. If you do wrong and you are punished, says Pierre, reason demands that you endure the punishment patiently—you should expect it: it is only what is coming to you. So any pain or sadness you have is not "veraye dolour." Boethius does have "veraye dolour," however: since he did not deserve this imprisonment, it is reasonable that he is sad:

> Boece dye que les mauuaiz homes sont bien depeciees et repetasees si le esmayent a faire, cest luire. Et les soes doulors sont verayes dolors sur touts doulors. Car puis quil estoit venu en tele chaitiuete et il ne les auoit pas deseruies, certes il se doloit raisonablement. Car qui fait aucun mal et en est punis, selonc rayson il doit porter cele peyne pacientement. Et se il dedeut [*sic*] sa doulor pas veraye. Et porce dit il que sa doulor est veraye, et quil ploure veraiement . . . ce quie il sostenoit il ne lauoyt pas teserui [for *deserui*]. Et dit encore Boece que ceans mauuaiz qui lont mene a perdition ne porent estre vencu por nulle paor de Dieu. Car il ne voloient pas estre accompagnies a nulle uertu.

18. William of Aragon, fol. 10r:

> ECCE MIHI LACERE, id est, dissute. Vel CAMENE, id est, Muse poetice DICTANT SCRIBENDA, dicuntur autem lacere in hoc modo dictandi propter causam dicendam, scilicet quia de proprietate dolentis est dissute diuersa tangere, de contumacione non curans; unde secundum poetas huic approperabantur ELEGI, id est, versus connominati sex et quinque pedum exprimentes miseriam et dolorem ad similitudinem dandi cautis qui in suo metro propter dolorem ostendit naturam. Et ideo sic dicit ET ELEGI UERIS FLETIBUS RIGANT ORA. Veri dicuntur fletus qui non sunt ficti, et causam videntur habere sufficientem.

19. Wheteley, fol. 19v:

> Poeta et philosophus cum sint artifices diuersi diuersum debent habere modum dictandi. Quia poeta debet fingere et modum dictandi lamentabilem et querelosum habere. Sed philosophus debet vera dicere et habere modum dictandi compendiosum. Qui modus debet magnum solacium verum conferre dictanti. Et sic patet quod non iniuste increpatur Boecius a Philosophia.

20. At this juncture, Travesio seems reluctant to admit that so worthy a man as Boethius should need treatment [*curandum*] (fol. 8r): "paciebantur enim in animo suo qui erat de fortuitorum bonorum amissione fortiter perturbatus; non credens hoc tamen esse in Boetio, sed est etiam opinio miserorum quos Boethius vult instruere ut se a malo proposito remoueant."

21. Note that the Anonymous of the Erfurtensis also considers the Camenae in a musical vein, but in a more exhaustive way than does Travesio. The Anonymous has a unique inter-

est in categories of music, which he may well assume to have been on the mind of Boethius, the author of *De Musica*. See Anonymous of the Erfurtensis, Silk's edition, 9:

> EC <CE> E MIHI LACERAE etc. Modos uocat qui sunt in musica, scilicet hos: Lydium, <*H*>ypolydium, *Ph*rygiu*m*, <*H*>ypo*ph*nygiu*m*, Dorium, <*Hy*>podoriu*m*. His modis musicis constat omnis cantus. Camenae dicuntur Musae quasi Canenae, scilicet a canendo dictae. Laceras uocat eas quasi laceratas quae non dictare ualent nisi si <*ngultim*> propter exilium, quia mecum exulauerunt; uel laceratas dicit quia priuatus erat omnibus bonis suis et retrusus in carcere non existens in statu suo. ELEGI id est miseri et flebiles. Inde elegiacum carmen lugubre dicimus carmen miseriae.

Camenae comes from *canendo,* the Anonymous informs us.

22. Reinerus, fol. 4r:

> Ecce assunt mihi Pyerides et Muse poetice canentes amene, que frequenter dicunt michi verba que scribere debeam apta meis doloribus, que etiam me ad hoc mouent ut totum wltum meum fletibus profundam, non fictis sed veris. @ Notandum quod Camene dicuntur quecumque sentencie delectabiles quasi canentes amene. Vnde quedam sunt integre, alie lacere. Integre dicuntur sentencie philosophorum et theologorum efficatissima racione et indissolubili veritate contexte. Et in hijs vera consistit consolacio. Alie sunt lacere, videlicet poetice fictiones inter vera falsibus dissute; et in hijs non est consolacio vera, dumtaxat apparens ut postea patebit.

Reinerus continues:

> Vltimum notandum quod elegi sunt cantus miserie ab "elegos" Grece. Vnde quidam sunt versus elegi, quos elegi mihi dudum sunt; . . . elegi, quia talia legi. Tertio notandum quod fletuum quidam sunt dolosi seu ficti, sicut muliebres: de quibus Juuenalis: "Flet si lacrimas respexit amici: nec dolet" etc. Vnde et Ouidius De remedio: "Neue puellarum lacrimis moueare caneto / Vt fleuerit oculos erudiere suos [689–90]." Hos metus excludit Boecius cum dicit VERIS FLETIBUS, id est, ex intima cordis afflictione prouenientibus. Et quasi alias diceret, "O Boecius, videtur quod hee Camene nichil prosint, quia tu idem vocas eas 'laceras.'"

23. Quotations for Tolomeo Asinari are from Vienna, Österreichische Nationalbibliothek Cod. 53; I have made frequent comparison to the only other known manuscript of Tolomeo's commentary, Paris B.N. 6410.

24. Tolomeo, fol. 6v:

> Ipse Muse sunt uane; ad delectationes corporeas moueant et distrahant a cognitione summi et ueri boni et respectu ad supremam et nobilissimam philosophiam. Ipse sunt uiles et obscure. Tamen non est opinandum eas esse malas, nec omnino tanquam inutiles uel dampnosas esse spernendas—tum quia omnis sciencia a Deo est, a quo omne datum optimum et omne donum etc., et a quo nullum malum procedere potest; tum quia in scientia non est vicium uel malum, sed solum in utentibus praue ipsis; tum eciam quia multe ex ipsis sunt necessarie, et quia eciam ille de quibus uidetur impius quam aliquem sit, in eis bonitas, sicut sunt ille que docent musicalia officia: fuerant ad laudem creatoris inuenta. Vnde Psalmista: "Laudate eum in sono tube, etc."

Tolomeo, fol. 7v:

> ET UERIS. Hic ponitur secunda racio quia dixit COGOR. Et dic "ueris," non "fictis"; quia uere suberat materia fletus, et per consequens [sic] scribendi lacere, non enim ipse finxit materiam sicut multi auctores fecerunt. ELEGI, id est, quia electa sunt. ORA, id est, uultus, ut sic contentum pro continente ponatur, quia os continetur in uultu. Uel dic "oris" appellatione totum uultum comprehendit, sicut etiam in pluribus locis ponitur, RIGANT, scilicet lacrimis. HAS SALTEM etc. Hic respondit tacite obiectioni que sibi poterat fieri auctor, dicens nullus dicat quod Camene non dictant michi scribenda, eo quod nullus quantumcumque amicus ausus est me sequi; quia iste nullo terrore uinci poterunt, quin me sequerentur. Et dic HAS, scilicet Camenas. Et nota quam bone sunt sciencie quia hominem non deseruerunt. Sunt enim uera bona anime, nec computantur inter bona fortune. . . . GLORIA Postquam auctor respondit tacite obiectioni. Confirmat quod dixit in duobus secundis uersibus dicens quod "dixi Camenas michi dictare, lacereque scribo bene dixi, quia uere eedem [eaedem] que michi fuere suadela gloriandi tempore iuuentutis, de prosperis; nunc suadent dolendum in mea senectute de aduersis." Et ordinat sic litteram. CAMENE que fuerunt OLIM GLORIA FELICIS UIRIDISQUE IUUENTE, id est, suaserant gloriandam tempore felicis iuuentutis SOLANTUR, id est, consolantur NUNC MEA FATA MESTI SENIS. Et dic fata, scilicet infelicia mesti senis, id est, mei qui senes et mestus. . . . fletibusque meis uerba dictantes etc. Et nota quod has Camenas representari susurrones quod secundum uarietates temporum uarianter et propseris suadent gloriandum, et in aduersis flendum.

At the opposite extreme of the fourteenth century, Pietro da Moglio (fol. 2r) says that the Camenae are "sciencie nostre temporales" who "non dicunt animas ad salutem nisi uera teologia." They are "sciencie lacerate." Pietro will not commend the Muses for faithfully sticking with Boethius in spite of terror. Yet the Muses have something else by which to redeem themselves (fol. 4r): "Et licet sit licitum poetarum sic dicere ficta. Et ea que uera non sunt, nichilominus in ficta latent bona. Id est, quamuis fabulose et fictiue loquantur, tamen habent in sententijs et in factis bonum et utilem, hoc est, effectus utiles et allegorie que colliguntur ex ipsis dictis poetarum." Pietro adds the caveat: "Licet ista poesis sit delectabilis, tamen non est omnino ductilis ad uitam eternam."

25. Guglielmo da Cortimiglia, fols. 96v–97r:

> CAMENE, id est, Muse poetarum quasi "canentes amene." Nota quod "Camena" est equiuocum: nam aliquando signat veneream delectationem, aliquando signat scienciam poeticam et carmina quibus delinitur . . . dulcedine cantus. Aliquando signat aliqua de novem Musis. CAMENE ergo dicuntur lacerate, id est, sciencie poetice propter diuersos modos. LACERE, id est, disrupte; uel etiam ipse Muse dicuntur LACERE ab effectu quia lacerant animos tam dicentium quam audientium et dispergunt in diuersas affectiones: nunc fletibus, nunc risibus, nunc honestis, nunc inhonestis deformant animum hominis; quia vt dicit Quintilianus, "Nichil est tam occupatum, tam multiforme, tam variis affectionibus quam mala mens." Sciencie autem naturales aut politice aut mathematice non lacerant mentem hominis sed componunt et orna[n]t ELEGI, id est, versus funebres facti de materia miserie et fletus RIGANT ORA MEA VERIS FLETUS, id est, non fictis aut adulatoribus sed miserabilibus. Vnde nota quod et cogebant Boecium versus flebiles facere. Primum erat dolor, qui fletu alleuiatur. Vnde *Seneca* tertio *Declamationum:* "Misero si flere non libet magis flendum est." Secundum est dulcedo carminis

alleuiantis . . . nota quod verum est fletum et vere miseri hominis esse dolorem
quando pro' mutabilitum rerum perdicione fleret; cum magis esset gaudendum.
Vnde dicit Valerius libro sexto: Caduca nimis et fragilia sunt que vires et opes
dicuntur; adueniunt enim subito et repente dilabuntur. In nullo loco, in nullo parte
stabilius iuxta radicibus consistunt; sed incertissimo flatu fortune huc et illuc acta
quos in sublime extulerunt inprouiso recursu destitutos profunde clade miserabili
immergunt. Vnde Socrates demergens aurum in mari ait, vt dicit Lactancius libro
de falsa sapiencia. "Abite," inquit, "in profundum male diuitie: ego vos mergam,
ne ego ipse mergar a vobis."

Arnoul Greban (fol. 8v) seems to see the Muses as hiding something beneath an *integ-
umentum* when he says that the Muses are "industrie sermocinales aliquid uerum sub falso
et delectabili sermone fingentes." Nevertheless, echoing many of his predecessors, he agrees
that the Muses draw the human heart away from constancy (fols. 4v–5r):

Ecce Camene, id est, Muse, a "canendo" dicte lacere, id est, non integre, sed
poetice, dictant, id est, monstrant vel frequenter dicunt scribenda, id est, que
scribere debeam mihi, scilicet vtilitatem meam, et rigant, id est, madefaciunt, ora,
id est, vultum. . . ." Notandum quod Camene dicuntur Muse quas poete . . .
fingebant, et dicuntur quasi "canentes amene" et designant quoscumque artes vel
sciencias. Quia ad modum cantus oblectant animam. Sci[encia] autem quedam
dicuntur integre, sicut artes et sciencie philosophice qui in integritate rationis et
constancia animi conseruant hominem. Quedam dicuntur "lacere" a "lacerando"
quia lacerant cor hominis et constanciam detrahunt cum, scilicet sine ordine ad
diuersa proposita ipsum inducunt et in verborum suauitate sine correspondencia
rei. Idem delectari faciunt. Jtem elegi sunt cantus miserie ab "elegos" Grece,
"miseria" Latine.

26. Bade d'Assche explains that *Lacere* is explained strangely: "laceratis et dissutis vestibus
et mesto vultu . . ." (aviijr). Shortly thereafter: "Camene, id est, Muse inuentrices carminum,
lacere: id est, pannose et laceris similes, dictant mihi scribenda" (aviijr). But, "Necque
Musas omnes damnat sed poeticas dumtaxat: quia philosophicis Musis eum curandum censet"
(biijr). Bade d'Assche concludes his discussion (biijv) with deliberately elegant balance:
"non opus habebat Musis delectationem inanem causantibus: sed veram consolationem ex
magnanimitate et sapientia gerentibus."

27. Guillaume, Royal MS 15.B.III, fol. 3v: "Sed has Camenas non potuit devincere [*ter-
rorem*]; semper enim concomitatur hominem sua sapientia quocumque siue quousque trans-
feratur." The slightly different reading in Munich MS 4603 does not really clear the air:
"Semper enim concomitatur hominem sua sciencia quocumque transeritur" (fol. 156r).
Guillaume has already said there are either poetical or philosophical *sciencie;* so the word
here could mean either.

28. Trevet, 17:

HAS SALTEM. Hic docet se in istis Camenis laceris, ad quas studium suum permu-
tatum erat, aliquale habere solacium. Et est sciendum quod de re ad quam homo
aliqualiter afficitur dupliciter consolacionem recipit: uno modo in quantum illam
secure possidet, alia modo in usu illius rei, sicut patet de cytharedo habente bonam
cytharam uel de milite habente bonum equum. Nunc autem Boecius pro statu in
quo fuit affectus erat ad scienciam poeticam, quia intendebat ea uti ad describen-

dum suam miseriam et ideo solacium ei erat quod eam secure possidebat, quia, cum non esset bonum corporale, non potuit persecucione temporali auferri.

29. William of Aragon, fol. 10r:
Quando enim sicut superius dictum est Boetius fuit captus et iudicatus exilio, tanta fuit nequicia Theodorici predicta quia omnia bona occupauit ipsius et neminem ad societatem vel servicium sibi notum dimisit. Et ob timorem tiranni nullus qui eum diligeret secutus eum, scilicet quod bona anime durante vita neminem derelinquunt nec possint predari manibus uiolentis, Camene impediri non potuerunt quin sequerentur eum. Et tam licet hoc proprium sit omnibus virtutibus et sciencijs; in hoc casu magis proprium Camenis existiri; homo enim pro dolore turbatur, et si non simpliciter saltem ad tempus priuatur alijs sciencijs et consolationis virtutibus. Et solum sibi assistunt ea quibus suos potest explicare dolores. Vnde cum hoc sit proprium poeticarum Musarum [ut] que solum docent modum exprimendi acute gaudium vel dolorem, ideo dixit ad perfectionem perfectam demonstrandam. HAS SALTEM etc. Alia enim [sunt] que virtutibus et alijs sciencijs pertinent que depressissent [*sic*] dolorem, [reading added from Gonville and Caius MS 309/707: *sed doloris turbacione memorie velabantur; licet absolute loquendo omnis ars et sciencia inseparabiliter sequuntur scientem. Vnde ait Cato, "Disce aliquid: nam cum subito fortuna precedit, ars remanet, vitamque hominis non deserit."*]

30. The liberal arts—especially the members of the quadrivium—of course represent some of the same subjects over which the classical Muses have jurisdiction: geometry, astronomy, and music. Conceivably, grammar from the trivium could include the study of some poetical matters, but if Wheteley does not accept purely poetic study as legitimate, his grammar must be a more linguistically based program of study. See R. Bolgar's discussion of the development of the liberal arts in *The Classical Heritage and Its Beneficiaries* (Cambridge: Cambridge University Press, 1954) (as a general guide, see as well Dionisotti's cautionary review of Bolgar's work in *Geografia e storia della letteratura italiana* [Turin: G. Einaudi, 1967]).

31. Wheteley, fol. 15v: "prosperitates vite mee prius habite in Romana ciuitate et suauitates amene habite in studio Athenensi . . . artes quas didici in etate iuuenili in studio Atheniensi"; fol. 19v: "Camene poetice mesticiam inferunt." The Anonymous of the Erfurtensis anticipates Wheteley's move at "Has saltem" by ignoring the grammar of *has* and saying that Philosophy will not desert him despite any imperial terror. Giovanni Travesio seems to get the grammar right; even the emperor cannot conquer the Muses. Yet Travesio (fol. 2r) also says here that "Sciencia numquam hominem derelinquit nisi grandis fierit mutatio," which would suggest that it is not the Muses but knowledge, or perhaps Philosophy herself, that will not abandon Boethius. They hardly console, though, "eo quod Boetius recordatur artis uersificatorie in qua inplebat suam miseriam describere." The Muses, Bade d'Assche says (aviiir–v), will not desert Boethius, even in prison:
"NULLUS TERROR neque mortis neque amissionis serum potuit PERUINCERE SALTEM HAS, id est, Camenas, licet notos et amicos peruicerit. Non potuit, inquam, eas peruincere quin, id est, quo minus (vel "qui non"), id est, vt non ipse existentes comites persequerentur, id est, ad finem vsque sequerentur nostrum iter etiam in carcerem."

32. Here many commentators describe the kinds of old age, usually "natural" or "accidental" (Boethius's is the latter), and the signs of old age: sagging skin, grey hair, and baldness.

33. Trevet, 17: "Consueuerunt enim iuuenes in tenera etate deputari ad discendam scienciam poeticam in qua proficientes gloriabantur in usu metrorum et rithmorum." Travesio, fol. 2v: "iste Camene solantur me miserum nunc, que Camene sunt pulcra iuuentus et recens." The Camene are also depicted in the Anonymous of the Erfurtensis (9–10) as not deserting Boethius at the line beginning "Gloria felicis," with this curiously elevating qualification: "Sciencia habita de supernis confert mihi solacium dolenti de mundanis."

34. Reinerus, fol. 4v:

> GLORIA FELICIS . . . Dicit quod certe presencia Musarum in preterito fuit et in presenti est michi summe recommendabilis. Nam tempore felicitatis et iuuentutis mee multum in illis gloriabar, et nunc in tempore aduersitatis et senectutis me consolantur. Vnde notandum quod Boetius dicit Musas fuisse suam gloriam effectiue; quia fecerant eum gloriosum assistendo consilio . . . et librorum compilationibus. Item FELICIS dicit, nam felicibus Muse conueniunt. Vnde Ouidius: "Ista decent letos felicia signa poetas," Juuentutem per methaphoram vocaret "florentem" quia ad fructum virtutis et sapiencie perducit. Simile dicitur Alexandris secundo ad fortunam de Alexandro: "Cur metis ante diem florentes principis annos?" Vltimum notandum quod licet iste Muse solentur ad tempus; tamen eorum consolacio transit vt ventus. Et dum tacent, hominem plus quam prius delinquunt deconsolatum, vt postea testatur Philosophia. Quare merito de modis suis dici potest illud Job 16: "Consolatores honerosi vos estis. Numquid habebunt finem verba ventosa?"

35. Most commentators note Philosophy's controlled anger, quoting the Psalmist: "Irascimini et nolite peccare."

36. Guillaume, fol. 8v: "Sceni[c]e [*sic*] vero dicuntur quasi 'theatrales.' SCENA enim dicebatur quedam pars theatri qua abscondebant persone et exibant; et ibi recitabantur opera poetarum. Ob hoc ergo dicuntur Muse poetice scenice, id est, 'theatrales.' Quia ad hoc erat sua tota intencio, ut in theatris recitarentur opera sua. Uel dic 'scenice,' id est, 'umbrales.' 'Scena' enim dicitur 'umbra.' Dicuntur ergo poetice Muse scenice, id est, 'umbrales,' quia sunt umbra sciencie et non vera sciencia: utrum uel quia obumbrant uel obnubilant corda hominum." Royal MS 15.8.III reads *ascendebant* here, but other manuscripts of Guillaume, such as Munich MS 4603, read *abscondebant,* as do a number of later commentators. *Abscondebant* also fits the sense of this discussion of *scenis,* since they are called shadows.

37. Trevet, 35:

> Vocat autem eas SCENICAS eo quod carmina poetica in scenis consuuerunt recitari. Scena autem secundum Isidorum, Ethimologiarum libro 18, capitulo de ludo scenico, erat locus infra theatrum in modum domus instructus cum pulpito. Dicitur a scena Greco uocabulo quod interpretatur umbra, unde dicebatur scena quasi obumbracio, quia ibi abscondebantur persone cantantes cantica tragica et comica.

In the Anonymous of the Erfurtensis (16), the fact that the Muses are "scenice meretricule" is not explained away. They are "scenice" either because their songs are recited in "scenis" (whatever those are) or because one known meaning of *scenis,* as far as this writer is concerned, is "make-up." This is and first appearance of this meaning: "Quidam uolunt ung<u>entum quo perungebantur meretrices, ut suis amatoribus gratum praestarent odorem sicque eos ad suam uoluntatem innectere possent. Ita ergo carmina poetarum se legentes ad suum amorem pertrahunt. . . ."

Similarly, the Pseudo-Aquinas of Munich (fol. 29v) explains that *scena* refers either to a place in which to recite the "dicta poetarum"—the place where people hid during their recitations—or the make-up used by prostitutes so no one will recognize them: "Scena fuit locus ubi recitabantur dicta poetarum, et dicitur a 'sceno' Grece, quod est obumbracio Latine; quia illi umbumbrant . . . recitantes laruis et pallis."

Little in Greban's commentary on 1 pr. 1 is original except that prostitutes use make-up (one of the meanings of *scenice* to the mind of some commentators) to keep their *lenones* [pimps or seducers] happy (Greban, fol. 8v).

We have seen Guglielmo's treatment of "scenice meretricule" and the Sirens before, though it is perhaps amusing to observe that the *scena* was the "pars theatri ubi poete ventilabant carmina in loco velato seu umbroso." "Shadow" is an appropriate translation for *scena* because of the nature of what poets do, for poetry is but the shadow of words:

> MERETRICULAS . . . sicut meretrix enim miscetur cuilibet non amore prolis sed lucri, sic poete scribebant de quolibet non amore sciencie sed laudis uel lucri. SCENICAS, id est, in scenis uel theatris recitatas. "Scena" enim est pars theatri vbi poete ventilabant carmina in loco velato seu umbroso. Vnde scena idem est quod vmbra. Vnde etiam poete in vmbra verborum ponere consueuerunt dicta sua uel qui eorum verba nichil extreme vel modicum habent sicut vmbra. Non ergo verba eorum vere consolantur dolorem, sed pocius augent et lacerent animum per diuersas affectiones.

38. Tolomeo, fol. 12r: "'Senecas' autem ideo appellat predictas Musas, quia in scena—quod est locus ubi ludibria exercentur—exerceri consueuerunt illa; taliaque docent dicte Muse, ut sunt cantus saltatrices et musicalia instrumenta; de quibus in principio huius libri dictum [est]."

39. Travesio, fol. 7v: "scenices . . . ab illo loco in quo congregabantur ad dictandum, uel quia pro maiori parte in carminibus senis, hoc est, habentibus sex pedes, dictabat. Scena locus est obscurus, uel scena recitatio est. Vel scena [est] materia exercitans q[uasi] in arte metrizandi."

40. Guillaume, fol. 8v: "Et nota quod poetice Muse dicuntur 'meretricule': alliciunt sibi hominem delectando et parum uel uidelicet nichil utilitatis conferentes, et satis penitentie siue penurie post saturitatem inferunt. Jtem sicut meretricule non amore sed spe lucri commiscent se cuilibet, ita poete non amore sciencie sed ut aliquid laudis uel premij extorqueant scribunt."

41. Heitmann ("Boethius' Verdammung der Musen im Mittelalter," 37–42) documents the interesting history of the commentators and translators trying to explain the very difficult words *scena* and *theatrum*.

42. Tolomeo, fol. 12r:

> HAS SCENESCAS MERETRICLAS [*sic*]. Hic appellat Musas predictas 'meretrices senecas,' per quandam similitudinem inuicem Musas et meretrices. Nam sic[ut] meretrices alliciunt sibi homines et abstrahunt a uero bone et sibi alligant per delectationes momentaneas, sic sciencie Musarum predictarum alliciunt animos hominum et delectant et faciunt humanum intellectum intendere ad ipsas sciencias, et abstrahunt a cognitione ueri boni.

Reinerus, fol. 9r:

> Notandum quod Muse poetice dicuntur meretricule scenece per similitudinem. Meretricule quidem pro vili precio se prostituentes lucra venantur et gloriam in pul-

critudine querunt: sic etiam poete plures scripserunt ut sibi prodessent lucro aut delectarentur alijs complacendo, iuxta illud Oracij: "Aut prodesse volunt aut delectare poete" [Horace, *De arte poetica,* line 333]. Vnde tangit et Ouidius quarto *Tristium*: "Scenece" uero dicuntur, id est, "theatrales." Nam scena erat locus theatri, id est, spectaculi publici Rome, ubi ficta poetarum legebantur. Vel scenece, id est, "vmbracules" quod est a "scena" quod est vmbra. Nam poetice Muse mentem obumbrant et obnubilant falsis figmentis ne possit ad vera documenta se subleuare; vt scenece, id est, falso colore redemito; nam scena secundum quosdam est vnguentum quo perungebatur meretrices ut suis amatoribus [se] prestarent gratas [MS gratos] colorem et odorem, sicque eos ad suam voluptatem inflecte[re] possent. Jta etiam carmina poetarum se legentes ATTRAHUNT SIBI que intendere faciunt. Meanwhile, the commentary given by the Anonymous of the Reginenses (43v–44r) on *meretrices* condenses what we have already seen in Guillaume but without any mention of *scenice;* the Sirens are not explained; they are simply called "delights, pleasures" [*delectationes*]. It is worth noting, though, the gloss to "barren thorns of passion" (Tester's translation of "He sunt enim que infructuosis affectum"): "He sunt licet vere infirmum redde[n]t infirmiorem."

In William of Aragon, the "scenicas meretriculas" in 1 pr. 1 are simply "sordidas meretriculas." Wheteley (fol. 19r) adds nothing new about *meretriculas* or *scenicas,* he mentions Isidore by name and gives the same description of the theater we have seen in William of Aragon. In Travesio (fol. 7r), the Muses are prostitutes chiefly because they are flatterers [*adulantur*].

43. Guillaume, fol. 9r: "Non enim est consolatio metrice dolorem scribere. Sed pocius est dolorem commouere. . . . Sed insuper propter hoc quod non possunt fouere remedijs dulcibus ALERENT UENENIS dolorem suum supple. Dulce uenenum vero est quod alicuius mentem allicit et non nocet [*sic* MS]; ad similitudinem huius metrica doloris descriptio dicitur dulce uenenum, quia et propter metrum placet et recordationem doloris nocet."

44. Anonymous of the Erfurtensis, Silk's ed., 16: "DVLCIBUS VENENIS, id est carminibus saecularibus uel desideriis, quae desideria saecularia sunt in praesenti dulcia sed in nouissimo amara."

45. Tolomeo, fol. 12r: "Vocat has sciencias uenenum quia sicut dulce uenenum est gustui sed tamen gustatum interficit; sic sciencie iste dulces sunt et delectabiles, sed quia per delectationes abstrahunt intellectum hominis a uero bone, ideo dicuntur uenenum."

46. Guillaume, Royal MS 15.B.III, fol. 94.

47. Guillaume, fol. 9r:
HEE SUNT ENIM etc. Modo probat quod nocent ille Muse. Et lege sic. Bene dixi quod nocent iste Muse. ENIM (pro quia) quia HEE SUNT QUE NECANT id est, auferunt SEGETEM UBEREM FRUCTIBUS RATIONIS INFRUCTUOSIS AFFECTUUM SPINIS. Et ad euidenciam horum notandum quod segetes appelantur hic perfectio anime quantum ad sciencias et uirtutes. Et appellatur seges per quandam similitudinem. Sicut enim seges ex agricultura iactato semine cum augmento crescit, ita sciencie et uirtutes anime exercitatione ingenij iactato semine, id est, doctrina alterius, cum augmento crescunt. Fructus racionis appellat bene cognoscere et bene operari. Quis enim est fructus hominis perfecti in scientijs nisi bene cognoscere? Et qui est fructus hominis perfecti in uirtutibus nisi bene ope-

rari? Nocent ergo iste Muse, quia necant segetem uberem fructibus rationis, id est, scientias et uirtutes anime que erant plene fructibus racionis, id est, bonis cognitionibus et operationibus, ut cognitio referatur ad scientias, operatio ad uirtutes. Cognitio enim facit scientem; bona autem operatio et frequens, uirtuosum. Dicit enim Aristoteles in Ethicis quod ex frequenti bene agere relinquitur uirtus.

Note the ultimate dependence on Guillaume in Reinerus's contribution (fols. 9r–v):

HEE ENIM QUE FRUCTUOSIS; hic Philosophia Musas redarguendas probat. Et dicit sic: bene possum increpare Musas; nam ipse Muse in mente plantant spinas affectuum, per quas spinas necant segetem, qui cum vbertate posset producere fructus racionis. Et tunc vtitur "efflexigesi" exponendo predicta, dicens quod ipse Muse faciunt mentes assuetas ad dolendum, et non liberant a doloribus sed magis confundunt. Notandum quod segetem vberem etc. vocat hic perfectione[m] anime quantum ad scientias et virtutes per methaphoram: sicut enim segetes ex agricultura iacto semine cum augmento crescunt, ita scientie et virtutes anime exercitatione ingenij iacto semine, id est, doctrina, cum augmento crescunt, fructus racionis appellat, vnde cognoscere et bene operari de hijs prius dictum est. "Ex fructibus eorum cognoscetis eos." Quis enim est fructus hominis perfecti in scientijs nisi bene cognoscere? Et quis perfecti in virtutibus nisi bene operari? Secundo notandum quod spina affectuum vocat quattuor affectiones anime; de quibus postea in fine huius primi, scilicet, gaudium, quod est de bene presenti; iram, de malo presenti; spem, de futuro bono; et timorem, de future male. Hijs enim affectibus fructus mentis seu racionis procediuntur de quibus infra huius primi metro finali scilicet Nubila mens est vincta que frenis hec vbi regnant etc. Hee etiam affectiones vocantur spine per similitudinem quia fructum impediunt et pungendo sanguinem extrahunt dum hominem anxium reddunt et animum eneruant. . . . reprehendo Musas enim (pro "quia") HEE, scilicet Muse, sunt ILLE scilicet QUE NECANT id est, corrumpunt et impediunt uel destruunt SEGETEM, id est, perfectionem anime quoad virtutes et scientias; VBEREM; id est, fertilem FRUCTIBUS RACIONIS, scilicet bonis cognitionibus et operationibus NECANT inquam SPINIS id est, per spinas INFRUCTUOSIS AFFECTUUM, id est, affectationum mentis, scilicet gaudij ire spei et timoris: quia nullum fructum bonum producantque (pro "et") . . . ASSVEFACIVNT, id est, consuetas faciunt MENTES, id est, animos hominum MORBO, id est, dolore ex iugi recordatione, et NON LIBERANT, id est, non sanant; quia scilicet nichil consolationis inducunt.

48. Anonymous of the Erfurtensis, 16–17: "HAE, scilicet Musae, NECANT, id est pessumdant, SEGETEM, id est mentem cuius que [sic] abundantem id est quae abundaret fructibus rationis, id est bonis studiis et uirtutibus. Perdunt quidem SPINIS, id est uoluptatibus, AFFECTVVM, id est terrenorum quae nullum fructum afferunt sed ASSVUEFACIVNT eandem mentem omnibus prauis studiis et NON LIBERANT eam MORBO, id est a terrenis uoluptatibus."

Travesio, fol. 8r: "Et talis est sciencia determinandi utilia qualia in hoc libro Boetius determinat." The thorns which harm these fruits are the "artes uersificationes in misero actu tali in quali Boetius erat uolens prius."

49. Tolomeo, fol. 12v:

INFRUCTUOSIS AFFECTUM, scilicet delectatione corporalium. Uel dic melius ibi, affectionum, que sunt quattuor, de quibus sit mencio in ultimo capitulo huius primi libri. . . . SPINIS: uocat delectationes corporeas et affectus terrenos "spinas,"

eo quod sicut spine suffocant semen quod inter ipsas cadit, sicut in Euangelio
dicitur. "Et aliud cecidit inter spinas, et spine suffocauerunt illud." Ita iste sciencie
racionem hominis (que implicatur hiis scienciis) necant et suffocant, et racionem
ita detinent, quod non potest intendere ad superiora siue uera bona consideranda.
Et hoc est quod subdit: UBEREM FRUCTIBUS SEGETEM NECANT, id est extinguunt
HOMINUMQUE MENTES ASSUEFACIUNT quia mentes deditas talibus scienciis uix
potest ad alia intendere. Sed quanto plus meis student aliquis, magis delectetur.
Tolomeo continues with a discussion of true knowledge and the reputation of the Eleatic and
Academic schools. These are a bit of a digression from the figure of the Muses, but similar
discussion appears in commentaries before and after Tolomeo; his treatment of this topic is
ample, and thus I have chosen to present it as exemplary (fol. 12v):

> AT SI. Hic Philosophia ponit causam sue indignationis quam Musas ostendit,
> dicens, AT SI PROPHANUM, id est, ignorantem siue ydiotam qui parum fundatus erit
> in scienciis uti UULGO SOLITUM, id est, sicut consueuerunt parum scientes in-
> tendere ad istas sciencias poeticas. UOBIS BLANDITIE UESTRE, id est, uos poetice
> Muse que blande estis detraherent MINUS MOLESTE FERENDUM PUTAREM. Ut subdit
> racio. Nichil quippe meo uestre opera lederentur, quasi dicat, "Non leditur si
> aliquis ydiota animum suum applicat ad tales sciencias. Sed quando aliquis habens
> intellectum eleuatum ad superiores sciencias et eis dimissis intendit ad sciencias
> poeticas." Certe in hoc dicitur Philosophia ledi; et hoc subicit, dicens: HUNC UERO
> ELEATICIS ATQUE ACHADEMICIS STUDIIS ENUTRITUM, scilicet detrahitis, quasi dicit
> hoc ferre siue sustinere non possum, quod nobis auferatis tam uirum nutritum
> tantis studiis. Et dic Eleatica et Achademica studia dici a locis in quibus studia
> philosophica exercebantur. Et dic quod dicta duo nomina ponuntur pro uno loco.
> Et secundum hoc dic "atque" (pro "id est") uel dic "poni" [*sic*] pro diuersis. Et
> Elea fuit unus locus ubi studium philosohie tenebatur ab Aristotele. Achademia
> fuit uilla in qua Plato tenebat studium. Vnde quia auctor iste studuit in libris
> Platonis et Aristotelis, dicitur talibus studiis enutritus. Uel forte Elea fuit locus in
> quo Boetius stetit in studio. Academia uero fuit uilla quedam distans ab Athenis
> per miliarium, frequenti terre motu, sterilitate ac peste concussa; quam Plato
> eiusque discipuli elegerunt ad studium ut metu sepe imminentium periculorum a
> libidine continerent et ab illicitis cessarent et ne per luxu et habundantiam rerum
> animi fortitudo mollescerent, et pudicicia conrumperetur. Vnde omnes secuti
> Platonem dicti sunt Academiis studiis nutriti. Jste autem auctor, scilicet Boetius,
> ualde Platonicus fuit; sicut inferioribus apparet.

Cf., e.g., Guillaume, fol. 158v; Trevet, 38; Pseudo-Aquinas of Munich, fol. 29v; William of
Aragon, fol. 14r; Wheteley, fol. 20r; Reinerus, fol. 9v; Pietro da Moglio, fol. 5r; Travesio,
fol. 8r; and Guglielmo da Cortimiglia, fol. 101v. Bade d'Assche is silent here. Only the
Anonymous of the Erfurtensis contains this unusual explanation of "Elis": "Elisa fuit filius
Nuba<e>, a quo Graeci primi citi sunt Elisei; sed postea uerso nomine Aeoles nuncupati
sunt. Elidae etiam uocantur Graeci ab Elide ciuitate" (17). Meanwhile, Pierre de Paris,
always original, comes up with the following (fol. 6v): "Estuides Eleatices et des achad-
ematienes. Cest a dire des sciences celestiales ou deuines. Car 'eleos' en gresois viaut dire
'soleill' en franceis. Et 'ycos' uuet dire 'science.' Et de ces ij. mos 'eleos' et 'ycos' est compost cest nom 'Eleatices' qui uaut autant a dire come 'science dou sollail.' Et 'achadema'
en grezois uuet dire 'liberal' ou 'franc' en francois. Et 'ycos' uuet dire 'science.' Et de ses
ii. mos (est assauoir achadema' et 'ycos') est compost cest mot 'achadematicjs' qui vaut tant
a dire come sciences liberalez. . . ."

50. William of Aragon, fols. 14r–v: "RACIONIS SEGETEM, id est, verum bonum NECANT, id est, obnubilant et impediunt ad passiones mouendum, HOMINUMQUE MENTE ASSUEFACIUNT MORBO, id est, vicio passione canto NON LIBERANT immo semper impediunt et perturbant."

51. Wheteley's glosses for "infructuosis affectuum spinis" (fol. 19v) are identical to one already mentioned.

52. Guillaume, fol. 9v:

> Sirenes sunt belue maris, quibus cantantibus multi falluntur. Fuerant autem filie Acheloi que legebant flores cum Proserpina quando rapta fuit a Plutone; que, cum doluissent de rapina Proserpine socie sue, miseratione deorum facte sunt dee maris. Et sunt monstra marina: partim fere, partim uirgines. Habent et alas et ungulas; que feruntur nauigantibus soporem immittere dulcedine cantus et naufragium inferre. Et vna earum canit voce, altera tybia, tercia cythara.

Cf. Ovid, *Metamorphoses,* 5.552 ff.; and Vatican Mythographers, I.186, II.101. (Quotations from Vatican Mythographers appear in *Scriptores rerum mythicarum latini tres Romae nuper reperti,* ed. Georg Heinrich Bode [Cellis, 1834].) The Anonymous of the Erfurtensis provides essentially the same information as Guillaume does (fols. 17–18):

> SIRENE<S> sunt deae in mare, quae cantibus suis multos deciperunt. Fuerunt autem filiae Acheloi, quae legebant flores cum Proserpina quando rapta erat a Plu*t*one. Sed cum perdoluissent de rapina sociae suae, scilicet Proserpinae, deorum miseratione factae sunt deae marinae. Et sunt monstra maritima partim ferae partim uirgines. Habent alas et ungulas. Quae feruntur nauigantibus soporem immittere dulcedine cantus et naufragium inferre. Et una earum canit uoce, altera tibia, tertia cithara. Vere tres fuerant sorores, quae sua pulcritudine amatores suos omnibus priuauerunt bonis. Alas et ungulas dicuntur habere, quia amor transit et vulnerat; et fluctibus dicuntur morasse, quia fluctus dicitur Venerem generasse. DVLCES dicuntur, quia usque in exitium delectant hominem ducentes eum in aeternam damnationem.

Tolomeo's Sirens (fol. 12v) are the same as those we have seen in Guillaume and the Anonymous of the Erfurtensis, with the addition that the Sirens eventually followed Proserpina to the underworld and sang beautifully. Notwithstanding, they were changed into marine animals. Similarly, the Muses make those tending towards God turn to other kinds of knowledge, killing their intellects and "submerging" them:

> SED ABITE id est, recedite POTIUS scilicet quam stetis hic (accipe hoc dici electiue ac si dicat "recedite" non autem hic stetis) SIRENES USQUE EXITIUM id est, locum mortis quasi dicit "ita recedite; quod amplius non redeatis." DULCES SIRENAS appellat dulces quadam similitudine: nam Sirene sunt quedam monstra marina. Scribitur enim in fabulis quod Pluto deus inferni rapuit Proserpinam quam Syrene eius pedissece secute fuerunt ad inferos; que, dulciter cantantes, infernali infeccione corrupte mutate fuerunt in pestem. Et deinde facte fuerunt monstra marina, de quibus dicit Claudianus: "in pestem uertere lyras" [Claudian, *De raptu Proserpinae,* 3.257] et dicuntur Sirenas ab "siren" quod est "atraccio." Nam dicitur quod pro dulcedine cantus nauigantes dormiunt et ommisso nauis regimine pereunt. Sic faciunt iste Muse poetice quia delectant adeo intendentes in eis quod omissis aliis scienciis maioribus racio et intellectus pereunt et submerguntur.

53. For Ovid and Vatican Mythographers references, see n. 41. Cf. Isidore, *Etymologiae,* ed. W. M. Lindsay, 2 vols. (Oxford: Clarendon, 1911), 11.3.30:

Sirenes tres fingunt fuisse ex parte virgines, ex parte volucres, habentes alas et ungulas: quarum una voce, altera tibiis, tertia lyra canebant. Quae inlectos navigantes sub cantu in naufragium trahebant. Secundum veritatem autem meretrices fuerunt, quae transeuntes quoniam deducebant ad egestatem, his fictae sunt inferre naufragia. Alas autem habuisse et ungulas, quia amor et volat et vulnerat. Quae inde in fluctibus conmorasse dicuntur, quia fluctus Venerem creaverunt.

54. Vatican Mythographers, 2.109:

Sirenes, Melpomenes Musae et Acheloi fluminis filiae, quum Proserpinam, a Plutone raptam, inquirerent, et eam minime invenissent, a diis novissime impetrarunt, ut versae in volucres, non tantum in terris, sed etiam in mari requisitam consequi possent. Quo concesso, diu quaerentes, novissime ad petram Martis, quae promixe imminebat pelago, devenerunt, ibique habitare coeperunt. His concessum quoque fuit, ut tamdiu manerent incolumes, quamdiu earum vox audiretur. Fuerunt autem parte volucres, parte virgines, pedes gallinaceos habentes. Harum una voce, alia tibiis, tertia lyra canebat. Quarum cantibus illecti nautae quum ad saxa accederent, in quibus illae residentes canebant, illisis in scopulis navibus, in naufragia ducebantur, et ab illis comedebantur. Has Ulixes contemnendo deduxit ad mortem. Nam quum illas praeternavigaret, omnium sociorum suorum aures, ne eas audirent, cera obturans, se jussit ad arborem navis religari. Ita et dulcedinem cantus illarum percpit, et periculum evasit. At illae adeo se victas doluerunt, ut se in fluctus praecipitarent, sicque mortem gustarent. Secundum veritatem autem meretrices fuerunt, quae quoniam transeuntes ducebant ad egestatem, his fictae sunt inferre naufragia. Σειρηνες igitur Graece, Latine trahitoriae dicuntur. Tribus enim modis illecebra trahitur, aut cantu, aut visu, aut consuetudine. Eaedem igitur volatiles dicuntur, quia amantium mentes celeriter mutantur. Inde gallinaceis pedibus finguntur, quia libidinis affectu quaeque habita sparguntur. Per Ulixem autem, qui quasi 'ὅλων ξένος id est omnium peregrinus dicitur, ad mortem deductae dicuntur, quia sapientia ab omnibus mundi illecebris peregrinatur.

Note also Fulgentius, 73. (References to Fulgentius come from *Fulgentius the Mythographer,* trans. Leslie George Whitbread [Columbus: Ohio State University Press, 1971]).

55. Trevet, 38: "Et ideo bene comparat eas Sirenibus, de quibus Isidorus, Ethimologiarum libro undecimo, capitulo 41 de portentis, dicit sic: Sirenes tres fingunt fuisse ex parte uirgines, ex parte uolucres habentes alas et ungulas, quarum una uoce, altera tibiis, tercia lira canebat, que illectuos nauigantes suo cantu in naufragium trahebant."

In William of Aragon (fol. 14r), the Sirens are mostly the same as in Trevet, though now they are "pericula marina." Just as the Sirens lure ships "dulciter canencia," then sink them, so the Muses "pulchre et ornate loquendo fructum rationis immergunt ad passiones trahendo"; thus William combines more strongly than any commentator has before him the notion of the Sirens with the fruits of reason. "SED ABITE POCIUS SYRENES USQUE AD EXICIUM DULCES. Appellat eas Syrenes methaphorice quod sicut quedam pericula marina dulciter canencia naues attrahunt et immergunt ad passiones trahendo, et ideo Philosophia suas Musas inducit."

56. Wheteley, fol. 20r: "tales pisces qui dulciter cantant in aqua ut nauigantes attrahunt *usque in excitium.* . . . Sunt enim pisces multum infesti hominibus . . . quod quando pluit et tempestas magna est in mari fore submersionem."

57. Guillaume, fol. 20r, explains that the Muses are like the Sirens because sweetness proceeds from one and the other, but in the end there is bitterness:

> quando est tempus horridum et plumosum quia post tempus horridum sperant habere tempus amenum. Item [or Ita?] flent quando tempus est amenum et pulchrum, quia post illud tempus expectant tempus horridum. Sed magis debet racio gaudii et fletus ipsarum assignari alio modo quo iam supradixi.

Cf. the Anonymous of the Erfurtensis. On the Muses as thorns (*supra,* n. 38).

The story of the Sirens in Reinerus, though (10r), is not original, combining the literal details of the Proserpina story as found in Tolomeo with the allegorical interpretations of Guillaume de Conches:

> SED ABITE POTIUS. In hac parte finaliter Philosophia Musas reprehensas licentiat et repellit. Dicit sic: "O Muse Syrenibus comparabiles, dulces usque in exit[i]um, multa turpia de vobis dicere possem. Sed non est dignum ut turpi uerbo os meum coinquinem; potius ergo abite et recedite, quia hunc non consolamini; sed RELINQUITE EUM MEIS MUSIS, scilicet suauibus philosophorum sentencijs curandum; quoad depulsionem morborum viciorum et dolorum et sanandum quoad restitutionem vigoris morum et virtutum." Notandum quod poetice dicuntur Muse "Syrenes" per quandam similitudinem; quia, ut patet secundo Methamorphoseos, Syrenes fuerunt filie Acheloy colligentes flores cum Proserpina dum raperetur a Plutone; que cum doluissent super raptu sue socie, miseracione deorum mutate sunt in monstra virginalem faciem reseruantes, alas uero et vngulas assumentes. Hee autem in mari habitantes dulcedine sui cantus nauigantes attrahunt, attractos dormire faciunt et tandem dormientes submergunt. Vnde secundum veritatem tres fuerunt sorores que sua pulcritudine multos alliciebant ad amorem. Alas dicuntur habuisse quia instabiles erant; vngulas autem quia ut alie meretrices suos procos et amatores bonis suis spoliauerunt. Amor enim transit et wlnerat [*sic*]. Et dicebantur dulces usque in exit[i]um. Vnde per methaphoram Muse poetice "Syrenes" dicuntur a "Syren" quod est "tractus"; quia metri dulcedine alliciunt, mestos ad magis dolendum incitant, et tandem doloribus et affectionibus confundunt. . . . Construatur. Multa turpia possem vobis dicere. Sed O SYRENES, id est, Muse Syrenibus comparabiles, DULCES, id est, delectabiles usque IN EXITIUM, id est, in finem exclusione sic quod non in fine dulces sed amarissime; ABITE, id est, recedite, potius, id est, magis, super quam adhuc turpiora audiatis que (pro "et") relinquite, id est, dimittite eum. . . . Boecium curandum quoad doloris expulsionem et sanandum, quoad pristine integritatis recuperationem meis Musis, id est, suauibus sentenciis philosophorum.

Pietro da Moglio (fols. 4v–5r) only paraphrases in the section on the Sirens:

> Postquam ego possum habere remedia uere philosophie. Et sic dicit: O Sirene, uel SIRENES DULCES, id est, delectabiles, USQUE IN EXITIUM, id est, mortem; ABITE, id est recedite potius etc. Sirenes: huius "Sirenes" declinatio Greca; sed Sirena: huius "Sirene" Latine; et "delfin," huius "delfin" Grece. Sed "Delfinus" in declinatione latine, etc. Et sicut Sirene ducunt homines in precipitum. Et ideo dicit "abite, uos que estis potius Sirenes Camene, et estis dulces usque in exicium usque in mortem anime," quasi dicit, "uos ducitis homines ad mortem eternam," etc. . . . Veniamus ad litteram. . . . SED ABITE: sed UOS, O SIRENES DULCES IN EXITIUM, id est, usque ad

mortem potius ABITE, id est, recedite, MEISQUE etc. que (pro "et") et O Sirenes
RELINQUITE EUM SANANDUMQUE (pro "et") CURANDUM CUM MEIS MUSIS.
For Travesio (fol. 8v) the Muses are like the Sirens in that "ars metrizandi delectabilis est;
in ea multa ficta et misera continentur. . . ." Fiction and misery are linked: "O SERENES quia
sunt tanquam Syrenes; nam proprietas Sirenarum in mari conuersantium est ex pulcris suis
cantibus attrahere [MS: fãce] nautas cum suis nauibus, postea submergunt; ita faciunt iste
Muse. Nam ars metrizandi delectabilis est; in ea multa ficta et misera continentur."

58. Bade d'Assche, biijv–biiijr:
Syrenes a Greco verbo "herein" mutata aspiratione in "s" litteram deduci constat.
Est autem "herein" connectere et retinere. Fuerunt, vt poete dicunt, tres Acheloi
fluminis filie ex Calliope Musa. He insulas quasdam iuxta Pelorum inter Siciliam
et Italiam habitasse scribuntur. Quod Ouidius etiam tetigit in xiiij Methamorphoseos [14.86–88] dum Enee transitum describens, inquit:
  . . . terrasque calenti
sulfure fumatas Acheloiodumque reliquit
Sirenum scopulos.
Harum vna voce (teste Seruio super V Eneidos circa finem), alia tibijs, alia lyra
canebat. Sed tanta dulcedine cantus transeuntes nautas afficiebant vt sopirentur:
quos cum sopitos persentiscerent [*sic*], submergebant, et deuorabant. Quare cum
iuxta illas transiturus esset Vlyxes, admonitus a Circe sociorum aures cera ob-
durauit, et ipse se ad nauis malum ligari iussit, atque sic quoque transiuit illesus.
Quod ille grauiter ferentes et ira succense atque dolore commote se precipitaue-
runt in fluctus, quod Juuenalis tetigit; apud quem dicit Neuola [*Sat.* 9. 148–50]:
  Nam cum pro me fortuna rogatur
affigit ceras illa de naue petitas.
  Que Siculos cantu effigit remige surdo.
Dicuntur autem tres fuisse: Parthenope, a qua ciuitas illa que nunc Neapolis, id
est, "noua ciuitas," dicitur, denominata est, cum illic sepulta esset, item Leucosia
et Ligia. Multa de his Claudianus et Uirgilius opuscula [Bade d'Assche: *opusculum*]
etiam confecit; sed potissimum Homerus in xij Odysee, vbi Syrenes dulcissimum
cantum habent, cuius sensus est: Huc ades inclite Vlixe, magna Achiuorum gloria:
hic nauem siste vt nostram vocem audias. Nemo enim vnquam hac iter fecit quin
nostri cantus suauitate demulceretur, qua oblectatus et plura doctus a nobis dimit-
titur a nobis. Haud enim nos fugit quid apud magnam Troiam Greci simul et
Troiani deorum voluntate gesserunt. Scimus preterea quicquid in alma terra agitur
etc. Hec verba suauibus quoque carminibus Cicero transtulit, quorum primum est:
"O deus Argolicum quin puppin fleetis Vlixe." Non opus est dicere "Syrenes,"
etiam dicti [Bade d'Assche: *dici*] apes imperfectas et inutiles. Jtem volucres in
India esse quarum cantu homines mulceantur, quos sono grauatos lacerent. Si
[Bade d'Assche: *sic*] etenim singula que de hoc vocabulo legerim transcribere
velim, nimis prolixus essem. Certum est autem quod scribit in prima syllaba per
"i" nostrum et longum quia Grece habet ei dipthongon. Dicitur hec "Sireni," huius
"Sirenis." In accusatiuo hanc "Sirena" non "Sirenem" et in plurali has "Sirenas"
quia in accusatiuo plurali nominis tertie declinationis ab accusatiuo singulari in
"a" habetur frequens accusatiuus in "as" ab "em" "es," et ab "im," "is." Quia
etiam obliqui Greci sepe in nominatiuos Latinos transeunt: vt delphines—arabus,
elephantus, a genitiuis horum nominum "delphin," "arabs elephas" mutando os in

"vs." horum nominum "delphin," "arabs elephas" mutando "os" in "vs." Jdeo ab accusatiuo "serena" fit etiam nominatiuus: hec "serena," huius "serene": sicut ab accusatiuo hanc cassida: fit hec cassida, etc.

59. Trevet, 38–39:

HIIS ILLE CHORUS INCREPATUS MESTIOR DEIECIT etc. Ideo mestior quia assuetus poeticis Musis cum difficultate eas relinquit. CONFESSUSQUE RUBORE VERE-CUNDIAM etc. Sapiens enim de aliquo turpi resipiscens [*sic*] de preteritis uerecundatur LIMEN id est curam studii mei TRISTIS EXCESSIT id est deseruit. De rubore autem ex uerecundia creato dicit ille Boecius in commento super predicamenta, capitulo de qualitate et quantitate, quod cum sit uerecundia in os, omnis sanguis egreditur et ueluti delictum tecturus effunditur. Ita quoque rubor fit ex sanguinis progressione atque in apertum effusione.

60. Tolomeo, fol. 13r: "Nota quod uultus rubescens indicat uerecundiam; pallor uero indicat timorem, et est ratio quia ob uerecundiam sanguis retrahitur ad uultum et fit rubens, timore uero retrahitur sanguis ad cor. Et sic uultus pallescit." Cf. Pietro da Moglio, fols. 5r–v:

Hiis ille corus. Ista lectio est parua et facilis. Postquam Boetius in precedentibus prefuit uerta mulierjs, scilicet Philosophie ad Musas, nunc ponitur effectus. Et duo facit. Primo ostendit effectum uerborum ipsius mulierjs. . . . dicit quod illa soci-etas Musarum sicut increpita, sic uerecundata fuit; dic cerus increpitus HIS, scil-icet uerbis, id est, reprehensionibus. DEIECIT, id est deorsum iecit et EXCESSIT, id est, transiuit LIMEN; CORUS, id est, societas—"uentus" [*sic*] quidam locus ubi can-tant fratres et presbiterij; est nomen cuiusdam instrumenti [*sic*]; sed hic accipitur pro societate; increpitus, id est, reprehensus. Dicit quod quando philosophus uidet quod inclinat se ad temporalia. Uiget quando studuit in Philosophia et alijs; tunc erubescit quando uidet se in temporalibus agere; confessus in rubore ipsemet considerauit quod esset sibi dedecus. . . . Veniamus ad litteram. HIJS ILLE CORUS INCREPITUS etc. JLLE CORUS, id est, illa societas, INCREPITUS, id est, reprehensus hijs uertis, MESTIOR (pro "mestus") DEIECIT UULTUM, HUMI, id est, ad humum, CONFESSUSQUE etc. QUE (pro "et") ILLE CORUS CONFESSUS UERECUNDIAM CUM RUBORE, id est, cum rubedine, EXCESSIT, id est, transiuit LIMEN, id est, introitum tristis; per similem copulationem regitur.

61. Anonymous of the Erfurtensis, fol. 7: "Musas quas inuocant illi qui saeculariter scribunt ut <H>oratius Virgilius et alii qui nouem Musas nouem deas fingunt et inuocant."

62. Persius, choliambic preface to his *Satires,* lines 12–14, quoted in Trevet, 35. The Oxford edition of Persius gives a rather different reading for the Persius citation (p. 3):

quod si dolosi spes refulsent nummi
coruos poetas et poetridas picas
cantare creas Pegaseium nectar.

63. For example, the Second Vatican Mythographer, 113.

64. Tolomeo, fol. 6r:

Novem sunt sciencie que Muse poetice siue "Camene" appellantur, quas "Mellenjs et Thespie," Jouis et Memorie filias, in Elicone monte fabule referunt habitasse.

Vnde quando aliquis poeta uolebat scribere librum de aliqua materia, ibat ad illum montem et inuocabat illam de cuius subiecto uolebat scribere; qui veniebat et adsistebat ei et uerba ministrabat. Alij dicunt quod Appollo cum hijs Musis sciencias poetis ministrabat in illo monte; de quo monte loquitur auctor Alexandro: ad illum cui scribebat sic totumque Elicona proprians [*sic*] doctrine sacram patefecit pectoris uel aulam.

65. Tolomeo, fol. 6r:

Prima scilicet Euterpe inuenit . . . tubas et tubialia instrumenta, siue que flatu sonantur. Secunda scilicet Merpomene: tragedias conscripsit. Tertia scilicet Ter[p]sicore: psalterium siue instrumenta cordalia. Quarta scilicet Caliope: commenta siue ficta dicta, et figuras siue literalem scienciam. Quinta scilicet Clio: istorias conscripsit. Sexta erat Erato: inuenit artem geometriam. Septima scilicet Pollimia [*sic*]: r[h]etoricam [invenit]. Octaua scilicet Talia commedias siue artem cantandi. Nona scilicet Urania: inuenit . . . astrologiam.

Tolomeo appends another list to this one, appearing thus in the Vienna manuscript (fol. 6r):

Prima tubas sciet Euterpe,

Tragicumque secunda Merpomene carmen.

Jnuenit Tersicoreque psalterium,

Sed Caliope commenta figuras.

Jstorias Clio dat,

Nos Erato geometras,

@ Rectoricos Pollumnia,

Comedosque Talia.

Ast Vrania sicque cepit astrologiam.

(B.N. MS 6410, fol. 7v, has a very odd reading attributing the invention of the tambourine to Vrania as well as astronomy: *Sistra Vrania sicque reperit astrologiam.*) This poem does not appear in the Vatican Mythographers. The Pseudo-Aquinas of Munich (fol. 29r) simply says that the poets believe the Muses to be nine goddesses.

66. Reinerus, fol. 9r:

Notandum primo quod Muse poetice sunt industrie mentales et ingenij ad describendum aliqua sermone pulcro et delectabili et ad fingendum delectabilia, licet nullius virtutis. Vnde etiam a poetis dicuntur esse nouem Muse iuxta fontem Elyconis residentes, et secundum quosdam dicuntur filie Jouis et Memorie; secundum alios tamen Memnonis et Testeadis, ut patet quinto Methamorphoseos. Hec autem industrie in quantum describunt ficticia dicuntur poetice, in quantum uero vtilia dicuntur philosophice.

Reinerus adds immediately some comments about Boethius's bed: "Secundo notandum quod Musas dicit astitisse thoro, id est, consciencie per similitudinem: nam sicut in thoro seu lecto sanus lasciuit [et] cruciatur; et estuat eger, sic homo bonus in consciencia sua gloriatur. Juxta illud Apostoli: 'Gloria mea est testimonium consciencie mee.' Malus uero in consciencia punitur vnde Juuenalis: 'Nemo nocens se iudice absoluitur.'"

67. Guglielmo, fols. 100r–v: "Nota secundum Ysodorum libro quarto Ethimologiarum, nimphe dicuntur, dee aquarum quasi nunina limpharum; et dicuntur a 'nephi' quod est nube[s] uel limpha. Nam aque motus musicam efficit. Deinde et Musa dicitur a 'moys,' quod est aqua, uel a 'muse,' quod est 'querere.'"

68. Cf. Vatican Mythographers, 36.82–83 and 210–11.

69. Cf. Vatican Mythographers, 2.24 (and 3.8.19–20):
       Versus Novem Musarum
Clio gesta canens, transactis tempora reddit.
Melpomene tragico proclamat maesta boatu.
Signat cuncta manu loquiturque Polymnia gestu.
Doctiloquos calamos Euterpe flatibus urget.
Terpsichore affectum citharis movet, imperat, auget.
Uranie caeli motus scrutatur et astra.
Comica lascivo gaudet sermone Thalia.
Plectra gerens Erato saltat pede, carmine ducto.
Carmina Calliope libris heroica mandat.

70. Bade d'Assche, biijr:
Muse a plerisque nouem ponuntur; quorum nomina et inuenta sic ponit Uirgilius:
Clio gesta canens transacta [Bade d'Assche: *transactis*] tempora reddit.
Melpomene tragico proclamat mesta boatu.
Comica lasciuo gaudet sermone Thalia.
Dulciloquis calamos Euterpe flatibus vrget.
Terpsicore affectus cytharis mouet, imperat, auget.
Plectra gerens Eratho saltat pede carmine vultu.
Carmina Calliope libris heroica mandat.
Urania poli motus scrutatur et astra.
Signat cuncta manu loquiturque Polymnia gestu.
[Note: these are rather imperfect hexameters, and they do not quote what we now recognize as part of Virgil's canon: it is possible that they belong to a medieval Virgilian commentary.]
Clio hystorias inuenit. Melpone [*sic*] tragedias. Thalia comedias. Euterpe tibias. Terpsicore psalterium. Eratho geometriam. Calliope litteras. Urania astrologiam. Polymnia rhetoricam. Hec Uirgilius. Sunt ergo Musarum nomina: Clio, Melpomene, Thalia, Euterpe, Terpsicore, Eratho, Calliope, Urania, et Polymnia. Quorum que in "a" exeunt declinantur more Latino, sicut "Musa," que in "e" et "o" more Greco [exeunt]; nam in "e" habent: genitiuum in "es," datiuum in "en," reliquos casus in "e," sicut "Penelope." Jn "o" autem habent Grecum in "vs," accusatiuum et vocatiuum in "o," reliqui autem casus in Latinorum vsu non sunt. Vt hec Clio, huius Clius, etc. Sunt autem omnes Muse inuentrices. Nam hoc nomen "Musa" secundum alios dicitur a "mosios," id est, ab indagatione vel inquisitione. Secundum alios a "myein" quod est docere. Clio interpretatur "gloria," dicitur enim "cleos," "gloria" apud Grecos. Hec hystoriam inuenit, vnde multum glorie et scribentibus; et ijs de quibus scribunt nasci solet. Cadmus autem Thebanorum rex primus hystoriam scripsisse secundum Plinium fiertur, sed non sine Musa, id est, inuentione et glorie cupiditate. Melpomene tragediam inuenisse dicitur, que mangno eiolatu [*sic*] agi solebat. "Melpo" autem idem est quod "canto." Thalia dicitur a "thalein," quod est florere: inuenitque comediam veteremque satyrum more lasciuis versibus constabat. Euterpe ab "eu," quod est "bonum": boni soni et tybiarum inuentrix dicitur. Terpsicore a "delectando" nomen sumpsit. Nam "terponie" dicitur "delector." Inuenit autem citharam cum choreis et saltationibus. Eratho ab "amore," quem "Erota" Greci vocant secundum quosdam deducitur; inuenitque geometriam et plausibus audit. Calliope dicitur "pulchra

veo" [*sic*]; inuenitque heroicum carmen. Urania dicitur ab "vrano," id est "celio" [*sic*]: et astrologiam inuenisse dicitur. Polymnia autem a "multa memoria" nomen sumpsit: vel a "multa laude." Nam "poly" multum et "hymnos" laus dicitur. Et rhetoricam inuenisse a Marone dicitur.

Bade d'Assche, biijr–v:

Ut autem Landinus recitat, Anaximander Lampsecenus et Xenophanes Heracleopolites dicunt poetas esse in tutela Apollinis (qui lyra canit) et nouem Musarum, in quarum medio ipse residet. Per Apollinem autem humanam vocem intelligunt que nouem instrumentis perficitur. Hec autem, Fulgentio teste, intelligunt quattuor anteriores dentes, quorum si quis desit, fibilius et non plena vox ex ore prouenit. Item duo labia; septimum est lingua. Octauum palatum: quod Greci "vranion" vocant; quoniam sit ad formam celi. Celum autem "vranos" appellatur, qua ex re octaua Musa dicitur "Vrania." Nonum instrumentum est gutturis profunditas per quam spiritus egreditur. Plato autem ille diuinus philosophus ponit quattuor furoris genera: inter que ponitur poeticus furor, quem a musis prouenire demonstrat. Musas autem appellat celestium spherarum cantus. Nam in libro de republica singulis spheres singulas Syrenas appositas dicit, motum ipsum spherarum ac sonum qui inde fit significans. Quapropter octo spheras, octo Musas, ac per illarum concentum nouam ponit, quam (quoniam harmonia [Bade d'Assche: *hermonia*] vna est ex omnibus suauissime composita) excellentissimam dicit Hesiodus. Ergo poesis a diuino furore, furor a Musis: Muse a Ioue eodem Platone teste proueniunt. Accedit ad hanc opinionem quod Phebum, id est, solem, qui medius planetarum est, in medio Musarum ponunt. Unde illud Virgilianum: "In medio residens complectitutr omnia Phebus." Qui quidem Uirgilius attestatur Musas Iouis filias cum dicit: "Adeste Muse maxime proles Iouis" etc. Alcineon autem et nonnulli alij eas celi et terre filias dicunt. Theodontius vero Thespie et Memnonis filias esse vult. Diodorus addit Musas fuisse octo puellas: quas Osyris orbem peragrans in exercitu duxit: eo quod cantu et alijs disciplinis essent insignes.

71. Bade d'Assche, biijr:

Muse a plerisque nouem ponuntur; quorum nomina et inuenta sic ponit Uirgilius:
Clio gesta canens transacta [Bade d'Assche: *transactis*] tempora reddit.
Melpomene tragico proclamat mesta boatu.
Comica lasciuo gaudet sermone Thalia.
Dulciloquis calamos Euterpe flatibus vrget.
Terpsicore affectus cytharis mouet, imperat, auget.
Plectra gerens Eratho saltat pede carmine vultu.
Carmina Calliope libris heroica mandat.
Urania poli motus scrutatur et astra.
Signat cuncta manu loquiturque Polymnia gestu.

Anonymous of the Erfurtensis, 7–8: "Sed in rei ueritate nouem Musae sunt quattuor dentes, duo labia, plectrum linguae, repercussio palati, anhelitus pulmonis; et sine istis perfecta uox reddi non po<t>est. Haec enim sunt instrumenta ad perfectam uocem formandam, quia , si ex his unum defuerit, numquam uox perfecta formabitur."

According to "true and philosophical reason," the Pseudo-Aquinas of Munich believes (fol. 29r), they are the nine instruments of the voice: "Sed iuxta ueram et phi[lo]s[oph]icam rationem, nouem instrumenta sunt vocis, sine quibus ulla vox perfecte formatur; scilicet, dentes medij, duo labia, plectrum lingue, repercussio palati, anhelitus pulmonis."

Tolomeo, fol. 7r: "Vel possumus per istas novem Musas intelligere novem instrumenta quibus uox formata profertur, que sunt dentes anteriores quibus lingua colliditur et duo labia, peltrum [for plectrum] lingue, palatus et anelitus siue motus pulmonis." Tolomeo continues: "mistice enim siue figuratiue dicuntur intelligi per Musas que dicebantur uerba poetis minstrare, quod quidem faciunt nouem sciencie predicte."

Bade d'Assche (biiiv) also identifies Apollo as the human voice itself, with the Muses again as its nine components. For the first and only time, one of these components is linked to a specific Muse: Urania stands for the palate: "quoniam sit ad formam celi; celum autem 'Vranos' appelatur."

The Muses as instruments of the voice may be found in Fulgentius on the Muses, 55–56. Cf. also the Vatican Mythographers (1.114).

72. Guglielmo, fol. 100v: "Sed Varro dicit . . . 3 esse Musas omnium sonorum que est materia cantilenarum, quorum formacio . . . voce aut flatu aut pulsu." Cf. Vatican Mythographer 3.8.22:

Musas esse concentum mundi etiam rustici apud antiquos cognoverunt, qui eas Camenas quasi Canenas a canendo dixerunt. Quia etiam caelum theologi canere conprobarunt, sonosque musicos caelestium sacrificiis adhibuerunt, qui apud alios lyra vel cithara, apud nonnullos tibiis aliisve musicis exercebantur instrumentis. Sane moys Graece aqua dicitur; inde Musa quasi aquatica. Aër enim per arterias canenti egrediens, humore aspergitur, nec unquam per gutturis fistulam nisi humoris adjutorio canitur. Secundum Varronem etiam ipsae sunt Musae quae et Nymphae; nec, ut ait Servius, immerito. Nam aquae, inquit, sonus musicen officit, ut in hydrauliis, id est aquaticis organis, videmus. Idem etiam Varro tres tantum esse Musas commemorat, unam, quae ex aquae nascitur motu; alteram, quam aëris icti efficit sonus; tertiam, quae mera tantum voce consistit. Harum rerum caliginosas ego diversitates meo censens ingenio onerosas, aliis discutiendas, sanaque interpretatione elucidandas propone, ne vel magnorum auctoritatibus parvitas mea refragetur, vel apocryphas promens traditiones, intelligendo faciam ut nihil intelligam.

Cf. Bade d'Assche, biijr.

73. Tolomeo, fol. 7r: "Alii dicunt per predictas Musas . . . representari 9 armonias celestes quarum 7 formantur ex reuolutione oribum 7 planetarum, scilicet Lune, Mercurij, Ueneris, Solis, Martis, Iouis et Saturni. Octaua formatur ex reuolutione firmanenti. Nona uero ex aliis componitur. Et de his tractat Macrobius super Sompnio Scipionis." According to Guglielmo da Cortimiglia (fol. 100r), the Muses may be the seven planets, plus the firmament and the Primum Mobile, the ninth member that Tolomeo does not mention explicitly. "Alii dicunt istas nouem Musas esse consonos armonicos: septem planetarum et firmamenti et primi mobilis."

74. Tolomeo, fol. 6v: "Primus uelle. Secundus delectari uolito. Tertius meditari in ipso. Quartus in intellectu capere meditatum. Quintus memorie tradere. Sextus aliquod inuenire simile. Septimus inuentum iudicare. Octauus de iudicato elligere bonum. Nonus illud bonum proferre."

75. Tolomeo, fol. 6v:

Primum facit Euterpe; mouet enim uoluntatem siue appetitum ad aliquid utile uel delectabile, ad quem omnis humanus appetitus inclinat et quia per scienciam maxime ad hec deuenimus. Ideo scienciam omnes appetimus. Vnde Philosophus in prime Methaphisicorum dicit quod omnes homines natura scire desiderant. Vnde ipsa interpretatur "bona delectatio." Secundum, scilicet delectari in uolito facit Tersicore, que interpretatur "delectans instructum"; quia delectamur in eo quod scire uolumus. Tertium, scilicet meditari, facit Clio, que interpretatur "meditatio rerum." Quartum, scilicet percipere intellectum meditatum facit meditatum Merpomene [Paris, MS B.N. 6410; Vienna Cod. 53 reads "percipere intellectum facit meditatum Merpomene"], que interpretatur "mediationem faciens"; quia tunc perficitur meditatio quando percipitur in intellectu; quod est meditatum. Quintum, scilicet memorari, facit Pollimia, que interpretatur "memoriam faciens." Sextum, scilicet inuenire simile, facit Erato que interpretatur "simile inueniens." Septimum, scilicet iudicare inuenta, scilicet utrum sint bene inuenta uel non, facit Talia, que interpretatur "subtilis et capax"; quia tunc reputatur quis subtilis et capax sciencie, quando scit bene iudicare de rebus. Octauum, scilicet eligere bonum et de inuentis et iudicatis, facit Urania, que interpretatur tanquam "celestis"; quia celestium est eligere bonum et reprobare malum. Nouum, scilicet modulate siue bono sono proferre, facit Caniliope que interpretatur "bonus sonus," quia data [*data* suggested from B.N. 6410; does not appear in Vienna Cod. 53] est in proferendo sono [*sono* added from B.N. 6410] et suaui tono loqui. Et sic per istos gradus ad perfectionem peruenimus.

Cf. Vatican Mythographers, 3.8.18. Cf. also Guglielmo da Cortimiglia, fol. 100r:
Clio que interpretatur "fama." Ideo enim sciencia poetica . . . queritur ut fama augeatur. Secunda Europe [*sic*], id est, "bene delectans"; quia etiam in sciencia poetica delectacio queritur. Tertia Melpomene, id est, "faciens meditationem." Nam primo volumus. Secundo meditamur. Tertio instando meditamus. Quarto Talia, id est, "capacitas." Quinta Polinna, id est, "multam faciens memoriam." Sexta Erato, id est, "inueniens simile." Post enim scienciam et memoriam oportet aliquod simile inuenire. Septima Tercicore, id est, "iudicium." Post enim memoriam et inuentionem oportet sequi iudicium. Octava Urania, id est, "celestis." Nona Caliope, id est "optime vocis": quia quod bene elegi, bene proferre oportet.

Another set of verses follows this allegory of the Muses as "gradus ad perfectionem"; they are laid out by the scribe of Vienna Cod. 53 as follows (see Tolomeo, Paris MS B.N. 6410, fol. 94):
@Euterpe bona delectatio sit tibi prima.
@Dulce canens tibi sit Melpomene musa secunda.
@Tertia Terticore [*sic*] quod rerum instructionem fertur.
@Caliope quasi "calofones" scilicet quarta uocatur.
@Quintaque tibi sit Clio quasi meditatio rerum.
@Ex similia similie quod reperit Erato fiet.
@Plurimumque dans Polumnia sic polis hoc manifestat.
@Tanquam celestis Urania tota transit etc.

Vienna ÖNB Cod. 53, fol. 6v, gives the following last lines: "Vltimamque dans Polumnia sic polis hoc manifestat / Tanquam celestis Urania nona transit." These verses do not appear in the Vatican Mythographers. This poem was apparently produced by the students of the twelfth-century grammarian, Eberhard of Bethune. See Doreana Wright, "Henryson's Orpheus and Eurydice and the Tradition of the Muses," *Medium Aevum* 40 (1971), 41–47.

76. Tolomeo, fol. 7r:

Sed postea perficitur istis mediantibus [or *meditantibus*?], scilicet ymaginatione, intellectu, memoria, sciencia, arte, studio, exercitio, sapiencia et uirtute. Nam primo ymaginatio rerum formas percipit. Deinde intellectus ea apprehendit et de ipsis iudicat. Tertio memoria ipsa iudicata et electa ab intellectu reponit et conseruat. Que sunt in memoria ducit sciencia in habitum, que cum producitur in actum dicitur "ars." Nam ars nichil aliud est quam sciencia in actu; postquam sequi debet studium ad sciencie conseruationem [Vienna Cod. 53: *conuersationem*] et augmentum et ad ingenium conseruandum ne ingrassetur. Juxta illud Catonis: "Exercere studium" etc. Et Cassiodorus dicit: Tepescit ingenium nisi iugi fuerit lectione reparatum. Et quia melius scitur et retinetur quod in exercitium producitur, sequitur excitatio ipsius sciencie; iuxta illud Thobie: "Doctrina scolaris intercisa perit; continuata uiget." Per predicta autem ad sapienciam deuenitur, que dat cognicionem celestium et iungit ipsam animam Deo, qui per frequenter bene agere acquirit sibi habitus uirtutum et sic efficitur ymago trinitatis.

Cf. Cassiodorus, *Variae* 11.8: "aegrescit profecto ingenium, nisi iugi lectione reparetur." My thanks to Professor James J. O'Donnell for identifying this quotation and for consultation on Tolomeo's wording at this point.

77. Tolomeo, fol. 7r:

Nam sensus primo percipit et illud representat imaginationi. Imaginatio uera illud representat cogitationi, que istud format. Jngenium autem illud representat cogitationi, que istud format. Jngenium autem illud inuestigat; racio iudicat, memoria conseruat, intelligentia comprehendit et ad contemplationem adducit. Contemplacio uera Dee iungit. Sicque anima perficitur.

78. Tolomeo, fol. 7r:

Prima est discernere inter honestum et turpe. Nam solius hominis est honestum prosequi, cum bruta non nisi utilia et delectabilia prosequantur. Secunda est passiones ordinare ad limitem racionis. Tertia est indiuidui intellectum eleuari ut sicut erectus ambulat corpore, sic in suum creatorem erigatur mente ut dicitur etiam in secundo libro, caput iij. ibi. Jn sublime etc. nam si per adhesionem nimiam ad terrenam inferiorem se fecerit, se commutat intellectiuam, ut dicitur etiam in 10 libro caput 2 in fine. Quarto est amicitiam habere secundum genus amicitie ubi differat a brutis que non habent nisi amicitiam que est delectationis et comutacionis et huiusmodi. Quinta est uerecundari turpi perpetrato propter quod in uerecundia dicuntur inemendabiles, quia in aliquo mutati sunt ab ordine racionis peccorinam naturam assumentes. Sexta est ut sit perfectio coniugalis quoad hec ut si contrahant nuptias eas faciant leges et consuetudines et ordinationes ceteras ciuitatis. Septima ut sit animal ciuile obseruando leges et propter racionis usum. Nona est ut sit animal mansuetum; nam ut sic differat ab illis brutis, quod mansuesere non possunt.

For the concept of "animal mansuetum" as a definition of a human being, see Aristotle, *De interpretatione* 2.20b. (My thanks goes to Professor Siegfried Wenzel for alerting me to this reference.) The seventh member of this series seems to be missing in Vienna Cod. 53; I have supplied a reading from Paris, B.N. MS Lat. 6410.

79. He quotes Ambrose, for example, on Luke's Gospel: "Mundana scientia, verborum ambitu fucata est; sapientia vero sacrae Scripturae, rerum veritate est magis subnixa" (Denis, 24).

80. In the student-teacher dialogue, Denis's pupil, John, worries about Boethius's dejection and sadness—for if he is sad, then he is a liar. He was a most learned man, yet he seems to have succumbed to passions and "animi motibus." Denis agrees that Boethius was a man of wisdom, but he was human, too, so his soul had both an inferior and superior part. His mournful song in 1 m. 1 uses the inferior part of his soul to communicate to the faithful just how many grave things he tolerated—exile, captivity, etc. Denis does not excuse him from venial faults, yet reminds John that Boethius was ultimately a martyr. Other holy men, Job and Jeremiah particularly, suffered greatly and spoke immoderately on occasions, yet were saintly (Denis, 29).

81. *Conservative* and *moderate* are meant to be relative terms, not political ones. I would almost rather say "green" and "purple" or "Calgarian" and "Edmontonian."

82. For a consideration of this tradition, see Seznec (*supra*), as well as Jane Chance, ed., *The Mythographic Art: Classical Fable and the Rise of the Vernacular in Early France and England* (Gainesville: University Press of Florida, 1990). See also Chance's *Medieval Mythography: From the School of Chartres to the Court at Avignon, 1177–1350* (Gainesville: University Press of Florida, 2000).

PART V

REEDITION OF
THE BOKE OF COUMFORT OF BOIS

THE BOKE OF COUMFORT OF BOIS
[BODLEIAN LIBRARY, OXFORD
MS AUCT. F.3.5.]
A TRANSCRIPTION WITH INTRODUCTION

Originally Transcribed, Edited, and Introduced by
Noel Harold Kaylor, Jr., Jason Edward Streed, and William H. Watts

Reedited here by Noel Harold Kaylor, Jr., and Philip Edward Phillips

Introduction

Description of the Manuscript

According to its catalogue, the Bodleian Library acquired MS AUCT. F.3.5. "not later than 1602." The catalogue gives the titles or brief descriptive information about the seven texts bound up in the manuscript, which can be summarized as follows:

1. (fol. 1). The first few leaves of a series of *Distinctiones theologicae*, or short articles on theological subjects.
2. (fol. 9). A text that ends with "Explicit tractatus artis predicatorie de compilacione domini Ranulphi [Higden] de ordinacione sermonum."
3. (fol. 26). A text that ends with "Explicit tractatus utilis de duodecim tribulacionibus secundum Petrum Blesensem."
4. (fol. 35). The *Mythologiae* of Fabius Placiandes Fulgentius, the grammarian.
5. (fol. 80). A text that ends with "Expliciunt opposiciones Petri Blesensis contra Iudeos."
6. (fol. 108). "Summa collacionum ad omne genus hominum edita a fratre Johanne Wallensi fratre Minore & sacre theologie doctore."

7. (fol. 198). Chaucer's version of the first book of the *De Consolatione Philosophiae of Boethius* ("Boysius"), here modified and paraphrased and to some extent accompanied by a commentary.

The binding of the manuscript, white sheepskin covering board, is in good condition. The catalogue dates this binding to about 1600. The pages are of parchment, with parchment tabs inserted to mark the beginning page of each of the seven texts. The pages are all 17.7 cm x 26.7 cm, except for those of text seven, which are 17.7 cm x 26.2 cm. The pages of the Boethian text each have thirty-four ruled lines contained within a space of 11 cm x 17.4 cm. Between folios 214v and 215r, two pages have been cut out, but none of the text is missing.

In several instances, the scribe repeats words or phrases and presents short passages in confused word order. This suggests that the scribe was probably working from a pre-existing copy or version of the text. The translation itself is, as the Bodleian catalog notes, dependent upon Geoffrey Chaucer's translation, the *Boece,* of ca. 1380. The scribe seems also to have had on hand some commentaries, which is evidenced by the *vita* of Boethius at the beginning of the text and by extensive glosses throughout.

Previous References to the Manuscript

Previous references to the manuscript include the following:
1. Mark Liddell, (Letter to the) *Academy,* March 7, 1896.
2. Friderich Fehlauer, *Die englischen Übersetzungen von Boethius' De Consolatione Philosophiae* (Ph.D. diss. Albertus-Universität–Königsberg, 1908).
3. Noel Harold Kaylor, Jr., "Factual Interpolations in the Oxford MS AUCT. F.3.5. 'Boke of Comfort of Bois,'" *Fifteenth-Century Studies* 23 (1997), 74–80.
4. Noel Harold Kaylor, Jr., "Boethius 'De Consolatione Philosophiae' didaktisch aufbereitet: Die anonyme mittelenglishche Übersetzung von Buch I in Ms. Oxford Auct. F.3.5.," *Artes im Mittelalter* (Berlin: Akademie Verlag, 1999), 187–97.

Editorial Notations

Within the manuscript, the scribe has indicated major transitions in the text with two vertical strokes, which we have reproduced as double uprights, "||." Words that have been broken at line breaks are usually indicated in the manuscript by a hyphen; where hyphens have been omitted in the manuscript, we have placed them in brackets, "[-]." Problematic passages that are discussed in the footnotes are enclosed in parentheses, "( )."

We have attempted as far as possible to maintain the integrity of this unique manuscript by retaining its idiosyncracies of syntax and orthography. Where the scribe has used "ff" to indicate a capital "F" at the beginning of a new sentence or a clause, we have maintained the double form, and we have kept the scribe's abbreviations: where raised characters were used, we have inserted superscripts. For example, an abbreviated *that* remains þ^t, *thus* remains þ^s, *with* remains w^t, *thou* remains þ^u, *the* remains þ^e, etc. When two words in the manuscript are clearly intended as one word, as in the case of *there inne* or *to warde,* we have left them separated. However, while the scribe has consistently joined the article *a* with the noun that follows, as in "ama^n," we have separated them. As in the example given, "ama^n," nasals are most often represented by a mark resembling a "~" above the word, which we render as a raised "m" or "n." For ease of reading, some abbreviations have been expanded, as in p^{ar}t.

We have made every effort to keep the punctuation in the edition as close to the scribe's punctuation as possible. Occasionally, for clarity, we have changed a comma to a period or vice versa, but generally the scribe's practice proves reasonable, and it is maintained.

Parallel lines and margin indications in the manuscript were scored prior to inscription of the text: thus, left and right margins are regular, and there are thirty-four regular lines centered on each page. We have added line numbers in the left margin. The lines indicated in this edition are faithful to those in the manuscript.

Throughout the manuscript, the scribe has provided indented spaces for ornate initials that were never painted in. A later hand has indicated what the initial letters should be, and we have maintained these, but enclosed them in brackets.

Dialect

The Bodleian catalogue dates this manuscript to the fifteenth century. We have found a close analogue to the scribe's dialect to be that of John Wyclif, from the southeast Midlands of the mid- to late-fourteenth century. For example, the use of *sche* as a form of *she* and the use of *fader* as a form of *father* places our scribe in the southeast Midlands, and in the late final quarter of the fourteenth century or the first quarter of the fifteenth century. Further indications—the fairly consistent use of the yogh (3) and the thorn (þ)—date the manuscript to this period, as does the occasional use of a *d* for a *th* and the use of *-aunde* as an ending for present participles.

The Text of the Manuscript

−198 r[1]−

	[F]	or als meche as eche aboke oweth worthily to be hadde
		in p^{ro}se, chargede and lovede aftur the worthinesse of his
		auttour, and the p^{ro}fite of the mater tretid thereinne, the -
		refore, as anemptes[2] the boke of coumfort the weche
5		with lowly subieccioun of myself to coreccioun of al -
		le wiser, p^{ri}ncipaly for ese of myself and thenne for other goode fre^{n} -
		des, I take in purpos to telle the menynge of hit in Engelische. ‖
		As nere to the entent of the auttour as I am disposide be grace of
		the goode lorde above, it is furste to wite for to put lekynge in re -
10		ders of hit, that the auttour of this forsaide boke was callide be
		dyvers names, and that for gret praisynge of him. ffor as the
		wers a man is, the more unacordyngely it is, that he have any
		name for name aftur the douet[3] hit puttes substaunce in a man
		the weche is refte hym be wise. Wherefore he schal worthily
15		lose his name, as be open ensample in the gospel of the ryche
		man, that was cladde in purpul and bise.[4] ffor thorutgh synne
		he was to be beryede in helle, as he that hadde lost the substau^{n} -

1. lower right corner of this page: "A.M." appears in a later hand

2. as regards

3. doubt

4. dark brown; gray

ce of grace, that schulde have kept hym therefro. Crist rehersede
of hym no name, as if he hadde none. Ry3t of the contraryouse
20   wise, the mo names and dyvers of worschepe, that are reherse -
de of a man, the more thay auttoryse hym and schewes hym
the more to be comendede and to be made of. || Thus kyngis
and lordes to magnefie thare a state apropirs[5] to hem in here stile
dyvers names. And for the same skille[6] in the titille of this
25   boke is Bois callide be dyvers names. Somme are to hym
p^{ro}pir names, summe names of office, su^{m}me names of auncer -
trye that he come of, and su^{m}me geve to hym o vertu, that
he most folewede. Thus thenne saith the titil of this boke.
[H]   ere begynneth the boke of coumfort of Anyte of Manle
30   of Severyne of Bois of the before counselour of ordy -
narie[7] of patrice, and be alle thaise names he menes o p^{er}sone.
ffurst he was callide Annycius, for he my3t no3t be bowed fro
ri3twisnes nether by prise ne be p^{er}ier.[8] He was callide Bois þ^t
is on Engelisch an helper, for he halp evere pore men in here

−198 v−

35   ry3t and nede. He was callide Severyne, and that is men sais was his
p^{ro}pir name, for he lefte nevere in iuggement the treuthe nother
for love drede p^{ro}fit ne mede,[9] he was callide Manlius of the ky^n -
red that he cam of. And he was callede Cyconsul of office that
he was inne. And he was callede ordynarie for he sette men and
40   and[10] ordeynde hem in here office. And he was callede patryce,
for he cam of the worthy fadres of Rome and be the maner
of hem he governyd.|| This worthy man hadde the gifte
of grete and passynge knowleche bothe of god and of creatures
and that he scheweth in the bokes that he made. ffor he made
45   of boke of the trynite of p^{er}sons in the godhede, and another
boke of Rethoryk, and another of musyk, and other of the te -

---

5. to assign as property to

6. ground; reason

7. title is explained below

8. perjury

9. need

10. *sic*

chynge of scoleres, and ylke on of thaise is dep^{ar}tid in two dy -
verse bokes. He levede in the ȝere aftur the Incarnacyou^{n}
five hundrede and xxiij, in the tyme that the tyraunt Theo -
50   doryk with the gothes soiecte[11] Rome to hem and p^{ur}posed the
slaughter and the destrucciou^{n} of the comu^{n} p^{ro}fite and his ȝe[12]
whos malicious entent this ryȝtwis man wisely and latou -
res[13] myȝthily w^{t}stode.‖ And therefore be malice of that
tiraunte acused of unlawful and vicious p^{er}sones of diver -
55   se false pointes, of the weche mynde[14] schal be made in
the boke plainly nouȝt araynede to be lawfully empeched
and put to answere, but in his absence he was falsly for [-]
Iugged and put in exile to papy[15] and in harde and foule pri -
soun. Thenne remembrynge hym self of the gret prosp^{eri} -
60   te and welthe that he was su^{m}me tyme inne, and on the
peyne and turment that he was thanne inne, nouȝt alone -
ly takynge hede to the sensualtie of his flesch that was lyk -
ly to be oppressede with myscoumfort that fortunes adv^{er}site
had sent to him, but also to other that myȝt falle to swe -
65   che wordly adv^{er}sites. That for defamite of coumfort myȝt
lyȝtly come to dispaire. Therefore in the foule place of his
p^{ri}soun destitute fro coumforth of alle outewarde bodely fre^{n} -
des he turnes him inwarde into him self, that is to his

−199 r[16]−

resoun and remembers him of olde wisdomes that he had sum^{m}e -
70   tyme seen, and lerid, and put hem in his boke callid Boke of Cou^{m} -
fort whereinne groose[17] he techeth this conclucioun. ‖ How the
soule of a man shal be mad stedfast in a wise meene betwene
the laughynge p^{ro}sp^{er}ite of unseker[18] Fortune and her adv^{er}sarie glo -

---

11. subject

12. scribe seems either to have added or omitted something in this sentence

13. no meaning can be assigned to this word

14. remembrance

15. Pavia

16. lower right corner of this page: "A.M." appears in a later hand

17. in large

18. uncertain

mynge,[19] nother be hir adv^er site to be broken ne drowned in
75 desolacioun ne kast doun in myscoumfort, ne to be enhyed[20] be
hir p^ro sp^er ite above the knowleche of him self. But ay to sta^n -
de stedfastly in a resonable mene withoute over mekel glad -
nes of welthy Fortune, or hevynes of hir unhappynes,
lokynge evere up with abrennynge desire to gete the evere -
80 lastynge goodes that may not faile, and forto dryve this co^n -
clusioun be acordynge menes, this man Bois schewes hys -
self. ffurst as a worldly wretchede p^er sone with holde w^t sen -
sualite of flesch that is desolate and gretly distourblede w^t
passions for disese of adversarie fortune come to him. ffor wa^n -
85 tynge of worldely welthfulnes and losse of temp^or al goode.
|| And thenne in his ymaginacioun he schewes him self as
a p^er sone w^t holde w^t wisdom and resoun that comes forth and
brynges acordynge remedies and consolaciouns. And this
dialoge in this oon p^er son as it were too, oon desolate and a [-]
90 nother full of coumfortht is dep^ar tid into fyve bokes. || In þ^e
furst he remembris his exile and his disese that he is fallen
inne, and that for innocentcy and not for gilt, ne be for tres -
pas, and for hie[21] wisdom as he rehercede. And he complay -
nes of fyve thynges, principaly as it schal be reherced. And
95 in the same philosophie begynnes to coumfort him be spe -
rynge homily of his seknes, and be his owne answere
sche discures[22] the causes of his maladies. || In the secun -
de boke ph^ilosoph ie begynnes to hele the soule of the seke ma^n
in the myscoumfort of dispaire, specialy for losse of foure
100 thynges, erthly riches, erthly ioye, erthly dignite of office,
and erthly power. And sche schewes that no man schulde troste
i^n fortune of fallynge to office, or of oþ^er worldly welthfulnes

−199 v^23 −

ne sorewe for the wantynge of hem. ffor sche schewes that thay

---

19. frowning
20. exalted
21. high
22. discovers
23. illegible marginalia: to the left of line 28; this occurs where summary of meter 1 begins

that ar most lekynge to a man in erthe, as golde silver, faire wif fai -

105   re horse or sweche other of p^{ro}phites to him of hevynes whenne thay
ar wantid be fallynge away fro him, and therefore whanne thay
arn had thay schulde not be charged. || He dep^{ar}tith the thirde in[24]
boke in too. In the firste p^{ar}tie sche schewes sovereyn p^{ro}fit goode ma -
y not rise ne stande no wise[25] in the goodes of this worlde. The

110   secunde partie schewith the p^{er}fite goode in the weche men schulde sette
here delite where that god is. The fourte boke schewes that goode
men ar alway my3tty, and evyl men with oute my3t al it other -
wise semes, and that the payne of evyl men schal nev^{er}e have
ende, ne the rewarde of goode me^{n}. And the cause why summe

115   tyme goode me^{n} ar disesed more thanne schrewes,[26] and schrew [-]
es sette in welthfulnes and goode me^{n} in hevynes, and thanne
schewes what goddis purvyaunce is, and what thyng desteny
is. || In the fift boke sche schewes what thynge men calle happe -
nynge. And whether free wille may stonde with desteny. And be -

120   cause that in this bokes corious pointes of clergie ar schewed
in askynge for coumfort that nedes answerynge to. Therefore
this boke is made as it were too p^{er}sons, the seke ma^{n} and
the leche, Philosophie the leche askynge, and Bois the seke
man answerynge, and su^{m} tyme agaynwarde,[27] Bois the seke ma^{n}

125   is the sensualite of fleshly thou3t that ay schurvys and he -
vyes[28] w^{t} disese. But Ph^{ilosoph}ie is the resoun, that w^{t} dyv^{er}se maner
of cunnyng and science makes defence to sweche a ma^{n} that he
schulde falle in despaire. And for comunly the seke pleynes[29] or
the leche p^{ro}fre his medicynes, therefore seke Bois thus be -

130   gynnes. || Allas I seke wepynge am constraynede to begyn [-]
ne verse of sorewful mater that sum^{m}e tyme was in florisshan [-]
d stodie likyngly makynde delitable ditees. Be halde thaise mu -
sis[30] that meryly synges, that were poetrie gladnes whanne

---

24. *sic*

25. in no wise

26. evil persons

27. vice versa

28. shivers and heaves

29. complains

30. muses

I was in my welthy stody, now haire[31] remembrau^{n}ce reves[32] my

135   herte and distractis fro stedfastnes, wetynge the vesage w^t veray

teres of me desolate wrecche.[33] And al if theodorik has ferdid[34] my

–200 r[35]–

bodily comforthis that thay schulde not felawschipe me in place of

my disese. Natheles this poetrye wisdom that sum^{m}e tyme I lerid

w^t no ferdnes[36] of the p^{r}ince may be lettyd, but thay wil folewe me

140   i^n the way of my exile, thay ware sum^{m}e tyme the gladnes of my

flesch and myrtheful in ʒouthede, and now they glade the weirdes[37]

of me agayn be[38] hevynes. ffor elde is comen unwarly upon me,

sodenly hasted be the harmys that I have so that sorewe has co -

manded his age to be w^{t}ynne me, that I have age be sorewe

145   schewes fallynge of my here before tyme that kynde i^n gladnes

cast hit. And my flesch tremlith as a womme^{n}is aft^{er} childynge.

That ded[39] is calde in comune speche of men blessede. || The we -

che in ʒeris of lekynge lyvynge p^{r}eses not unto ma^n, but holdes

him away, and that same ded is callyd blessed, that redily co -

150   mes to ham that ar i^n hevynes besily called aftur of ham.

But allas allas, ded that so desired unto wrecches callyd eft^{er}

of tham in here hevynes, fro me wrecchedly dysesed and fast

callynge aftur hir, turnyth here heryng ere, and to me hir deth[40] ere

and as a cruel encresser of my paynfulnes sche denyes to spe -

155   re my wepynge eyn. Allas whilke unfaythful fortune faverd

me in my p^{ro}sp^{er}ite, with the goodes of this worlde that ar light

---

31. their

32. rives

33. woe

34. destroyed

35. illegible marginalia: to the right of line 20, between lines 14 and 15 and lines 27 and 28; lower right corner of this page: "A.M." appears in a later hand

36. fears

37. fate [OE *wyrd*]

38. perhaps *from heaviness* is intended

39. in this manuscript: *d* sometimes has the value of *th*; probably *deth* is intended

40. probably *deaf* is intended

and sone[41] blowyn away. That tyme the hevy oure of deth
had almost drowned my hede und[e]r the erthe, but now sone
sche hath w[t]drawe hir begylynge and clowdy semblaunde
160   and chaungynge hir chere of welthfulnes unto disesy nede [-]
fulnes, my unkynde bodily lif drawes alonge and agayn my
wille is abidynge in me. || Here it is the cause that he spe -
kes before of the dissayveable semblaunde of fortune. That
fortune be wis poetis was discryved in lickenes of a lady with
165   too vesages, on before and that was whi3t in colo[ur] and þ[t]
betokenyth p[ro]sp[er]ite, and a blak face on the back half, that be [-]
tokenyth adv[er]site, this lady sat in myddis of a while.[42] The
whele sche was contynuly turnande aboute, the weche is
undurstande hir variaunce and chaungeablenes, and i[n] this
170   whele was writen in ten p[ar]ties thereof. In the first hono[ur]

–200 v–

and worschipe, and that sche wolde sum[m]e tyme w[t] the white face
and ri3t hand schewe to many and sodeynely or[43] me[n] were ware
the whele schulde be chaungede to the blak side and w[t] the blak
face liftande and glomande countinaunce sche schewed writen
175   to the same schame and reprove, sum[m]e tyme of the forside, w[t]
the white face and the ri3hande schewynge writen grete ruthes[44]
and worldely welthe, and sodeynly sum[m]e tyme on the blak sy -
de sche wolde schewe writen povert and beggery, sum[m]e tyme
hele, sum[m]e tyme sekenes, sum[m]e tyme lif, sum[m]e tyme deth &[45]
180   alle men to forse hem to clymbe on this whele, and whanne
thay wende to have comen up be the p[ar]t of worschipe, sche so -
denly put hem to the p[ar]t of schame and of reprove. ffro the
p[ar]t of riches, to the p[ar]t of beggery and pov[er]te, fro hele into
sekenes, and fro lif into deth. Thus sche with hir dissayvable
185   chaungeablenes wolde nev[er]e be stable ne suffre no ma[n] to stounde

---

41. soon

42. wheel

43. before

44. compassions

45. character in manuscript resembles an ampersand

stably in the stede.[46] To this unseker begilynge fortune Bois to -
ke hede and thus contynuede his complaynynge. || O ȝe fren -
dis ȝe have dissayvede me, why callede ȝe me sum^{m}e tyme
happe and blessyd, he that sone slode and felle dou^{n}n, as I
190   have now dou^{n}n, stode he nevere stable in stede.
        [T]   hus whille Bois contynues in hevynes and leves spe -
            kynge entres, as he witnes Wisdom his comforture in
skilles licknes of a womma^n, and this licknes was acordyn -
ge for two skiles. ffirste sithen a womma^n that was fortune
195   had brought him in sekenes, hit was semely that a wom -
man^{n}s wisdom schulde returne him, be ensample of Eve
and Marie. || The secunde skile for womma^n throrew ten -
dre kepynge of the seke geves him gretter coumfort thanne
a man. Thus thanne Bois sais, in the meenewhile that
200   I recorde this forsaide mater of hevy co^{m}plaint be myself,
and for thenkynge on I wrote my weply and sorewful com -
plaint w^t a pointel. And so dede I alle man^{er} be the weche a ma^n
may schewe his grife,[47] and þ^t is in thre wise, in thenkynge spe -
kynge and writynge. I saw a womman of grete revere^{n}ce bese -

–201 r[48]–

205   meland[49] that stode above my hevede, that is to mene wisdom and a [-]
cordyngly he assignes hir standyng above his hedde. ffor al wisdom
com fro god, as the wise sais. The weche is hed of alle creatures.
Also for be ph^{ilosph}ie in a mannys hed is the sete of wisdom, and þ^t
w^{t}in thre scelles[50] of thre p^{ar}ties of the hede in thre chaieres. ||
210   ffurste scho[51] sittes in the scelle of the forme[52] p^{ar}tie of the hedde in
the sete and in the chaier of undurstondynge, in the celle of þ^e
myddis p^{ar}t of the hed in the sete and chaier of discrecioun and
resonable demynge. In the celle of the hynder p^{ar}t of the hede,

---

46. in that place

47. grief

48. lower right corner of this page: "A.M." appears in a later hand

49. appearance

50. cells

51. *sic*

52. foremost

in the sete and chaier of mynde and fast on thenkynge. And for
215   al wisdom is schewede be oon of thaise thre, understanding
discrete demynge, and haldynge in mynde acordengly, he sais
sche apperid above his hede w^t flawmynge eyn brennynge &
clerly lokynge ov^{er} that other comu^{n}men my3t see, be weche he
discryveth wisdam as passynge in knowynge and undurston -
220   dynge. ffor be ph^{ilosoph}ie colerik complexioun that disposes a man^{n}es
eyn kyndly to the p^{ro}purtes before sayde arguse in him grete
sotilte^{53} of wit to take knowynge of thynges, the weche know -
ynge the comunite of men comes not to. And therefore he sa -
is sche lokid more clerly thanne com^{m}on men my3t. || W^t a love -
225   ly colo^{ur} and strenghy^{54} that my3t not be ov^{er}comen the lovely
colo^{ur} is the fare^{55} speche and eloquence of wisdam that gretly
embelesshes wisdam. That hir strenghe may not be ov^{er}come,
betokenes hir plentyuowsnes i^n wit, that ferther and besier
a ma^n sekes i^n hir, he schal nev^{er}e ov^{er}come hir, for ev^{er}e the ferther
230   he sekes, the mo dou3tes he schal fynde, and the more he schal
thenke that he hath nede to lere. And al if sche were ful of so
gret age, that hit was nou3t like that sche my3t have betrow -
ed^{56} of our elde. The stature of hir, natheles was of dowtes iug -
gement, for sum^{m}e tyme sche litild and schrynkid hirself, like
235   to the comu^n mesure of me^n. And sum^{m}e tyme hit semede that
sche towched hevene, that the si3t of ma^n mi3t not loke to
hir. || Here we ar tau3t furst of þ^t age of wisda^m, þ^t sche was be -
fore ma^n and ay w^t him, as þ^e wise ma^n sais. I wisda^m passid forth

—201 v^{57}—

fro the mouthe of the hiest before begynnynge of ma^n. ffortheremo -
240   re be the dowtouse stature of hir that sum^{m}e tyme was like to
comu^{n}me^n, sum^{m}e tyme touched hevene, sum^{m}e tyme p^{er}cid heve -
ne above the si3t of ma^n, betokenes thre degrees i^n knowynge,

---

53. subtlety

54. strength

55. fair

56. betrayed

57. illegible marginalia: to the left of lines 14, 28, 29, 33, and 34, and between lines 25 and 26

be wheche a ma^n schal go up to knowe the maker of alle. || ffurst
the wise ma^n must knowe wisdam of the maker i^n the comune
245   stature of ma^n, that is furst to have perfi3t knowleche of bodily
creatures, aftur go hier and touche hevene. In takynge hede
to hevenly creatures, and knowe wunderfully causes of hem,
that makes the wundurful and dyverse wirkynges in bodily
creatures, and thenne in the thridde degre p^{er}se hevene, that is to
250   passe ov^{er} mannes resoun unto hidde p^{ri}vatyes of the thre p^{er}sones in
godhede, and for thaise causes sche schewed hir so dyv^{er}se in stature.
Here clothes were made of the lethiest^{58} and smallest thredis of a lasta^n -
de mattere by sotyl^{59} craft. The weche clothes sche hadde woven and
madde w^t hir owne handes, as I knew wel aftur be the tellynge of
255   hirself. Thaise clothis of wisdam ar the sevene siences w^t alle prac -
ti3ynge of speculacioun that be mannes craft or wit is drawen ou3t
of hem, the weche hydes w^{t}inne hem self the curyoustes of wisda^m.
As clothes covers mennes bodily sustenaunce. The lethy thredis
and smale is wisdam sponnen, and schewede ou3t in wordes and
260   writynges. The weche is of a lastande matere that is the desire of
cunnynge, thaise clothes sche spanne and madde w^t hir owne han -
des, that ar hir philisophres, that were wundurful spekers wry -
ters and wirkers of wisdam. || But now he saith the clothes ar
made dym and derke w^t elde that is nou3t sette by, as the smoke or
265   reeke is wount to make ymages dym that hanges therein. This
betokenes in his menynge that for necglygence of me^n that have
left stody of wisdam and drawes hem to lustes. Wisdam as sche
were an olde cloth is cast away, and not set by and so is dymmyd.
ffor sche is al besmoked with the reeke of synne in vicyous ly -
270   vers, that ar rekeles in knowynge of goodnes. In the lowest
skirtes of this cloth was redde wryten a ˙P˙ of greike, and on hye
in the colere of the cloth was redde wryten a grykysh ˙T˙ betwene

–202 r^{60}–

weche lettre ware sette degrese craftily wrou3t in the maner of led -

---

58. most supple

59. subtle

60. illegible marginalia: to the right of lines 1 and 29 and between lines 3 and 4 and 30 and
31

275

280

285

290

295

300

dres,[61] be weche degrese men my3t clymbe fro the netherest letter unto the heyer, be thaise lettres he betokenes too partes of wisdam that comprehendes al wisdam, of the weche p^{ar}tes the lower begyn^{n}es with ˙P˙ of greik, and is callyd p^{ra}ctyse wisdam in outwarde wisda^{m} wirkynge callyd in comu^{n} speche lyf actyf. The heyer p^{ar}ty of wis - dam begynnes w^{t} ˙T˙ callyd theoryk and that is wisdam inward thynges callyd in comu^{n} speche lyf conte^{m}platyf. ffro the lower he schal go to the heyer, fro actyf to contemplatyf, fro outwarde wir - kynge to goddis lovynge but not agayn warde,[62] levynge the hyer for the lower. This goynge upwarde may not be in wisdam sodein - ly fro the toon[63] to the tother. But he muste clymbe soburly be þ^{e} degrese of a ledder set betwene hem. || The furst degre is that he enforme his owne soule to goode lyf and honest. The secu^{n}de set to travayle be goode ensample and techynge to p^{ro}fite thy ney - bore. The thrydde w^{t}drawe frele men with lawful blamynge fro vycyous lyf, and w^{t} vertuous governaunce demeene hem and sta - ble hem in vertuous levynge, thaise thre degrese longes[64] to actyf lyf. || Go thanne heyer on the ledder, and thenke how thou kanne love god and his creatures in his my3t, for he made hem in his wisdam, for he ordeynede hem and set hem in his goodnes. ffor the ende to the weche he made hem consyderynge the cause, the mann^{er}, the p^{ro}p^{en}sytes, the ordre, the multitude, the kyndes, and the bewte[65] of alle creatures. Arettynge[66] al to the love of god, for the goodnes of here maker. || The heyest degre is that thou kan ov^{er}passe alle creatures and love and reste in the goode lorde with p^{er}fyte forgedy^{n} ge of al thynge, that is not he al oonly absorte and ravyscht i^{n} his love for himself, and 3it hast thou the heyest p^{ar}t of wisdam that is pure contemplacioun of god. ffortheremore Bois saith, that the handes of sum^{m} me^{n} hadde schorne the cloth be vyole^{n}ce, and ylke of hem bare away pecys[67] that he my3t gette, thay schare þ^{e} clothis of wisdam that wenes that oon liberal scyence my3t

---

61. ladders

62. the reverse

63. *sic*

64. belong

65. beauty

66. attributing

67. pieces

305   p^{er}fyly[68] be cowde,[69] or my3t make a p^{er}fyte wise ma^n w^{t}oute another.
       Or elles thay that wenes that goode dede my3t make hym vertu -

−202 v[70]−

       ous with reklesnes of alle other goode dedes. But thay take here pecys
       be vyolence for hit is not wisdom his entent to make sweche men
       wise. This womma^n forsayde bare bokes in hir ry3t hande and i^n hir
310   lefte hande a septre. That is to meene, that wisdam is to geve al
       worldely p^{ro}mocyouns, but spirytual undurstandynge be the bokis
       and temp^{or}al undurstandynge be the septre. Also sche berith bokis
       for hem that ar symple and wolde be goode are unkunnynge, the
       bokis of wisdam is here techynge to sweche the septre betokenes
315   auctoryte of ponyshynge of hem that arn evyl. || And whanne sche
       sawe he saith thaise poetycal muses, the weche he callyd his de -
       lyte, that he hadde to wryte in metre of poysy is mysfare.[71] Wha^n -
       ne sche sawe swech delyte of wrytynge stande aboute my bedde,
       endytynge wordes to my wepynge, sche was a lityl amovyd
320   and glowed w^t cruele eyn, that is to meene, whanne veray wis -
       dam saw him set his wisdam and lekynge wisily[72] to remembre
       him sorewfully of hevynes that he was fallyn to, and to kepe
       hit in mynde in writynge sche was movyd. ffor that wolde a[73] re -
       mouvde hit ou3t of here soule, and with kastynge of hir synne
325   o[74] syde as it is the condicyoun of hem that are wroth. || Sche say -
       de, who suffrede this foule comu^n womma^n come so nere to thay -
       se seke men, to whylke not aloonly aswages not his sorewes and
       his hevynes with no remedyes. But thay wolde fede and norys -
       che him up with swete venym, this delite that Bois hadde þ^s
330   in meter to discryve his sorewe, wisdam calles comu^n womme^n
       of a place callyd theatre. In weche place poetes made here wry -

---

68. probably highly abbreviated form for *perfectly*

69. known

70. illegible marginalia: to the left of line 22 and between lines 12 and 13, 13 and 14, 24 and 25, 25 and 26, and 26 and 27

71. unfortunate

72. with determination; knowingly

73. have

74. out

tynges to be knowen and rehercyd, for ry3t as a comu^n womma^n
drawes a ma^n to lust and geves none, or elles lityl and schort
whyle abydynge, thanne leves to hym in longe abidynge pay -

335   nefulnes. Ry3t so do thay and thay abate nou3t his sorewe but
rather encresyd, and therefore sche calles hem swete poysun,
swete for the lekynge metere that the wordes ar set in. But the
mettere is poysun abidynge paynefully, and ay the more that it
is hadde in mynde the weche is set in sweche wordes of delyta -

340   ble metter. And therefore sche saith folewyngly, that sweche mu -

–203 r^{75}–

ses holden hertis of men in usage, that is of sorewe, and why wisda^m
spekes thus agayn thaise muses sche telles, that for they with
thornys, be the weche he menes foure fleschly affecciouns. ||
That is gladnes of p^{re}sent goode. Gru^n chynge^{76} for p^{re}sent evyl, hope

345   of goode forto come. And drede of evyl forto come. Thay prycke
so thaise affecciounes unp^{ro}fitably, that thay distroye the corne
and the plentynouse fruyates^{77} of resoun the weche are wisdam
and vertue, for thay kepe a man in usage of sorewe. || Now wis -
dom directis hir speches unto thaise muses, that is to meene,

350   this wisdam Bois p^{er}sevynge him self in errour, for as meche
as he couthe not aswage his hevynes with vertue and wisda$^{m.\,.}$
But rather encrese hit, he blames him self in spekynge to hir
muses in the p^{er}sone of wisdam on this wise. Hadde 3e muses
with 3oure flateres withdrawe fro me any unkunynge and un [-]

355   p^{ro}fitable ma^n, as men be wount comu^{n}ly to fynde amonge the pe -
ple I wolde wel have suffrede it lasse grevously. ffor my wittis
and myn ententis in sweche on that hadde hem nou3t hadde
nothynge ben damaged. But this man that 3e wolde take fro
me, hath be norischede and brou3t up in scolis and studies of

360   eleaticis and of akademycis^{78} in greece. Akademe was the toun
that aristotillis maister plato leryd and tau3t his philisophie
inne. And Elys was another toun in the sweche florischede

---

75. illegible marginalia: to the right of lines 4 and 13, and between lines 5 and 6

76. expressing discontent; complaining

77. fruits

78. reference to Eleatics and Academics

specyaly the study of wisdam, and therefor it is ap^{ro}peryd[79] to Aris -
totil, because thenne, that thaise too were pryncis and pryn -

365 cipal of philisophies wisdam and comendynge of Bois excel -
lensis in the reherseile of thaise too studyes Eleaticis and A -
kademycis, sche makith him p^{ar}tyner of both here cunnynge.
And for his cunnynge sche puttes to him more blame, that
he schulde complaynely take his disese. || And ferthermore

370 thus blamefully, sche spekes unto the muses saynge þ^s.[80]
Go now away ȝe meremaydenes, that with ȝoure swetnes
brynges men to myscheveous deth, and suffre this man to
be curyd and helyd[81] with my muses. That is to mene, riȝt
as a meremayden that is a mysschapen thynge in the see.

−203 v[82]−

375 ffor the over p^{ar}t is like to a womma^n, and the nether p^{ar}t to a fisch, with
hire swete syngynge syttynge on a roche drawes schippis to wrak
and men to p^{er}rele[83] of drownynge, riȝt so do ȝe poetical muses, that
with delitable metres make sotil soules, to sette in hem here hevy -
nes and so drownes in sorewe. Goth therefore away, and suffre this

380 ma^n to helyd, with my muses that arn vertues and resouns of wis -
da^m, that are synguler cures and remedies to sweche. Thus tha^n
ne thaise poetical muses blamyd be wisdam, wrothly cast here
semblelande to the erthe. And there schame schewyd be redy -
nes of coloure. Thay passyd ferther over the threswalde. This

385 betokenes that Bois was aschamyd that he schulde be over -
come be any passioun, and not geve ententfully to wisdam.
And than Bois sais whos siȝt was drownyd in teres. ||
Was so dymmyd that I miȝt nout knowe what womma^n
that was so imp^{er}ial aucttorite. His siȝt of resoun and undur -

390 stondynge was drownyd in teres of sorewe and hevynes for
losse of worldely goode. And therefore he myȝt not knowe the
auctorite of wisdam. And therefore as astonyede he saith, I a -

---

79. assigned

80. thus

81. probably *to be helyd* is intended

82. illegible marginalia: to the left of lines 20 and 32 and between 22 and 23

83. peril

bode stille in silence and lokyd to the erthe. What ferthermo [-]
re sche wolde do, thanne come sche forth, and set hire upon
395   the uttermost corner of the bedde, wisdam comyth towarde ma^n
on foure wise. ffurst whanne he removes him fro alle charge
and cure that is unp^{ro}fitable and nedeles. The secunde wise
whanne a ma^n begynnes to have lekynge in wisdam. The
thridde. Whanne he is besily sought of whom a ma^n may lere
400   wisdam. And the fourte[.] Whanne a ma^n may take exercysce of
execucioun of wise werkis. || The bedde is a consience and
the vertuouse p^{ar}t, is the begynnynge and the prynciples of
wisdam, the weche be besy exercyse and encrese, wil come
nere to the mynde of the soule that is to p^{ro}fite knowleche and
405   love and werkynge thereof. Or elles thus. In the soule is
foure my3tes. Oon is callyd a kyndely my3t by the weche a
man hath fre kyndely power, to say a thynge, here it, or wirke
it. The secunde my3t, ables the soule to knowleche of thyn -

–204 r^{84}–

ges. Be the thridde my3t thynges that are passyd and so forth to
410   come, are fastnyd in the mynde, and be the fourte my3t, is the sou -
le mad possible to returne and calle agayne thynges forgetyn,
and in this p^{ar}t sat ph^{ilosoph}ie. And behaldynge my chere, that was
hevely cast unto erthe ful of sorewnes and wepynge. Sche co^m -
playnede the disturblelaunce of my thou3t, with thaise wor -
415   des that folewes. || Allas sche sais, now the thou3t of man
drownyth and ov^{er}thrawen with worldley besynes, dulles the
soule, and lettis it fro his own p^{ro}pir clernes, that is the bry3t [-]
nes of wisdam and of undurstandynge. And makes him to
go into outwarde derkenes of ignoraunce and unknowynge.
420   As ofte as noyful^{85} besynes waxes upon him withoute mesu [-]
re, the weche is drevyn to and fo, with wordley wyndes.
Here he callith noyful besynes, besynes aboute some passynge
thynges of the worlde. The weche whanne thay are wantyd,
and gendrys in a man paynful longynge aftur and desire, and
425   had gret yrkesomnes with drede of losynge of hem and hevy -
nes. And therefor thay are callyd noyful, the weche are drevy^n

---

84. illegible marginalia: to the right of lines 9 and 21 and between lines 7 and 8

85. annoying

to and fro, with worldley wyndes. Be thaise wyndes, sche
meenes the prosp^{er}yte and adversite of fortune, the weche ry3t
as a wynde blowith up ly3t thynges, and kast doun hevy. So
430   the p^{ro}sp^{er}ite of fortune blowith up folis and unwise me^n, unto
forgetynge of hem self, and hire adv^{er}site castith hem and drow -
nyth hem in care. || Thanne wisdom turnis hire specialy
to Bois schewynge furst, in what wisdom before he hadde ly [-]
vyde inne, aftur how temp^{or}al losse, hath distroublyd him fro
435   that wisdom. Thus thanne sche saith, this ma^n that sum^{m}e
tyme was free, that is to say, loos fro temp^{or}al cure. Whil he
was in floures of his p^{ro}sp^{er}ite, to whom hevene was opene
and knowen, and he wount forto go into hevenly pathes. ||
Hevene is callyd open to hem that thenkis on hevenley thyn -
440   ges, spekis of hem, or in goode lif goth to hemwarde, and to Bo -
is is callyd open for clernes of undurstondynge þ^t he hadde i^n he -
venely thynges, his goynge i^n to hevenly pathes, tokenys his be -

–204 v–

synes enserchynge of the course of the planetis of the movynge
of the firmament and of sternys,[86] of div^{er}s hyd vertuse and wir -
445   kynge of hevenely bodies has in the erthe benethe of the foure
elementis. ffyre, ayre, watur, and erthe, and of here p^{ro}purtis
and wurkyngis, of thaise forsayde Bois was wount to then -
ke, dispute, and wryte. fferthermore wisdom saith, that he
sawe the ly3tnes of the redde sonne, and the sterenes of the col -
450   de mone, that is to meene, he sawe the skyl[87] why the sonne schew -
es more rede in the morne and eve, thanne in the myddis of the
day. And he fonde this the cause, for as mekyl as in the myd -
de of the day he sendis forth his bry3t leemys[88] the weche dulles
the scharpe p^{er}sevynge of mannys sy3t, that he may not so p^{er} [-]
455   ce so p^{er}fytly unto the sonne, for excesse bry3tnes of his beemys
as he douth in morne and eve. Whanne the sonne sendis not
forth, but gaderes and kepis his owne bry3tnes, withinne hy^m
self, and he calles the sternes of the olde mone, the dwelly^{n}g

---

86. stars

87. reason

88. probably *beemys* is intended

460 place that the mone goth to in his movynge, and other sternes in hire speres, and he calles him calde, for he is nether to
the elementis watur and erth, thanne any other hevenely
body. And therefore he into his wirkynge takis more of the
colde of there kynde, thanne any other body above him. fferther -
more sche saith. That Bois sum^{me} tyme wist wel, what ster -
465 nes in hevene usyd wanderynge, courses, movynges, and retur -
nynges, be dyverse speres, the weche he ov^{er}come, hadde com -
prehendyd, be the countynge of astronomye, this is to mene,
that Bois wist wel that the firmanent, in the weche the ster -
nes that we se are festenyd, and thus for it is calde the sternye
470 of hevene Celu^m stellatu^m. Of his p^{ro}per kynde meves fro the west,
i^n to the est, taryinge him self fro the vyolent movynge that þ^e
hevene above him drawes aftur him fro the est the weche, mo -
bile or celu^m cristallu^m. || Hevene c^{ri}staline is called. In a hundreth
ȝere the space of sweche agre^{89} as thre hundreth and sixty co^{n}tenes^{90}
475 the sercle of hevene that in astronomye is called, ȝodiacus, and
so he wist that be noumbrynge of astronomye i^n multipliande

−205 r^{91}−

of ilke a degre of thre hundreth and sixty be a hundreth ȝere this fir -
mament forsayde be mevynge of him self eche a hundreth ȝere
a degre, fro the west into the est schulde in six and thritty thousa^n -
480 de ȝere sette himself, and other moveable bodies in the same sta -
te and degre that thay were inne. In here furst creacioun. || And
this space of six and thritty thousande ȝere, is callyd the grete
ȝere of the worlde, as witnes, affrican^{92} and tholome,^{93} too grete
auctors of astronomye. || Also he wist the kyndly movynge
485 of the sevene planetis, fro the west into the est, agayn the vyo -
lent movynge of the firmanent, he knew also be the nou^{m}bre
of countynge of astronomye, in what tyme thay fulfilde here

89. agrees

90. contains

91. illegible marginalia: to the right of line 4 and between lines 2 and 3, 11 and 12, and 12 and 13

92. Africanus

93. Ptolemy

course, that is to say, how saturne that is heyest of the seve -
ne fulfilles his course in o ȝere, and Iubit^{er} his course i^n xii ȝere, ma -
490   rs in too ȝere, the sonne in o ȝere. || Venus and mercurie almoste
ocupyes the space of the sonne, the mone in sixe and twenty
dayes and sixe houres. Wisdom ferthermore comendynge Bois
of natural ph^{ilosoph}ie saith, that he was wount to seke the causes
of the hote brennynge wyndes that steres[94] so movyndly the
495   smothe wat^{er} of the see, that is he wyst that the sonne be the
beemes of him, makes the erthe hote and dry, and drawes
to himward drye vapours of the erthe, and lyftes hem up to
a colde place of the ayre callyd in ph^{ilosoph}ie, mediu^m instertiau^m aeris.
And for the drynes of there vapours is contraryous to the kyn -
500   dely moystnes of the ayre, therefore thare fallith a distourbela^n
ce i^n ayre, sweche as is callyd blastes. Also wisdom saith, that
Bois was wount to encerche what spirit turnyd the stable he -
vene, as who say, he wist wel that þ^t spirit was not a soule
of the worlde as sum^{m}e philisophes seynede. But it was the
505   myȝtty wil of the maker. Also sche saith, sche[95] was wount
to wite why the sterne ras ouȝt of the est and falles doun in
the west. || And what temp^{er}s the lusty wederis[96] of ver.[97]
The wheche is the furst som^{er} sesoun that ourneth[98] the erthe
w^t floures of roses, as who say he wist because it is mee -
510   ne betwixe the caldist tyme of wynt^{er} and hattist of som^{er}

–205 v[99]–

begynnynge i^n the tent day that ouȝt passynge of marche, and las -
tande unto thre and twenty day of the monouth of Iune. In the
weche space the tyme is merye wyndes blowen soberly. Snow -
es relentis, moysture ryses fro rotes unto braunches of trees,
515   cornes waxes, medewes ar grene. Bestes are gendryd, and all
thynge is best disposyd. ffor thay may not be hyndryd be over -

---

94. steers

95. probably *he* is intended

96. weathers

97. [*the*] *vernal* [*season*]

98. turns

99. illegible marginalia: to the left, between lines 17 and 18

meche colde because of hotnes of som^{er} that is comynge. ||
Ne w^t ov^{er} meche hete because of coldenes of wynt^{er} that is but
late past. And therefore in that tyme is alle thynge sette i^n the

520   best meene. Also sche sais, he knew who makes autumpne i^n
sale[100] ʒeris to flowe ful of hony grapis, autumpne, is tyme of
ʒere that begynnes at the foure and twenty day of Septembre,
and lastes unto the to and twenty day of Decembre. In that ty -
me comu^{n}ly vynes ar ful of grapis þ^t ar gaderyd. Also sche saiþ

525   he was wount to telle of dyv^{er}se causis that were hydde i^n kyn -
de, that is now, how p^{ri}vely kynde werkis dyversly i^n sondry thy^n -
ges, and thanne wisdom co^{n}cludis pleynyngly hou fre so grete
wisdom.[101] ffor he cannot bere losse to temp^{or}al welth, he has lost
his chere, & thus sche mournes for his unwit. Allas now sche

530   saith, he is p^{ri}vyd[102] the lyʒt of sweche thouʒt that is co^{n}templaci -
oun of wisdom and liʒtnes his soule, and he hath his necke
threste doun w^t hevy cheynes. That is w^t the movynge of his
fleschly affeccioun. He beris his chere bowed dounwarde, that is
his love to erthly thynges, that he has lost, and for grete vyce he

535   is co^{n}strayned to loke doun to the erthe, that is for losse of worldly
goode, he is constrayned to loke to the foltes[103] erthe, that is to the^n -
ke on his losse, the weche marres him and makes him foltise[104]
i^n his wit. Sʒ mediane &[105] thanne a wise ma^n a wise p^{er}son that
wil not longe tarye i^n plenynge, sche ordeynede to him remedy

540   for his disese, and lokyd upon him w^t al hire eyn, of ful cum -
fortede agayne his sorewe, sayinge, art þ^u not he, q^{uo}d sche, þ^t was
norischede and brouʒt up w^t my mylke, fed w^t my metis, and

---

100. probably *fale* or *full* is intended; perhaps scribe has mistakenly transcribed an *f* as an *s*

101. precise nature of Wisdom's complaint is obscure in this passage; she seems to object to the manner in which Boethius has greeted her

102. deprived of

103. foolish

104. faulty

105. this passage contains obscure symbols and irreconcilable words (for example, *mediane* seems to refer to Philosophy's medicine); parallel passage in Chaucer's *Boece* (1 pr. 2: "'But tyme is now,' quod sche, 'of medicyne more than of compleynte.' Forsothe thanne sche, entendynge to meward with al the lookynge of hir eien, seyde: 'Art nat thou he,' / quod sche, 'that whilom, norisshed with my melk and fostred with myne metes, were escaped and comyn to corage of a parfit man?'")

throwe hem come to þe[106] corage of a p[er]fyte ma[n]. || Thus wisdo[m]
askis of Bois, forto styre his soule to coumfort, and sche calles

o—o—o—o—o—o
| hire mylke[107] |
o—o—o—o—o—o

−206 r[108]−

545   hire mylke, the techynge that he hadde, whanne he began to bere
with here, and hire fode or metis sche callith his p[ro]fyte in hire scole
and be curage of ma[n] his p[er]fytenes in al hire scyence. And thanne
sche sais, I gaf the sweche armours, the weche if thou had not
kast away, thay schulde have defendede the, puttynge the i[n] sekir -
550   nes that may not be ov[er]come. Sche calles hire vertue and the
p[er]fyte knowleche of hevenly thynges and of erthly w[t] drede of
god and knowynge of sothfastnes the armours of wisdom the
weche forsakis nevere a ma[n]. Or a ma[n] have forsaken ham, if thay
be kept, thay suffre nev[er]e a ma[n] to be ov[er]come, with any worldly adv[er] -
555   site. || And for he helde him stille, and gaf not answere sche than -
ne saide, knowist þ[u] me nou3t. Why art þ[u] so stille. Is it for scha -
me or for stonyenge and wondrynge, I hadde lever sche saith it
were for schame. But me semes that wond[er] has oppressid the.
Sche had levere he held his pes for schame thanne for stonye[n]
560   ge of hire wordes, for thanne that wolde seme, that he coude a[n]
swere if he wolde. And whanne sche saw me not aloonly stil -
le, but as it were w[t]oute tounge al doumbe, sche put sofly
hire hande to my brest and felde me. Here sche dide the maner
of a leche, that by touche asaith, if the seke be curable. Here
565   is no p[er]ele[109] sche saide. In sekenes, is dispaire of herle[110] p[er]ele of
hevynes is dispaire of coumfort. He is quod sche fallen i[n]to li -

---

106. scribe has not superscripted the *e* in the manuscript

107. note occurs: middle of the bottom margin; follows after usual thirty-four lines of text;
probably in the hand of the scribe who produced the text; framed as shown here with dashes
alternating with small circles; two such notes occur manuscript, each features the two words
that begin the text on the succeeding page; probably not inscribed as reader's prompts

108. lower right corner of this page: "B.M." appears in a later hand

109. peril

110. word *herle* makes no sense here; perhaps *herte*[,] is intended, or *healing*[,]

targe the weche is a comu^n sekenes, to hertis that are dissay -
ved. Sche calles litargye, sekenes of forgetilnes i^n his dise -
se of olde wisdoms. || In tokene thereof sche saith ano^n, he
570   has a litil forgetyn him self, but he schal li3thly remembre
him if he have know me or[111] now. A ma^n hath too substau^{n}ces
body and soule, the dedly body and undedly soule the te^{m}p^{or}al
welth of the dedly flesch as Bois had tho, truly he had sum [-]
what forgetyn him self, but w^t remembraunce of the diffe -
575   rence of the soule, fro the body he is curable. And therefore
wisdom saith, that he may so do, I wile wipe his eyn ali -
te the weche are derkened be the cloude of mortale and ded -
ly thynges. And whanne sche has sayd thaise wordes sche

–206 v–

dryed my eyen ful of wepynges w^t the lappe of hire garnement
580   plityd toged^{er}. The plityd lappe of hire garneme^{n}t is curiouses sen -
tenses and many taken of dyv^{er}se science of wisdom, w^t the weche
sche wipes away the cloudy derkenes of the undurstandynge
of mannes soule, dullyd w^t any unresonable worldly hevy -
nes, and that witnesses Bois in the next metre.
585   [T]   hus thanne saith Bois, aft^{er} that Wisdom had wipid my
lites, the weche are my resoun and my resonable wille,
thanne the derkenes of ignoraunce I unkunnynge left & forso -
ke me. This ignoraunce Bois calles a ny3t that cloudis a ma^{n} -
nes undurstondynge. But that ny3t discussed thorw the infor -
590   macioun of Wisdom, the strengthe of knowleche wille sone
come agayne to the spiral ly3tes beforesaide of a man^{n}es sou -
le, and this is p^{ro}vyd folewyngly be ensample, for ri3t as wha^n
the sonne is hydde, and sternes are coverede w^t cloudes thorw
blowynge of a wynde. That is a syde wynde callyd choras &
595   the firmame^{n}t standes derke, be watry cloudes so that the ster -
nes apperen not on hevene, thanne semes the ny3t spradde
up on erthe. || In this ensample is wisdom lekenyde to
to[112] the sonne. ffor as be absence of the sonne the ayre is derke
and the worlde hath no ly3t, ri3t so be absence of wisdom, the

111. before; probable erasure under the letter *r* indicates character perhaps originally
transcribed mistakenly as *3*

112. *sic*

600   lesse worlde, that is a ma^n is derke in his undurstondynge.
       Riȝt as this absence and hidynge of sonne is caused be the
       reyny side wynde callyd chorus, the weche makes cloudes
       before the sonne. On the same wise a man^{n}es resoun and
       his undurstondynge is derkyd be worldely adv^{er}site. That
605   settes before hem the cloudes of sorewe and hevynese for temp^{or} [-]
       al losse. But this maner of hidnes of the sonne it is nouȝt
       kyndely to hit. Ne sweche maner of hevynes to the soule is
       not kyndely but viciouse, hit is p^{ro}fitable to a ma^n to have swe -
       che man^{er} of cloudes removyd away, and how that may be,
610   schewes Bois be ensample sayande, that if the wynde that
       hiȝt Borias, the weche is contr^{ar}youse to the wynde sayde be -
       fore Chorus, be sent out of the cavernys fro the cu^{n}tre of Trace,

−207 r^{113}−

       it wile bete the nyȝt and chase it away and discovere the day, thanne
       schynes phebȝ with a soden lyȝt, that is the forsaide sonne and eyn of
615   men merveles he smytes so w^t his bemys. Be ph^{ilosoph}ie natural there is
       sum^{m}e wyndes that gadres cloudes and sum^{m}e that brekis and dis -
       parilys hem, Chorus is oon of the furst, Boreas oon of the secu^{n}de.
       Boreas sent ouȝt of the kav^{er}nes fro the cuntres of trace. It is a ma^n
       nes reme^{m}braunce of his begynnynge and of his ende. This schul -
620   de breke and disparel the cloudes of myscoumfort, for any te^{m}p^{or}al
       disese, this schal make the sonne to schyne, that is to put his sou -
       le in coumfort thorow clere knowleche that he may not come to
       a blisful ende, but by a payneful mene. ffor be witnes of apos -
       til. Be the menes of tribulacioun it is nede to entre i^n to the
625   kyngdom of hevene. And this tauȝt crist i^n dede. It nedid crist
       to suffre, and so to entre hevene. Remembraunce thanne that
       abidynge blis may not be geten but be sweche sufferaunce
       schulde put away the cloude of sorewe and of hevynes and
       make Phebȝ to sende forth his beemys, that is with wisdo^m
630   to take it so gladely and coumfortably that men^{n}es eyn may
       m^{er}veyle of it. ffor riȝt as it is m^{er}veyle i^n kynde, how eftur so
       depe a derkenes of the nyȝt, there folewith sodeynly a sely^{114}
       briȝtnes, so it is m^{er}veyle i^n p^{er}sevynge of ma^n. How aft^{er} mater

---

113. lower right corner of this page: "B.M." appears in a later hand
114. innocent

of so gret hevynes a man thorow wit and wisdom may sone
635   falle to coumfort and gladnes, how that Bois did that and
on what wise it is scheweyd for thus he saith. || The
cloudes of my sorowe and hevynes dissolvyd so and on non
othur wise I toke hevyn and receyvede mynde to knowe þe[115]
vysage of my leche and of my phisician. Here by he mee -
640   nes playnly, that he my3t not have hevyn that was his
ende or elles of hevenly thynges, but he suffrede matere
of disese that was his exile and losse of temporal welth.
And therefor he saith 3it the cloudes of sorowe and hevy -
nes was brokyn and put away. And so on no nother -
645   wise he toke hevene and knew the vysage of his phisician.
The vysage of wisdom is love of goodnes and knowyng

–207 v–

of sothfastnes, ffor as a man is know be his face, so wisdomes is knowe
in a man be thaise too. And of the knowynge of this face, I led my eyn
to hirewarde he sais and lokyd fast on hire. And I behelde my no -
650   risch philosophie in whos houses I was brou3t up fro my 3outhe. || This
meenes whanne Bois turnyd frowarde sorowe to love of god &
knowynge, he sawe be propir skil, that sorowe was but foly, and
therefore he turnyd preseneantly unto Wisdom. And that betoke -
nyd his fast lokynge on hire. Whanne he callyd his norisch for
655   sche brou3t hym forth wt litil techynge. And therefor covetyn -
ge for to have a new homlynes he begynnes his tretynge wt
hire wt this questioun. O thou maistres of alle vertues, that art
comen doun fro thy sodeyn sete.[116] Why art thou come fro thy[117] solitarie
place of my exile, art thou ought made gilty wt me of any fals
660   trespace. || Here Bois knowleches himself innocently ponysch
and for mekil as in himself he leris be experience that the innocen -
tly goodnes of wisdom is alday giltyd and fylid[118] be the envyou -
se malice of hem that have it nou3t. He specyd[119] this questioun

---

115. scribe has not superscripted the *e* in the manuscript

116. parallel passage in Chaucer's *Boece* reads *sovereune sete*

117. probably *fro thy* should be read as *to my*

118. defiled

119. spoke

to the weche sche coumfortably answerith. O thou my norie[120] schul -

665 de I forsake the now, and not be p^{ar}t betwene us too in comune
travaile, the hevy charge of disese. The weche for envye of my
name thou hast suffrede. Here is schewed the gentryse[121] of wisdo^{m},
that leves not him that sche brou3t up, but wil have disese w^{t}
him i^{n} comu^{n}, and so li3ten him of his hevy charge, and therefor

670 sche saith ano^{n}, that it were not sittynge[122] ne leveful to ph^{ilosoph}ie to
leve the way of him w^{t}oute cu^{m}panye that is a innoce^{n} t. And
therefore philisophes thorow no^{n} other beleve. But of love of
goodnes v^{er}tues and knowleche of truthe, thay mythly[123] gladly
& w^{t}oute disese of herte sufffrede, som exile, som deth, som pri -

675 soun, som turme^{n}trye, and som othir. So that here Wisdom
dischargede hem of alle here hertly grunchynge and therefore
Wisdom saith. Schulde I, sche saith be aschamyd of blame in -
nocently put up on me, as a new thynge were fallen, as who
say it is in custu^{m} ev^{er}e wisdom to be pursevede of folye and so

680 sche saith, triste þ^{u} nou3t ph^{ilosoph}ie be now o fust assayled i^{n} piles[124] be

–208 r[125]–

folk of evyl maners and foly levynge, have I stryve^{n} sche saith w^{t}
ful gret stryf, i^{n} olde tyme before the age of my plato agayn the fol -
hardynes[126] of foly. And in tyme of lyf of the same plato socrates
his maister hadde victorie of unri3tful dede, in my owne plesence.[127]

685 || Here ph^{ilosoph}ie curtesly in purpose to coumfort Bois telles, how
sche has in custu^{m} to be in felawschipe in^{n}ocent suffres. And sche
saith sche straf ful sore in olde tyme before hire owne plato
tyme agayn foly.[128] And sche saw hire owne Socrates slayn in

---

120. nourisher

121. nobility

122. suitable

123. mightily

124. probably *periles* is intended, although no abbreviation indicated in the manuscript

125. lower right corner of this page: "B.M." appears in a later hand

126. foolhardiness

127. probably *presence* was intended

128. before her own Plato's time against folly

hire owne p^{re}sence. And that was as clerkis telles be a fals acu -
690   sacioun of his owne discipline, the weche acusyd him. ffor he
made a boke of o god, and not of many goddis. Therefore he
was mad to drynke poisoun in the name of that o god, and
he kept him fro deth. Thanne he made him drynke i^n the na -
me of many goddis. And thanne he dyede poysounde. And for
695   he dyede on that wise innocent. Sche callyd him victor of
deth. But it may be askyd. Why ph^{ilosoph}ie calles plato, my plato,
to the weche it may be answerde. As it is said before in the
garnement of ph^{ilosoph}ie were too letteres ˙P˙ and ˙T˙ practyf and
speculatyf, or actyf and co^{n}templatyf. Sum^{m}e philisophre red -
700   de the first lettre, but not the secunde. As Socrates dede plato his
maist^{er} tau3t hou a ma^n schulde his levynge be vertues wirky^n -
ge. Sum^{m}e redde the secunde and not the first, as dede Puta -
goras that tau3t hou a ma^n schulde ex^{er}cise his wittes i^n stody &
encres his kun^{n}ynge. But plato p^{er}fitely redde hem bothe, for
705   in his tretynges he dep^{ar}tes ph^{ilosoph}ie into thre p^{ar}tes Ethyk Phe [-]
syk and Logyk. Ethyk telles how a ma^n may be vertues in
wirkynge. Phesyk teches a ma^n to contemplatyf in know -
ynge be kyndely wit and undurstandynge. And Logyk teches
a ma^n in truthe fro falshede to have a resonable demynge. ||
710   And therefore sche calles my plato. Also thaise othur phili -
sophres in here tretynges passyd not creatures, that is rechid
not up in here wittes to the maker of alle. And thay wann -
tyd the pryncipal p^{ar}t of wisdom. ffor plato over ham spak
of godhede, as it is playnly schewede in his boke Times[129]

−208 v−

715   placens,[130] were[131] he arettis plainly to the my3t of the godhede, ma -
kynge of alle thynge, to the my3t of the godhede ordre and set -
tynge of alle thynges, to the goodnes of god, the ende of alle
thynge, he calles him rewarde of al that triste^n in him and
worschepe him, and many other p^{ri}vytes of holy wrytte
720   he tretis in that boke, and other as it is sayde in the seve -

---

129. *Timeus*

130. no meaning can be assigned to this word

131. where

nete[132] boke of policraticon the capitre and the hiest myst^{er}y
of oure faith, the weche comp^{re}hendis alle wisdom made
and unmade, bothe of god and of creatures. The weche
Ion eva^{n}gelist soke of the brest of veray wisdom of the Fa -

725   dur of hevene that is. || In principio erat v^{er}bum, was
founden in his bokes unto a certyayn place. Sum^{me} sayn
to that place, Et lux i^{n} tenebris lucet. Sum^{me} sayn to that
place, v^{er}bum caro f^{a}c^{tu}m est.[133] And therefore of alle philisophirs
that acordynge Wisdom callith him hire owne plato, whos

730   heritage sche saith of Socrates that is his doctrine in o -
pynyoun of felicite. Whanne the peple epicuriens and
stoiciens and many other, put hemself to ylke of tham
to have it be raven for his p^{ar}t, this is to say, that ylke of
hem wolde drawe to defence of his opynyoun to the last

735   wethfulnes[134] callyd felicite. The wordes of soc^{ra}tes thanne
for I cryede and debatyd agaynes hem, thay raf and alto[135]
drowe my clothes, the weche I hadde wouven w^{t} my
handis, and with the cloutes that thay hadde ravyd out
of my clothes, thay went away wenynge that I hadde

740   altogedur gon with hem. || ffor the undurstondyng
of this is to wete, that soc^{ra}tes maister unto many wise
philisophres purposyd sweche a sentence. Voluptas est
sum^{m}u^{m} bonu^{m}. That is lust is the sov^{er}en gode. And aftur
fel that there was too sectes of philisophres [,] oon was

745   callyd Epicuriens folewers in lerynge of a ma^{n} callyd E -
picure, that was before discipline unto soc^{ra}tes. The secu^{n}
de were callyd stoiciens whos maist^{er} was sevene phili -
sophres, also disciple unto soct^{ra}tes, the toon maner[136] of

−209 r[137]−

philisophre harde the sentence of that saide before. And Epicu -

---

132. seventh

133. Latin quotations from the first chapter of St. John's Gospel, verses 1, 5, and 14

134. perhaps *we[l]thfulnes* was intended

135. also

136. the one school [the Stoics]

137. lower right corner of this page: "B.M." appears in a later hand

750   riens saide that soc^ra^tes undurstode that bodily lust that standis
in fleschly lekynge is the sov^er^en gode that stoicie^n^s saide that
soc^ra^tes ment of the lust, of the undedly soule, the weche he
weche he[138] saith is hadde whenne the soule withoute any dis -
turbelaunce is in gladnes and quyete. Thus eche of thaise

755   wolde ravysche the doctrine of soc^ra^tes to his p^ar^t. And so thorw he -
re cont^ra^riousenes thay tare my clothes, and eche of hem wend
fully I hadde ben with hem, as who saye thay hadde me not.
Natheles because that sum^me^e semyd som^me^e traces and step -
pes of my abyte[139] in the Epicuriens and stociens, the foly of

760   men supposynge that thay hadde be familyar with me, tho -
row the errour of the wickede and unkunnynge multitude
of hem pursued ham, that is to say, for thay semyd wise
philisophres, thay were pursuede unto the deth and slayn.
|| And if thou have not knowen the the[140] exilynge of Anaxa -

765   gor[141] ne impoysnynge of soc^ra^tes, ne turmentis of ʒeno,
ffor in case thou haldist hem straungers, thou myʒt knowe
the Senycye^n^s[142] the Canyous[143] and the sorancis[144] of whom the
myndes[145] nother halde[146] ne unsolempte.[147] ffirst ph^ilosoph^ie calles Anax -
agor the weche for wisdom was exiled out of his owne cun -

770   tre. And soc^ra^tes and ʒeno straungers unto Bois, because tha -
y were grekis and he a Latyn ma^n^. But the tothir[148] there that
sche brynges in coumfort to Bois, were of the birthe of
Rome and hadde mekil of wisdom. And therefore thay were
gretly pursuede unto the deth. And as ph^ilosoph^ie anon aft^er^ saith,

775   there was nothynge elles that brouʒt hem unto deth but

---

138. *sic*

139. habit; clothing

140. *sic*

141. Anaxagoras

142. Seneca

143. Canius

144. Soranus

145. memories [are]

146. old

147. uncelebrated

148. the other school [the Epicureans]

oonly for thay were enformyde of the maners of hire, &
were most unlike to the studyes offe wickyd me^n, as Bois
saith, þ^u schilde not m^{er}veyle ne wondre though the bitt^{er}
see of this lif, dryve me with tempestes blowynge abou -
780   te, as who say, thynges that hath ay ben usede schulde
nou3t be m^{er}veylede, as goode men to suffre of schrewes.
ffor as the see, that he receyves castith it to and fro and ma -

–209 v–

kes the hyest p^{ar}t of it lowist and agaynward. So in the worldely
varyaunce, now lowe thynges are hyede, and hye thynges are lowyd.
785   And he telles the cause, why goode me^n are lowyd with schrewes.
ffor the p^{ur}pose of wisdom in hem is and a wise to be ay to dysple -
se wickede men.[149] ffor wisdom lovys his lyke, and hatys his con -
trarye. The weche wickede men be there nevere so many, thay are
to dispice, for thay are not ledde ne governyd be resoun. But with
790   errour foly and flytynge. And if thay sche saith sum^{m}e tyme or -
deyne an ofte[150] agaynes us. That semyth strenger thanne we,
thanne oure ledere schal drawe to gedere his riches into his toure.
|| The leder of wisdom is callyd here resoun, his tour is contempla -
cioun of god and of hevenly thynges, the riches that schal be
795   brou3t thereto, is the thou3tes of the soule with mynde love &
knowleche. Thanne lat alle worldely adversites ordeyn evyl
men on the strangist wise agayn sweche a man. Thay schal
not disese him. ffor as wisdom saith, thanne thay are ocupy -
ede for to distroye unprofitable sechelse.[151] And thanne we that we
800   are aboven sekurly closyd in sweche a palays, fro here woodnes,
for it is not lefful to sweche chaterynge foly to come, we do
but skorne sweche raveners and hounters of the foulyste
thynges. ffor a man sette in the heghte of wisdom con -
templacioun of god and hevenly thynges closyd therein w^t
805   even and o lyke takynge of all worldely prosp^{er}ite and adv^{er}sy -
te all sensuale movynges in a man to the contrarye, whos
sterynges are callyde here chaterynges, foly and unp^{ro}fitable ra -

149. perhaps something omitted in scribe's transcription of this sentence

150. a host

151. satchels

venes, that wolde spoyle fro a ma^n vertue, and clernes of kno -
wleche, and other wise dulle him in dysese. Or kast him on
810   loft above knowynge of himself, schal sone be lytel set
by, and with the roprove[152] of skorne schamefully put abak.
And he sadly schal abyde in the forsaide toure as a victour.
Therefore it folewes in the next metre on this wise, he that
is clere of vertue, sadde and wel ordeynede in his levynge
815   that can put undur fote destenyes and werdis,[153] and loke
up o lyke ov^{er} other fortune, he that may halde his chere undis -

–210 r–

coumfyted. Before is schewed how p^{er}secuciouns that foly doth
to wisdom, sensualite to resoun, and worldely adversite to ma^n -
nys soule schal not be dredde. || Here begynnes sche to schew -
820   not the maistry, in the weche lessoun p^{er}secuciou^{n}s are lekene -
de the wode see to brennynge fyre and to wastynge leveny^n -
ge[154] aftur holy wri3t evyl lyvers other[155] thay are lechoures, &
thenne thay are undurstonde be the wodenes of the see, or tha -
825   y are covetous that is undurstandynge be the brenny^{n}ge
fire, or proude, that is undurstonde be the wastynge leveny^n [-]
ge. Also all p^{er}secuciou^{n}s are gendryde other of envye undur -
standynge be the wodenes of the see. That contynuly destro -
ies the londe that lyth aboute it, or of wrecche and malyn -
830   coly undurstondynge be brestynge ou3t of the fire ou3t of þ^e
mount vesave,[156] or elles of pryde, undurstandynge be was
tynge of levenynge. Or elles thus al dysese that comes to a
man, othir it comyth be wordes, undurstondynge be the
wodenes of the see, for his soundynge or elles of bodely
835   hurtynge, undurstonde be the fire for his wirkynge. Or el -
les be takynge away of temp^{or}al possessioun, undurstounde
be the levenynge for his wastynge. But thanne saith
ph^{ilosoph}ie, if a man be clere in vertue, sadde and wel u^{n}durston -

---

152. reproof

153. destinies and wyrds

154. living

155. either

156. Vesuvius

de in his levynge, that can put undur fote the proude

840 werdis and loke o lyke on othir fortune. That is in the
same degree take adv^{er}site and prosp^{er}ite. Thanne schalt þ^{u}
holde the clere undyscoumfyted and sche telles, for nother
thenne the manas,[157] ne the wodenes that kestes up heete
fro the grounde of the see . Be weche as I sayde is undur -

845 stondyn the p^{er}secuciou^{n}s of unclene and lecherous levers.
Or that comes to a man be envye, or malyncoly of wordes.
Ne the unstable mountayne that hyght vesavus, the we -
che out of his brokyn chynnes[158] sendes smokynge fyres.
Be weche is undurstonde p^{er}secuciou^{n}s caused of covetyse,

850 or of the fire of ire, and hridde[159] rancoure of herte of dedely

–210 v–

hurte. Ne the way of thoundris li3t the weche is wount to smyte
hie[160] toures adoun. That is p^{er}secucyou^{n}s caused of p^{ri}de and of prou -
de men, weche be raveyne castith doun many that were hye be
ryches. None of thaise sche saith schal styre or move sweche

855 a ma^{n}. ‖ Here it is to wyte that the forsayde hyl, vesavus, is an
hyl of ynde[161] full of fire. Sum^{me} tyme brennynge inwarde and not
p^{er}seyvyd ou3twarde, sum^{me} tyme he brestith ou3t at finale creves -
ses and sendis ou3t a gret flame of fire that brennyth al the pla [-]
ce aboute it. Aftur this wisdom and ph^{ilosoph}ie schewes playnly,

860 that because that power of grete men of erthe extendis no ferther
but other to gene worldely goode, or ellis to take it away. The -
refore he that rekkenys not to have or to lose, he schulde drede
non erthely power. ffor on no wyse he may be dysesed be hit.
And therefore he callyth hem wrecches that other for to have good

865 or elles for drede of losse of goode frely soiectes[162] hemself, unto er -
thely power, and if thay be afturwarde dysesyd thay schole not

---

157. menace

158. chimneys

159. horrid

160. high

161. *sic*

162. subjects

merveyle, for here owne fre and subieccyoun[163] geve to the toþ[164]
power. And who so with whakyng dredyth losse, or defycet
any thynge that is not stabyl of itself, that man hath cast
870   away his schelde, that is evenly takynge of fortune. And
therefore he is removyd fro his place, that is restful contem -
placyoun of wysdom. And he hath suffred hymself frely to
be bounden with a chayne, that is with foure fleschly affeccyou[n]s,
Gladnes, Wreccche, Hope, and drede, be weche he hath abylded[165] hy[m]
875   to be drawen into sorewe and hevynes of soule. ffor al this ȝit
lay Bois and sobbyd in his sorewe, and that felyd ph[ilosoph]ie and
blamyngly sayde, felyst thou not quod sche thayse thynges
ne entur thay not into thy soule, art þ[u] quod sche lyke an
asse, that herys the sounde of a herpe, and conceyves no melo [-]
880   dye thereof. ffor þ[u] herys so my delectable wordes and takest
no coumfort of hem. Why wepest þ[u], why flowest þ[u] out in
teres, if þ[u] abyde aftur a leche, telle and dyscovere thy sekenes.
Thus thanne Bois movyd be ph[ilosoph]ie to telle his dysese as
he sayth, he gadryd togedre his strenghe. And as it schal be

–211 r[166]–

885   schewede be signes. ffyve causes of his wepynge and his greves.
ffurste for he that oryble[167] place of prysun that he was in thenkynge
on himself, that he hadde nevere dyscervyd[168] sweche payne but p[ro]fy -
table rewarde. The secunde skyl of his wepynge was for his cau -
se that he was prysounde. ffor whos[169] thankeful vertuouse riȝt
890   wyse, and hadde not deservyd payne. The thrydde cause of his we -
pynge was, for he was convycte be sweche vycyouse p[er]sones,
as be ryȝt and lawe schulde nother acuse ne bere wytnes. The
fourte cause was, for the iugge was so unryȝtful, that he wolde
dampne him wythoute cause lawfully p[ro]vyd. And the fyfte

163. subjection

164. ther [to those who hold power over them]

165. abled

166. marginalia to the left of this upper case *N*; written in later hand; possibly an initial *I*

167. horrible

168. deserved

169. who was

895   cause was, that the peple schulde be so frendeful of the tyraunt
        to suffre innocencry in his p^{ri}sone to be fyled[170] and gylted.[171] And tha^n -
        ne he complaynes of god that schulde suffre it. || Thus than -
        ne furst he sayth unto ph^{ilosoph}ie. What nedis it to reherce or schewe
        the, more of my dysese the scharpnes of woode fortune, that wex -
900   is agaynes me, schewes not the self opynly ynow. Art thou
        not movyd to see the face, or the maner of this p^{er}sone, and this
        place. Was this the lyberarye that is. Was this foule p^{ri}soune
        that hous of wysdom, that þ^u sum^{m}e tyme ches for thyself, and
        disputyd ofte with me of the scyence of thynges, that touches
905   godhede and creatures. Was thanne my abyte[172] sweche as it is
        now. Was my face or my chere sweche as it is now, whanne I
        saw with the Socrates of kynde. And þ^u enformyd al my lyf be
        ensample of the ordre of hevene. And thanne he concludys ster -
        nefully. (Is[173] this the rewarde and the warysoun,[174] þ^u geves me
910   N this speche be forme Bois makis || for my servyce.
        his rehersel in p^{ri}sone of grete welthy men of the worlde that)
        are fallen to unwelthynes concludynge in sentence of his spe -
        che of alle degres of welthynes, that there is no disese so me -
        kyl, as forto have be in gret ease, and now be nouȝt. And so Bois
915   of that he hath ben inne, he complaynes his disese the weche
        now he is inne & wantynge of it. And for that, he saith be co -
        mune speche may be understonde savynge that clause, hou
        man is enformyd by ensample of ordre of hevene. ffor to knowe

–211 v–

        how, that it is to wyte that be hevene he undurstondes alle the mekyl
920   worlde. As made be ensample of the more worlde. In weche lyckenes

---

170. defiled

171. rendered guilty

172. habit; clothing

173. proper word order for this passage: "Is this the rewarde and the warysoun þ^u geves me
/ for my servyce. / In this speche be forme Bois makis his rehersel in prisone of grete welthy
men of the worlde that. . . ."; confused word order results from scribe's practice of leaving
indentation for the ornate initials; scribe has placed the words of what would be a short
preceding line at the end of the following indented line; however, here scribe has failed to
indent, evidenced by presence of an *N* that should be preceded by an initial *I;* margin to the
left: missing initial letter appears in a later hand

174. wealth; possessions

in mannes p^{er}sone his hevyd is, as it were hevene heyest. ffor ry3t
as in hevene god in thre p^{er}sones is as governowre above alle crea -
tures. So in the hevyd is the resonable soule in thre my3this.[175]
Mynde, wille, and undurstondynge, to governe alle the lower

925   p^{ar}tes. The firmament in mannes p^{er}sone is his vysage, the too
grete li3ttys of hevene, sonne and mone is in mannys p^{er}sone,
his too eyn. The ri3t as the sonne, the lefte eye as the mone.
The sternys of hevene in a mannys p^{er}sone, is the inwarde wi3ttis
of a mannys brayn, that are callyd in ph^{ilosoph}ie the comu^n witte, fan -

930   tasye, ymaginacyoun, estimacyoun, and mynde. || To the weche
fyve inwarde wittis, the fyve outewarde wittis arn as it were ha^n -
demaydenys[176] and servauntis. The li3t of hevene is the u^{n}durston -
dynge of a mannys soule, and the planetis is the affecciouns
of the soule. Ioye and wrecche, hope, and drede. The element of

935   fire is a mannys stomak, to sethe his metis. The eyre[177] is i^n the
brest, and as in the eyre are sum^{m}e tyme derke cloudes, sum^{m}e ty -
me cler. So in a mannys brest is sum^{m}e tyme hevynes, sum^{m}e
tyme gladnes. Watur is in the bely, and erthe in the fette,[178] and
also as it is p^{ro}vyd be the sotilte[179] of astronomye. But if the swift

940   movynge of planetis were restrayned, be the contraryous movy^n -
ge of the firmament above, thynges benethe, that takes here
influence schulde be ravyschede with hem out of here kynde, and
so thorw swift movynges of the sonne, we schulde nother ha -
ve abidynge day ne ni3t. Ri3t on the same wise, the passiou -

945   nys of mannys soule, that are callyd the fyve fleschly affec -
ciouns, were thay not restraynede, be the gostly vesage of ma^n,
that is the firmament of resoun. Thay schulde move man to
many unresonable desires, and ravysche to here condicioun
alle the vertues of a mannys soule. This may be callyd the

950   ordre of hevene. That Bois saith, wisdom hadde enfurmyd
him aftur. || fferthermore he reherces hou he was servysable
unto wisdom. Certes he saith thou enfurmyd this sentence be

---

175. powers

176. handmaids

177. air

178. feet

179. subtlety

–212 r–

the mouthe of plato, that blessed is that comu^{n}ite were[180] the governow -
res are wise men, or elles besy to stody aftur wisdom. ffor gover -
955   nowres schulde be as the sonne, or the mone in vertuouse bri3t -
nes, more to comu^n p^{ro}fyte thanne to singuler, and that thay may
not have withoute wisdom, the weche may be knowen in he^m
be thaise tokenys. If thay excuted lawfully ri3twisnes, if thay
stere soiectes[181] to ouyde in saule[182] in truthe eche of hem to other
960   and sothfastnes. If thay demene[183] hem with wise counselis. If
thay ensample honest lif of vertues and goodnes. And if thay
have in al this a wille set and groundyd menynge. And Bois
reherces, that wisdom saith be the mouth of the same plato,
that it was necessarye to sweche wise men, to take governaun [-]
965   ce of comu^n thynges. That the governayle of comu^n Cytees we -
re not left in the handis of man sleers and evyl men. The
wheche wolde brynge in pestelence and distruccioun to goode
fook. Sethyn thanne philisophres alonly steryd be kyndely
resoun, tau3t thus men endewyd[184] with with[185] wisdom, not al -
970   only to leve ham self, but also tyl other. || Meche more
we schulde leve vertuesly to other, that arn within the bryd -
des of cristes be leve, knowande be faith oure rewarde. There -
fore saith Bois, that he folewynge the worde of plato, desy -
ryd to put forth tho[186] thynges in execucioun in comoun admin -
975   instracioun that he hadde leryd of wisdom, in his pryve restyn -
ge whiles. And thanne saith Bois, thou and god that put
the in the thou3tes of wise folke, knowes that nothynge brou3t
me to ministry ne dignite. But the comu^n stody of al goodnes.
Here Bois teches playnly how a man schulde come to maist^{er}
980   be stody that is to say, of al goodnes, for he that schal gover -
ne worthily, he muste stody to bye the pees of the peple. The

---

180. where

181. subjects

182. no meaning can be assigned to this phrase; perhaps "to avoid insulance" was intended

183. judge

184. endowed

185. *sic*

186. *sic*

defence of the citee or cuntre, the armoure of the folke. The
hele of the seke, the gladnes of alle heritage of pore men.
The coumfort of children and to himself, hope of evere -
985   lastynge blis, knowynge that if he come to governayle w^t [-]
oute stody of goodnes. As he is furst in worschepe, he schal

–212 v–

aftur be furst in payne. And therefore biddis god that a man schal
not seke to be a nige.[187] But if he may with his vertue destroy oþ^{er}
mennys wickydnes. || On foure wise there be made governow -
990   res in the peple. Sum^{m}e tyme be ordynaunce of god, as Saule p^{ri} -
mo regum et David p^{ri}mo reg^{um} XVI^{co}.[188] Sum^{m}e tyme be auctorite of
holy churche as in figure, Moyses callyd Iosue,[189] and badde him
lede the peple of god Deutronom^{ie} t^{er}cio. Sum^{m}e tyme be successi -
oun of lynage, as Salomon entrid aftur his fadur David t^{er}cio
995   regum scdd. Sum^{m}e tyme be comu^n choice and eleccioun of the pe -
ple as Vaspanyan[190] was chosen to the empire of Rome, and
on what wise that he entrid, but he stody for goodnes, he forfe -
tis the worthynes of his astate. And whether in his governau^n -
ce his stody be to goodnes or nou3t, he schal wete[191] be that as Bois
1000   saith next, he saith because I studyede to goodnes betwene wyc -
kede folke and me, were grete discordes that non p^{ra}yeres[192] my3t reles,
thus wyckednes seces[193] nevere to pursue goodnes. Natheles he
saith that consience hath that fredom, that he hath dispised al [-]
waye the wratthe of my3ty folke, for salvacioun of the ry3t.
1005   That menys, that al if the discordes betwene wickede me^n and
him my3t not be relesyd on no wise. ffor he on non wise
wolde consent to here folies and unry3twisnes. Ne thay my3t
not be drawen to consent to his vertues and goodnes. Nathe -

---

187. miser

188. reference to 1 Kings 16, in which Samuel is sent to inform Saul that David will succeed
him as king of Israel

189. Joshua

190. Vespasian

191. know

192. prayers

193. ceases

les the salvacioun and kepynge of ryche was to him, so leky^n -
1010 ge that al that he suffryd therefore was to him unpayneful.
|| Were thay nevere so my3tty in worldly power, and that he
proves be ensample anon aftur of many my3tty p^{e}sons and sais.
How ofte saith he with stody I do man callyd Conygaste,[194] that
wolte evere more have hyndrid and disesid the goodly fortunes
1015 of goode feble folke. This Conygaste was on of the my3tty me^n
of Rome, busy ay to displese pore me^n. And in rehersel of his
p^{er}son Bois makes us to wete, thay he withstodde the wron [-]
ge. The weche be the gret ry3gleders[195] of citees were purpo -
sed to pore men, and not alonly he agayn stode the grete of cy -
1020 tees, but also unry3tful officeres of lordes, and therefore he saith

–213 r–

hou ofte saith he have I kast and lettyd Trygewiff[196] pryncipale of -
ficer of the kynges house, bothe fro the wronges that he had begon -
ne do, and the weche he hadde do in dede. That menys, if he wolde
do wronge Bois lettyd him. And if he hadde do wronge, he dede
1025 him make aseth,[197] and fro he has tolde how he agayn stode the ma -
lice of the grete. He telles how he fordede the nede of the pore.
And saith, hou ofte saith he have I koverede and defended the
pore be myn auctorite put agaynes peryl, that is hou ofte ha -
ve I put my^n auctorite in peryl for to delyvere wrecched pore
1030 folk out of grevaunce and disese, out of noumbre that thay
in,[198] and to kepe hem fro the ponyschynge and of the tormentynge
purposed unto hem be the covetyse of straungers. He calles hem stra -
ungres[199] that were of birth and bryngynge up of other cuntres
and late comen to Rome, to wham because of eloquence, or el -
1035 les sum^{m}e what semyd p^{ro}fitable, were taken in the citee to digni -
te of office. Thaise stodied faste to covetise for thay wolte plese
the grete with giftes, and therefore, for goode thay ponysched

---

194. Conigastus

195. instigators of civil strife; ringleaders

196. Trigguilla

197. satisfaction; compensation; amends

198. perhaps verb *were* has been omitted

199. strangers

and oppressed the pore. But agayn sweche Bois ay defendid
the pore. And therefore he saith, for ham he put his auctori -
1040   te in peryl, that menes, that he the forsaide straungers mo -
vyd the grete to pryve[200] Bois degree of his office, as unworthy
to have it, because he toke hem to his defence as innocentis
the weche thay hadde giltyd of malice. But for al that peryle
he saith. There was nevere man my3t drawe me, fro ry3t on
1045   to wronge. As who so say, where to schulte I tarye alday to
telle my innocentcy, be specyal ensamples I say at ouns. ‖
I wolde for no man do wronge. But whenne I saw the for -
tunes and ryches of the peple of the provynces be har -
myd and hyndryd other be private raven or comun tribute, I
1050   was sory therefore as thay that suffryd the harme. Here he me -
nes, that Theodorik toke unri3tful tribute of the peple of the
provynces. The weche he calles his anccre men of Rome put in
thraldom be the quest of the forsaide kynge. The weche teraunt
knowynge a grete hungur in Campayne[201] made gadre alle the cor -

–213 v–

1055   nes of the cuntre unto his awarde[202] and kepe it so straytly, that there
schulde no man have of it, with oute a grete pris of mony. And
with that he schulde bynde him self to servage therefore. But
this maliciouse unresonable tyrauntrye, Bois my3tyly and
wisle lettede. And so he saith anon in the text folewynge. ‖
1060   Whanne it was he saith in the sorwe hungre tyme, there was
cryede agrevous and untellable coempcioun. He calles coempci [-]
oun, the forsaide pryce and servage. That men saw wel it wol
be gretely turne to damage of alle the cuntre of Campayne,[203] and
therefore I take strif agayn the grete officeres callid provost of the
1065   prethorye[204] for the comun profite. And for that the kynge knew of it, 3et
I overcome it, so that the coempcioun was not askyd ne toke ef -
fecte, the provost of the pretorye was an officer in the Citee, the we -

200. deprive

201. Campania

202. custody; wardship

203. Campania

204. Praetorian Prefect or Provost

che was ordeynede inwarde in the Cytee to acorde ham that dis -
cordyd and governe here batayles outewarde agaynes here ene -

1070   myes. And he schulde make distribucioun inwarde, to the peple
of sustunaunce and monye. fferthermore he saith Pauline[205]
a counselo[ur] of Rome. Whanne the houndis of the palays,
that he calles the officeres of the court wolde have devowrede
for covetyse of his ryches, I delyvede him fro ham. And for as

1075   meche as the accusacioun put agayn Albyn[206] annother coun -
selo[ur] of Rome, schulde not sodeynly ponysch him wrongwis -
ly, I put me fully agayn the hates and the indignaciounes
of the accuser Cyp[ri]ane,[207] this Cyp[ri]ane accusede falsly this forsai -
de albeyn, and made him withoute answere to be foriugged.

1080   And therefore Bois put him to defende him. And sythin I ha -
ve put me agayn the malyce of so many, for the god and in -
nocentis, is it not now wel sene, that I have purchased grete
discordes agaynes myself, but I au3te to be the more seker,[208]
that I kept nevere non evyl, of the courtyours of the kyng[es]

1085   halle, undiscovered, for I wolde be the more seker. Him thyn [-]
ges[209] here he schulde have ben the more seker fro disese. Be [-]
cause he consented not to the wronge of evyl men as he has
declared. But he saith he is the more unseker. And therefore

o—o—o—o—o—o
| his accus.[210] |
o—o—o—o—o—o

−214 r[211]−

his accusacioun, of thre unworthy p[er]sones, he reherses ano[n] sa -
1090   ynge. That thorw the accusynge of the same accusers I was co[n] -

---

205. Paulinus

206. Albinus

207. Cyprian

208. certain

209. perhaps *thynkes* is intended

210. see the note 107 above for "hire mylke"

211. lower right corner of this page: "C.M." appears in a later hand

dempnyd of the noumbre of the sweche on Basilius,[212] the weche
for untruthe was put out of the kynges servyce, and now is
he compellid for mone,[213] to accuse mo. Also Opylyon[214] and Gau -
dencius[215] the weche be the kyngis iusticis, were demyd to go

1095   to exile for here frauds and falshede wᵗoute noumbre. To the
weche iuggement thay wolde not obeye, but fledde into seintua -
rye.[216] And whanne the kyng wist it, he comaundede that but thay
avoydede the Citee of Raven[217] withinne a certain day assignede þᵗ
men schulde merke hem on the forhede with a hooke of iren,[218]

1100   and chase hem oute of towne. || What thyng thenne myȝte
this cruelte be lyckenede to, for certes the same day was recey -
vede the accusynge of my name, be thaise same accusoures.
As if he saye, truly sweche accusoures schulde not have ben
harde to accusede. That so worthy for here owne trespas was

1105   accusede, and if it were supposede that I were worthy for my
owne trespas to be accusede, al if sweche accusers schulde not
have ben harde to accuse me, therefore I aske what may be sa -
yde hereto, hath my connynge and my stody desernyd thus.
Or ellis the forsaide dampnacioun of me hath it made thaᵐ

1110   riȝtful accuseres, as who say nay, was not fortune thanne
aschamyd of this. Thanne he tellis how fortune schulde
have be aschamyd. Certis al if fortune had not be aschamyd
that Innocence was acusyd, ȝit aughte sche to be aschamyd
of the filthe and the unworthynes of myⁿ accusoures.

1115   But aske þᵘ of what gilt I am accusyd. Men say that I wol -
de[219] the cumpany of the senatoures, and wilt þᵘ here iⁿ what
manere I am accusede that I schulde have disturblyd the
accusour of the senate to bere lettres, be the weche he schul -
de have made the senatoures gilty agenys the kyngis ro -

1120   yal mageste. O, þᵘ maistres, what demes þᵘ of this saith

---

212. Basil

213. money

214. Opilio

215. Gaudentius

216. sanctuary

217. Ravenna

218. brand them

219. verb *to save* has been omitted

Bois to ph[ilosophi]e. Schal I forsake this blame, that it be no scha -
me to þe,[220] as if he say nay, for certis he sais I have ev[er]e

–214 v–

wolde it, that menes the salvacioun of the senate, ne I schal ne [-]
vere lette to weele[221] it, and that I confesse and am a knowe.[222] But
1125   the entent of the accuser schal acese, for schal I saith Bois cal -
le it a felonye or a synne that I have desirede the salvacioun
of the senate, al if he say I doute wheþ[er] I schal or nou3t.
3et hadde the same senate done to me thorw here decree and here
iuggement, al if it were synne and felonye. That is to say.
1130   ffor to desire the salvacioun of hem for this, it is to wete, that
be charite eche man is holde for to desire the gostly hele of other.
And also his bodely hele and welefare. If he be corigible of his
trespas. But if the trespas be so maliciouse that thorw bodi -
ly welfare it schulde be continuede rather thanne stynte, tha[n] [-]
1135   ne with desire of soule hele, thorw lawful ponyschynge the
bodely hele schulde be occasioun of continuaunce of trespase
oweth with charite to be withdrawe. But let foly saith Bois
lye to him selfe alway, and 3et schal it nou3t chaunge the
merit of thynges, ne I trowe he saith, be the Iuggement of
1140   Socrates that it were leeful to me, to hide the sothe, and to a -
sent to lesynges. But certis how that evere it be of this, I
put it fully in Iuggement of the, and of wise folke, of the
weche thynge al the ordenaunce and the sothe for folke þ[t]
be to come, aftur oure daies schole knowe it, I have put
1145   it in scripture and remembraunce. || ffor towchynge the let -
teres that were falsly made, be the weche I am acusyde, that I
schulde av[223] hoopede[224] the fredom of Rome, that menes, for to ha [-]
ve delyverede fro thraldom of the tyraunt Theodoryk. What
p[ro]fites it me to speke there of. Of the weche letteres the frau -
1150   de and gile hadde ben schewede openly, if I hadde had fredom

---

220. scribe has not superscripted the *e* in the manuscript

221. will

222. confess and acknowledge

223. have

224. hoped for

for to have ben at the confessioun of myn acusores, I wolde
thanne have answerede, be the wordes of a man that hight
Canyus. That was in his tyme oon of the wise gover -
nowres that was in Rome. ffor whanne he was acusede
1155   of Cesar gayus Iermayn sone,[225] that he was knowenge and
consentynge of a coniuracioun[226] made agaynes him, this

–215 r[227]–

Canyus answerde thus, if I hadde wist it, þ^u haddist not wist it.
In the weche thynge sorewe has not so dullyd my wit, that I pla -
yne oonly, that schrewed folke susteynes schrewedenes agaynes
1160   vertuis. But I wondre gretly, how thay may p^{er}forme thynges
that thay have supposede for to do, for why to wilne[228] schrewedenes
that comes p^{er}aventure of oure defaute. But it is like to a mons -
tre that is a myschapen thynge and a mervel. How that in the p^{re} -
sent siȝt of god sweche thynges may be p^{er}formyde as ev^{er}y maliciowse
1165   schrewe has conceyvede in his thouȝt agaynes conscience and Inno -
cence, that menes, that schrewes schal have power for to disese
goode vertues folke. ffor the weche thynge oon of the famylieres
not unskilfully askede thus. If goode is, whennes cometh evyl thy^n -
ges, and if goode is not, whennes comyth goode thynges. But al if
1170   it had ben lefful that schrewede folke that now desiren the blode
and the deth of alle goode folke, and also of alle the senate, have de -
sired to distroye me, whom thay have sen alway batayle and de -
fence goode men, and also alle the senate, ȝet hadde I not deservede
of the fadres, that menes of the senatowres, that thay schulde de -
1175   sire my distruccioun. Thou remembres wel as I suppose saithe
Bois to ph^{ilosoph}ie, that whanne I wolde do or say anythynge thou
reuled me. At the Citee of Verone,[229] whenne the kynge that was
gredy of comu^n slautter kest to put oon al the ordre of the senate
the gilt and the trespas of his ryal mageste, of the weche gilt,
1180   Albine was acusede with how grete p^{er}ele unto me, defendede I al

---

225. Caligula

226. conspiracy

227. lower right corner of this page: "C.M." appears in a later hand

228. desire

229. Verona

the senate, and for it my3t be supposede that Bois avauntede[230] to
meche himself, he saith to ph^{ilosoph}ie, þ^u wate wel that I say soth,
ne I avauntede me nevere in preysinge of myselfe. ffor alway
whanne a man resceyves fame in avauntynge of him self.

1185   Of his werkes he abates, the sekernes of his conscience, that me -
nes he loses his mede.[231] But now he saith þ^u may wel se to what
ende I am come for myn Innocence I receyve payne of false
trespas in rewarde of veray vertue. And what open confessiou^n
of trespas and felonye hadde evere Iugges so acordynge in cruel -

1190   te, that menes, as myne acusynge has, that errour of mannes

–215 v–

witte, or ellis condicioun of fortune that is uncertayne to alle ded -
ly folke. Submyttyd not sum^{me} of hem, that menes to have pite
and compassioun for al if I hadde ben acusyd, that I wolde bren [-]
ne holy houses, or strangle prestes with wickede swerde. Or that

1195   I had ordynede deth to alle goode men. 3et the sentence shulde
have ponyschede me p^{re}sent confessede or quyte. || But now I a^m
removede fro the Citee of Rome almost fyve hundrede thouson -
de passe, I am with out defence dampnede to exile and p^{ro}scripciou$^{n.}$
And to the ded, for the studies and bountes that I have don to

1200   the senate. Thanne he sais on skorne. O wele be thay worthy
of mercy, as who so say nay. There my3t nev^{er}e 3it non of hem
be quytte of sweche a blame as myn is. Of weche trespas my^n
acusoures saw ful wel the dignite. ffor thay wolde derke it w^t
medelynge of sum^{me} blame. Thay bar on me and lyede that

1205   I hadde pollute and defoulede my conscience with sacrilege for co -
vetyse of dignite. And certes sais Bois to ph^{ilosoph}ie, thou thy self
that art plantede in me, þ^u chacede away ou3t of my corage alle co [-]
vetyse of mortale thynges. Ne sacrilege hadde nev^{er}e leve to ha [-]
ve place in me before thyn eyen. ffor þ^u droppede every day in

1210   my eres and in thou3t the comaundement of pyttogoras.[232]
That is to say, menne schal serve to god and not to goddes.
Ne it is not nede to covenaunt to take helpe of the foulist spi -

230. boasted

231. mean; balance

232. Pythagoras

rites. I that þ^{u} hast ordeynede to sette in sweche excellence that
me like to god and ov^{er} this, the ri3t clene seker chambre of my

1215   house, that is to say my wife and the company of my hon [-]
est frendes, and my wifes fadre as wel holye as worthy to
be reverencede throrw his owne dedes defendeth me fro alle sus [-]
pecioun of sweche blame. And thanne he cryeth ou3t on mali -
ce and saith. But O malice, for thay at[233] acusede me takes of

1220   the ph^{ilosoph}ie feyth of so gret blame. ffor thay trowe that I have
had affynyte to enchauntementes and sorcerye. Because that
I am fulfilde with thy techynges. And enformyde with thy
maners, so that in him vertue was p^{er}sevede for vyce. And
thus it suffices not only that thy reverence availe me nou3t.

−216 r[234]−

1225   But if þ^{u} of thy fre wille rather be blemyschede with my grevau^{n} [-]
ce. But certes to the harmes that I have, there betydes 3et this
encreses of harme, that the Iuggement of meche folke lekes no [-]
thynge to the decertes of thynges. But only to the aventure[235] of
fortune. And thay deme, that al only sweche thynges are pur -

1230   veide[236] of god. The weche that temperele welthefulnes co -
mendes, as thus. That if a man have p^{ro}sp^{er}ite, he is a goode
man and worthy to have that p^{ro}sp^{er}ite, and who so have adv^{er} -
site, he is a wickede man. And god hath forsaken him, and he
is worthy to have that adv^{er}site, this is the opynyon of su^{m} -

1235   me folke. And thereof comes it, þat[237] goode fortune first for -
sakes alle wrecches. || Certes it greves me to thenke ri3t [-]
now, the dyv^{er}se sentences that the peple saith of me. And
thus meche I say. That the lest charge of fortune is. That
whanne any blame is laide upon a man. Men wene that

---

233. that

234. lower right corner of this page: "C.M." appears in a later hand

235. accident

236. foreseen

237. that

1240   he hath he hath[238] deservede to suffre it. As if he say, and ȝet al
       day. ffor cause unknowen many suffres withoute deserte.
       And I, he saith, that am put away fro goode men and despo -
       ylede fro dignytes and defoulede of my name, have suffrede
       tormentes for my goode dedes. Certes me thenges[239] that I
1245   se felawschepes of wickede men al bounden in ioye & glad -
       nes. And I se that every lorel[240] schapes him to fynde ouȝt
       newe fraudes. ffor to accuse goode folke. And I see, that goode
       folke ben overthrowen for drede of perele, and eche a lecherouse
       tormentoure dar[241] do al ille unpuyschede, and thay are strayne -
1250   de[242] thereto be giftes.[243] And Innocentes are not oonly robbyde
       and spoylede of sekernes, but also of defence, and therefore
       me lust to crye to god in this manere. In the weche cryes
       Bois. Sithen god disposes and levles alle thynges bothe
       in hevene and in erthe, why he for sakes the werkes of man,
1255   and leves ham to fortune, thus thanne he begynnes.
       [O]   thou maker of the wheele that berith the sterris the
       weche art fast to thyne evere lastynge chaier. That
       menes. The weche art ay in thy self stedefast tho -

–216 v–

       rew thyne evere lastynge beynge, the weche turnes the hevene, that
1260   menes. The firmament with a ravischynge swyȝth,[244] and constreynes
       the sterres to suffre thy lawe. That menes, to move aftur thy ordi -
       naunce of thy purveaunce. That he ensamples first of the mone
       so that the mone sum^me tyme schynynge with here fulle hornes
       metynge with al the bemes of the sonne. That is whanne sche
1265   is undur the sonne, here broþ^er. Be weche is ment the sonne, hides

---

238. text reads, "he hath he hath," with dots under each letter of the second "he hath"; two
lines below, "he saith" appears, also with dots under each letter; perhaps indicating that the
second "he hath" in the phrase above should be read as "he saith"

239. perhaps *thenkes* was intended

240. scoundrel; rogue

241. dare

242. encouraged

243. rewards

244. motion [sway]

the sterres, that are lesse, for the more liȝt vanysches the lasse is
it. And sum^{m}e tyme whanne the mone is pale with here derke
hornes drawes nere to the sonne. Sche loses hire liȝttes. ffor
undurstondynge of this, it is to wite, that as alle philisophres
1270   acordes, the mone hath no liȝt ne briȝtnes of himself. But sche
is in here kynde polischede as it were a meroure, that the briȝt -
nes of the sonne whanne it falles up on it, it may schyne.
The cause why sche hath no briȝtnes is. ffor if sche hadde briȝt [-]
nes of kynde sche schulde have hete of kynde, and sythen sche
1275   is next the erthe of alle planetes, sche schulde cause every mo -
neth a wynt^{er} and somer, as the sonne doth ouns in the ȝere.
‖ ffor whanne movynge be the singes of the ȝodiake scho^{245} co -
mes to the token callede the crabbe if sche hadde hete of here kyn -
de. Sche schulde cause som^{er} as the sonne dos. And sche comyth
1280   in here monythlye movynge to a signe callede Caprycorne sche
schulde cause wynt^{er} in coldenes. And so sethen every moneth sche
passes, movynge be thaise to tokenes, it foleweth that every
moneth if sche hadde briȝtnes and hete of kynde, sche schulde
make bothe wynt^{er} and som^{er}. And so schulde alle waxynge and
1285   beynge thynges benethe be destroyede, therefore it is concludyd
that sche hath nother of here self hete ne briȝtnes. But sche rece -
yves briȝtnes of the sonne, and for meche as the kynde of a briȝt
body is, to liȝtten the p^{ar}t of another body, that is next to it, and
to cause a schedew in the contrary p^{ar}t as we see every day be exp^{er}i -
1290   ence of the sonne. Therefore whanne the sonne is riȝt even a -
bove the mone, thanne is the ov^{er} p^{ar}t of the mone nerre to the
sonne al liȝt. And the p^{ar}t touwarde the erthe is al schadewede as

–217 r^{246}–

it is in tyme of coniuccioun^{247} and thanne it nys not sene. But when -
ne begynnes to move on side fromwarde the sonne, thanne falles
1295   here briȝtnes that sche takes of the sonne sum^{m}e what downwar -
de, and the more sche remeves fro the sonne, the more sche
schewes us ful briȝtnes. And therefore in the ful mone wha^{n} -

---

245. *sic*

246. lower right corner of this page: "C.M." appears in a later hand

247. conjunction (explained in the following lines)

ne sche is ferrest fro the sonne, sche schewes here al bri3t. And
as it li3tnes dounwarde, it schadewes upwarde and agayn

1300 warde unto agayn it come evenly undur the sonne. The we -
che tyme is called co^{n}niunccioun. ‖ Also saith Bois, and
that the even sterre Esp^{er}us.[248] The weche in the first tyme of
the ny3t brynges forth here colde arysynges comes est agaynes
here usede courses. And is pale in the morewen at the rysyn -

1305 ge of the sonne. And is thanne callede Lucifer. Be this Bo -
is saith, that it is a wondre ordynaunce of sterres, for the
same sterre that folewes the sonne at even and is callede Esp^{er} -
us. It gos before the sonne at morewe and is callede Lucifer.
Also þ^{u} restraynes seth Bois the day be schorter duellynge

1310 in the tyme of colde wynt^{er}, that makes the leves to falle,
that is for fernes of the sonne ferrer fro us in wynt^{er} thanne
in somer. Also he saith thou dep^{ar}tes the swift tydes of the
ny3t, whenne the somer is comen. Thy my3t atempres þe[249]
variaunt cesouns of the 3ere, so that 3ephirus the sobre wy^{n} -

1315 de, that is the south wynde. Brynges agayn in the first so -
mer sesoun the leves that the wynde that hy3te Boreas the
northwynde hath refte away in autu^{m}pne, that is to saie in
the laste ende of somer. And the seedes that the stere that
hi3te Arthurus[250] sew ar waxen hye cornes. Whanne the sterre

1320 Ciryus[251] eschafes[252] hem. There is nothynge he saith unbounden
fro his olde lawe. Ne flees fro his owne p^{ro}pur estate. O[253] thou
governo^{ur} governynge alle thynges be certayn ende, why refu -
ses þ^{u} only to governe the werkes of man by dewe maner.
‖ Why suffres thou that slydynge fortune mysgoverne

1325 thus thynges, that the payne that worthily schulde ponys -
che schrewes, ponysches innocentes, and folke of wickede

---

248. Venus

249. scribe has not superscripted the *e* in the manuscript

250. Arcturus

251. Sirius

252. dries out

253. scribe does not emphasize the beginning of this meter, but gives unusual emphasis to
the ending

−217 v^{254}−

      maners sittes in here chaieres. And cursede folke treden unrytfully
      in the neckes of holy men. And vertue that is clere and schyny^n -
      ge naturaly. Is hudde^{255} in derknes, and the ri3tful man berith
1330 the blame, and the peyne of the schrewe. Ne the forswerynge
      ne the fraude that is colo^{ur} of a fals colo^{ur}. Noies^{256} not to schrewes.
      The wheche schrewes whanne hem lust to use here strenghe tha -
      y reioyce hem to put undur hem the sovereyne kynges, the
      weche that peple with oute nombre dredes. O þou thanne
1335 saith Bois. What so evere þou be that knyttes^{257} alle boundes
      of thynges, loke on thaise wrecchede erdes, We men that are not
      a foule p^{ar}t. But a faire p^{ar}t of the grete a werke we are tormen -
      ted in the sea of fortune. || Thou govern^{or} thanne with draw -
      e and receyve thy ravyschynge flodes, and fest and make stede -
1340 fast these erdes with the same that þou governes with the
      hevene, that is so largee.^{258}
      N^{259} this next p^{ro}se spekes ph^{ilosoph}ie to Bois, and schewes him whe -
      reinne he hath erode.^{260} And that is in that, that he saide that
      mannes werkes were not disposede be god. But only be for -
1345 tune, and sche schewes be diverse ensamples that it is not so.
      || And thanne sche remembres of thynges of the weche he
      made his complaint, and sche telles, how he muste furste u [-]
      se soufte medecynes and easy. Thus thanne begynnes this
      speche. Whanne I hadde with a contynual sorewe sobbet and
1350 broken ou3t theise thynges, Sche with here pesable^{261} chere no -
      thynge displesede, with my complaintes saide thus. Whanne

---

254. marginalia appears to the left: between lines 16 and 17

255. hid

256. annoys

257. knits

258. scribe leaves last two-thirds of this line blank, indicating an indentation for an ornate initial had been considered; no indentation appears, but occurrance of a solitary upper case *N*, where word *In* is clearly intended, suggests space for an initial *I* was accidentally omitted

259. marginalia to the left of this upper case *N:* written in a later hand; appears to be an initial *I*, but substantiates the reading suggested in the previous note

260. erred

261. peaceful

I sawe the quod sche sorewful and wepynge I knewe anon
that þ^u was a wrecche and exilede. But I wist nere hou fer thy
exile was. If þ^u hadde not tolde it me, (him[262] ph^{ilosoph}ie calles exile he -
1355   re, the weche folewes fortunes chaungeablenes into hevynes
thorw adv^{er}site and into p^{re}sumpcioun thorw p^{ro}sp^{er}ite fleede utter-
ly so, fro resonable menne that schulde his owne cuntre.) ||
But certes saith ph^{ilosoph}ie to Bois. Al if þou be fer fro thy cuntre,
ȝet art þou not put al ouȝt of it. But þou hast failede of thy
1360   way, and go amys. And if þou have lever to wene that þou

–218 r–

be put ouȝt of thy cuntre, thanne hast thou put ouȝt thy self rather
thanne any other. ffor no man but thy self myȝt have done that to
the, and that sche p^{ro}ves on two wise. ffor if thou remebre of
what cuntre thou were borne, that is hevene, hit is not goverde
1365   be emperoures, ne be governayle of multitude as were the cun -
trees of Athene. But oon lorde oon kynge that is god. He is lor -
de of thy cuntre. The weche lorde reioyses[263] him and is gladde
of the duellynge of his Cyteȝenes, that menes in his Cytee of
resouⁿ. And he ordeynes nouȝt to be put ouȝt into exile of the
1370   weche lorde, it is a sovereyne fredom, for to be governede be the
bridel of him, and to obeye to his ryȝtwisnes. Hast þ^u forgete
saith ph^{ilosoph}ie to Bois, the ryȝt olde lawe of the Cytee, in the
weche Cytee it is ordeynede and enstablede that what man
has lev^{er} founde there his sete or his house, thanne elleswhe -
1375   re, he may not be exilede by ryȝt fro that place. ffor who so is coⁿ -
tente and contenede withinne the palayce of that Cytee of
resoun. There is no drede of exile, for the lawe is there, that
there schal non be exilede thennes but he that frely wille
be exilede, and therefore sche saith. That who so loves
1380   wel for to enhabite and duelle there, and for to be cyteȝen
of that Cytee, he may be exile so that I say that the face
of his place moves me not so mekil as douth thyn owne
face. Ne I aske nouȝt saith ph^{ilosoph}ie, rather the walles of thy

262. grammar in this passage is confused; possible reading is: "Philosophy calls him exiled
who, following Fortune's changes through adversity into heaviness and through prosperity
into presumption, is fled utterly from a reasonable mean that should be his own country"

263. rejoices

librarye apparalde and wrouȝt with yvory and with glasse,

1385   thanne aftir the sete of thy thouȝte. In the weche I put not
whilom bokes. And certes sche saith, of thy decertes that
was evere aboute the comu^n p^{ro}fite, þ^u has sayde south.[264] But
aftur the multitude of thy goode dedes, þ^u hast sayde fewe, and
of unhoneste and falsnes of thynges, that ben purposede

1390   agaynes the, þ^u hast remembrede thynges that are knowe to al [-]
le folke, and of the falshede and fraudes of thyne accusoures,
I have touchede it for sothe riȝtfully and schortly. Thou hast
also blamede gretly and complanede of the wrongful dede
of the senate, and þ^u sorewede for my blame, and þ^u hast wepede

–218 v–

1395   for the damage of thyne name, that is appayrede, and thyn last sorew -
folnes agayn fortune. And þ^u complaynes hire rewardes, that ar^e
not evenly ȝolden[265] to the decertes of folke. And in the later ende
of thy wode muse þ^u prayede that ilke pes, that governes the
hevene, schulde also governe the erthe. ‖ But for many tri [-]

1400   bulaciouns of affecciouns hath assaylede the, and sorewe and
ire and wepynge to drawe þe[266] dyversly, as þ^u art now feble
of thouȝt, myȝttier remedies schulde not ȝet touche the, for the
whilke we wil use somdel liȝtter medicynes so that tho[267] pas -
siouns that ar waxen harde in swellynge, be p^{er}turbaciouns

1405   folewynge into thyn thouȝt, mowe waxe esy and soft to res -
ceyve the strenghe of a more myȝtty and more egre medicyne
be a esyer towchynge.

        [N] ow for meche as it is sayde that it is p^{ro}fitable to Bois.
        ffurste to assaie esy medicynes, sche confermes the

1410   same be dyverse ensamples schewynge alle thyn [-]
ge that schal wel be don, must be don in accordynge tymes
for elles thay schal not be don p^{ro}fitabley. Ensample of seede
the weche is unp^{ro}fitable sowen, but if it be sowen in his
tyme. Thus thanne sche begynnes to schewe here pur -

---

264. truly [sooth]

265. yielded

266. scribe has not superscripted the *e* in the manuscript

267. *sic*

1415   pos. Whanne the hevy sterre callid Cancer is enchasete[268]
       be the beme of phebus. That menes whanne that phe -
       bus the sonne is in the signe of Cancre, who so geves tha^n [-]
       ne largely his seedis to the feldes. That is in the monyth
       of Iuly, let him go begylde of truste, that he hadde to his
1420   cornes to acornes or okes. As if sche say. That tyme of
       the ȝere is resonable to fynde inne okes akernes and not
       to sowe feldes. And other ensample also, if þ^u gadre violet -
       tes. Go not to the pure wode whenne the feldes chyteres[269]
       of colde, be the felnes of the wynde that hyȝt Aquylo.[270] ||
1425   That menes, go not to gadre floures in felnes of wynt^{er}.
       An other ensample also, if þ^u desire or wil grapes use se -
       ke[271] not with a glotonsle hande to streyne and presse the
       stalkes of the vyne in the furste somer sesoun callede vern[272]

–219 r[273]–

       for bachus that is god of wyn, hath rather geven his ȝiftes
1430   to autumpne the latter ende of somer, thenne sche telles,
       for what purpose sche saith thus. ffor god sche saith assignees
       alle tymes ablynge hem here p^{ro}pre office. Ne he suffres
       not the tymes the weche he hath deptede[274] to be mengyde[275] to -
       gedre. ffor ilke a thynge hath his owne p^{ro}pre tyme. (And[276]
1435   therefor he that loves certeyne ordynaunce of doynge[277] be a -

---

268. warmed

269. shivers

270. Aquilo, the North Wind

271. seek

272. vernal; spring

273. lower right hand corner of the page missing, due to defect in the hide

274. perhaps *dep^{ar}ted* was intended

275. mingled

276. passage is confused because scribe continues sentence preceding the indentation on the second half of the first indented line; proper word order: "And therefor he that loves certeyne ordeynaunce of doyng be acordynge tymes, he hath no gladde syne ne ende of his ordenaunce & werkes. [F]erthermore in this next p^{ro}se ph^{ilosoph}ie purposes to Bois, foure questionnis, and sche. . . ."

277. doing

cordynge tymes, he hath no gladde syne[278] ne ende of his {or
[F]   erthermore in this next p^{ro}se || denaunce} i^n werkes.
ph^{ilosoph}ie purposes to Bois, foure questiouns, and sche)
descures[279] pleynly the cause of his sekenes. And tha^n [-]

1440   ne at the laste sche comfortes him affermynge, that there
is ȝet life in him. ffor he hath kyndely heete thorw the we -
che he is curable. Thus thanne begynnes ph^{ilosoph}ie to speke
to Bois. ffurste wilt þ^u suffre me to touche and assaie the sta -
te of thy thouȝt, be a fewe demaundes. So that I may und^{er} -

1445   stande what is the maner of thy curacioun^n.[280] || Aske me q^{uo}d
Bois at thy wille what thou wilt. And I schal answere.
Thanne saide ph^{ilosoph}ie thus, whether wenest thou q^{uo}d ph^{ilosoph}ie,
that this worlde be governede be folies happes and fortu -
nes. Or elles wenest thou that there is in it any governa -

1450   unce of resoun. Certes q^{uo}d Bois I trowe not in no man^{ner}.
That so certayn thynges schulde be movede and governe -
de be fortunose fortune. But I wot wel, that god maker
and maist^{er} is govern^{er} of his werke. Ne there was nev^{er}e
ȝet day, that myȝt put me ouȝt of the sothnes of the sen -

1455   tense. So it is q^{uo}d ph^{ilosoph}ie, for the same thynge sounge[281] thou
alite[282] here before. And thou sorwede and wepte. That
only men and here werkes were put ouȝt of the cure of
god. ffor of alle thynges thou doutede not but thay were
governede be resoun. But how saith ph^{ilosoph}ie, I wondre gret -

1460   ly certes why that thou art seke, sethen that thou art
put in so holsum a sentence. But lat us seke depper, I
deme thare[283] lackes. But I not[284] what, but say me this.

---

278. sign

279. discovers

280. final *n* of *curacioun* is indicated, but standard mark indicating abbreviation appears above it in the manuscript

281. sung

282. a little

283. therein

284. know not

–219 v²⁸⁵–

Sithen thou douȝtest not but this werlde is governede be god,
with what governaunce takes thou hede, that it is governe -
1465   de. Bois answers, unnethes he saith, knowe I the sentence
of thy questioun. So that I may not ȝet answere to thy de [-]
maunde. Thanne saith ph^ilosoph^ie, I was not dessayvede saith
sche. But there failes summwhat, be weche the maladie
of p^er^turbacioun is cropen into thy thouȝt. But say me this.
1470   Remembres the ouȝght what is the ende of thynges, and
whether the entencioun of alle thynge purposes at the en -
de. I have harde tolke it sum^m^e tyme saith Bois, but drerynes²⁸⁶
and sorewe hath dullyd my mynde. Certes q^uo^d ph^ilosoph^ie thou
wotest wel, whennes alle thynges be come and p^ro^cede, I
1475   wot wel, q^uo^d Bois, that god is the begynnynge of alle.
And how may this be q^uo^d ph^ilosoph^ie. That sethen thou know [-]
est the begynnynge of thynges, that thou knowest not
the ende of thynges. But sweche be the custome of p^e^rtu -
baciounis and this power thay have, that thay move a
1480   man fro his place. That is to say, fro the stabilnes and
knowynge of p^er^feccioun. But certes thay may not alle
aliene him in alle. But I wolde that thou wolde answe -
re to this. Remembres the ought that thou art a man.
Why schulde I not remembre that saith Bois. May thou
1485   not telle me thanne saith ph^ilosoph^ie, what thynge is a man.
Aske thou not me q^uo^d Bois. Whether I be a resonable best
mortale, I wot wel, and I confesse that I am it. Wist þ^u^
evere ȝet þ^u^ were any other thynge q^uo^d ph^ilosoph^ie. No q^uo^d
Bois, nowe wot I wel q^uo^d ph^ilosoph^ie other cause, of thy male-
1490   die and that ryȝt grete. Thou hast left for to knowe thy self,
what þ^u^ art. Thorw the whilke I have founden the cau -
se of thy maladie. Or elles the entre of resceyvynge of þy
hele. ffor why, for thou art confoundyd with forgetynge of
thy self. Therefore þ^u^ sorewes that þ^u^ art exiled fro thyn
1495   p^ro^pur goodes. ffor thou knowest not what is the ende of
thyne thynges. Therefore thou demes that wrecchede

---

285. see note 273 above

286. dreariness

$-220 \ r^{287}-$

1500
1505
1510
1515
1520

and wickede men, be my3hty and weleful. ffor thou hast for -
geten be what governaunce the worlde is governede. There -
fore thou wenest that thaise chaungeynges of fortune ar left
with out governo^{re}. Thaise ben grete causes, nou3t only to
maladie. But certes gret causes of dede.[288] But I thanke the
auctour, and the maker of hele, that nature hath not alle
forgeten the, but sche kepes gret noryschynges of thy hele.
And that is the sothe governaunce of the worlde. That thou
beleves that the governaunce of hit is not soiette[289] ne under -
put unto folie of theise avterouse[290] happes. But to the resou^{n}
of god. And therefore doute the nothynge. ffor of this lityl
sparge[291] thyne hete of lyf schal sprynge and schyne. But for
as mekil as it is not tyme 3et of fester and gretter remedies.
And the nature of thougtes that are desceyvede is this. That
as ofte as thay kast away sothe opynyownes thay clothe he^{m}
in false opynyownes. And thanne the falsnes of p^{er}turba -
cioun waxes up that confoundes the veray insy3t. And that
derkenes schal I asaye soumwhat to make thynne and way -
ke[292] be ly3t and menely[293] remedyes. So that afture at[294] there
derkenes of desceyvnynge desyrynges is don awaie. Thou
may knowe the veray schynynge of ly3t. That menes,
whanne desires of worldely goodes is put away, that derke -
nes the ly3t of resoun and of gostly goodes. Thanne schal
thou clerely se the p^{ro}fite[295] of gostly goodes of vertues of resow -
nes of ilke a soule.

[F]   or as meche as ph^{ilosoph}ie hath schewede that p^{er}turbacio -
un of fleschely affeccioun derkes the ly3t of the sou -
le. Therefore in this last metre of this furste boke

---

287. lower righthand corner of the page is missing, due to a defect in the hide

288. death

289. subject

290. *av^{en}terouse* or chance

291. spark

292. thin and fragile

293. moderate

294. that

295. perhaps *p^{ro}fite* is intended

1525   sche p^{ro}ves that be ensamples. ffurst of the sonne. That
the sonne may not clerly schyne, whil it is koverde with
cloudes. The secounde is of the see, that may not be cler,
whil the trumblynge sotherne wynde blowes thus. Than -
ne sche begynnes the sterres koverde with blake cloudes,
1530   may geve downe no ly3t. If the trublely wynde that hight

–220 v^{296}–

auster,[297] stormynge and walewynge the see medeles[298] the heete, þ^t
is to say. The boylynge fro the grounde of the see, thanne the
waves that sum^{m}e tyme were as clere as glas, and lyke to the
faire bry3t daies, withstande anon the sy3ttes of men. Be the
1535   fylth and unclene matere that is resolvede. And the fletynge
streme. That rowles doun dyversly fro hye mountaynes, ys
arested and withstanden ofte tymes. Be the sounterynge[299] of a
stone that is dep^{ar}tede and fallen fro the roche. Thanne be thaise
ensamples sche brynges in here purpose. Therefore if thou wil
1540   loke and deme soth with clere li3t, and holde the way of aly3t pat -
the, put away ioye dryve fro the drede. ffleme[300] away hope, and
lat no sorewe come nere. That is to say. Lat non of thayse fou -
re passiowuns overcome the or blynde the. Noyther glad -
nes in havynge of worldely welthefulnes. Ne drede of losy^n -
1545   ge. Ne hope forto have in tyme comynge. Ne sorewe ne
despayre for wantynge of worldely goodes. ffor ful clowdy and
so derke is that sowle and bounde with streyte brydeles, whe -
re as thaise foure reygnen and have the maistrye. FF.
Explicit p^{ri}mus liber st^{a}diu^m Boysium de Consolacone Phi -
1550   *losophie.*

Seal of the
Bodleian Library

þþ

---

296. see note 287 above

297. Auster, the South Wind

298. stirs up

299. meeting

300. put to flight

CONTRIBUTORS

William J. Asbell, Jr. earned his Ph.D. in Classical Studies at Vanderbilt University. He has taught Latin and Greek literature at Vanderbilt and the University of Houston.

Ann W. Astell (Ph.D., 1987) is Professor of English at Purdue University. She is the author of *Job, Boethius, and Epic Truth* (1994) and of numerous other books and articles on medieval literature, spirituality, and rhetoric. Her most recent book is *Joan of Arc and Sacrificial Authorship* (2003).

J. Keith Atkinson is an emeritus Reader of medieval French language and literature of the University of Queensland, Australia. His primary research focus, from the time of his post-graduate work at the Université of Neuchâtel in 1968 (under the tutelage of Professor Jean Rychner) until the present, is the medieval French tradition of Boethius's *Consolatio*. Apart from a number of analytical articles and articles relative to the manuscript tradition and dialectal variations, he and his doctoral students are responsible for critical editions of six of the medieval French translations of the *Consolatio,* three of which have been published.

Romanus Cessario, O.P. teaches theology at Saint John's Seminary, Brighton, Massachusetts. Among other publications, he is the author of several books in Christian ethics and of a brief history of Thomism. Father Cessario is a Fellow of the Pontifical Academy of Saint Thomas Aquinas.

Glynnis M. Cropp is now Professor Emeritus (French) and an Honorary Research Fellow in the School of Language Studies, Massey University, Palmerston North, where her long academic career has included the positions of Dean of the Faculty of Humanities, 1987–97, and Head of the

School of Language Studies, 1998–2001. Her main research interests are in three fields: the courtly lyric poetry of the troubadours of the twelfth and thirteenth centuries, the medieval French translations of Boethius's *Consolatio Philosophiae,* especially the most widely known translation *Le Livre de Boece de Consolacion,* and related writing of the fourteenth and fifteenth centuries.

Graham N. Drake has taught medieval literature at the State University of New York College at Geneseo since 1989. He co-edited *Four Romances of England* (1999) and is currently working on an edition of William of Wheteley's commentary on Boethius.

Christine Herold has taught medieval and Renaissance literature in the Department of English at The College of Saint Rose, Albany, New York, for the past eleven years. She earned her B.A. at Williams College in 1987, and her M.A. and Ph.D. at the University of Massachusetts at Amherst in 1991 and 1994. She specializes in Chaucer, medieval mystical literature, tragedy, and post-Jungian archetypal theory.

Christoph Houswitschka teaches English literature at the University of Bamberg. He has published on English literature of the fifteenth, eighteenth, and twentieth centuries. He is particularly interested in literature and politics (e.g., Love and Politics in the *Morte D'Arthur;* the High Treason Trials of 1794, and the Literature of Democratization).

Noel Harold Kaylor, Jr. is professor of English and chair of the English Department at Troy University. He authored *The Medieval Consolation of Philosophy: An Annotated Bibliography* (1992) as well as numerous articles on Chaucer and Boethius, and he recently coedited John Bracegirdle's *Psychopharmacon: A Translation of Boethius' "De Consolatione Philosophiae"* (1999). With Philip Edward Phillips he is editing Queen Elizabeth I's translation of Boethius. He is the executive director and founder of the International Boethius Society and coeditor of its journal, *Carmina Philosophiae.*

† **Michael Masi** was associate professor of English at Loyola University, in the Department of English, where he taught medieval literature and, especially, Chaucer. His *Chaucer and Gender* was published in 2005. Other publications include a collection of essays on Boethius and the Liberal Arts and a translation of the *De Arithmetica* of Boethius.

Philip Edward Phillips is associate professor of English at Middle Tennessee State University, where he teaches medieval and early modern British and European literature. He earned his Ph.D. at Vanderbilt University. With Noel Harold Kaylor, Jr., he is editing Queen Elizabeth I's translation of the *Consolation of Philosophy*. He is the secretary of the International Boethius Society and coeditor of its multidisciplinary journal, *Carmina Philosophiae*.

Krista Sue-Lo Twu is associate professor of English at the University of Minnesota, Duluth, where she teaches medieval literature. She is currently the editor of the *International Boethius Society Newsletter*.

Francesca Ziino graduated in Rome (1992) in Romance Philology and earned her Ph.D. in Naples (1997). She has studied the Medieval Spanish tradition of *De consolatione*. She is currently working in a public library in Pavia, Italy.

INDEX OF MANUSCRIPTS

GENERAL INDEX

Abbey of St. Victor, 53
Academics, 15 n. 41, 207 n. 49
Achelous, 182, 183
Agamemnon, 18, 25
Agrimi, Jole, 105 n. 33
Aeschylus, 28 n. 1
Aguiló, Angel, 103
Albareda, Anselm M., 103 n. 16
Alain de Lille, *De planctu naturae,* 148
Alcañiz, 87
Alcinous, 10, 13 n. 19, 16 n. 52
Alexander of Aphrodisias, 15 n. 39
Alfonso, King (the Magnanimous), 85
Alfonso X, King, 83
Alfred, King (the Great), xiii
Ambrose, 219 n. 79
Ammon, 118
amour, 111
Anaximander, 187
Anonymous of St. Gall, 195
Anonymous of the Erfurtensis, 174, 180,
   181, 182, 185, 187, 193, 198 n. 21,
   202 n. 31, 203 n. 33, 205 n. 44, 206
   n. 48, 208 n. 52, 210 n. 57, 212 n.
   61, 215 n. 71
Anonymous of the Reginenses, 173, 193,
   205 n. 42
Anonymous of the Vaticanus latinus, 193
Anonymous Oxford, xvii
Apollo, 169
Apuleius, 13 n. 19
Aquinas, St. Thomas, 87, 91, 112, 153 n.
   3
areté, 6
Arianism, 159, 160, 161, 162
Aristotle, xii, 4, 5, 6, 8, 15 n. 41, 26, 45,
   46, 47 n. 12, 144, 145, 154 n. 7, 164,
   171, 189, 218 n. 78; *Categories,* 83;

Metaphysics, 13 n. 18;
   Nichomachean Ethics, 8, 14 n. 24,
   15 n. 37; *Rhetoric,* 6, 8, 14 n. 25;
   tripartite soul, the concept of, 26
Arius, 161
Asceticism, 6
Ascetics, 9
Aspasius, 15 n. 39
Atkinson, J. Keith, 69 n. 1, 84, 90, 102,
   102 n. 5, 105 nn. 26, 37
Athenian schools, 177
Atherton, Béatrice M., 58, 69 n. 1, 70 n.
   10, 71 n. 18
Augustine, St. (of Hippo), 30 n. 16, 34,
   46, 47 nn. 7, 10, 48 n. 19, 112, 153
   n. 3
autarkeia, 3, 4, 5, 6, 7, 11, 12, 13 nn. 10,
   15

Babbi, Anna Maria, 102
Bade d'Assche, Josse, 176, 183, 184, 187,
   196, 201 n. 26, 207 n. 49, 211 n. 58,
   214 n. 70, 215–16 nn. 70, 71
Badia, Lola, 103 n. 10
Baraut, Cebrià, 103 n. 16
Barrett, Helen M., xiii
Basil of Caesarea, 6, 14 n. 27
Benson, Larry, 153 n. 2
Benveniste, Samuel, 101
Berlioz, Jacques, 107 n. 52
Bible, 120
Blamires, Alcuin, 113
Blanca (daughter and heir of King
   Charles III of Navarre), 87
Bode, Georg Heinrich, 106 n. 51
Boethius, Anicius Manlius Severinus,
   xi–xvii, 3, 4, 7, 8, 9, 10, 11, 17, 19,
   20, 21, 22, 23, 24, 26, 35, 64, 66, 75,

Typeset in 11 pt. Times New Roman
with Perpetua Titling display
Composed by Juleen Audrey Eichinger
for Medieval Institute Publications
Manufactured by Sheridan Books, Inc.

Medieval Institute Publications
College of Arts and Sciences
Western Michigan University
1903 West Michigan Avenue
Kalamazoo, MI 49008-5432
www.wmich.edu/medieval/mip

 WESTERN MICHIGAN UNIVERSITY